The Paperbark Tree

Born in 1938, Les Murray grew up on a dairy farm
at Bunyah on the north coast of New South
Wales. He retired from outside employment
in 1971, making writing his full-time career.
His other books include *The Daylight Moon*
(Poetry Book Society Choice), *Selected Poems*
(Poetry Book Society Recommendation),
Dog Fox Field (Poetry Book Society Choice)
and his verse novel *The Boys Who Stole
the Funeral* (Poetry Book Society Recommenda-
tion). In 1992 Minerva published his *Collected
Poems*.

LES MURRAY

The Paperbark Tree

Minerva

A Minerva Paperback

THE PAPERBARK TREE

First published in the Great Britain 1992
by Carcanet Press Limited
This Minerva edition published 1993
by Mandarin Paperbacks
an imprint of Reed Consumer Books Ltd
Michelin House, 81 Fulham Road, London SW3 6RB
and Auckland, Melbourne and Singapore

*The publisher acknowledges financial assistance
from the Arts Council of Great Britain*

A CIP catalogue record for this title
is available from the British Library
ISBN 0 7493 9861 2

Printed and bound in Great Britain
by Cox & Wyman Ltd, Reading, Berks

Contents

Preface

This book presents a sample of the other writing I do. It isn't as important as poetry, it isn't sacred, and it isn't as much fun. It does have its uses and its satisfactions, though. It helps me to think, and to find out what I think; it gets things off my chest; it sometimes starts the bird poetry from her covert, and occasionally it attains a measure of poetry in its own right. The selection of my prose which I have made reaches back over seventeen years to the era of my early book reviews for the *Sydney Morning Herald*, and illustrates most of the themes and aspects of my essay–writing. It shows a gradual shift away from book reviews to the commissioned article, the lecture and the speculative essay, and, as its only departure from reprinting pieces whole, gives three excerpts from my only full–length prose book, *The Australian Year*, a study I wrote in 1983 of the seasons of our continent, which both are and are not the traditional four.

Throughout this book, readers will encounter the debris and discarded maps of wars I have been conscripted to fight in, now alongside, now in distant parallel with mainly black and Celtic allies. These are the wars against Culture, and against the Athenian, Roman and British empires, by all of which I mean the war against Metropolis. In some respects, this war has now been won. Only in certain redoubts do I still need to ask Would you dare patronize me in that way if I were black? The distribution and promotion of art are still controlled in large measure by Metropolis and its servants, but first–rate work is at last allowed to be done anywhere. Indeed, first–rate work is the price one must pay to go home, or to stay at home.

Another war which has left its traces in this book is my struggle, often without any visible allies, against the police-minded ideological rectitudes which have so largely captured the spirit and culture

7

of my time. This is the suffocating ethos which affects to value poetry but really seeks to harness and suppress it, lest it disrupt whatever Big Final Poem people may be living in and defending. I have given this ethos many names over the years, and right now I tend to call it the East German Plastic Bag. The term seems apt for that clammy sheath of expected allegiance and enforced style which is still jammed over your head as soon as you come near the world of literature or commentary. As you slowly asphyxiate in it, out through the vapour and distortion of its slick folds you can dimly see the ordinary human world in all its irrecruitable variety. To that world, though, even your muffled cries for help are apt to sound like just so much more exhortation, so much more incomprehensible scorn of fellow humans.

In a way, I would be far happier if my battle were only against the ideologues; what is more painful is that it is also in part a war against my friends. As will be clear, I am deeply troubled by the relationship of poetry to education. I'm in the position of a farmer half of whose friends work tirelessly and, they believe, for his benefit in a pesticide factory which is poisoning his land. In spite of their best efforts, it does seem that education trains a small public for poetry but loses us a large one. Educators are mostly reluctant to concede that education functions for most people as a large relegation machine, apt to estrange them from older values and their own background, while at the same time providing the terms by which they will see their lives fall short. It is surely dangerous for the reception of poetry that nearly all people now encounter it first, and exclusively, in places where they are sent to be humiliated.

Assimilation of the age-old figure of the poet to that of the modern revolutionary intellectual seems to have caused a catastrophic fall in the number of poetry's readers, and removed it from anything like an earlier normal place in the world of books and reading. It is in the light of this disaster, and what looks like an ongoing campaign in modern times to replace poetry altogether by criticism and theory, that I have tried, through introspection and using my own *ad hoc* terms, to examine the claim that poets are the unacknowledged legislators of the world. As will emerge from the relevant essays towards the end of this book, I end by modifying this insight a bit, seeing poetry itself as the more likely candidate, and then mostly in a transferred sense under which most of the 'poets' wouldn't see themselves as such at all. On the other hand, I do contend that poetry is the deep pattern by which humans organize reality, and the only lens through which we ever see anything. Art models the process I am talking about, and art alone is capable of distilling it to a point beyond conflict, beyond action, which is really to say, beyond human sacrifice.

Because I tend to think in afterthoughts, several of the essays in this book have been expanded in the past. Since they have now attained their final forms, however, I have generally not modified them further for their first British outing. The only substantial exception is the first extract from *The Australian Year*, which has had to be adjusted from its function as the preface to another book and made to work as an essay in this one. I have also not done any updating, preferring to let each piece remain true to the time in which it was written. Anything else might have nullified any sense of personal evolution this book may contain, and subjected the essays themselves to unbearable strains of anachronism.

As an example of how received thinking has altered on one particular topic since I first wrote about, accounts of Aboriginal culture have recently, in part due to the campaign for land rights, turned sharply away from the content of local legends to examine the way these are disposed in the landscape and related to geographical features, along the Dreaming paths which Bruce Chatwin re-named 'Songlines'. Pressure against cultural and artistic borrowing from Aboriginal sources has increased, while alcohol and the dying off of elders have caused a further catastrophic loss of sacred knowledge. We have seen the beginnings of a separatist Aboriginal intelligentsia with its own imperatives, among them an insistence that attention should now be devoted to modern, English-language material from acculturating groups, rather than to traditional culture. At the same time, there has been the world success of Western Desert art based on the earth-painting and body designs of the past. This art is fully readable only by initiate tribesfolk; for the rest of us, its significance resides in its great formal beauty and the sense that it does contain complex meanings. We have thus arrived, for the time being, at a constrained but genuine reverence for closed boxes, whose original contents may be evaporating even as we admire them. My own earlier essay 'The Human-Hair Thread' thus does not reflect current doctrine, but is amplified by frequent recourse to Aboriginal concepts in my writing since, recourse based on their profundity and high importance. Another essay, 'Filming a Poem', was written to be translated into French for the Cannes film festival, and so I thought it wise to update the poem's pre-1914 Australian street slang for the translator's benefit. I have now left my updated versions in place as a courtesy to British readers! I don't imagine any other such glosses will be needed elsewhere in the book: we're not yet quite foreign to one another.

Les Murray
Bunyah, NSW
April 1992

Celebrating the Fields

Complete Poems of Andrew Young (Martin Secker & Warburg, 1974)

Although he lived until 1971, Andrew Young belongs to a world before the recent servitude of poetry to intellectual tastes. As that world survived longer in Australia, perhaps, than elsewhere, he is of special interest to us, particularly if we compare him with John Shaw Neilson, another very fine and dedicated poet whose quality, though admitted, is obscured by current canons.

Born in Elgin, Scotland, in 1885, Andrew Young was a country parson and amateur naturalist. Probably the biggest event in his life was his shift from the ministry of the United Free Church of Scotland to the priesthood of the Anglican Church. Having thus moved, as it were, from faith to religion, he emigrated to England and spent the rest of his life there in a quiet country parish, going up to London only rarely and never for more than a day, as he disapproved of the values of London.

His flavour is his own, but if I set up a triangle of names, I think it would fall substantially between them. The names would be Douglas Stewart, John Shaw Neilson, and Emily Dickinson. Perhaps the figure would need to be a square, with the name of John Clare at the fourth corner, though somewhat strangely Young didn't wholly admire Clare. Quotation is better than geometry, though:

> I listened to the grasshoppers
> Like small machines mowing the hay,
> Hot and content to think myself
> As busy and idle as they
>
> from 'The Old Man'

or one might cite 'The Haystack', in full:

> Too dense to have a door
> Window or fireplace or a floor,
> They saw this cottage up,
> Huge bricks of grass, clover and buttercup

11

Carting to byre and stable
Where cow and horse will eat wall, roof and gable.

Young is no simple nature poet – there aren't any of those. He is a miniaturist, a poet in a long and honourable English succession, celebrating the fields and streams, the mountains and villages and wildflowers of Britain in delicate verse too well-knit to admit intrusive analysis.

Where he is weak, the verse grows wispy, and the conventional rhymes *look* conventional. There are quite a few pieces, in what is a thick book, which I must admit look as thin and hackneyed as hymn texts without the music. But the good ones, and there are many of those, too, all have the light touch which still conveys solidity and texture. Occasionally, too, a gentle but bone-deep irony that I can't help placing as Scottish comes through. Imagine a Christian minister writing 'Cuckoos':

When coltsfoot withers and begins to wear
Long silver locks instead of golden hair,
And fat red catkins from black poplars fall
And on the ground like caterpillars crawl
And bracken lifts up slender arms and wrists
And stretches them, unfolding sleepy fists,
The cuckoos in a few well-chosen words
Tell they give Easter eggs to the small birds.

Young's handsome paperback *Complete Poems* contains one whole mystery play and salvaged bits of a couple more, as well as two very interesting long poems, 'Into Hades' and 'A Traveller in Time'. These lie somewhere between J.B. Priestley, C.S. Lewis, and in the case of the latter, MGM. I don't think either succeeds, but the better of the two, 'Into Hades', does have an authentically ghostly feel, and some patches of real terror.

The strength of Andrew Young doesn't lie in his mystical or visionary writing, however, nearly as much as in his ability to take a common object or scene and draw out its significance till it resonates deep in the mind. If you're undecided about buying the book – so many books of verse have snubbed you, perhaps – let me tempt you with another sample, 'Fenland':

Where sky is all around
And creeps in dykes along the ground,
I see trees stand outlined
Too distant to be tossed with wind.

And farther still than these
Stand but the tops of other trees,
As on the ocean's rim
Vessels half sunk in water swim.

Where there is so much sky
And earth tip level to my eye,
Trees and trees farther hide
Far down the steep world's mountain-side.

Pound Devalued

The Pisan Cantos, by Ezra Pound (Faber and Faber, 1973)

Members of Ezra Pound's circle in Italy, I've heard, were expected to be able to identify without hesitation any passage from his immensely long meditative-polemic poem sequence, the *Cantos*. They played this game among themselves, and to be stumped brought grave loss of face. Other poets have also had their heelers, of course, but I like the inner-circle flavour of that yarn. All the humourless, competitive owlishness of discipleship is in it. The outer circles of the same cult run through nearly every university and college in the Western World.

Pound is still regarded by many as one of the heroes of the modernist breakthrough in poetry, and his imitators are legion. Better and more intelligent men than Ezra Pound have devoted years of study to his texts, and written immensely complex books about them. He is a mainstay of the lit. crit. industry, and a major influence.

All establishments exist to compel acceptance and to deflect, for as long as possible, the question of absolute quality. In both respects the Pound establishment has been highly successful. In an era of the political test in literature, they have even been able to gloss over their hero's fascism. There is an unpleasant sense in which Pound has been forgiven much because he is the universities' man; the wealth of thesis material in his texts has made it inexpedient to judge their poetic quality too scrupulously, and the story of his arrest for treason and subsequent committal to a mental hospital in the US has redounded to his credit among the romantically alienated.

For my own part, after having once long ago thought Pound's interminable heaping up of recherché allusion intriguing, I now believe that old Ez was a pathetically colonial, phony-rumbustious biblioholic from Philadelphia who made a lot of noise, did a crucial piece of editing on Eliot's *Waste Land*, but never achieved poetry in his own right. In mitigation of this, I should perhaps add the view of the American critic Yvor Winters that 'Pound is a talented man who has quite obviously been off his trolley for a great many years; he is a backwash in the development of modern poetry, and about 75 years behind his time.'

The *Pisan Cantos*, numbers LXXIV to LXXXIV in the overall sequence, have now been beautifully reprinted by the court publishers to the 1920s literary establishment, Faber and Faber. They have the same structure and exhibit the same bag of tricks as those which precede them. On an approximately trochaic metrical base, Pound does all his tiresome tricks of counterpoint and apposition, of mimicry and echo, of sudden shifts of sense and language. He will start a line with a quotation from some obscure US senator, drop in a phrase or two in Italian, turn the result on a Greek word (either romanized or in the original script), go on for a couple of lines in archaizing English, add a Chinese ideogram, follow it with a line in contemptuous phonetic spelling meant to represent the speech of the uneducated – but the whole never reaches any sort of resolution, let alone the fusion-heat of poetry. In these late Cantos we don't even encounter the odd passages of sustained rhetoric – the famous one against Usura is an example – which, in the earlier Cantos, were Pound's nearest approach to poetry.

Now complex, allusive, inclusive poetry is nothing new; from Virgil to Dante to the Goethe of the Faust plays to MacDiarmid and Francis Webb, the list is a long one. It is the high manner of our art. Perhaps the main difference between modern practitioners and most, though not all, past ones has lain in the moderns' greater readiness to leave some of the roughnesses in, lending a feeling of multiplicity and struggle to the work and highlighting the resolutions which they arrive at. The battle for redeeming insight and the perplexities of our information-sodden, prescriptively despairing times are enacted during the course of the work, rather than being chiselled into lapidary utterance from the beginning.

Pound's contribution has been to loosen the whole method and make it wilful, a flaccid grab-bag that will take any amount of ill-digested book-learning. His verse is thronged but never dense, obscure but never concentrated. It is a rhetoric of hints and nudges, of half-considered ironies and juxtapositions, of reliance on accident and exegesis. These late Cantos are what may one day be seen as the typical 'poetry' of an age in which an audience of commentators, ambitious and eager for a slice of poets' action, invited us to a new form of corruption: be wild and colourful and slapdash; half-do your work and we'll complete it by interpretation.

The achievement of the Pound-Eliot breakthrough was to deliver us into such hands. They ensured that, in the English-speaking world more than anywhere else, the appeal of poetry would be to a self-consciously intellectual audience, with consequent atrophy of its appeal to readers of any other kind. They, more than anyone else, made a certain slangy-mandarin tone dominant in poetry, though Eliot did, in later life, retreat from the colloquial and make his tone more traditionally mandarin.

Pound went on to promote the ideal of the bohemian guru standing over against the Establishment, an ideal which led on to the grotesqueries of Messrs Ginsberg, Ferlinghetti, and a score of others. The Sharon Tate murders may be said to have consummated that line of historical development.

In making poetry an art for intellectuals and scholars, Pound and Eliot handed us over to an establishment to which the question of quality is, finally, irrelevant. To a scholar, a work of art is an artefact; its importance lies in the amount of cultural history it contains, in the number of profound matters it raises, not how well it raises them or what beauty it wrings from them. It is no accident that one of the most fruitful digs in modern archaeology was done on the Chicago city dump.

Again, the central business of scholarship is with the assigning of credit: who did what first, under what influences and to what effect. The importance of Pound, Eliot, and their European coevals was therefore always the breakthrough they made, not the quality of the verse they produced. This attitude, coming to dominate criticism as it has done, has meant that authors are granted the ultimate accolades for innovation rather than for quality.

The approach is historical and progressivist, concerned more with state-of-the-art than with art. It is better to be new and daring than to write well. The resulting damage to poetry from all this has not been fatal, of course; the more grievous damage has been to its reception by readers. People have been confused and scared off and misled, taught to look for the wrong things – to confuse a poet's biography with his work, for example – and worse, have been allowed to overlook whole classes of poetry not readily susceptible to scholarly analysis.

The worst effect on writers of the link with the intellectual class has been a pervasive temptation to élitism and alienation; we are lumped in with the intelligentsia, and many of us, perhaps all but the best, forget our older dignity. The result is an endless succession of writers estranged from and often contemptuous of non-literary mankind as it exists in the industrial age. The central question of art becomes one of flies and fly-bottles. The compassionate élite response is to hate the bottle and seek to get the fly out; the response of Pound and very many more, particularly from the New World, has been to scorn the fly for being in the bottle.

I mention the New World for a purpose. Both T.S. Eliot, whom I consider a real poet, and Ezra Pound came to Europe in advance of the wave of American literary *émigrés* of the twenties. The wind that impelled them across the Atlantic was blown, long before, from the cheeks of Alexis de Tocqueville, when he spoke of the difficulty of reconciling excellence with the ideal and practice of human equality. In a profound sense, Eliot and Pound were in flight from equality – which I take to be the central theme of the New World, explicit with the Americans, a matter of folk tradition with us – towards an ideal of high culture. The result was almost always self-falsification and defeat.

Eliot became a facsimile English gentleman and wrote less and less well, and the career of Ezra Pound ended in a kind of tragedy which I think the *Pisan Cantos* exemplify. He was crushed by the weight of what he embraced. His verse, increasingly with the years, has a sort of interminable cunning obliquity common to the socially insecure and the mad, in so far as both desperately want to be heard but are terrified of giving themselves away. Everything is allusion and significant winking, every impending lucidity in the Cantos is hurriedly deflected by magpie philology, in case any of the sophisticated readership which the writer courts and fears should ever impute a barbarian simple-mindedness to the clever boy from Philadelphia.

Of all the recurring themes in these pieces, perhaps the obsessive anti-Semitism comes closest to outright statement – but that has precisely the force of obsession to drive it. Unlike Eliot, Pound did not drop that particular potato when it grew hot; by the thirties and forties it had become pretty well the staple food of his imagination and the squashy touchstone of his view of history. It was this that led him to broadcast for the Axis powers during the Second World War and caused his post-war sufferings. In the end, the aspect of European culture which he mastered and made his own was a grubby paranoia.

The Lost Inheritance

An Introduction to Gaelic Poetry, by Derick Thomson (Victor Gollancz, 1974)

Not long ago, I was at an Irish-Australian party in Sydney – most parties here are at least a bit Irish – and a visitor from the Republic sang a very beautiful song in Gaelic, the old royal language of Scotland and Ireland. He was pretty well ignored. The descendants, at only three or four generations' remove, of Gaelic-speaking Irish immigrants had totally lost that side of the tradition they were trying to celebrate. And yet many of their attitudes, even their turns of phrase, were only really comprehensible in terms of that lost inheritance. Their education had been concerned with other things and had failed to draw out and elucidate the elements of their past for them.

Although from the beginning white Australians have been an Anglo-Celtic rather than an Anglo-Saxon people, and although we have gradually become a people of richly diverse origins, our education remains overwhelmingly English, with a Franco-American bohemianism being picked up by some as an extra-curricular alternative, mostly at university level.

Now, certainly, English law, English tradition, English literature and the values of the old Empire have been central in forming our culture, and would be well worth studying even if they hadn't. The insistence of the Anglo-Australian Establishment, however, that our education be based almost exclusively on the priorities of the gentry and merchant classes of England, on the English bourgeois interpretation of history, is out of date for us now, a colonial hangover – and paradoxical in a country that claims an egalitarian temper. Only the sternest upholder of popular Darwinism, that curious nineteenth-century theory which glorifies bullies and winners, could claim that, although the ancient Celtic cultures were native to the ancestors of perhaps one half of today's Old Australians, they weren't worth studying because they had been defeated.

And yet, to date, no Australian university has a chair of Celtic studies, any more than it has, say, a chair of Aboriginal studies (as distinct, necessarily, from a department of Anthropology). The closest we've come to getting a Celtic department was probably eight or nine years ago, when the Australian National University acquired the late Archbishop Duhig's splendid collection of Gaelic books in return for a promise to set up such a department; the books were immediately salted away in the Menzies Library and the promise forgotten. In the schools, of course, there's nothing, and there won't be until the universities give a lead.

If they ever do give such a lead, I can't imagine a better introduction to at least one of the Celtic traditions than Professor Thomson's clearly written and comprehensive account of Scottish Gaelic poetry from its beginnings as an independent tradition down to our own day. I can't imagine a better introduction for the general reader, either; the book is far from being a dry academic text, though the scholarship is impeccable. Derick Thomson, a Lewisman, is head of Celtic studies at the University of Glasgow, founder of the magazine *Gairm*, and, under his Gaelic name of Ruaraidh Mac-Thomais, a highly regarded modern poet of Gaelic-speaking Scotland. A quotation from one of his own poems will demonstrate his quality:

> That night
> the scarecrow came into the ceilidh-house;
> a tall, thin black-haired man
> wearing black clothes.
> He sat on a stool
> and the cards fell from our hands,
> one man
> was telling a folktale about Conall Gulban
> and the words froze on his lips.
> A woman was sitting on a stool
> singing songs, and he took the goodness out of the music.

Plenty of peoples around the world, victims of the empires and the missionaries of Calvinism, progress and the like, would understand this poem very well.

Huge amounts of the older poetry of Gaelic Scotland have been lost to us; poems were memorized and passed down orally, and only occasionally were some of them written down and preserved in books. Many of these books were lost or destroyed with the passage of time, destroyed not least by Gaelic-hating Calvinist preachers eager, like Lowland schoolmasters, to eradicate the language of popery and Jacobitism and get rid of an administrative inconvenience. The surviving literature, however, presents us with pictures of a social order perhaps more interesting to the present generation than it might have been to those just past. By contrast with urban societies in which nearly everyone is technically literate but in which only a few appreciate art of any quality or are free from a pitiful inarticulateness of spirit, this was a rural society in which art, eloquence, and a clear sophistication of mind were commonplace even among the illiterate majority.

This was, and some extent still is, a result of the strong tradition of oral learning common in all Celtic cultures. The bardic system, however, had something to do with it, too. As the old tribal order passed away – it was dead on its feet well before Culloden – the bards, whose function it had been to uphold society by praising and commemorating the chiefs and celebrating high deeds, became obsolete, and their closed-shop traditions of poetic craftmanship and technique broke down, to be replaced by simpler metres and a diversification of subject matter. The bards had, however, trained an audience, and the high standard of craftsmanship they had upheld stayed in the collective memory of the Gael. Poetry of a high order remained popular, a natural and accepted vehicle for expressing what was important to the society.

Even the master-poets of the old schools had often turned their hands to songs and poems outside their usual ambit of genealogy, eulogy, and elegy. Here, from around the year 1600, are the first and last stanzas of a love poem by Niall Mor Mac Mhuirich, of the great McCurrie line of bards – I wish I could cite the whole poem:

> Farewell forever to last night;
> swift though it passed, its joy remains;
> though I were hanged for my share in it
> I'd live it over tonight again. . . .
>
> Mother Mary, of fostering grace,
> since poets look to you for light,
> save me now, and take my hand
> farewell forever to last night.

If you have ever wondered why the popular songs and ballads of Scotland and Ireland often seem more elevated and complex in their language than those of, say, England and America, this is a large part of the reason. A popular culture does not have to be crude, nor do its songs need to be always monosyllabic and simple to the point of illiteracy. From the time of the collapse of the old tribal order right down to the terrible dispersions of the Gael all over the world, a period of nearly two centuries, Gaelic culture was perhaps the highest 'folk' civilization in Europe.

Perhaps the other most striking thing which Professor Thomson demonstrates is the strength of Gaelic poetry in this century, in a time of catastrophic decline in the numbers of people speaking the language. I would go so far as to say that England herself, with her millions of people, has not, at least since the last war, produced any poets superior to those who have been writing for a potential audience of only ninety thousand or so in the Scottish highlands and islands. Poets such as Sorley Maclean, George Campbell Hay, Iain Crichton Smith, Donald MacAulay, Catriona and Morag Montgomery and many of the upcoming generation are introduced to us, and are well worth following up.

They have proved that Gaelic poetry can engage modern themes and complexities while retaining much of its characteristic flavour and that piercing clarity which has always given the lie to notions of Celtic twilight. For the first time, some of today's poets are Lowlanders who have learned Gaelic as second language and have chosen to write in it. Despite the continuing decline in the Gaelic-speaking population, the author is optimistic for the future of Gaelic poetry in this century at least.

To illustrate the clarity we spoke of, though, and the timeless beauty of the best poetry still being written in the language of Lachlan Macquarie and my own ancestors, here is an excerpt, slightly abridged, from the poem 'Turas' (Journey) by the young poet Iain Macdonald:

> High tide near
> and the seaweed beginning to float.
> We begin to collect it.

> It was not too large a raft of seaweed
> but it was thick, well-packed.
> It would grow enough potatoes for us.

> We set off with it,
> tied to the thwart,
> the gathering held, did not give way.

It had grown cold
before we got home, a red splash
in the west growing larger.

A pale moon
rising, a petticoat
of clouds below it, a high tide calm.

That was another night, another year.

A Folk University

Cole of the Book Arcade: A Biography of E.W. Cole, by Cole Turnley (1974)

Aside from official universities, whose real if unadmitted courses might be listed as Caste, Debunking and Alienation, Australia has had a small number of what might be called folk universities. One was the famous Carnegie library at Borroloola, in the remote Northern Territory, where the books, stored in the cells of the local lock-up, served to educate a generation of outback drovers and drinkers. Another was E.W. Cole's famous Book Arcade in Melbourne.

In its heyday in the last two decades of the nineteenth century, Cole's Book Arcade had over a million books on its shelves and a host of supporting attractions that included a monkey house, a band to supply music, a tea salon, a bazaar complete with Indian hawkers, and an Ornament Exhibition billed as 'the prettiest sight in Australia'.

Best of all, it was the policy of the Arcade that anyone might read the stock to his heart's content without being asked to buy. An autodidact's paradise! There was nothing like the Arcade anywhere else, and it was the heart and pride of Melbourne throughout the boom years and the 1890s depression alike. It was also a very personal creation, and depended for its life on the wonderfully humane, eccentric, moralizing spirit of its founder. Within ten years of his death in 1918, at the ege of eighty-six, the great Arcade was gone, and only the unique *Cole's Funny Picture Books* survived as its memorial, being 'among the oddest, oldest and most deeply rooted of Australian traditions', as the poet Randolph Stow has described them, and a publishing phenomenon with few parallels. Never out of print since Cole's own day, they have sold over three million copies.

Edward William Cole was born in the village of Woodchurch, near Tenterden in Kent, on 4 January 1832. His father, a farm labourer named Amos Cole, died when Edward was three or four years old, and the boy's mother subsequently married a man called

John Watson, a strict Wesleyan but a kindly man, who always treated Edward and his elder brother Richard as though they were his own children, and taught them to read from the family Bible before sending them to the village school. Here young Edward came under the influence of a schoolmaster who was something of a freethinker and who introduced the boy to astronomy. Reproved sternly by his stepfather when he voiced doubts about the biblical story of creation, Cole nevertheless grew up with an independent and questioning mind.

Given his half of the forty sovereigns the boys' father had left them, he considered joining his elder brother on the Californian goldfields, but fear of crossing the ocean caused him to seek his fortune in London instead. There he hawked sandwiches, almost starved, very nearly took the Queen's Shilling – he was a quarter of an inch too short, and was told by the recruiting sergeant to 'come back when you're not so tired and slumped-like' – and finally migrated, first to South Africa, then to Australia.

Melbourne, when young Cole landed there, was a raw frontier town in the grip of gold fever. Cole and a mate went to the Forest Creek diggings, where the mate died of a combination of typhoid and dysentery known in those days as Colonial Fever. Alone again, as he preferred to be – all his life, Cole was happiest, he said, in 'the company of one' – the ex-digger found he could earn more by selling lemonade to the miners than with his pick and shovel, and thus set up the first of the stalls which he was to run and out of which, more than a decade later, the Book Arcade was to grow.

A many-minded, thoughtful, and energetic man, Cole combined his business ventures with a programme of omnivorous and meditative reading which included anything he could get on the great religions of the world. He became what we would call a syncretist, convinced of the validity and value of all the great religious traditions, and the earliest of his many attempts at educating the public in tolerance and the broader view was a pamphlet titled *The Real Place in History of Jesus and Paul*, which he brought out in 1867. Then, and on the many subsequent occasions on which he trotted it out, this pamphlet, like most of his other serious philosophical writings, only achieved any substantial circulation when its author gave it away for nothing.

From the quotations which his grandson Cole Turnley scatters through his affectionate and very well-written biography, one can see why. For the most part, though the ideas aren't all bad, the tone is naïve, sentimental and preachy, though the last-mentioned quality shouldn't have mattered in an age very nearly as preachy as our own. The style is all wrong for intellectual readers, too programmatic and simplistic by half, while some of Cole's ideas may well have seemed too much in advance of their time for the general reader. He did have the satisfaction, though, thirty-odd years after he had predicted it, of seeing heavier-than-air flight achieved.

Cole had a fervent belief in the coming federation of mankind, and supported the federation of the Australian colonies as a step towards it. Accordingly, he was bitterly disappointed by the adoption of the White Australia policy, and fought against it in a stream of books and other writings, all to no avail.

Many of Cole's serious concerns, his lifelong opposition to the evils of racism and smoking, for example, left their deposits in the *Funny Picture Books*, but his yearning to be listened to and regarded as a thinker and man of letters, rather than merely as a highly original merchandiser of books, went almost totally unsatisfied. Melbourne and Australia thought of Cole as perhaps the supreme eccentric of his times: they were delighted by the original things he did, and by his Book Arcade with its rainbows and its notions. They loved to recall the story of how he advertised for a wife, and got one, but they took less notice of his achievement in getting right through the Hungry Nineties without sacking any of his staff.

But I won't pre-empt all of the good things in the book. It is very well produced, and a lesson to publishers in the art of producing illustrated books which *are* books and not merely coffee-table extravaganzas. The cover carries a reproduction of the cover of the first *Funny Picture Book*: only one very valuable specimen of this edition is now known to exist.

Let your last thinks be all thanks

Thank You, Fog: Last Poems, by W.H. Auden (Faber and Faber, 1974)

Jaunty, Mozartian in its easy mastery, and permeated by the spectre
of approaching death, W.H. Auden's last collection contains the
poems that he completed after leaving New York in the spring of
1972 to return to his native England.

The book is a compound of farewells and acknowledgements and
the graceful closing of accounts. He addresses Fog:

> Grown used to New York weather,
> all too familiar with Smog,
> You, Her unsullied Sister,
> I'd quite forgotten and what
> You bring to British winters:
> now native knowledge returns.

As is proper to age, memory is summoned and summed up; in
'A Thanksgiving', he gives us most of the biography we need to
know about any poet:

> When pre-pubescent I felt
> that moorlands and woodlands were sacred:
> people seemed rather profane
>
> Thus when I started to verse,
> I presently sat at the feet of
> *Hardy* and *Thomas* and *Frost*.
>
> Falling in love altered that,
> now someone, at least, was important:
> *Yeats* was a help, so was *Graves*.
>
> Then, without warning, the whole
> Economy suddenly crumbled:
> there, to instruct me, was *Brecht*.

> Finally hair raising things
> that Hitler and Stalin were doing
> Forced me to think about God.

> Why was I sure they were wrong?
> Wild *Kierkegaard, Williams* and *Lewis*
> guided me back to belief.

Of course autobiography at this level is a composed thing, with the twists and turnings and quirks smoothed away. For today's poets, an orderly succession of influences like the one Auden gives might seem strange; our influences come in from all sides, and simultaneously. 'After the Industrial Revolution, all things happen at once', as Robert Bly says in one of his poems. Auden goes on:

> Now, as I mellow in years
> and home in a bountiful landscape,
> Nature allures me again.

> Who are the tutors I need?
> Well, *Horace*, adroitest of makers,
> beeking in Tivoli, and

> *Goethe*, devoted to stones,
> who guessed that – he never could prove it –
> Newton led Science astray.

> Fondly I ponder You all:
> without you I couldn't have managed
> even my weakest of lines.

A lot of us have worked through all these influences and more in less than a lifetime – but how many of us have profited so much from them, or surpassed so many of them and remained capable of gratitude? Of course, he is cheating a bit, to leave out Lord Byron, whom he once called 'master of the airy manner'. Byron's lightness and grace echo in Auden's own later work, and help to make him the abolute master of airy, civilized verse in our own day. In a time of high if often strident solemnity, Auden's dancing seriousness, with more warmth in it than Byron ever managed, may be the thing we'll miss most about him.

Notice, by the way, the capitalized *You* in the poem above, and the subtly odd use of *home* and *allures* in the stanza at which I took up the poem again. A certain courtly if ironic usage of capitals and a wilful confusion of the parts of speech, as well as a deliberately recherché vocabulary, are trademarks of the later Auden. But how beautifully he does it:

> What disastered a city,
> volcanic effusion,
> fluvial outrage,
>
> or a human horde
> agog for slaves and glory,
> is visually patent,
>
> and we're pretty sure that,
> as soon as palaces were built,
> their rulers,
>
> though gluttoned on sex
> and blanded by flattery,
> must often have yawned.
>
> from 'Archaeology'

I quoted you that piece to demonstrate a technique, but the coda of the same poem is even more worth quoting for a different reason. I offer it to militants and military men alike:

> From Archaeology
> one moral, at least, may be drawn,
> to wit, that all
>
> our school text-books lie.
> What they call History
> is nothing to vaunt of,
>
> being made, as it is,
> by the criminal in us:
> goodness is timeless.

The book, you see, isn't all valedictory; even the farewelling pieces often engage the current books and theories people are talking about. Auden was a great partaker in the intellectual conversation of mankind. There is, for example, a poem called 'Ode to the Diencephalon', which takes up current controversy regarding the lack of harmony between the 'older' and 'newer' structures, from an evolutionary point of view, in man's brain.

Another, called 'Unpredictable but Providential', dedicated to the biologist-philosopher Loren Eiseley, is derived, I would imagine, from a review article on Eiseley's work which Auden published in the *New Yorker*: this one contains a passage which I treasure and dedicate to, I suppose, the Progress Party:

> As a rule, it was the fittest who
> perished, the mis-fits
> forced by failure to emigrate to
> unsettled niches, who
> altered their structure and prospered.

When Auden died, on 29 September 1973, *Thank You, Fog* existed in typescript and had its title, but it remained only about half as long as the average Auden volume.

To make up heft, the publishers have added two fragments from Auden's and Chester Kallmann's libretto for the musical comedy *Man of La Mancha*, which they were commissioned to write in 1963, but which, in the end, was written entirely by others, and the text of Auden's last work for the stage, an antimasque called *The Entertainment of the Senses*, again written in collaboration with Kallmann, as an introduction for James Shirley's masque *Cupid and Death* (1653). This was performed for the first time in February 1974 at the Queen Elizabeth Hall, London, with music by John Gardner.

The *Man of La Mancha* fragments include one song lyric that is at least jaunty and singable in the Broadway style, but really it's a pity that this padding material had to be put in at all. The antimasque is full of clever things but so cumbrous and artificial in its structure that it can't survive reading on the page, and would be far too much of a jewelled-and-gowned piece of antiquarian High Culture to appeal to anyone much nowadays.

Perhaps the most moving of Auden's last poems is 'Lullaby', with its lovely mocking refrain of 'Sing, big baby, sing lullay'. When I came upon this one last year in the *Listener*, it moved me deeply. 'Let your last thinks be all thanks', it goes – but I'll give you the whole last stanza:

> Now for oblivion: let
> the belly-mind take over
> down below the diaphragm,
> the domain of the Mothers,

They who guard the Sacred Gates,
without whose wordless warnings
soon the verbalising I
becomes a vicious despot,
lewd, incapable of love,
disdainful, status-hungry,
Should dreams haunt you, heed them not,
for all, both sweet and horrid,
are jokes in dubious taste,
too jejune to have truck with:
Sleep, big baby, sleep your fill.

A North Coast Poet

Creekwater Journal, by Robert Gray (University of Queensland Press, 1975)

Hitherto, I've avoided reviewing Australian poetry, mainly to avoid any appearance of mutual backscratching between myself and other poet-reviewers. I'm prepared to abandon even stuffiness, however, to write about Robert Gray's new collection. I'm most enthusiastic about it.

Mr Gray has an eye, and the verbal felicity which must accompany an eye. He can use epithet and image to perfection and catch a whole world of sensory understanding in a word or a phrase. *Creekwater Journal* is full of examples:

> a flock of pigeons
> walking. Nothing else around.
> The pigeons pedal off in all
> directions, eyes backwards –
> they keep pecking
> the air in front of them
>   from 'Church grounds'

or again, a haiku, one of many in a book which pauses every so often to pour out dozens of brilliant short pieces, *aperçus*, haiku, tiny imagistic poems:

> 4 am; the Milky Way
> is blown along, high over the forest.
> A truck changes down.

and, from the first poem in the book, titled 'Journey: the North Coast', a more complex effect, but done with the same inventive rightness:

> Now the man's gone
> who had the bunk below me. I swing out,
> cover his bed and rattle up the sash –

there's sunlight teeming
on the drab carpet. And the water sways –
solidly in its silver basin, so cold
it joins together through my hand.

Robert Gray is thirty this year and comes from Coffs Harbour.
Creekwater Journal, a title which delights me (and I'm fussy about
titles) appears in the generous Paperback Poets series put out by
UQP, and contains a few poems resuscitated from Mr Gray's earlier
Lyrebird Writers collection. I wish more had been retrieved: there
was an excellent piece in that book called, if I remember rightly,
'The Idiom', in which the speech, and through it the world, of North
Coast country people was caught perfectly. But I can't really com-
plain. His new collection catches very much more of the life Up
Home with equal or greater finesse. Take 'A labourer', for instance;
the man comes out to the woodheap at dawn, still half asleep:

a bone-smooth axe handle pointing at him. It lifts the block
on a corner of beetled, black
earth. The logs are like rolled roasts,
they tear apart on red-fibred meat. The axe squeaks out.
Lifting it –
the head pulls backwards –
now he sinks to where he is. And the new tile roofs
encroaching about
in the thin water of the sun;

The North Coast in Gray's poems is always slightly sad, slightly
valedictory, a simpler world that has achieved all of its possibilities
and reached a standstill:

Seeing these small towns, it brings to mind
the lives of old women
            . . . .
In those houses is the smell of bottled vegetables,
and of something else –
it is the sexual hatreds, stored away
like china or cuff links,
that will never be spoken.
                    from 'Within the Traveller's Eye'

Mr Gray's poetry doesn't stick to the North Coast exclusively; it
moves in and out of the cities, touching the world of boarding-
houses, of dead-end jobs taken to raise a stake, of suburbs and

working people, and the pigeons who rose in the air at the crash of Ronald Ryan's hanging.

Everywhere, though, without being monotonous, the slightly autumnal note I spoke of in the North Coast poems reappears. It is a tone familiar to us from many modern writers, from Camus and the existentialists perhaps most of all: that almost affectless equanimity of the uprooted modern person which can come out as deep melancholy. With its almost hallucinatory clarity and very cool use of common-life objects, it is a tone we strike in Gary Snyder, where Snyder is not being coverly polemical, and in many other American poets of recent times.

No other Australian poet has so completely mastered the lessons of Donald Hall's *Penguin Book of Contemporary American Poetry*, a collection which, from its first appearance in 1962, has had a considerable and much-advertised effect on Australian writers. The note Mr Gray strikes, the signature of his poetry as it were, is one well beyond the élitism and class warfare of so much other modern writing, but I suspect the path it is following is a dead end for Western poets, and that Mr Gray himself will turn aside from it fairly soon.

I refer, of course, to Zen. Mr Gray has been to school to the Zen masters, at the usual removes of ocean and language, but with more than usual benefits. All the same, there is a sense in which Zen can be a knack, a 'sound' as rock fans might say, which, once you master it, enables you to turn out neat, spare, portentous strings of free-form imagery till the cows come home. Gradually, you may lose touch with that Homeric many-mindedness and sense of wrestling with complexities of sense and music that has been the spinal strength of Western poetry, and increasingly write poems that read like rather knowing translations. Mr Gray hasn't starved his art in this way as yet, but I think he will need, and want, to develop an ear in his future work so as to give his writing that richness of aural and rhythmical effect which to some extent it now lacks.

Having made this one stricture, I don't intend to talk futurity any more, or to use the insufferably condescending epithet *promising*. Robert Gray's poetry, as presented in this book, has no need to appeal to the future for its justification. It's right here, and a pleasure to read.

Sydney Morning Herald, 10 May 1975

From a Neighbour's Bowl

Contemporary Indonesian Poetry, edited and translated by Harry Aveling (University of Queensland Press, 1975)

A long time ago, Harry Aveling and I were fellow students in the department of Indonesian and Malayan Studies at Sydney University; that year, though, was the Winter of my Discontent, and I dropped out. Harry went on to become a leading scholar in the field and perhaps the best-known translator into English of Indonesian poetry.

Some years ago, when we met again briefly, he very kindly gave me a booklet of his translations of W.S. Rendra, the fiery Catholic poet who introduced a whole range of new styles, including a kind of talking blues, into Indonesian verse. I think I wrote him a thank-you note then; if not, he is assured that I was, and am, grateful.

Rendra, as a poet, isn't entirely my cup of brandy (I prefer brandy and dry, myself) but he's a hard spirit to ignore, once tasted, and he has intoxicated many. His 'Prostitutes of Jakarta Unite' is famous in Indonesia and beyond:

> Sarinah!
> Tell them
> How you were called to the ministerial suite
> And how he spoke long and deeply to you
> About the national struggle
> Then suddenly – without even finishing what he was saying
> Calling you the inspiration of the revolution
> Undid your bra.

Rendra has plenty of the sort of vulgarity which some readers confuse with forthright honesty, but he is often a powerful poet for all that. The quieter and more fastidious writer Ajip Rosidi brackets him with Mayakovsky, which is just, if perhaps a little hard on Rendra. His diction in Bahasa Indonesia is, as Harry Aveling translates it, free verse held back from being outright chopped prose

34

only by a certain rhetorical intensity. The vulgarity and the power seem to be inseparable, however. A long poem called 'Swan Song', for instance, in which a prostitute named Maria Zaitun, thrown out of her brothel to die of disease in the streets, contains vulgarity but also contains some really harrowing evocations of desperation in streets more destitute and terrible than any we know. In the end, when Maria has a blissful carnal interlude with the Bridegroom, who is Christ, we don't know whether to laugh or to cry.

One of the striking things about this collection, which represents the wave of poetic energy and achievement that burst forth in Indonesia around 1967, is the amount of Christianity in it. Subagio Sastrowardojo, who teaches in Salisbury, South Australia, even has a fine short hymn-like lyric on the birth of Christ. Partly, of course, this is a reflection of the fact that what this book is ultimately concerned with is an imported, European form of 'high' art radically different from older native literatures. It is a poetry of the European school and the university, of the Europeanized, Westernized side of an educated Indonesian's personality. This is not to ignore the millions of good Christian Indonesians, people who put so many of today's whingeing, well-fed Australian agnostics and residual Christians to shame. Christianity is a minority religion in Indonesia, but not a new one.

All the same, of the many attempts by different poets in this collection to build bridges across from the learned to the traditional culture, all but one are defeated by a sort of clever, shamefaced sophistication, or by a tone of slightly antiquarian artificiality. The exception is Ajip Rosidi's beautiful 'Memory of a Masked Dance from Cirebon' (*C* represents the English *CH* sound in the new orthography, by the way; the same place used to be spelt Tjirebon):

> As I watch the masked dance in the Summer Palace
> I remember the beauty of the Cirebon masked dance.
> As I listen to Tang-ak, my body gently at rest
> I remember the beauty of the gamelan of Bali.
> The further I travel, the more I see
> The more I value my own, carelessly wasted.

This, by the way, is one of the few poems in the collection which really resonates for me when I read the original text. One of my rationalizations for giving up Indonesian was always that the sound of the language didn't excite me; it seemed staccato and monotonous, all atap and rattan and rambutan, with few of those deep, strange resonances which draw one to a language. Maybe the insensitivity is all mine, therefore – but I can't free myself of the impression that few of these poems have much verbal music or aural subtlety to them.

Perhaps it would be surprising if they did, considering the extreme youth of Indonesian as a literary language. Fifty years ago, we must remember, what was to be Bahasa Indonesia was still a Malay lingua franca spoken around the islands; it entirely lacked the formal grace of, say, Javanese or peninsular Court Malay. It has thus come a very long way in a short time.

Space, or the lack of it, prevents me from mentioning all seven of the poets represented in the collection. The one I liked best was Sapardi Djoko Damono, who entirely escapes the stricture I made above; his language seems as finely turned as his sensibility is subtle and civilized. His poetry treats of religious struggle and yearning, returning again and again to the figures of Adam, Abel, and Cain as they appear in the Bible and the Koran. Linking the two traditions is easier in Bahasa Indonesia, where the Christian religious vocabulary, like the Moslem, consists for the most part of borrowed Arabic words. I will quote his 'Two poems with One Title' in its entirety, so much do I admire it:

1
The blood spills in the field. Who
is the sacrificial-animal this time, brother?
Then silence. How many ages have suffered
since He drove us out of There.

The small clouds recognise it, they shout:
Abel has been butchered, his blood cries out to God
(I am at your side, brother, look ahead
though sharp the smell of blood. We go to the world).

2
if You are Non-being, it is well that we meet
in the middle of the day: after I have killed him.
In the middle of the plain I remain alone
enduring beneath the Sun.

the trees remain stiff, they understand the bitterness
of a faithful man swept to one side

true, I killed Abel, the recipient
of nature's bitterness, of humanity's first hatred
the clouds in the sky still move, the wind
still fills the leaves; all in your name: Non-being.

What strikes home deeply here, of course, is the desolation of that phrase, 'We go to the world'. In the original, it is simply *Kita ke dunia*, the succint form in which the preposition *ke* ('to') does service for a verb.

This, it seems to me, has a classic brevity and spareness rare in the collection, and recalls the aphoristic concision of such older classical Malay literature as I've seen. Here, I suspect the language's own resources are being plumbed, whereas elsewhere it is often being forced, at the cost of some verbosity, into European thought patterns.

Mr Aveling's collection, with its very helpful preface and notes, appears in the University of Queensland Press Asian and Pacific Writings series, which is under the general editorship of Michael Wilding. It is, for my money, the most interesting book so far in the series, though comparisons are probably unfair, given the large differences between the various books and authors. It will doubtless be a valuable textbook for schools, CAEs and universities, but this in no way reduces its very real interest and suitability for the general reader. The translations are very well done, spilling little of the poetry, so far as I can judge, as they pour it from the Indonesian to the English bowl.

A lesser but still remarkable miracle is the price. Perhaps Australia's publishers have begun to repent and learn loving kindness. My only cavil at the book, which is otherwise beautifully produced, is the extreme tightness of the binding. All of the Asian and Pacific Writing series suffer from this irritating fault.

Sydney Morning Herald, 19 July 1975

An Irish Poet

High Island, by Richard Murphy (Faber and Faber, 1974)

In the introduction to his important history of Irish Letters, *Gaelic Literature Surveyed*, published in 1929, Aodh de Blácam wrote:

> In effect, the Gael found a way of life long ago, and a religious faith, that satisfied him then and forever.... His literature, therefore, contrasts in a remarkable way with that of a country such as England, where the writings of every generation mirror some philosophic change. Gaelic literature intellectually is a literature of rest, not of change: of intensive cultivation, not of experiment. It is, moreover, the image of a civilisation half heroic, half pastoral, that continues down to the present day, [one] that has never accepted industrialism and the city.

Turning firmly aside from the fascinating if distant light this casts on many aspects of Australian life, it is interesting to look at modern-day writers working through the medium of English in Ireland and in the countries to which the Irish have emigrated, and see to what extent they have kept some contact with the deep continuities of their ancestral culture.

The same goes, of course, for the Scottish Gaels, though the religious question is more complicated there. Looking at him from this point of view, Richard Murphy seems to me to be a poet who writes better the more closely he cleaves to the traditional life of Ireland, and less interestingly the further he wanders away from it. The farthest he wanders is to his childhood in colonial Ceylon:

> He's tired of winding up the gramophone
> Half way through the Three Little Maids
> And waiting for the rickshaw to return from the bazaar.
> The monsoon teems on the compound.
> A coolie, splitting cocoanuts on an iron spike,
> Stoops to wring the water from his loincloth,
> The boy picks up a box of matches.
>
> from 'Firebug'

Fair enough, I suppose, in a slack, story-telling sort of way; any magazine editor receives heaps of such near-prose every week, and, *faute de mieux*, publishes the best of it, which is usually to say that which is least long-winded and has the best central idea. But now look at 'Sunup', a woman's cry straight out of a tradition which has produced some of the greatest laments ever written:

> I kiss you both, like the sun,
> I kiss your hands and your feet,
> Your ears and your eyes,
> Both your bodies, I bless them both.
>
> Do you feel this when you make love?
> Do you love her as I loved you?
> Will you let her steal all you have
> And suffer her to leave?
>
> Meet me today! We'll find a wood
> Of blackthorn in white bud:
> And let me give you one more kiss
> Full of sun, free of bitterness.

Not all of Mr Murphy's Irish poems are of this very traditional sort, with deibhidhe and all (*deibhidhe?* that's when you rhyme a stressed with an unstressed syllable, as in kiss/bitterness, though there's more to it than that in the old strict Galic prosody), but you probably have to be able to produce something of this quality in Connemara if you claim to be a poet there. The High Island of the book's title refers to the island off the Connemara coast where Mr Murphy now lives and works. Most of his best pieces use a mask; they are dramatic poems, poems through which a person other than the author is given utterance, though there are some very good personal poems, mainly meditative ones set off by the poet's environment. 'Walking on Sunday' is an example; it begins:

> Walking on Sunday into Omey Island
> When the tide had fallen slack,
> I crossed a spit of wet ribbed sand
> With a cold breeze at my back

and 'Brian Boru's Well' is another, even better poem of the same sort, which I won't injure by excerpting. Closely related to these are the animal and bird poems, though none of these is really good except the first piece in the collection, 'Seals at High Island'. This one is superlative, and contains, among much else, the best use of the word *carnelian* in all literature.

Mr Murphy is probably best known outside Ireland for his last book, *The Battle of Aughrim*. This was a long verse sequence of epic plainness, hardness, and impersonal compassion, and was deservedly praised by Ted Hughes and many other good judges. Something of the same classic spareness and force emerges in 'Pat Cloherty's Version of The Maisie', one of the most deeply respectful heightenings of popular speech I've ever read, and one which puts most self-consciously 'proletarian' poets to shame. Excerpting this poem would be sacrilege; you should read it, and read it whole.

Of course, we should not delude ourselves that these poems are 'popular' art in any sense. The élite journals in which they appear, on both sides of the Atlantic, aren't the ordinary reading of Connemara cottars and fishermen – unless I'm very much misinformed. They are artifice, high art made by reworking and heightening traditional popular elements.

This, to my own infinite regret, is how it probably has to be for some time to come; the old popular audience for poetry is gone, or nearly gone, destroyed by industrial values and industrial entertainments I'm neither simple-minded nor snobbish enough to despise, and snubbed by a rootless modernism I'm perhaps too Gaelic-minded to admire. While we are in exile from the people, however, one of my final standards for judging the worth of a poet is his attitude towards those who will probably not read him. Applying this test to Mr Murphy, I get the right response; his work is full of the music of an un-hieratic, undivided humanity. Even though his new book is one of those tight little Faber paperbacks that you have to hold open by main force, I recommend it warmly.

The Deluge

Louis and Antoinette: A Biography, by Vincent Cronin (Collins, 1974)

We live in the winter of the monarchies; the few that remain are compromised, near-impotent curios or tourist dollar-earners buying up shares in multi-national companies against the day of their ouster. Almost any royal biography of recent times is apt, therefore, to have at least an autumnal flavour, and accounts of Louis and his queen, Antoinette (like all of Maria Theresa's daughters, she was christened Marie before her personal names, but she was never called Marie Antoinette in her lifetime), are inevitably coloured by their death on the scaffold. Vincent Cronin's sympathetic joint biography of the royal couple who were to atone for the indifference and excesses of the earlier rulers of France is one of the best biographies I've read, and corrects many defamatory untruths which are still believed.

Louis and Antoinette probably did more to promote charitable works than any earlier rulers of France, and though the queen might be slandered at court, she was popular with ordinary French people right up to the eve of the revolution, despite her Austrian birth. Charity is never enough, of course, but the royal couple did set something of a fashion for benevolent works and foundations. The king added to his unpopularity at court by paying for relief schemes out of deductions from court pensions and household expenses. Contrary to persistent legend, the queen never exerted an undue influence on the royal government, neither in her own nor in Austria's interests. The king firmly banned her from government business, and she accepted the restriction with only slight demur.

Despite the devaluation of the status of the French queen during the two preceding reigns – under Louis XIV and Louis XV alike, mistresses were exalted into play-queens and *de facto* setters of the tone while the proper queens were relegated pretty well to the pious production of legitimate heirs – Antoinette did a good deal to change and, all too late, to reset the style of the world's most influential court.

41

Co-operating with the king in his welfare and economy drives, she also expressed her own spirit in the simple, uncluttered styles of dress and ornament she favoured. Manufacturers, whose activities Louis tried to stimulate in a country of feudal agriculture and hidebound, uninventive technology, complained that the queen's fashions deprived them of work. Antoinette's real character survives in the beautiful lines, the simplicity and the gaiety of the Louis Seize style. Far from being a parasitic butterfly playing milkmaids at the Petit Trianon – to the extent that this picture isn't merely propaganda, it is a vulgar confusion of décor with life – she actually saw to it that the royal farms at Versailles ran at a profit.

Louis XIV inherited a medieval system of government in which the reforms he attempted were largely stifled by provincial jurisdictions, class privileges, and ancient bodies such as the *parlements* which, under the divine right of the Crown, could not themselves rule but could obstruct rulers. In the end, since Louis was his reserved, self-doubting self and not a royal firebrand, the system proved irreformable and was swept away violently, with the king and queen perishing as its scapegoats.

He also inherited a court as remote from the life of France as, say, Canberra is from Australia, and he and his queen tried to live against the bad traditions of that court and so reform it. In the end, the spirit of the Sun King's pleasure-park won out, and died of the victory. The style it had set for all of cultivated Europe during the eighteenth century was sophisticated, worldly, irreligious, and mad on protocol and on fashion. Childish in the shortness of its attention span and prey to any aberration so long as it wasn't conventional, the court would run after any charlatan and disdain anything so ordinary as going to church. Similarly, marriage, even royal marriage, was dull and *démodé* compared with promiscuity and intrigues.

What ennui, to have to put up with a monogamous, mass-going royal couple! Cronin is particularly worth reading on the moral and artistic background of the Revolution. He points out how the art of the epoch was incapable of expressing or dealing with man's darker side. Evil was scouted as an amusing Gothic fantasy or a priestly imposture; every cultivated person knew that man was naturally good and noble, the more so the more closely as he approached a state of savage innocence. There was a moral vanity abroad matched perhaps only by the New England Puritans of the seventeenth century or the student revolutionaries of recent years. Intellectuals, as a class, first took up their caste-strategy of comfortable disaffection during the lifetimes of Louis and Antoinette, and the work of scientists and encyclopaedists in classifying phenomena in new ways had the effect of breaking down older hierarchical modes of thinking. Alphabetical order was a revolutionary innovation in its day. Again:

> Lack of faith in God engendered a prodigious faith in man, and in quasi-religious panaceas; it had weakened faith not in monarchy but in divine right monarchy. Save among the peasants, there was little churchgoing, yet many a nobleman had his pet theosoph.

Perhaps the most poignant side of Cronin's story is his account of the way in which court gossip about the early difficulties the royal couple had in consummating their marriage – royal sex lives, being quasi-priestly, are necessarily quasi-public – and about the queen's imaginary infidelities were spread about and worked up by pamphleteers until the unfortunate woman could be believed by the ignorant to be a monster of lust, capable of incest with her son. Some of the pamphlets are quoted in an appendix, and they are degraded stuff, aimed at stirring the fears and jealousies of classes far removed from the court. In a real sense, the queen's death was made possible by the scandals and the pamphlets. They were a means whereby she could be pulled down into the dark whirlpools of the popular psyche and dealt with as a demon rather than as a human being.

Some odd commonplaces date from the last reign of the old order: potato chips, the colour puce (from a dress of Antoinette's which Louis called 'flea-coloured'), our own La Perouse, the convention of Left and Right in politics. Cronin says there is more, however. Although France has rejected any idea of a constitutional monarchy in recent years, still in that country, 'Louis and Antoinette resemble those exploded stars astronomers call black holes: invisible, but sending out powerful gravitational waves.'

Maybe so. Australians, dazzled perhaps by *la gloire* towering into the clean air above Mururoa Island, might be pardoned for suspecting that Bonapartism was a much more powerful occult star in contemporary French life.

Sydney Morning Herald, 9 March 1976

The Australian Republic

Waiting for the Australian republic is like waiting for the other shoe to drop. We all know it is coming; according to one's convictions, the waiting is therefore either a sour and uncreative delaying operation or a sort of null interregnum in which all energies are frustrated. There can be a measure of real terror, for the civic-minded, in either alternative. The human figure in a recent poem of mine, who has a fairly shadowy, infinitive sort of existence, is sitting in a nearly dry creek-bed between rains and suffering a touch of the mid-life crisis. One of the horrors facing him is that of suspension between epochs, of being

> here with your country, that will waken when it wakens,
> that won't be awakened by contempt
>   or love:
> to know you may live and die in colonial times

Many writers and others must feel something like this dread just now; Xavier Herbert notoriously does. On the other hand, there is the very real fear felt by people who can only imagine *civitas* under its present or inherited forms. Traditionally inarticulate about values, and lately more or less bullied into silence by progressives and radicals, these people were easily persuaded that a socialist republic was the only kind in prospect, and that indeed the very idea of a republic for Australia was a leftist goal. This of course is an expedient political lie, whichever side it may come from. The grain of truth in it is, rather, that the republican idea and the labour movement here grew out of roughly the same soil. Last century, before more pragmatic short-term techniques were evolved, protest against bad conditions and oppression often took a republican turn, with New World rhetoric. Eureka is the great example of this. The Labor Party has fitfully known, during its history, that severing the British connection and bringing in a republic would release much energy and lead to a great deal of change – a daunting prospect for an increasingly conservative party. It can now be argued that Labor's failure to declare

44

a republic in 1973 when the time was ripe for it was a failure of vision and of nerve which would ultimately betray many of their other initiatives in the field of national identity and self-confidence. The republic, pushed through then, would have made so many other innovations irreversible.

It may be necessary to distinguish the republican idea, with its goals of completed Australian sovereignty and the abolition of obeisances, from all current political streams here, while forcefully urging it on all parties and promoting it among the people. If, in the wake of the Vietnam war, the intelligentsia here would adopt the sort of nationalist orientation taken up by their coevals in, for example, Scotland and Wales, the colonial hangovers which subtly cripple much of our life might soon be swept away. I see little hope of this, however. Many older Australian intellectuals have a pretentious, roundabout, finessing style characteristic of late colonial times, when one is concerned not to appear unsophisticated. Straightforward nationalism might not appeal to these people; they'd be afraid of making themselves appear foolish in front of overseas guru-figures (who aren't looking, but are imagined to be). For many left-oriented people, nationalism is something for Third World peoples, not for white-skinned bourgeois ones. For most politicians, of course – and I'm not quite lumping them together with the intelligentsia – nationalism and similar ideas have a certain rhetorical charm, but are also faintly childish; they aren't insiders' currency, but rather the sort of thing which at once misses the point and pricks the conscience. For similar reasons, they tend to be rejected with scorn by the sort of people, usually clever first-generation types, who wish to be thought insiders. The attitudes of vernacular Australia, that is to say of the people who know they're not in on the action, are as always subtler and more various, though intense defiant patriotism and intense fear of seeming to talk bullshit or to be taken in by it are contending spirits there. All in all, this picture is what I have in mind when I use terms like late-colonial; many of the attitudes are probably similar to those existing a century and more ago in Europe, at the start of the various movements for national independence, though our distrust of rhetoric is probably greater and more typically twentieth century. Raw rhetoric and superheated hyperbole have tended to follow the wave of active nationalist struggle as it spreads farther and farther out into the former colonial world from its European beginnings. One could say that much of our national timidity and frustration as a people stem from an inhibition in language: we keep snubbing ourselves out of speaking the liberating word.

It would be altogether simple-minded to assert that republicanism of the ordinary sort would suffice as our liberating word. In at least two very different ways the republic is already here. It can be aruged that we have been a republic of sorts since 11 November 1975. Anyone who believed that the Crown might still act as some sort of ultimate talisman of political decency was undeceived that day, and his illusions were then trampled underfoot by the English monarch's reply to the appeal by the Speaker of Federal Parliament, Mr Scholes. Since this final Singapore of the monarchical remnant in Australian politics, we have been a sort of Establishment republic lightly disguised as an absentee monarchy. It is almost overt: even the restoration, since Labor's downfall, of a few monarchical trappings has been half-hearted and inconsequent, and there is much disarray in what has been restored: knighthoods *and* the Order of Australia, a choice of five national anthems, no return to the English monarch's portrait on postage stamps – it all bespeaks a style on the verge of passing away, and in which no one any longer believes. The republic, on the other hand, is held back from having its catalysing and liberating effect on the national life by being kept covert, implicit, undeclared. The situation is the worst imaginable, but may be of value if it forces us to take a slow, deep look and recognize the other main way in which the republic already exists and has indeed existed for a long time. This other republic, the one we have to discern, is inherent in our vernacular tradition, which is to say in that 'folk' Australia, part imaginary and part historical, which is the real matrix of any distinctiveness we possess as a nation, and which stands over against all of our establishments and colonial élites. This is the Australia of our deepest common values and identifications, the place of our quiddities and priorities and family jokes. The Melbourne Cup and the Fair Go and a myriad gum-trees live there, along with equality and Anzac Day and the Right Thing. It is the strain of denying or pretending to be indifferent to this stratum in our psyche that gives the prose style of many of our more conscientiously disaffected intellectuals and artists its unmistakeable shrill, hectoring note. It is this stratum which the Whitlam victory touched in 1972, with results that may be irreversible for all that has happened since. It is hard to forget the return of all those expatriates, often having no very real prospects here but all full of a sort of excited, overflowing love of country they might have disclaimed if they'd been taxed with it – and which was too obvious to need much comment anyway.

Not that the vernacular republic consists merely in a tribal excitement. It is the subsoil of our common life, and to live consciously outside it or in opposition to it, without expatriating oneself, is a crippling strain. A few genuine royalists, deeply romantic folk on the edge of eccentricity or over it, should probably be added to the list of groups that choose to bear this strain. The position of the remnants of Australia's abortive gentry caste must be an especially bitter one, full of the mockery of sharing their rituals and knighthoods with the sort of people who uphold a later *status quo*, and empty of any hope for the future. A more common and less admirable form of disaffection is the one typical of many aspiring to succeed the older social élites. The characteristic note is sounded, in a moderate way, in Ray Ericksen's book *West of Centre*:

> I had tried, almost desperately at times, to search out reasons for wanting to come back to Australia. They were few and hard to find. It had been much easier to list reasons for staying away. The aesthetic poverty of our cities and the deadly non-life of our suburbs, the incompetent larrikinism of our politics, the weak villainy of our foreign relations, the hypocrisy and brutal results of our colour prejudice, our intolerance of the non-conformist individual, our dreadful pubs and overrated beer, our complacent materialism and our witless imitation of many of the worst features of one of the worst models in the world; there seemed to be no end to the list of deterrents and some of them were basic and truly alarming.

The tune is familiar enough – hatred of country has always been a part of Australian patriotism – but what is new is the strident insistency with which it has been played in the last dozen years, and how quickly the educated classes have moved towards a position of all-out war on vernacular Australia. Just how far this can go, as we approach the radical lunatic fringe, is well illustrated in the filmmaking sequence in Frank Moorhouse's *The Electrical Experience*, one of the most chilling things in our literature. From the crowing pack-brutality described there to the youthful SS *Sonderkommando* having a bit of fun before shooting their victims is almost no distance at all.

Although usually presented as a generation conflict or a set of more or less parallel revolutionary struggles over values, what we are really in is a sharp little class war which may already have passed its climax. A struggle between the vernacular and the privileged cultures has been endemic in Australia for a very long time, at a fairly low level of intensity. It may have been hotter in the 1890s than we now remember; Henry Lawson's angry dismissal of his 'cultivated critics' sounds like an incident in such a war, and is interesting as an early clash between the vernacular culture and the mandarin branch of the Establishment rather than the entrepreneurial or the legal branch. Since then, of course, the educated caste has been able to free itself from the older Establishment and become a dominating, oppressing power in its own right.

A new class often cannot or will not see itself as a single entity, and has to be identified and named by those outside it. Our new class, in Australia as elsewhere, would probably stress its internal conflicts and divisions, which are admittedly often very broad, but it is none the less as clearly a single class as, say, the aristocracy in pre-revolutionary France or the gentry in eighteenth-century England. It has as yet no name, though many have been tried on for size: the Left, the trendies, the epigoni (in poetry and the arts), the radical intelligentsia, Bohemia, and a dozen more. None quite fits, because none gets all the emphases right and all the constituent phenomena in. Borrowing a term from Irish history, I would suggest we speak of the Ascendancy; this at least connotes both the foreign-derived oppressiveness of the new class and its *arriviste*, first-generation flavour.

The new class is the natural upper class of a socialist world order, and has come into existence as it were in anticipation of that order. In it, tertiary education plays a part analogous to that played by land ownership in past ascendancies: it is a central but not an entirely exclusive organizing principle. Just as a university degree or some ability in the general field of letters or the higher fornication could gain one a place in the English gentry of two centuries ago, a certain radical style can get one into the new class now. Style, in fact, is probably the broadest common denominator of the new ascendancy, and one of its most important cohesive principles. Another feature that is diagnostic for the whole class, above and beyond all of its apparent divisions, is its tendency to see all opposition to it as being right-wing, and to use fashion as a weapon of defence and attack. It is in common responses of this sort, in fact, that the coherent entity of the new class can be recognized.

The new ascendancy has, if we want to be dramatic about it, captured most of education, much of the arts, and much of fashion in Australia. Under the Whitlam government, its style became very important in policy-making and administration, and some of its preoccupations were expensively promoted. Irritation at the ascendancy's style, in particular, was obviously a large factor in the Labor government's unfortunate downfall. Just after the elections, I remember a game which spontaneously came up during a dinner at our place: every time someone would use a new-class word, the company would hoot 'The people voted against that word!' and dissolve in laughter. 'Well, there's no hassle —' 'Watch it! The sovereign people has rejected *hassle*!' And we'd all of us voted Labor. I expect that the new class will get into the corridors of power again, after its present setback, though whether it will do so again under the aegis of a Labor government is less clear; socialism in Australia may have finished with Labor. The new class, however, is too interested in rule and power to be permanently excluded from government. It will survive its present exile partly because of a powerful psychological safeguard built into its belief system, the image of itself as a valiant, downtrodden band bearing aloft the torch of enlightenment against all oppression. We have reached the age of privileged, often subsidized martyrs.

Not that the ins and outs of all this matter much to people whose only culture is the vernacular one. Whoever dominates the Establishment, or has captured bits of it, the situation is basically the same; it doesn't matter whether bosses bully you or suck up to you. To borrow a word from the hardest-pressed section of vernacular Australia they're all *gubs*. The term is derived from *governor*, and refers to the most salient and persistent characteristic of white men: they try to run you, to change you, to rule you, and even when they're nice to you, the bastards always know better.

Formal education and high culture in Australia, as in any other colonial territory, are systems of foreign ideas imposed from above whose usual effect is to estrange people from their own culture and injure their rapport with their own people. They are ways in which the ruling élites recruit people to their purposes. Some few think their way through the imposed ideas and overcome their alienating effect, but most are caught for good in their estrangement, and convert it into privilege or virtue. It has never been possible to get a distinctively Australian education through institutional channels. You must either give yourself one, or be taught by your elders in a more or less informal way outside the institutional system. This is the way all the vernacular cultures of Australia — Aboriginal, immigrant, and mainstream — *are* in fact transmitted, though the mainstream one does also get disseminated to a limited extent through books and other media. The most comfortable way to educate oneself is to do it at a university; the library there tends to be better stocked than that famous and perhaps mythical one in the cells of Borroloola lock-up, which is said to have educated a generation of Queensland and Territory wanderers. I used and resisted my university in this way, though I don't claim much credit for it: it was an instinctive and precarious balancing act which I didn't really understand at the time and which must have looked merely perverse to many of my contemporaries. All I knew was that if ever I snubbed or denied my fellow country people, those who hadn't had the education I was getting, I would be lost.

The tragedy of a colonial situation in the things of the mind is that thought itself can come to seem alien and oppressive; the vernacular culture then retreats into rituals and semi-autistic meditation. All of the main new ideas taken up by the educated classes in this country in recent times, however, have been imports and most have been given a strong anti-popular twist here. Even so good and necessary an idea as conservation has often been used as a stick to beat ordinary Australians. It has been argued, in this connection, that ecological concern is a luxury which the privileged and protected can afford, and represents an attempt on their part to preserve a pleasant environment for themselves because the yobbos wouldn't appreciate it anyway. I've never liked this line of argument; what saddens me is the way strong concern for ecological values seems to erode human sympathy and destroy balance. Even Judith Wright seems to have lost all her compassionate understanding of country people since she became an activist. Her work has lost its intimate linkage with the vernacular traditions it used to draw on, and has become strident. She seems to have denied the pioneers and lost her Dreaming, and it's a tragedy. Trying to make not so much 'high' as rich and flexible art out of traditional and vernacular materials is a lonely enough pursuit these days, without seeing one's best colleague go over to the colonial party. In Pelagian times, hope too often seems to destroy charity.

Hidden purposes destroy charity, too. While, at its best, the main vernacular culture in Australia has always tended to revere the Aborigines, however mawkishly, as a sort of gold-standard of Australian-ness, a recent stream of intellectual opinion has taken them up as the *only* licensed Australians, and used the tragic fact of their cultural crisis as a weapon against, in particular, country people. Now, if your intention is to persuade white countryfolk to be more decent toward black and mixed-blood people, and to promote the subtle rapprochements which are in fact going on between them, surely you don't do it by hysterical accusations, by overstatement or by a sort of proxy racism. If, on the other hand, your real intention is to strike at the main vernacular culture, then it's natural to go for the country people, since the bush is the traditional reservoir of distinctive Australianities. The assault can be crude or subtle, depending on the attacker and his milieu. Somebody wrote in *Quadrant* a few issues ago about the failure of Australian writers to produce a literature of rural contentment and happiness, despite the rapidity and success of farming settlement along the east coast and in its immediate hinterland; we had only produced a picture of half-idiotic clown figures such as Dad and Dave, and otherwise we had been dominated by a despairing tradition of suffering and defeat based on the experience of the dry frontier. This had become the prevailing flavour of rural literature, and was traceable to hidden guilt at our conquest and displacement of the Aborigines. I must say I felt quite abolished. I had written in vain. So had David Campbell, and Eric Rolls, and the younger Judith Wright, and many more. In point of fact, the gloomy tradition of outback suffering and heartbreak, which is adequately explained by the facts of settlement in the outside country and the misery of some sensitive or socially ambitious figures involved in it, is pretty much a thing of the past, preserved nowadays mostly as an anti-popular icon by some intellectuals and academics.

There is an equally strong, or in fact stronger, tradition in our literature of respect for outback people and almost mystical reverence for the land; this runs through Upfield and Idriess, Durack and Xavier Herbert and dozens more, and shades off into 'high' art in myriad ways I lack the space here to follow up. Among the vernacular artists, it often contains a large element of that love of eccentrics and 'characters' which has become so much the dominant component of the Northern ideology, as celebrated voluminously by Xavier Herbert even when he is decrying the bitter effects of racist and paternalist attitudes on the Aborigines. Herbert is an excellent example of what I call the vernacular stream of Australian writing; his self-educated tone, his inability to understand the real inwardness of intellectuals, foreigners of any kind (including Englishmen) or the real otherness of Aboriginal culture, despite all his huffing and puffing and heaping up of lore, are the limitations of an older Australia. On the other hand, his deep identification with the land, his Dickensian celebration of its types and his adumbration of the North as a possible vigorous Creole nation of the future probably do reflect very accurately the beliefs and hopes of our tropical third, at least as held by liberal people there, and cast an interesting light on the rest of our country. He is a hideously uneven and often self-indulgent writer, but the depth and direction of his concerns cause me, for one, to see him as a natural ally. He is as haunted and frustrated by the slowness of our spiritual decolonization as I am.

In a sense, it is tempting (and very self-congratulatory) to see the best flowering of the Australian republic so far in the work of writers and artists of all periods who have resisted colonial alienation and kept faith with the main vernacular culture. Around my own age (though I disapprove of the mindless age-stratification so common here) and citing only the poets, I should name Bruce Dawe, Roger McDonald, Geoff Page, Robert Gray, and some of the very exciting new poets of the *Canberra Poetry* group. Many other poets display a similar unstraining respect and sympathy when they write on specifically Australian subjects. Geoffrey Lehmann (surely the most scurvily neglected of all our major poets) has it in many of his long *Ross's Poems* sequence, and elsewhere. Chris Wallace-Crabbe has it often, especially in his very interesting *Shapes of Anzac*. I must, however, stop counting heads, and resist the suggestion of looking around for a gang; the republic must never become an establishment. In a way, a greater acceptance of and interest in vernacular Australia was bound to come about in recent times, particularly during the Labor government's term-and-a-half in office. I imagine plantings of Australian trees in Canberra and elsewhere went up during the same period. Australianity, often of a crude sort, became chic: the Establishment had to create a new sneer to keep their more vulgar countrymen in their place. The result was the now-famous *ocker*, allegedly invented by an Adelaide bookseller. The word does have its uses, of course, if we narrow its signfication a little and use it only to refer to people, in show business and elsewhere, who crudely parody features of the vernacular culture to amuse the privileged or who mask unpopular or alien political purposes behind an exaggerated pose of matey Australian-ness. Old-style communists are particularly prone to this. The effect on the real vernacular culture of a country of Marxist-style popular-culture promotions, which may often be sincere in their intent, can be utterly withering. The Czech novelist Milan Kundera, in his superb book *The Joke*, illustrates this extremely well.

The vernacular republic is not solely rural or working-class; poets as diverse as C.J. Dennis, Douglas Stewart, the later Slessor, Ronald McCuaig, and Bruce Dawe (the list isn't exhaustive, and apologies are proffered, etc.) have kept us in mind of this. In many ways, the urban and middle-class ramifications of the vernacular tradition are among the most interesting to trace and meditate upon, because they are subtler and less clichéd. As we decolonize, we must learn to understand all the strands of our vernacular culture, as well as seeing it as a unity over against past and present streams of dependence. I have long wanted to see an anthology of Aboriginal poetry in translation, which is to say a collection of song texts of every level of solemnity translated at a proper literary standard from the original languages. There isn't as yet much decent Aboriginal poetry in English, but some of the material I have seen in translation from the Aborigines' own languages is superb; the *Moon-Bone Cycle* of the Wonguri Sandfly clan of Arnhem Land, in Professor Berndt's translation, is one of the very great poems of Australia, and ought to be a part of every secondary school syllabus, as much as *Five Bells* or *The Wind at Your Door*. There is bound to be much more material of a similar standard, if we will look for it. Some is around already, in the stiff or literal sort of translation that suffices for scientific journals. A collection of translations of scrupulous scientific accuracy which still manage, often, to flower into poetry of a high order, is T.G.H. Strehlow's *Songs of Central Australia*; a huge and vilely expensive book, it covers only a part of the oral literature of one tribe, the Aranda. The whole extent of the literature we might still retrieve must be truly stupendous.

This is something I can do, or at least suggest as a venture. Parallel ventures, differing greatly in kind perhaps but fitting the needs of the different component traditions, might be put up by others. As I have preached before, Chairs of Celtic studies and of folklore studies, despite the clear dangers inherent in the latter, need to be set up in our universities; the main vernacular tradition is full of Celtic elements we need to bring out and understand if we are to get our picture of ourselves right. This is not England; we don't need to snub and suppress and deny our Celtic inheritance – though we mustn't be colonized by it, either. It, too, belongs to the past. We aren't Europeans any longer: some of us never were.

I am perhaps unlikely as a poet and newspaper book reviewer to found a distinctive republican school of literary and social criticism, though I have been practising a loose sort of republican critique in my reviews. A republican critique would by no means be antipathetic to all innovation or cultural borrowing; quality, in particular, would always be able to get past its guard. It would stress the native traditions and the 'set' of the national mind as touchstones by which innovation should be judged, and differentiate between what was useful borrowing and what looked more like sterile importation for the sake of excitement or keeping up with whoever were the current overseas Joneses. As applied to home-made productions, it would probably be immensely unpopular for the hard truths it would have to tell about cultural cringe and colonial imitation, about exaggerated Australian-ness and our rather pitiful tourist cosmopolitanism. Ultimately, of course, the severest republican critique of all is practised, silently or angrily or with ribaldry, by the vernacular nation itself. All alien things show the strain of this, through the embitterment or growing unbalance of their proponents; you can judge when an innovation has begun to be accepted by the return of its supporters to tolerance and largeness of sympathy. The tragedy, of course, is in the way good things have to suffer by association with reject tissue. The obvious example is the way in which even poets who keep faith with their people are isolated and ignored because the people have come to see *all* poets as being in collusion with intellectuals and other establishment types who despise the common herd. Our arrangements are still so aristocratic, so courtier-like, and yet we have uttered the great words *equality* and *democracy*. The people heard, especially in the New World (of which Australia is a part as much as America), and they will keep us to them. The wider vernacular republic which exists beneath the surface of the whole industrialized world, and which has historically come closer to the surface in Australia than perhaps in any other country, has punished modern poetry savagely for its pretensions. The wilder gestures of avant gardes everywhere, with their increasing mental and spiritual squalor, can be seen as the death throes of a long-lived and much adapted historic class system, just as the alleged ugliness, anti-intellectualism, and larrikinism of the vernacular republic can be seen as intransigence, and as cultural self-defence. The mutual hatred and rejection can go very deep. Over against it, the republican idea is above all one of humility, of reconciliation; it says the people are sovereign and means it.

Republicanism is neither a party nor an ideology in this country, and it may be better if it always remains a principle. As such, it is one we would do well to examine during the null time before the *de jure* republic comes into existence. We need to develop a consciousness that will at once hasten the end of our present situation and equip us to deal fruitfully with the new one. And this will be an altogether healthier pastime for the years ahead than frantic efforts to discover new patterns of dependence for our country – the most pathetic try so far has been the attempt to pretend that Australia is really a part of Asia. We are more deeply colonial than we know; it may take centuries to straighten our back, but we will straighten it more quickly if we know it's bent and that we would be healthier walking upright. Our nationhood in the past has often been something we only discovered through disasters, including disasters our dependences dragged us into. The First World War was the supreme example of this. In return for sixty thousand dead men and the destruction of one of our most interesting vernacular sub-cultures, the German one, we gained a slight, fragile but vital new confidence in a few of our qualities and gave the main vernacular culture some new themes. We have come some distance towards independence since then; not merely the realities of economics and global strategy but also things now true to our spirit would prevent us from once again rushing like lemmings into a European war. I doubt our establishments could now, for a while at least, even get us into an Asian war. The republic, however, is a principle whereby our further advance toward independence does not require any catastrophes.

Without republican thinking now, we may easily see the *de jure* republic betrayed in any of a dozen ways when it does come in. I think the idea of the vernacular republic underlying the formal, juridical one might be a worthwhile theme for us to develop – it may suit the set of our mind the way stated and declared principles appear to have suited the American republic, and clearly it already does influence our whole national life. To articulate it might be a contribution to political and social discourse which the New World can still make. In a local framework, republican attitudes will help us to cure an obsession with identity and nationality which is one of the great cripplers of intellectual life and tappers-off of spiritual energy among late-colonial peoples. In this sense, though only in this sense, the republican idea is self-consuming; the embarrassingly insistent side of it fades when it is no longer needed.

On Sitting Back and Thinking
About Porter's Boeotia

Sometime in the eighth century before Christ, so the tradition goes, a youth named Hesiod, son of an immigrant farmer from the Greek colonies in Asia Minor, was guarding his father's flocks on the side of the sacred mountain Helikon, in rural Boeotia. The mountain had probably been a Wunger-place (to use an Australian term) since long before the Aeolian Greeks trekked down from the north with their shaggy cattle and their Indo-European sky gods. Perhaps the most potent magical site on the mountain was the spring named Hippokrene, the Horse's Fountain, supposed to have been set flowing by a touch of Pegasus' hoof, but probably a ritual spot long before the flying horse and his heroic Greek rider were heard of. It may have been a mother-goddess site; springs with names alluding to a horseshoe or hoof often are. This would explain the compensating presence near by of an altar dedicated to the father god Zeus. Somewhere near this altar and spring – that is to say, in a place where the two religious principles were in balance – the young Hesiod had a vision in which the Muses, immortal maidens begotten by Zeus upon Memory, gave him a staff of flowering laurel, breathed a 'godly voice' into him, and commanded him to make poems.

Real or metaphorical – and many poets have had similar visionary inductions into their craft – the experience led to the creation of two long poem cycles, the *Theogony* and the *Works and Days*. These poems are second only to the two great Homeric epics in the number of progeny they have generated and the cultural influence they have had. The *Theogony* is the source of much of our knowledge of Greek religion, and this alone makes it one of the great historic resources of the Western mind, a sublime marble-quarry of imagery and myth for well over two thousand years. The *Works and Days*, in turn, stands at the beginning of a long literary succession coming down through Theocritus and Virgil and the high vernacular poetry of the Middle Ages to Wordsworth and Frost and a hundred more in modern times; most recently, in Australia, it surfaces in David Campbell's own *Works and Days* and Geoffrey Lehmann's *Ross's Poems*. In a much wider sense the work of Hesiod stands on one side of a rift that runs through the whole of Western culture, a fundamental tension which for convenience we may call the war between Athens and Boeotia. Peter Porter's superb poem 'On First Looking into Chapman's Hesiod' is concerned with this rift at once on a cultural level and on a personal level, and in this essay I will be concerned mainly to dilate upon the background and cultural implications of the themes he raises, though I may venture to argue respectfully with him towards the end, as the 'side' he chooses is the opposite one to my own.

What is at issue are two contrasting models of civilization between which Western man has vacillated; he has now drawn the rest of mankind into the quarrel, and resolving this tension may be the most urgent task facing the world in modern times. In the past, Athens, the urbanizing, fashion-conscious principle removed from and usually insensitive to natural, cyclic views of the world, has won out time and again, though the successes of Boeotia have been far from negligible. Now, I think, there are senses in which we may say that the old perennial struggle is coming to a head, with Australia finding herself, very much to her surprise, to be one of the places in which some sort of synthesis might at last be achieved. If this is to happen here, though, we will need to clear our heads of many remnant colonial obeisances, and look at things clearly and straight. Let us start by looking at the origins of the struggle, in their artistic dimension.

From the time of its rise in the sixth century BC urban-minded, slave-holding Athens was always scornful of rural, traditional-minded, predominantly small-holding Boeotia. The Boeotians, living to the north-west of Attica, were held to be rude, boorish, and stupid, their country swampy and cheerless, their arts old-fashioned and tedious. The conflict went deeper than mere rivalry between Aeolian and Ionian Greeks; Athens and Thebes, the chief city of Boeotia, were competitors and occasionally enemies. Even the great Boeotian Pindar, honoured all over the Greek-speaking world for his eulogies of victors in the great Pythian and Olympic games, fell foul of this enmity. When he wrote his famous lines in praise of Athens:

> O thou shining, violet-crowned, most-worthy-of-song
> bulwark of Hellas, glorious Athens, city of the gods,

his own city-state of Thebes imposed a fine on him.

Above and beyond its artistic dimension (as if anything could be!) the rivalry may have threatened Athens more seriously than we now realize. The vehemence of Athenian scorn at least is suggestive. Later, Athenian dominance as an educational and cultural centre, particularly during Roman times, may have caused the disappearance of works which might otherwise have revealed a more brilliant Boeotian tradition than that which we can now trace. There is evidence that a specifically Boeotian style of poetry, called by that name, may have existed in Homeric times and later. Some elements in the *Iliad*, especially, may be Boeotian. The famous catalogue of ships is a case in point. The catalogue seems to be a typically Boeotian device. Athenians *count*, we may say, while Boeotians *list* and *name*. The distinction makes for a profound difference in cultures that follow one model or the other.

For all the scorn heaped on Boeotia by progressive Athens, two of the three greatest and most influential poets of classical Greece came from there; both Hesiod and Pindar were Boeotians, as was the woman poet Corinna. The third great name, of course, is that of Homer, who may not have been one person at all. After Boeotia, we would have to look to Alexandria for a comparable cradle of poets and poetic modes. By contrast, the only great Athenian poets were dramatists. Athens's glory lay in her drama, her philosophers and her political theorists. All of these are urban and, in our expanded sense, typically 'Athenian' pursuits. Boeotia, in her perennial incarnations, replaces theatre with dance or pageant – or sport; philosophy she subordinates to religion and precept, and in politics she habitually prefers *daimon* to *demos*. Mistrustful of Athens's vaunted democracy – which after all involved only a minority of voters living on the labour of a large slave population – she clings to older ideas of the importance of family and the display of individual human quality under stress. If aristocracy is her besetting vice, that of Athens is probably abstraction. Each has its price, artistically, and it may be that poetry, of all but the dramatic sort, is ultimately a Boeotian art. It often has that appearance, seen over against our modern, increasingly Athenian art. Conflict and resolution take the place, in a crowded urban milieu, of the Boeotican interest in celebration and commemoration, modes that perennially appear in spacious, dignified cultures.

We have been mesmerized during the last few centuries by evolutionary ideas that contrast 'primitive' with advanced, progressive with stagnant, dynamic with decadent – the basic metaphor has been stretched many ways. It has taken the Second World War and the decolonization after that of much of the world to reveal the iniquities perpetrated by Western cultures, using these sorts of ideas as their cover and justification, on traditional cultures. We are beginning to be conscious of a nexus of thinking and of oppression here which extends all the way from personal to international relations, and goes far beyond the bounds of art. In terms of our polarity, Athens has recently oppressed Boeotia on a world scale, and has caused the creation all over the world of more or less Westernized native élites which often enthusiastically continue the oppression. Athens has again overborne Boeotia on the same old basis as that used in classical times, and has again made herself the ally and preceptress of Rome, that is to say, of imperialist force.

Within Western culture itself it is possible that not only the oppressive use of contrasts such as *modern* versus *old-fashioned* or *cultivated* versus *rude* but even the very notion of such polarities may ultimately derive from the submerged and almost forgotten conflict between Athens and Boeotia in early classical times. Again, the ultimate coercive success of the Athenian model may be said to have been confirmed and greatly strengthened by Rome. We may say, altering the adage, that when Rome conquered Greece, she was herself conquered not by Greece but by Athens. Always, predominantly, Rome accepted Athenian and Alexandrian biases and standards, and added themes of her own to them. The contrast between *metropolitan* and *provincial* is a case in point; this was only an implicit element in the older, decentralized Greek culture. Rome also greatly narrowed the field of 'high' culture, and initiated that removal of high art out of the purview of the great mass of the people which has been a recurrent curse in subsequent Western cultures. In classical Greece, art was a matter of public performance and concern; since Roman times it has persistently tended to become a luxury product, a matter for coteries and high society. Rome is the great exaggerator of Hellenic tendencies; she is Athens without proportion.

Almost the single notable exception to what we have been saying is Virgil, who worked his way as it were backwards through Arcadian art – an Athenian style evolved to deal with Boeotian material in an emasculated way – in his Theocritean *Eclogues* to the pure Boeotian mode of his *Georgics* and thence to the epic. This is a fruitful path which has been followed many times since. Present-day conservationists and urban drop-outs often follow it, turning to the country for romantic, basically Arcadian reasons and discovering harder Boeotian truths there. Because of the atypical nature of Virgil's works, Dante's evocation of him was appropriate and not culturally disruptive in the Middle Ages – a period in which the highest Boeotian civilization in Western history flourished. Classical allusion, when passed through a Virgilian filter, did not interfere with Dante's deeply Boeotian purpose of creating a vernacular poetry capable of handling sublime matters.

The revival of classical learning on a large scale, the so-called Renaissance, was of course and by contrast deeply disruptive. It coincided with and aided the centralizing of power in royal courts and the end of the old decentralized life of Europe. Athens always tends to capture ruling classes when they become estranged from their territorial bases of power, and the urban merchant classes, cut off from the land from which their forebears probably fled, naturally confuse eminence with excellence and ape their betters. In Europe, the great autochthonous arts and fresh beginnings of the Middle Ages were dismissed as 'Gothic' and replaced by self-conscious Roman-Athenian revivals, which eventually generated new high styles that remained dominant until the muddled upsurge we call the Romantic Revival. This last, of course, was not so much a Boeotian revival as a confused eruption of Boeotian and other elements, which the dominant classicizing styles had threatened to refine, or snub, out of existence. The romantic period has not yet ended, of course, though it has become repetitive, decadent, and sometimes actively violent. It has placed a number of cultural, as well as literal, bombs in our luggage. Boeotia, made desperate and driven to seek strange allies, becomes Nazi Germany, or present-day Cambodia, or some of the more fanatically anti-Western (but still irretrievably Westernizing) of the new African states.

Within our civilization we repeatedly see a pattern of autonomous, distinctive art at the beginning of each people's cultural history, followed by the importation and imposition of the general Roman-Athenian cultural inheritance. In some cases the native tradition will live on more or less vigorously at the level of folk art, with idiosyncratic works of a strongly 'popular' flavour surfacing from time to time within the purlieus of the 'high' culture. Sometimes the native art, and the Boeotian order that it carries, will prove resistant. In the Gaelic-speaking world of Ireland and Scotland, it took the effective destruction of the native language to break the stubbornly Boeotian cultural preferences of the people. Again, in each of the newly conquered and newly settled countries of the New World, the same pattern is repeated. Each New World people gets, as it were, a short period of anarchic, makeshift cultural independence in which to produce its Chaucers and Langlands and its literary and artistic Gothic cathedrals, or at least the foundations for them. With the consolidation of an élite of the European sort in the country, and the establishment of the kind of educational and cultural set-up that goes with that, the period of distinctiveness normally comes to an end, or at least becomes embattled. If the new country is lucky, it will produce distinctive figures or themes during its 'Boeotian' phase whose influence is powerful enough to modify the form the 'Athenian' civilization takes there when it is brought in. Whitman, a deeply Boeotian poet, is an example of such a figure. The tradition he founded is still productive and part of the reason for our being able to speak of a distinctive American poetry. At best, these fruitions of distinctiveness, these new departures full of idiosyncrasy and character, are the treasures of nationality, and are among the few justifications there can be for the existence of nations and separate peoples. Athens is lasting, but Boeotia is ever-new, continually recreated, always writing afresh about the sacred places and the generations of men and the gods.

Written from the vantage of Peter Porter's personally necessary and long-maintained exile in London, his poem is a work of high importance as a cultural document, as well as being vivid and lively. However, I suspect that its argument will be widely resented, or evaded, in Australia. The judgement that it passes on Australian culture is precisely the one that many home-grown Athenians have been at pains to deny or deplore. And yet, in any sense broad enough to admit the great majority of Australians, our culture *is* still in its Boeotian phase, and any distinctiveness we possess *is* still firmly anchored in the bush. However we may resent the fact, too, we are seen almost universally in this light by others, and held to our stereotypes with affection and scorn. Colonially obedient in so many ways, we yet fail to heed the metropolis when it tells us to be ourselves. Perhaps the fact that the advice often comes in the form of a dismissal may make us reluctant to take it.

Porter's poem is an ode with a flexible but never sloppy three-beat line, set out in thirteen-line verse-paragraphs. It is not metrically complex or highly wrought; although he is a profound student of music and opera, Peter Porter does not usually seek after musical effects or dense interweavings of sound in his verse, though the construction of his poems often follows a quasi-musical logic. In most of his work he will establish his metrical base early in a poem and then stick with it right to the end. He is clearly more interested in phrase and reference, in the poetry of what is said. He once worked in advertising – not entirely a bad training for a poet – and perhaps this sharpened his appreciation of phrase-making and succinct for-mulations. More than any other poet now writing, I think, his work has the metropolitan tone, at once intellectual and colloquial, at home with rapid shifts of level, sudden deflations and witty jux-tapositions. A Porter poem often works by heaping up a crucible-full of arcane and stylish references (he has the true urban and Athenian appreciation of style, and of shifting stylistic resonances, developed to a very high degree of discrimination) and heating it with sheer intelligence till a clear drop of unforgettable imagery or wisdom, most often elegaic, flows out. As I have said elsewhere, Porter is one of the best writers of last lines in the business.

At first sight, 'On First Looking Into Chapman's Hesiod' seems more discursive than is usual in Porter's work, and it is more relaxed on the surface – until you notice that not a word in it is superfluous. It carefully matches up epithets from Hesiod's *Works and Days*, often in quotes, with strongly flavoured bits of Australian vernacular cul-ture, and all the matchings are dead right. As far as the lore is con-cerned, I am a bit worried by the reference to kerosene in honey tins: Up Home it was mostly honey in kerosene tins. But let that pass. The poem is deeply Australian in many other ways, too. There is, for example, the reticence which prefers to say 'within myself' where another culture might speak frankly and, we fear, gaseously about the soul, the spirit, etc. And there is the way it catches, with just the right harsh image about 'kelpie yapping', all the features of Boeotian art and tradition here which so grate on the sensibilities of our respectable Athenians. There is, finally, a very hard implicit suggestion for such people contained at once in the last two lines of the poem as a whole; this is the suggestion that Athenians do not really belong in Australia and might as well follow Porter's own example of self-exile. Nowadays, I imagine, the direction of such exile would be more often America than London.

Above all of the poem's many felicities, though, I believe that it is its cultural relevance that makes it fascinating and, in the critical sense, enormously productive. Once it raises the part-historical, part-metaphoric conflict between Athens and Boeotia, and identifies Australian culture as essentially Boeotian, its radiance, to use Aquinas's term, spreads out in all directions and illuminates all sorts of things beyond those explicitly mentioned in the text. One even begins to notice the ultimate non-urbanity of works we had thought were secure classics of high Athenian art here. Slessor, for example, can suddenly be seen as a poet whose work followed the classic Virgilian progression from willed Athenian literariness slowly but surely towards a profoundly Boeotian achievement, culminating in the great funeral ode 'Five Bells' and in the democratic funerary commemoration of 'Beach Burial'. He is a city poet, but not, we begin to see, a metropolitan one. Rather, his work at once constitutes and points to the possibility of a kind of urban art appropriate to Australia, with her wide, scattered, half-Boeotian garden cities, and to modes of literature which might yet help us to counterbalance other, dangerously cosmopolitan imports. All this becomes a little ironic, when we remember Slessor's strong concern, and the concern of that whole *Vision* school of Lindsayite Arcadians, to oust the bush from what they considered to be its excessive pre-eminence in our literature. What they ultimately achieved was to extend the range of a strong unitary culture when it needed extending.

Whether the pre-eminence of the ballads and other vernacular poetry was excessive at one time or not, it is true that these sorts of writing remain the core of whatever specifically Australian poetry the nation's people still value and refer to. And it is here, with the position of the people to whom Athens perenially offers nothing and whom she disdains as *hoi polloi*, the ockers, 'your average suburban yobbos' and the like, that I have to begin to fight against Peter's poem, or rather against its untimely, if personally valid and honest, conclusion. I cannot believe in that 'permanently upright city' of willed disengagement from the past and unending personal development. And even if I could, surely now would be the worst possible time to go seeking it, at least among the liberal metropolises of Europe. Peter says all this for me, however, with the phrase 'Europe's entropy', implying that an almost Old Testament fear of the wicked metropolis still held by some Australians is merely a theme of ours, a convention one can subscribe to or not.

Fair enough. So let's come at it another way. One of the few Athenian features that have 'taken' in Australian society has to do with the image of the artist. In Boeotia he is a craftsman, with some remnant of priestly dignity. In Athens, he is an intellectual, a member of a class for which entropy and the corrosive analysis of value are principles of life. Or he is a Bohemian, a licensed buffoon, a disruptive element expected by Platonists of all persuasions to threaten the public order, usually pretty harmlessly, and to generate new styles of behaviour and adornment. Just as Romano-Athenian art, in its decay, tends towards excessive satire (Rome's only distinctive contribution to literature), towards Dada and the absurd and the ultimate scrambling of all values, so our modern Athenian artists are subtly encouraged to abandon the Works and cultivate the Life, and the

Death, as a performance. The metropolis can offer the fierce excitements of entropy, but no real cure for the decays it continually exposes. And even the virtues of its faults now seem to be disappearing. A few years ago, the metropolis could still offer intense intellectual satisfaction in artistic form, but now the age of the great intellectual aerialists seems to have almost passed away. With W.H. Auden dead, Porter himself is one of the few really first-rate intellectual poets left. As the older European values crumble away, Europe's artists begin, often, to look simple-minded and lacking in subtlety; under socialist influence, many are making self-consciously 'proletarian' gestures and trying, often clumsily, to express attitudes that we have been articulating and refining for generations in the New World.

Perhaps I am being simple-minded myself, in seeming to confuse Peter's upright city with any literal metropolis. The ideal city is ultimately in the mind, and is glimpsed in the art a person produces. This makes Peter's position a lonely one, and I think many passages in the poem give us a sense of loneliness, of isolation sought and accepted. This may be how it has to be. To shift our parallel just a bit, Athens can't be restored, as a city of art, in Hellenistic times. Still less during a period of barbarian irruptions. Peter is a more overtly personal poet than I am, and we have argued some of this before, notably at the *Poetry Australia* Write-In at Macquarie University in 1975, when I advocated a public and 'bardic' function for poets which he took in a narrower and quainter sense than I had intended. I think there is wisdom in Australia's Boeotian-ness; it may be a good sheet anchor for us during the period of collapse of many of our parent cultures – I say many, because not all of our culture derives from Europe, just as not all Australians are of European descent. Some, the black Australians, have been here for tens of thousands of years, and their culture is a Boeotian resource of immeasurable value for us all. Again, the idea of our deliberately remaining Boeotian is full of exciting possibilities. It would be something indeed, to break with Western culture by not taking, even now, the characteristic second step into alienation, into élitism and the relegation of all places except one or two urban centres to the sterile status of provincial no-man's-land largely deprived of any art or any creative self-confidence. This is what is at stake. The centre of Athens isn't the Parthenon, but the Agora, the chatty, educative market-place – but the centre of Boeotia is every place held sacred by any Boeotian. Interestingly, we have admitted this as a definite principle in favour of one of our sub-cultures, that of the Aborigines.

This may be a brake on our denying the principle outright as regards our other constituent cultures. Perhaps in saying that we are still Boeotian in the essentials of our culture, Peter's poem has put its finger on a real if subterranean reluctance to take that second and fatal Western step. And this despite the fact that our education system is Athenian from top to bottom, and generates a terrific pressure in favour of the centralizing metropolitan pattern of culture.

A nation, a people, is always of more value to the rest of mankind if it remains itself – where else are new ideas and new models for living to come from, if not from idiosyncratic human variety on a scale large enough to command attention? It may be reserved for us to bring off the long-needed reconciliation of Athens with Boeotia, and create that lasting organic country where *urban* and *rural* no longer imply a conflict, and where one discovers ever more richly what one is and where one stands and how to grow from there without loss or the denial of others. But our ultimate choices in this will be made by deep movements in the life and mind of our people, and may in fact be made irrevocably before anyone detects what road has been taken. Some years ago, before Peter Porter's very candid and generous reconciliation with his homeland, I remember reading an interview with him in which he said, 'I've kept my Australian passport; I don't quite know why.' Pindar of Kynoskephalai (literally, Dog's Heads – perhaps not a bad equivalent for post-war Brisbane, the city Peter left to go to London) also travelled far from home for professional reasons; he paid his fine, too, for praising a splendid city which deserved praise, and likewise never renounced his Theban citizenship. However hard I may have presumed to argue with the last eight lines of Peter's poem, it will be clear that I regard it as one of the central works in our literature, on a par with the very finest poems we have to show. Its wider significance, as I have tried to demonstrate, goes well beyond our place and time.

From *Australian Poems in Perspective*, edited by Peter Elkin (University of Queensland Press, 1978)

James McAuley – a personal appreciation

James McAuley, who died yesterday, was one of the three or four best known and deservedly eminent poets in Australia. Of all the scholar-poets, he was the most incisive and provocative theorist. An enemy, sometimes a merciless enemy, to much that seemed to him shoddy and wrong-headed and mean in literature and politics alike, he could still write in his first editorial in *Quadrant*, the magazine he founded in 1956: 'In spite of all that can be said against our age, what a moment it is to be alive in!'

Much that this clear-minded and passionately engaged man did and said will survive him. Above all else, he wrote one of the two best religious poems to have come out of this country – McAuley's 'Jesus' and Judith Wright's 'Eli Eli' are the two I mean – and five or six other poems which will be read as long as English is spoken here.

My list of Jim McAuley's Greats is pretty much the conventional one: 'Envoi', 'Terra Australis', 'Jesus', 'The True Discovery of Australia' (not the slightly vindictive coda, but all of the Gulliver part), 'Pieta', and 'Because'. All but a very few readers of Australian poetry will know these.

Some might add other pieces to the list; a dozen others came to my mind while I was thinking about it. One was 'Father, Mother, Son', with its evocation of the heartbreak brought to so many by religious division back in the days when, as someone has said, the religions of Australia were Catholic and anti-Catholic:

> For fifty years this one thread – he has held
> One gold thread of the vesture: he has said
> Hail, holy Queen, slightly wrong, each night in secret.
> But his wife, and now a lifetime, stand between:
> She guards him from his peace. Her love asks only
> That in the end he must not seem to disown
> Their terms of plighted troth. So he will make
> For ever the same choice that he has made –

Another was the similar and tragic 'Tabletalk', how many decent suburban childhoods have been like this:

> What is the wisdom that a child needs most?
> Ours was distrust, a coating behind the eye
> We took in daily with the mutton roast.
> The corned-beef salad, and the shepherd's pie.

I was also tempted to list any number of bits, parts of longer poems, isolated stanzas like the final verse of 'The Sixth Day', in which the vision and the tone are as pure and childlike as the best of Shaw Neilson:

> Enormously strange it is,
> Forever to be you and I,
> Not to die, not ever to die.

Making up a personal list of Jim McAuley's very best poems – as it were totting up his score – has of course been a way for me to avoid thinking about his death, even though, in my best moments, I share his faith in the Resurrection. I did not know him well – we met perhaps three times – but I valued him, and I am saddened by the fact that now we won't, in this life, have the conversation I had always hoped to have with him. He is now his work, and his further poetry won't be published on earth.

I can, of course, admire and argue with him on paper. For instance, I disagree with him when he writes, in a poem called 'In the Twentieth Century':

> Christ, you walked on the sea,
> But cannot walk in a poem,
> Not in our century.

This is a momentary loss of faith, not in Christ but in poetry. If it is in the power of irreligion and intellectual fashion to do the central work of revolution (not that all revolutionaries are irreligious, by any means) which is to change the subjects of permitted discourse, and thus to alter the world, it is also in the power of poetry to reverse their work and bring old truths, including the supreme ones, back to vivid life. And McAuley himself has done it, not in this superb poem, but in his 'Jesus'.

> And people moved before him undisguised;
> He thrust his speech among them like a sword.
> And when a dove came to his hand he knew
> That hell was opening behind its wings.
> He thanked the messenger and let it go;
> Spoke to the dust, the fishes and the twelve

> As if they understood him equally,
> And told them nothing that they wished to know.

This is not a conformist's vision of Jesus, and Jim McAuley was anything but a conformist in the age he lived in. All the same, I couldn't quite include any of his polemical poems in my presumptuous short list; not the valedictory poem for Roy Campbell, not even the 'Letter to John Dryden'. They are often full of good things, but they fail to escape that slightly peevish tone that has so bedevilled much Catholic and conservative writing in the last century or so, that defiant making of brilliant points to a public one knows deep down is not listening. A certain despairing preachiness insinuates itself and deadens the language even when it is most affirmative. The salt hasn't lost its savour, but people no longer inclined to taste it certainly won't take it from what they feel to be outdated and suspect cruets.

McAuley realized this, ultimately; grace can't be communicated through argument; it must find other channels that are beyond disputation, channels of inspiration and splendour. As he writes in the Dryden poem:

> Incarnate Word, in whom all nature lives,
> Cast flame upon the earth: raise up contemplatives
> Among us, men who walk within the fire
> Of ceaseless prayer, impetuous desire.

In his own case, it was communicated best through the personal poems, mostly written late in life, in which even the most painful matter is infused with forgiveness and charity, and through some of the great early public pieces, with their visionary richness of language. Space won't permit too much quotation, so let's take the finest of the personal pieces, a poem which bowled me over when I first read it and has never diminished in my mind. This is the poem 'Because', with its famous opening:

> My father and my mother never quarrelled.
> They were united in a kind of love
> As daily as the Sydney Morning Herald,
> Rather than like the eagle or the dove.

No better account of the emotional ravages of self-withholding puritanism has been written, but there is no bitterness, no taking revenge on the dead or outgrown parents:

My mother sang Because and Annie Laurie,
White Wings, and other songs; her voice was sweet.
I never gave enough, and I am sorry;
But we were all closed in the same defeat.

People do what they can; they were good people.
They cared for us and loved us. Once they stood
Tall in my childhood as the school, the steeple.
How can I judge without ingratitude?

One set of poems I never contemplated including among Jim
McAuley's best was the Ern Malley series. Unlike some conciliatory
critics, I can't regard these as any more than they are, a hoax got up
to discredit a movement. They were successful for a while in that,
but it has to be faced: they did hurt a number of people, and condemn
an enthusiastic editor to a lifetime of assertive and slightly pathetic
self-justification, and they did bring about a temporary narrowing
and deadening of the arts in Australia, and prolong the life of some
pretty lousy anti-artistic attitudes here.

This was the uncharitable side of a campaign McAuley waged all
his writing life, a campaign which it would be too narrow to describe
simply as anti-modernist. He was concerned to assert and to restore
the primacy of reason and a certain classical clarity in art over against
romantic portentousness and formlessness, and he fought to revive
the high style. In the former aim, he had some success for a time;
he and one or two others made a certain 'Augustan' tone dominant
in Australian poetry for more than a decade after the Second World
War. In the latter, he never really prevailed against what I think is
the central and best tendency of Australian poetry, an enlightened,
inclusive, civil mode of writing which belongs ultimately to the
middle style, but allows itself to dip up and down at need, and at
best abolishes all the levels by reconciling them.

Against this fundamentally democratic style, the long, almost epi-
cal 'Captain Quiros' and other consciously splendid poems of his
middle period seem overblown and their language rings dated and
dead. When *Surprises of the Sun* appeared in 1969, it seemed, to some
lovers of McAuley's earlier work, almost like a rebirth. Professor
McAuley was dead; long live James McAuley.

Now he is gone. There is much more I could have praised in him.
I could have commended his superb translations from the German
– he made all too few of these. I'm sure people who studied under
him, both in government at the Australian school of Pacific

Administration and in English at the University of Tasmania, will have tributes to bring. He expressed a great many things: real splendour (before he started trying hard), rigorous standards, a deep concern for poor, deluded futility-haunted mankind. In 'The True Discovery of Australia', he expressed better than anyone that loathing of country that is part of the patriotism of colonial nations, but his love for Australia was deep and lasting, and comes out in poem after poem. Even in 'The True Discovery', he makes a vivid and passionately comic fiction out of Australian mediocrity: we become more wonderfully dreadful than we are. That is the grace of art, transcending judgements and positions; as Jim wrote himself in his 'Credo'.

> For the world's bare tokens
> We pay golden coin.
> Stamped with the king's image;
> And poems are prophecy
> Of a new heaven and earth,
> A rumour of resurrection.

Sydney Morning Herald, 16 October 1976

The Human-Hair Thread

It may seem strange, and immodest, for a poet to embark on a lengthy account of one of the elements in his own work. My justification for tackling it is threefold: first, I was asked by the editor of *Meanjin* to do so, second, it will tend to use my writing as a springboard for talking about matters of wider interest, and third, its centre of gravity is not so much what I have been able to do with one of the great Australian cultural heritages, but rather what that heritage has given me, and how it has contributed and may yet increasingly contribute to a richer and more humane civilization in this country.

Since the demise of the Jindyworobak movement, this resource has been largely neglected by writers; the main effect of Aboriginal culture on the general Australian consciousness in the last twenty-odd years has tended to flow through the conservationist movement and, to a lesser extent, through painting and perhaps music. Growing politicization of the Aboriginal question has also, perhaps, made many non–Aboriginal writers wary of charges of exploitation, paternalism and the like. It will be a tragedy if the normal processes of artistic borrowing and influence, by which any culture makes part of its contribution to the conversation of mankind, are frozen in the Aboriginal case by what are really the manoeuverings of a battle for political power within the white society of our country, or by tactical use of Third World rhetoric by jealous artists trying to damage each other professionally. Artistic borrowing is quite unlike the processes of finance from which the metaphor is drawn: it leaves the lender no poorer, and draws attention to his riches, which can only be depleted by neglect and his loss of confidence in them; these cause them to be lost. Borrowing is an act of respect which may restore his respect for his goods, and so help to preserve them. And he is at all times free to draw on them himself with the benefit of his own superior understanding of his treasures.

There has been an Aboriginal presence in my work almost from the start. This is natural enough, in one coming from the country. Until quite recently, the original Australians were almost exclusively

71

a country people, and the white culture they had to resist or assimilate with was the Australian rural one. Growing up outside the cities, one couldn't fail to be conscious of them, living on the fringe of things, mostly in poverty, hanging around the pubs in Taree or walking the two hot, dusty miles back out to Purfleet Settlement. In my part of the north coast of New South Wales, they were not really poorer or more broken down than the poorest farm families or seasonal workers. All the same, one was dimly conscious of a difference that went beyond the often slight differences of skin colour. One knew there were special laws about the Aborigines – to some extent, the modern Aboriginal people is a *creation* of discriminatory laws working against the declared policy of assimilation – and one heard they could be treacherous, apt to repay slights exorbitantly after long and patient delay, though I don't remember any examples being given. They had a way of looking stately in tattered clothes, walking along the road to Taree, but one had no idea then of the warmth with which they supported and cared for their own. Nor any idea of their tradition of sharing. Ugly, contemptuous words were used to refer to them: coon, darkie, koori, black-gin. My mother, a city woman, prohibited these words in our house, and it was only years later, in the city, that I learned that *Koori* was what the black people called themselves. About the term gin, I remember hearing the story of Constable Crotty, of Taree, who was caught *in flagrante* with a Purfleet woman down at the Manning River car ferry, in the days before the Martin Bridge spanned the river; a six o'clock curfew was imposed on Aborigines in Taree in those days, and Mr Crotty was supposed to be seeing that all the black people were across the river by that hour. For a long time afterwards, in all the pubs of the town, a gin-in-milk was known as a 'Crotty's'; the word drove Constable Crotty to leave town.

The Aborigines were partly a people, partly a caste, partly a class, though really that last term is inaccurate: they were actually part of a larger class of the rural poor, and it is still often more useful to see them in that light than in currently fashionable radical-racialist terms. We, my family, were in the same class ourselves. The Murrays were among the earliest white families in the Manning district, but my father was a tenant-at-will of *his* father, who, before letting him rent a hived-off segment of his large property and farm it, had exploited his labour as a bullock driver and timber cutter for eight years with no pay beyond gruff promises of future rewards, Grandfather John Allan Murray, called Allan to distinguish him from his wildly generous and hospitable, if feckless, father Johnnie Murray, the first white settler at Bunyah, was always a man to do well out of family loyalty, but he was not at all unusual in that, in his time and place. Until it was pulled down some years ago, our house on the farm never had a ceiling, or lining on the walls; summer and winter, the wind through the cracks in the plank walls provided us with air-conditioning. As my father says, 'We were poor people – hardly had a roof to our mouth.' I suppose we were heirs to the unadmitted guilts of the white conquest of Australia, though I don't remember our being conscious of them at all. Perhaps we were too poorly educated. A certain slight shyness on my part when meeting Aboriginal people may stem from subterranean feelings of guilt, however; indeed, I almost hope they come from there. They may be no more than an outgrowth of learned liberalism, or a residue of childhood fears. Really, I am not at all sure about white conquest-guilt; it may be no more than a construct of the political Left, that great inventor of prescriptive sentiments and categories. It certainly isn't a reliable sentiment for outsiders to invoke among country people.

We may also have been heirs, tangentially, to guilts about miscegenation, a topic on which many older country people of all colours are deeply and ambiguously touchy, in part because of real tension between racial scorn and ordinary decency, in part also because it has been a stick used by urban élites, past and present, to beat us with. Then, as now, the sunny, self-righteous, generalizing confidence of urban commentators was inimical to rural Australians. When I was growing up, the injustice of urban attitudes was shifting from the black people (feckless, primitive, a doomed, inferior race) to the white rural population (bigoted, conservative, ignorant, despoilers of the environment, a doomed, obsolete group), though it had not reached its present levels of intensity.

I grew up in what had been the country of the Kattang people, a region lying between the Manning and the Karuah Rivers and extending westward towards Gloucester and Dungog. This is the country which formed me, and I have celebrated it many times in verse. When I was a child, though I did not know it then, there were still initiated men living at Purfleet, men who had risen through the ceremonial stages of the Bora, that ancient religion whose name means resurrection and rebirth. I read about these men much later in the memoirs of Mrs Ella Simon of Taree, who was one of the last fluent speakers of Kattang, as well as a recognized keeper of family trees and traditional lore. Mrs Simon was one of the informants in Nils M. Holmer's study, published in two parts by the Australian Institute of Aboriginal Studies in 1966–67, of the Kattang and Thangatti languages. Her autobiography, titled *Through My Eyes*, will correct and greatly amplify anything I could say here about the life of the Aboriginal people Up Home, and people wanting an account, from the inside, of relations between the races in the Manning region are advised, most warmly, to look out for this book, which was published by Rigby in 1978. Mrs Simon was a great lady of my country, the first Aboriginal Justice of the Peace in New South Wales, and a person of immense wisdom and justice; she knew where all the corpses were buried. She would certainly have known who the old black man was who stood by the roadside in Purfleet with his hat in his hands and his eyes lowered the day my mother's funeral passed by on its way out to Krambach cemetery. I was twelve then, but that man has stayed with me, from what may well have been the natal day of my vocation as a poet, a good spirit gently restraining me from indulgence in stereotypes and prejudices. Or trying to. I don't know who he was. He could have been one of the Bungey family, a relation of young Cecil Bungey who jumped into the Manning from Queen Elizabeth Park in Taree one night when the police were after him and drowned. This tragedy, in the mid-1950s, was an important event in the district, because the indignation it caused among black and white people alike led to some curbing of police oppression of the Purfleet community and beginning of social change in the settlement. He could have been a Saunders, or a Lobban, a member of that Scottish settler family of a century ago which seems to have no white members left now. Or he may have been one of the Syrons, visiting from Minimbah.*

In tracing the black thread as it runs through my work, I am conscious of many mistakes, shortcomings and impositions of myth on the facts. Leaving aside a couple of short stories I wrote while at university, heavily programmatic tales which were really about the tension between individuality and community values, and not about real Aborigines at all, the first poem of those I have kept which deals with an explicitly Aboriginal subject is one titled 'Beside the Highway', written in about 1962 or 1963. It is an outsider's view of an Aboriginal settlement of the old type, and is, of course, based almost entirely on Purfleet and the life I saw or imagined going on there, the heat, the ennui, the sense of dereliction and aimlessness – in other words, very much the conventional white liberal picture,

---

* I have since found out who the Aboriginal man was who doffed his hat for my mother's funeral. His name was Eddie Lobban, one of the last fully initiated men of the Biripai (Shark) section of the Kattang people, and our cousin by marriage.

enlivened by an eye for detail. The thing in this early poem which gives it some fleeting originality is the image of cars on the highway, which 'approach like missiles / and scatter glare as they pass'. Purfleet used to be bisected by the Pacific Highway, exposed to the constant intrusive passage of cars and trucks that violated its inwardness. It must have been a fearfully dangerous place for little children – though they grew up into public-spirited youngsters capable of putting out placards on the approaches to warn motorists of police speed-traps – and one can imagine the disruption and chronic restlessness which the endless glittering stream of vehicles must have provoked in the people there. Mrs Simon says in her memoirs that Purfleet should be bulldozed now; it had value in its day, and was a step up from the squalid riverbank blacks' camp it replaced, but the need for a refuge, a separate community, in effect a ghetto, has now passed. The poem is stitched shakily together by the imagined figure of Mad Jess, who owes more to Wordsworth and Yeats than to actual observation; this figure is made to bear the burden of Significance in the poem:

> "And I was dreaming,"
> says old Mad Jess to herself, "flash cars was coming
> at me like hailstones, cutting me to pieces."

What this highly literary figure allowed me to do, I see now, was to use the rural dialect I had grown up speaking, but which I was as yet too conventional to employ in my verse. Perhaps the most perceptive touch in the picture of Mad Jess, though, is the image of her contemplating her shoes. This image, with its concomitants of remembered barefoot freedom and of lore and magical practices connected with tracks, recurs in a much later poem, 'The Ballad of Jimmy Governor'. Images of the ground and of tracks abound in the poem, and in one place the half-caste outlaw ironically refers to his full-blood accomplice Jacky Underwood as having 'already give back his shoes'. The implication is that the only footwear Underwood ever owned was that given to him by the prison officials in Dubbo for his appearances at court. Now he has been hanged and the shoes have been taken back. The Governor Ballad is written entirely in the dialect, or more properly sociolect, of the rural poor. I have heard it read in an Aboriginal accent by the actor Bob Maza, and the effect chilled even me!

In a poem written while I was living in Wales in 1967, entitled 'The Wilderness', there is a reference to the day my friend Peter Barden and I, watched by curious peak-hour crowds, trotted down Wynyard Concourse in Sydney towards the railway ticket barriers,

excitedly pointing out imaginary animal tracks in the dust and pausing to make more with our knuckles in the manner of Aboriginal
hunters discussing the finer points of their trade, while all the time
exchanging remarks in an Aboriginal-sounding gibberish. We even
avoided sibilants in our mock-Aranda, knowing dimly that these
don't occur in Australian languages. The yen for travel to the Outback and for what Barden called the 'clean country' of the Centre
was strong on us that day. And it was a good stir. In the poem,
which is about a hitchhiking trip through the Centre which I'd done
in 1961 to while away the hungry months of the Credit Squeeze
that year, I refer to our gibberish as mock-*Arunta*, and thereby fall
into the same sort of error as the old Jindyworobak poets, Rex
Ingamells, Ian Mudie, Flexmore Hudson, Max Dunn, Roland
Robinson and the rest, who lacked the really first-rate scholarly
sources available to us now. The spelling 'Arunta' comes from the
writings of Sir Baldwin Spencer and F.J. Gillen, who carried out
valuable but faulty anthropological studies in Central Australia in
the late nineteenth and early twentieth centuries. The people these
men were principally concerned with were the *Aranda*, who pronounce their tribal name with the stress on the initial A. The common
white Australian mistake of pronouncing the 'Arunta' form with
the stress on the medial *u* probably stems from popularizing material
derived from Spencer and Gillen.*

The Jindyworobak poets were very prone to romanticize the
Aborigines, but their really worthwhile project of fusing Aboriginal
and diverse European elements into a new and genuinely Australian
poetry was made more difficult by the shaky incomplete source
material they had to work with. Roland Robinson, the greatest of
the Jindies, is of course an exception, largely because he did his own
original research. Many of the best modern studies only appeared
at the end of the Jindyworobak period or even later, in the late forties
and early fifties; T.G.H. Strehlow's monumental and superb *Songs
of Central Australia* only came out finally in 1970. Before the Second
World War, for those who read German there were accurate poem-
texts in Carl Strehlow's *Die Aranda- und Loritja-Stämme in Zentral-
Australien*, published between 1907 and 1920, and other accurate
texts could be found in odd articles by E.H. Davies and the young
T.G.H. Strehlow in *Oceania*. Other texts, whose reliability I cannot
judge, existed in George Taplin's 'The Narrinyeri', a chapter of *The
Native Tribes of South Australia* (1897), in A.W. Howitt's *Native
Tribes of South-East Australia*, and in a few other old books. Older

* A new orthography that has now largely replaced Strehlow's spells the word as *Arrernte*.

texts were often clumsily literal, or else rendered Bill Harney-fashion into totally inappropriate English traditional rhyme and metre, which smothered their tone and flavour and usually made them look merely banal. Mary Gilmore's renderings are a partial exception, as Judith Rodriguez points out in a recent review article in *Contempa*. To digress for a moment, it would be wonderful if we could recover the transcriptions of native, probably mainly Wiradjuri, songs Mary Gilmore's father is said to have made; these were allegedly most painstaking, and were glossed by Mr Cameron in his native Gaelic so as to avoid missing nuances, before he made his English versions. It was not until 1945 that R. and C. Berndt published the results of their early field work in the Ooldea region, and not until 1951 that Ronald Berndt published his study, with sensitively translated texts, of the Arnhem Land Djanggawul cycle. Similarly, the younger Strehlow's authoritative *Aranda Traditions* only appeared in 1947. The Jindyworobak poets also suffered from too great an emphasis on only one Aboriginal tribe, the Aranda, important and fascinating as the traditions of the Aranda are. Pretty well their whole understanding of Aboriginal metaphysics and philosophy comes, it is clear, from Spencer and Gillen's often shaky understanding of Aranda belief.

If this last point is true of the Jindyborowak poets, it is even more true of the hazy ideas of Aboriginal philosophy and religion held by most white Australians. A particularly good example of this is the term 'Dreamtime'. This term, taken from Spencer and Gillen's studies of Central Australian tribes and applied indiscriminately to all Aboriginal groups in Australia, is analysed incisively by T.G.H. Strehlow in his *Songs of Central Australia* (pp.614–15):

> Spencer and Gillen's *alcheringa* (altered in *The Arunta* to *alchera*), which has been mistranslated as "dream time" and popularised by them and others in this sense, owes its origin to a confusion of *altjíra ráma* and *altjíranga* (*ngámbakála*). The English "dream time" is therefore a vague and inaccurate phrase; and though it has gained wide currency among white Australians through its sentimentality and its suggestion of mysticism, it has never had any real meaning for the natives, who rarely, if ever, use it when speaking in English. "Dreaming", or rather "dreamin", which is commonly used by pidgin English and Northern Territory English native speakers means *totem* only, and is a translation not of *altjíranga* but of *kngánakála* (= someone who has originated). Thus "emu dreamin" would be a translation of *ilia kngánakála* (= someone who has originated as an emu).

Strehlow discusses the word *altjíra* in some detail; it is apparently a rare word used only in a few fixed phrases, and its root meaning seems to be 'uncreated, sprung out of itself'. The suffixed form *aljíranga* means 'from all eternity', and is given as an answer to questions about the origin of the world. In the Aranda view, the earth and the sky have existed *altjíranga*, that is, from all eternity. So have the supernatural beings who created the features of the earth and its human and animal inhabitants, and who continually reincarnate themselves in them. Some of the immense dignity of traditional Aborigines, when seen outside of degrading circumstances, obviously comes from their sense of being the present forms of eternally existing beings. A man who 'owns' a certain ceremony or set of verses belonging to a sacred site does so because he *is* the supernatural being who indwells in that site. The only slight connection between *altjíra* and dreaming, in our Western sense of the word, is through the idiom *altjíra ráma* 'to see altjira', that is, 'to dream'.

I place great reliance on Strehlow's accounts of Aranda matters because unlike other scholars to date he spoke Aranda as a native; it was one of his mother tongues. In a private discussion, Emeritus Professor A.P. Elkin of Sydney University told me that Strehlow was really the only white man who had ever learned an Aboriginal language. Spencer and Gillen, on the other hand, had to rely on native informants speaking a limited pidgin English, because they themselves spoke no Aranda at all. This led them into many mistakes, notably their belief that the sacred chants attached to the different sites (for ritual scarcely exists apart from the places in which it must be performed) were in fact nonsense verses which the Aborigines themselves did not understand, a sort of ritual glossolalia! As an example of the long survival of misinformation, I remember in 1961 being told dogmatically by a well-read, rather pedantic and in fact somewhat scary truck-driver that sacred Aboriginal verse was all meaningless noise-making. As we were crossing the Nullarbor at the time, I did not persist in arguing with him when he showed signs of irritation.

The first poem in which I attempted to capture some of the rhythm and feeling of Aboriginal poetry was 'The Rock Shelters, Botany Bay', written in early 1968 (we were living in Scotland then) and published, like 'The Wilderness', in my second book *The Weatherboard Cathedral*. It is a rather pallid poem, 'poetic' in a bad sense, and reads like a counterfeit of another culture's poetry rather than a genuine re-creation of it. It fails to catch the tone and style of Aboriginal poetry of any sort, in the way in which, say, Tom Keneally caught them in the short extempore songs he put into the mouth of the young Jimmie Blacksmith in his fine novel based on the Governor outbreak. I was perhaps too far, in every sense, from my sources. The only real point of interest in the poem is the mention of people averting their eyes from the track of a 'kingparrot man', the ill-omened spoor of a soldier dressed in a red coat. It was a guess of mine that, in the first days of contact, people accustomed to ritual body painting would take figures in red coats to be spirit-figures associated with a familiar creature. Apart from possum-skin cloaks for wearing in cold weather, most Aborigines in traditional times scarcely had a concept of what we may call secular clothing. Decoration with blood, paint and the down of birds was a festive or religious act. The poem alludes to the common eastern Australian idea, reminiscent of Melanesian belief, that the white invaders were actually ghosts, a truly horrifying thing for a people with as deep-rooted a fear of the dead as Aboriginal Australians possessed. Ghosts garbed as crimson rosella (kingparrot) men would thus be an attempt to make sense of white figures garbed in red upper-body decorations.

My next attempt to describe, amongst other things, the effect of absolute culture shock was in 'The Conquest', written in 1969 and published in *Poems Against Economics*. This is a more successful poem, I think, and deals with black-white relations during the first years of settlement at Sydney Cove, the period of Phillip's governorship. This period is very important, in that events and reverses which happened then went far towards setting the pattern of black-white relations for more than a century afterwards; the poem outlines some of these and then, in its last two sections, moves into a more general depiction of white myth-making about the Aborigines, both in the past and today:

> A few still hunt way out beyond philosophy
> where nothing is sacred till it is your flesh
> and the leaves, the creeks shine through their poverty
>
> or so we hope. We make our conquests too.
> The ruins at our feet are hard to see.

Early in the poem, the failure of understanding on both sides is presented in terms of perception; neither side can *see* the other at all accurately, because neither side can understand what it is seeing. The failure is presented from both sides, with the Aboriginal side predominating in the early sections and then fading away as white incomprehension, brutality and myth-making take over. The tribesmen see, with difficulty, what look to them like 'blue parrot-figures wrecking the light with change' (Royal Navy officers and bluejackets are meant) and they see 'man-shapes digging where no yam-roots were', a solecism against the proper order of things in many ways, not least because most digging was women's work. Later, the Governor addresses the tribesmen in English and they reply, naturally enough, in Dhuruwal, the language of the people south of Sydney Harbour. Marines stand solidly there, with their firelocks at the ready, obeying the customs of their culture and their service, and the warriors obey *their* customs by ritually biting their beards as a sign of defiance and challenge. Beard-biting with this significance was, it seems, pretty well universal throughout Australia, so it is not inappropriate to cite an Aranda example. It comes from the sacred song associated with Ankóta, a northern Aranda dingo-totem centre on the Burt Plain in the Northern Territory; 'he' refers to the dingo ancestor Ankótarínja:

> Angrily sucking his beard into his mouth
> He follows up the scent, moving his head from side to side.

Nothing comes of the confrontation ('glass beads are scattered in that gulf of style'), and soon convicts are crying out for protection against the imaginary violence of naked 'Indians', the common eighteenth-century term for all New World indigenes, who 'circle them like birds'. Exasperated with the unresponsiveness and menacing mien of the Aborigines, the Governor forgets his earlier unrealistic projects of racial harmony and orders that they be driven off, and so they disappear carrying the germs of unknown European diseases which will sweep through them like fire through blady grass. In the forest, dogs feed on the corpses; 'it makes dogs furtive, what they find to eat'. Later, finding that the colony cannot support itself, Phillip changes tack again and orders that some natives be captured, partly in order to get information about native food resources, and partly to train as emissaries capable of interpreting the benevolent white Governor's wishes and intentions to their fellow indigenes. The poem thus records Phillip's swings from benevolence to exasperation and back, and his final outburst of savagery when his personal huntsman, named McEntire, is speared. The punitive expedition he orders on that occasion is a complete failure, but it sets a deadly pattern for the future:

> The punitive squads march off
> without result, but this quandong of wrath
> ferments in slaughters for a hundred years.

As the Aborigines themselves fade from view as an independent 'side' in the confrontation, their place is taken by various stereotyped European views of them. Paralleling the Governor's shifts from benevolence to anger, the image of the Noble Savage in very early drawings and accounts is replaced by scornful pictures of degraded black beggars in Sydney Town, capering drunkenly for pennies or rum in a now totally desacralized world. They have gone, in a few short years, from being unencumbered with possessions to being destitute, 'poor for the first time', and their culture goes underground, becoming a matter of fading traditional lore spoken softly in languages which most white men do not trouble to listen to or learn. Colonial reality is something which can be, and is, expressed entirely in the conqueror's language. Perhaps because of a personal interest in linguistic things, I have made more, I think, of the linguistic dimension in black-white relations than most other Australian writers.

Matters of language are very much to the fore in the very next poem I wrote, a few weeks after 'The Conquest'. This was 'The Ballad of Jimmy Governor', and the tension in this poem is between the rough nineties ballad-metre in which it is cast and the horrific anti-white and anti-pioneer sentiments of the Aboriginal outlaw who speaks it. I tried to write the poem, though, in the only poetic mode Jimmy Governor might have been expected to know, the rough folk-poetry of the settlers and battlers, and there is possibly some pathos in the way his language is precisely theirs, right down to the dialectcal forms such as 'give' for 'gave' and 'soon be' for 'it will soon be', the slang is turn-of-the-century too, as in the use of 'plant' for 'hide'. This, and the other forms, are still current among older people in my region today. There are cruel punning references to Black Velvet (Aboriginal women, as sexually exploited by white men) and White Lady, a dire mixture of methylated spirits and powdered milk still drunk in shanty settlements to this day. The only references to traditional belief are fairly oblique, and refer to traditional lore about the balefulness of tracks and other traces left by evil men and, more specifically, by traditional revenge parties. I've noticed that white readers don't tend to notice or 'hear' these parts of the poem, though a couple of Aboriginal people who have heard or read it have reacted to them. I may just have got something right, and succeeded in creating a real Aboriginal character. Interestingly, Tom Keneally also refers to footprint-sorcery, and to the concomitants of shoe-wearing, in his *Chant of Jimmie Blacksmith*. Tom was writing his novel at the same time as I was writing this poem; this was a subject for mutual surprise and head-shaking later on.

The first poem in which I deliberately incorporated large amounts of actual material of a traditional sort was one called 'Stockman Songs', which forms part of a long sequence entitled 'Walking to the Cattle-Place'. This sequence forms more than a third of *Poems Against Economics*, and goes into enormously ramified detail about cattle and their place in human history and consciousness. The element of surprise in the poem is that the stockmen aren't white Australians singing Country-and-Western songs, but black men chanting the sort of non-sacred nonce-verses which Aborigines compose on the spur of the moment to celebrate the casual events of the world around them. The only Aboriginal terms I know for this style of song-making are *djabi-dja*, which comes from one of the languages of the Kimberleys, or *tabi*, a term from Ngumal, one of the languages of the Pilbara. The place names in the poem are Aranda ones: Pmolangkinja is known as Palm Valley in English, Tnórula is Gosse's Range and Rúbuntja (or Urúbuntja) is Mount Hay. There is a reference, of a joking sort, to the grass-seed totem, and a couplet in near-traditional style referring to the semi-sacred Rúbuntja fire totem ceremony. Strehlow tells the story of this ceremony in an article published in the *Inland Review* (vol. 3, no. 12, September-November 1969):

> A large group of fire ancestors was living at the beginning of time around Urúbuntja or Rúbuntja, now known as Mount Hay. Some of the fire ancestors accidentally started a bushfire which rapidly engulfed the whole countryside. Finally the fire ancestors themselves were set ablaze. The older men among them thereupon turned into sacred objects. The younger men – who were still wearing their hair tied into long cones in the manner of Aranda novices – rose towards the sky. With their hair aflame and their bodies charred and blackened, they were carried by the fire-heated gales many miles away. Some landed near Tnorula, and changed into grass-trees; others came down in Pmolangkinja, where they turned into palms and cycads... The mountain of Urúbuntja never regained its trees, and the surrounding burnt-out country turned into Mitchell grass plains.

As well as being metaphorically vivid, this story makes good sense as history, and depicts what probably happened many times in the past as Central Australia dried out and became deforested. The Aborigines almost certainly assisted in the work of dessication and deforestation by careless use of their firesticks – like the Bedouin, they may be as much fathers of the desert as sons of it – and even the picture of the grass trees and palms 'flying' into sheltered places is an accurate image, when you consider that the flora of sheltered, well-watered spots in the Centre consists of remnants of sclerophyll forest and even rainforest. The description only lacks a time scale, but then mythologized history usually does. Written only a couple of years after 'The Rock Shelters', and slightly revised in 1981, this poem works very much better, I think, as an attempt to capture some sense of the inwardness of another culture and its ways of looking at things.

There follow a number of poems, written over the next few years, in which there are passing references to Aboriginal themes and culture, or in which Aboriginal figures appear. In 'Lament for the Country Soldiers' war memorials are called 'The stones of increase'; they are, as it were, sacred sites from which a spirit, if not the spirits of the dead soldiers themselves, can be reborn, and the names incised on them are a sort of *tjurunga* of a past world. In one of the poems of the cattle cycle, 'Novilladas Democráticas', 'shirts of landless red' refers to the often gorgeous garb of black stockmen in the Outback, and in the last poem of that cycle, a black woman remarks, after the somewhat puritanical country women have explained the reasons for their narrowness and coercive use of the power of community feeling, that Jesus said all hidden things would be revealed, a profoundly true insight of His in which I have great and even sardonic faith. In 'The Mitchells', I have a suspicion that one of the two Mitchells is an Aborigine, because of the 'pain and subtle amusement' with which he announces his name. But this is perhaps a country point, and too much stress should not be placed on it, as some critics have tended to do. The point of the poem is its depiction, from the outside, of an Australian vernacular culture and its shared private understandings. The two Mitchells – if they *are* both Mitchells – know what they are conveying to each other. We, the readers, are never going to be told, since we don't need to know. In the poem 'Escaping Out There' there are references to imaginary place names constructed on an Aboriginal model – the Flying-Fox Cooking-Place and Praising White Moth Larvae – along with other local names constructed on a not dissimilar rural white model: Where The Old School Got Burnt and Where The Big Red Bull Went Over. The latter is an actual place on the island of Tristan da Cunha in the South Atlantic, but it is so like nonce-names for familiar places Up Home that it fitted in perfectly. It may be evidence for a good deal of commonality in rural place-naming in widely separated parts of the world. The name All The Bloodwoods also occurs in the poem, but I would not like to speculate whether that one is white or Aboriginal. The same poem contains a reference to unadmitted, and therefore probably black, grandmothers, and their benign effect on mountain farm families who might otherwise have been too stiffly respectable and hard-working for their own good. In 'The Action', finally, a meditation on history and minorities spoken by a man floating at his ease in Coolongolook River in my country, there is a reference to a sacred flying fox increase-site said to have existed nearby. Both Coolongolook River and the red-headed fruit bat are important sponsors of my writing. It was while sitting in the now-vanished timber mill at Coolongolook and contemplating the river, one evening in the mid-1950s, that I first realized that I was going to be a writer; rivers in my work often have a lot of Coolongolook water in them. The metaphoric appropriateness of the flying fox, a nocturnal creature who sleeps upside down during the day and flies out for miles at night in search of 'grown and native fruit', to the general situation of poets in this country has a compelling force for me. I examined this in a poem written in 1974 and entitled 'The Flying-Fox Dreaming, Wingham Brush, NSW'. That poem connects the metaphor with the ancient ritual and economic significance of the flying fox in my country. Along the Manning in pre-white days, there seems to have been a seasonal ecology of native figs, flying foxes and Aborigines. The fruit bats are very nearly my 'dreaming', in the half-serious, half-joking way that Douglas Stewart identified his totem animal as the bandicoot while claiming David Campbell's was a big red fox. This is not quite so jocular as it looks, though it can be taken too seriously. I remember, from devouring back issues of *Oceania* in Fisher Library when I was a young student at Sydney, that people of the east coast tribes were supposed to discover their dreamings for themselves through a sort of waking revelation. I know of a parallel to this, from a very different region of Australia, in which a baby's aged initiate relative discerns its dreaming for it. In a poem called 'Lalai', translated by Andrew Huntley from a prose version by the anthropologist Michael Silverstein and published in *Poetry Australia* (no. 58, 1976), the Worora elder Sam Woolagoodjah says:

> In its own Wunger place
> A spirit waits for birth –
> "Today, I saw who the child really is –"
>
> That is how a man
> Learns to know his child.

Namaaraalee made him,
No one else,
No one.
But not all things are straight
In this day.

As I looked at the water
Of Bundaalunaa
She appeared to me:
I understood suddenly
The life in our baby –
Her name is Dragon Fly.

Without pressing the point farther than it will go, I know I would be most reluctant ever to hurt a flying fox. The same poem also speculates about a possible origin for *tjúrunga*, the sacred objects in which ancestral spirits inhere; a dead and shrivelled flying fox is spoken of as 'becoming a clenched oval stone'. But this is a guess, based on little more than the way dead things in a dry country are apt to shrivel and even become mummified in the sun, and it may apply more to the Centre than to the coast.

I suppose the next poem of mine, after the cattle cycle, in which a major Aboriginal component appears is one with the very long title 'Thinking About Aboriginal Land Rights, I Visit The Farm I Will Not Inherit', written in 1972. This sonnet describes how the bush would reoccupy and obliterate our old farm, and how the potentials for such an obliteration lie everywhere in the landscape. It does not overtly refer to our having lost the farm – my father was too hurt and proud to buy it when his father didn't leave it to him, and so his brother bought it and gave it to his own son, who eventually evicted Dad from it – but rather counteracts a feeling of dispossession by talking about dimensions, intimacies, knowledge of the place which dispossession cannot touch. The speaker is thus in a rather Aboriginal position, *vis-à-vis* the usurper, and this is underlined by his becoming in effect a totem ancestor in the last line; like the figures in the legends, 'I go into the earth near the hay shed for thousands of tears'.

The human–hair thread thickens as we approach the present. In another, much longer poem written in 1973 after a tour in Western Australia the previous year, and entitled 'Cycling in the Lake Country' (the Wordsworthian echo is not without mischievous intent), there are several allusions to Aboriginal matters, and the

Aboriginal presence is pervasive throughout the poem. It is most explicit in Sections 2 and 6, though Section 8 has a reference to the sacred song associated with Ilbálintja Soak, a bandicoot totem site in Central Australia. In the special poetic language used only for sacred verses, the bandicoot initiates chant the words of the great sire Károra describing his *pmára kútata* or 'everlasting home' (cf. Sam Woolagoodjah's *Wunger* place) at Ilbálintja: again and again, he refers to the rings of soil and clay and stone revealed in the soak as the water dries up in drought time:

> The crimson soil is grating under the heel;
> The white creek sand is grating under the heel.
>
> White creek sand!
> Impenetrable hollow!
>
> White limestone band!
> Impenetrable hollow!
>
> Rich yellow soil!
> Impenetrable hollow!
>
> Red and orange soil!
> Impenetrable hollow!
>
> Plain studded with whitewoods!
> Impenetrable hollow!
>
> White salt lake!
> Impenetrable hollow!

When I was looking for a way to describe the successive tide-lines left by water drying up in limestone doline-lakes well south of Kambalda, this was the obvious allusion. It seals, as it were, the description which precedes it, and helps to sustain the sense of Aboriginal presence.

In the second section of this long poem, which is based on an imaginary bicycle trip from about Leonora south to the sea at Esperance, there is a reference to the Central Australian belief that sacred quatrains and couplets (called *tjúrunga rétnja* or 'tjurunga-names' in Aranda; each is regarded a a compound epithet by which the initiate addresses and invokes his spirit ancestor) have no human authors; they were composed by the great sires themselves as they did their deeds of creation, wandering over the country and pausing at various spots to rest and perhaps to dance and shake off thousands of tiny feathers from their ceremonial body decorations. These feathers became the spirits of their myriad progeny, and when their human incarnations shake off their showers of down in ceremonial performances, the totem species are renewed again and made to multiply. This process is described in the poem, which then goes on, in its allusive impressionist way, to invoke one of the most riveting of all Aboriginal ceremonies, the Northern Aranda circumcision rite, and make contemporary sense of it. I am conscious here of falling into the old trap of overdependence on Aranda tradition, but this was the way the poem unfolded itself to me, and I gather that initiation ceremonies all over the desert regions of our continent tend to be very much more severe than those in the gentler country; Aranda initiates had to undergo circumcision, subincision and even sometimes the tearing off of one or more fingernails: no wonder they referred contemptuously to coastal men as *wía*, or boys! Perhaps the Aranda ceremony is not too much out of place in the context of the Western Australian desert, though.

The ceremony is a very brutal one, and appears to revolve around the theme of violence, particularly sexual violence and the tension between the sexes. In the timeless creative age, a large party of *lákabára* hawk men were travelling over the country devouring quails on the wing, when they heard the sound of a shield being beaten on the ground and saw a number of female wallaby ancestors, many of them deformed, preparing to circumcise their boys with burning brands of bark. This utterly infuriated the hawk men, who flew down, assuming the form of men, and killed the women. Then, with angry violence, they circumcised the boys themselves with stone knives, after which they released the wallaby men from a ritual ban of silence, flew up into the air and continued on their way. This may well be mythologized history, too, but we have no way of checking that. What is certain is that ever since, the ceremony of circumcision, called *atuélama* (to make a man), *látnua ultákama* (to cut off the prepuce) or, most suggestively, *pára ultákama* (to cut off the penis), has been carried out among the Northern Aranda with great roughness and violence, reproducing the fury and cruel joy of the hawk men. By contrast, the rite of subincision, splitting the urethra, is carried out in a context of rather idyllic verses, some of which have a comic, teasing note. In tribes farther to the north and west, the Rainbow Serpent replaces the hawk men in the story, and the women are not killed, but merely told that this is the new ritual, to replace ordeal by fire.

When I was writing the poem, it seemed to me that the circumcision rite had a significance not unlike that which it has in the Book of Exodus, a sacrifice of a part to propitiate forces which might otherwise demand the whole. Or, perhaps, remembering the idiom *pára ultákama*, it might have a suggestion that the prepuce is 'enough'. Of course, if the theory held by some anthropologists that circumcision was introduced by Moslem fishermen from Macassar in recent centuries and then spread inland from the northern coast is well founded, then the connection with Exodus and ancient Semitic practice becomes a direct one. Many Aboriginal self-mutilating acts have an element of propitiatory sacrifice in them; one offers one's blood and one's pain to satisfy harsh demands which might otherwise become exorbitant. Central Australian people still gash their heads and bodies after a death to demonstrate their grief and their innocence of murder; without such demonstrations, the dead person's relations might come and kill them. In our own culture, the instinct and need for sacrifice, the whole complex of motive and pattern in it, were for a long time resolved and discharged through the sacrifice of Christ on the Cross, as re-enacted every day in the Mass. For many people, especially intellectuals, this is no longer acceptable however, and they are forced to face the question again, willy nilly, and either work their way through it afresh or face destruction by it. As a parallel to my poem, it may be instructive to look at one of the quatrains in David Campbell's superb 'Kuring-gai Rock Carvings' sequence:

> The kangaroo has a spear in his side. It was here
> Young men were initiated,
> Tied to a burning tree. Today
> Where are such cooling pools of water?

Well, Christians could tell him – but many white people will now not look our way. I may have been disputing with David in this passage of my poem, though I can't remember now whether the argument was conscious or not. It is relevant to mention here, though, as the media never do, that recent census figures show a very pronounced movement of Aboriginal Australians into the Christian churches; suddenly, Aboriginal Christianity is one of the great growth areas of our faith, on this continent.

In the sixth section of 'Cycling in the Lake Country', I use the figure of Lionel Brockman, a West Australian Aborigine who twice escaped from Fremantle Gaol and took to the bush with his family, sparking off the most intensive manhunts in the State's history.

This part of the poem does not bring in any specifically traditional material, apart from a slightly tongue-in-cheek allusion to shape-shifting as a method of concealment, but talks about Australian vernacular culture and the need to rid oneself of bossy *gubba* attitudes if one is ever to achieve the humility and the silence necessary to understand Australia and belong deeply to it. The Aboriginal slang word *gubba*, supposedly derived from *governor*, means a white Australian, particularly one who always knows better and wants to push people around. This leads on to the consideration of the true, latent Australian republic in the following section, and the need for much patient listening in order to discern that republic among the faint, shy, ironical or harshly intransigent indications. The whole poem contains a great deal of reference, and relates all of its points to the landscapes in which it is progressively located. It was one of the poems in which I worked out many of my beliefs about Australian civilization and the opposition between our derivative 'high' culture and our more distinctive 'vernacular' cultures. I am more often a meditative than a lyrical poet, and the organizing principle of this, like many others of my poems, was the meditation. It is a whole meditation with colloquy and all.

An even more intensely meditative poem which contains hardly any specific references to Aboriginal culture, traditional or modern, but which is none the less relevant here is 'The Returnees', composed in 1975. It is relevant because, as part of its working, it attempts to come to terms with the common ground of human experience on this continent, the ground of perception and influence from which Aboriginal and white reactions to the country necessarily spring. The discovery of this common ground is done in terms of *sound*, the sort of thing film-makers call 'wild sound', which is to say that low, aggregate susurrus which emanates from living landscape and which has to be put on the sound track of any outdoor film; if it were not there the audience would probably not be able to put their finger on what was wrong, but its absence would probably unsettle them. Down beneath consciousness, we know that nature is never wholly silent, and we are apt to be awed when it approaches silence, but disturbed when total silence supervenes. The poem catches:

> a lifelong sound
>
> on everything; that low fly-humming
> melismatic untedious endless
> note that a drone-pipe-plus-chants or

(shielding our eyes, rocking the river)

a ballad – some ballads – catch, the one
some paintings and many yarners summon,
the ground-note here of unsnubbing art

If I had to find epithets for this partly synaesthetic signature-note of the Australian countryside, I would probably fumble with phrases like 'beautiful monotony' or 'belonging subtlety' or some such. I hear it very clearly in Aboriginal music and chant, a humming intricately enwoven with rhythmic liquid notes of the clap sticks and with undulating high-pitched, rather nasalized notes that rise and fade, echoing bird cries and the sharps and flats of midsummer blow-flies. At least, this is how it has come to me, hearing it on recordings and also at odd times in Central Australia and the north west. That peculiar pitch of Aboriginal men's singing, somewhere between a man's voice and a woman's, has long fascinated me. It is the high-pitched light voice of the figure ancient alchemists called the Herm-aphrodite, something we might expect in a religion involving the priesthood of all (male) believers. This is of a piece with the strange custom of subincision among the desert tribes, by which initiates are given a sort of mock vagina while remaining male. We achieve the same image of the hermaphrodite by making priests remain celibate, and having them celebrate the sacred mysteries in an ambiguous quasi-feminine garb. It is a very deep and necessary thing: a priest, to perform his rites properly, must stand in a difficult balance between the sexes, resolving the primal tension at the heart of all our dualities.

It is more than a decade since I first read R.M. Berndt's translation of the great Wonguri-Mandjikai Song Cycle of the Moon Bone. It stunned me when I first read it, and it may well be the greatest poem ever composed in Australia. Of course, it isn't *one* poem, but a cycle of traditional couplets in a sort of telegraphese verbal shorthand meant to be filled out by music and dance, rendered into long, syntactically complete lines by Professor Berndt, celebrating the life of the people and animals around Arnhem Bay in north-eastern Arnhem Land just before the start of the monsoon season:

In here towards the shade, in this Place, in the shadow
of the paperbarks.
Sitting here in rows, those Wonguri-Mandjikai people,
paperbarks along like a cloud.

Living on cycad-nut bread, sitting there with white-
stained fingers,
Sitting there resting, those people of the Sandfly clan...
Sitting there like mist, at that place of the Dugong, and
of the Dugong's Entrails...
Sitting resting there in the place of the Dugong...
In that place of the Moonlight Clay Pans, and at the
place of the Dugong...

After the prescriptive despairs and alienations of Western literature, which are so often merely matters of class identification, it is good to immerse oneself in this great peaceful poem, with its total acceptance of an intimately known and coherent world. Some may find its Edenic calm almost frightening, for it calls so much human effort and history into question, and presents an idyll wholly opposed to and perhaps impossible in a crowded technological civilization. Again, it expresses that total harmony and communication of all living creatures which we remember from fairy tales, but which we resist in adulthood because it carries the dangerous nostalgia of Paradise:

At that place of the Dugong, of the Tree-Limbs-Rubbing-
Together, and of the Evening Star
Where the lily-root claypan is...
Where the cockatoos play, at that place of the Dugong...
Flapping their wings they flew down, crying, "We saw
the people!"
There they are always living, those clans of the white
cockatoo...
And there is the Shag woman, and there her clan:
Birds, trampling the lily foliage, eating the soft round
roots!

Judith Rodriguez puts the matter well, in a book review in *Contempa* (no. 2/4, 1977):

Is it a sickness of sophistication to long for that "Always there" which occurs through the... ritual cycles, to find in that universalising imagery of climactic annual ritual chant something that makes our own sacramental feast of blood and flesh and our own uses of sex seem secondhand, tawdry and difficult to live by? Certainly in the Aboriginal rituals there is an assurance inaccessible to us; and our civilisation has made it inaccessible to the very people who told it to Ronald Berndt at Yirrkala in 1947.

And yet I would venture to disagree, not only about our own sacramental feast (and I have an abhorrence anyway for our modern uses of sex), but also about the alleged inaccessibility of that assurance. It is perhaps an inaccessibility that is most marked for intellectuals. I know some other white Australians who possess this assurance almost in its purity, in terms that are their own. And it is not a sickness to long for that 'Always there', but a real health of the spirit; it is sickness to reject it. One of the triumphs of Berndt's translation is that it renders the Aboriginal poetry into a language deeply in tune with the best Australian vernacular speech, and reveals affinities. The tone, as well as the images, is profoundly familiar. It has perhaps been the tragedy, the sickness, of poetry here that it has so rarely caught precisely that tone, and that our audiences have been trained not to expect it from us.

Around Christmas 1975, I conceived the idea of writing a cycle of poems in the style and metre of Berndt's translation of the Moon Bone Cycle. As I thought about it, I realized it would be necessary to incorporate in it elements from all three main Australian cultures, Aboriginal, rural and urban. But I would arrange them in their order of distinctiveness, with the senior culture setting the tone and controlling the movement of the poem. What I was after was an enactment of a longed-for fusion of all three cultures, a fusion which, as yet perhaps, can only exist in art, or in blessed moments when power and ideology are absent. The poem would necessarily celebrate my own spirit country, the one region I know well enough to dare comparison with the Arnhem Landers. In the final stanza of a poem called 'The Gallery', I had made what was in effect a trial flight, teaching myself to handle the rhythm and spirit of the Moon Bone Cycle. Fairly soon, I lighted on a device by which the projected poem could be launched and ordered: this was the annual exodus of many urban Australians to the country and the seaside resorts, people, many of them only a generation or two away from the farms, or even less, going back to their ancestral places in a kind of unacknowledged spiritual walkabout, looking for their country in order to draw sustenance from it. Or newcomers looking for the real Australia. Or people going to seek unadmitted communion with the sea, with the bush and the mountains, recovering, in ways which might look tawdry to the moralising sophisticated eye, some fragments of ancient festivity and adventure.

The poem took about six weeks to write, in two bursts approximately a month apart; the hiatus came, I remember, between Sections 6 and 7. It may be relevant to examine each of the sections in turn – there are thirteen of these, as in the Moon Bone Cycle. Section 1 starts by evoking the southern limits of the region and the different styles, interests and ways of speech of small-town people and country people, then moves into a description of the preparations being made for the return of those who have gone away to live in the cities and finally enumerates some of the legendary, and in one case suggestively notorious, associations of their ancestral region. In Section 2, the Pacific Highway in peak holiday time is described ironically in terms of a great fiery but all-giving Rainbow Snake writhing over the country and throwing out deadly little offshoots of excitement into the districts up back roads. Section 3 begins the process of rediscovery of intimacy with landscape and familiar creatures, though there is some residual violence in it. Names of creatures begin to be capitalized, in a way recalling the capitalized substantives in the first section; a sort of affectionate, quasi-totemic empathy is suggested by this, a kind of casual sacredness in well-known things. The process of recovery continues in Section 4, with a growing renewal of powers of observation in the returnees. Section 5 broaches the subject of ancestors. This is a purely white matter; Aboriginal religion, with its reincarnationist schema and its taboo on mentioning the dead, is quite at variance with white reverence for particular, successive ancestors. In the poem, though, the particular pioneer ancestors are, as it were, given the aura of the great ancestral sires of the Central Australian sacred sites, and the timelessness of these founding ancestors is stressed as against their successivity, so there is convergence. Premature judgment of them in modern terms they never heard of is rebuked – one may not preach without a sacrifice – but jokes are permitted, because of the affectionate intimacy they evince. Communion with the dead, of a slyly laconic sort, is established by recalling their *words* and the values behind them through the image of their great animal, the horse. Section 6 celebrates genuine popular pleasures of which the conservation-minded might disapprove, but the vigour, the beauty and the meaning of those sports is discerned because judgment is put aside in favour of *looking*, without prejudices. Non-judgmental looking, if you like. In Section 7, there is an unobtrusive mingling of memory and perception which makes it possible in the end to discern a pattern of human work and settlement going beyond the ambit of one person's sight. Section 8 is almost pure celebration, though it is bound together by the image of blood exacted from all the inhabitants of the forest by one creature's need of it. Blood is a condition of reproduction for mosquitoes, and by inference for other creatures as well. In Section 9, a human type perhaps especially prominent in the New World in recent times, though it isn't confined to the New World, is examined and presented through its characteristic words, the *tjúrunga rétnja* of its values, and the section ends in a sardonic antinomy, with the working men watching boys, new recruits to their non-privileged world, 'who think hard work a test, and boys who think it is not a test'. You can't win in that game except through real maturity and personal independence. Section 10 is again almost unalloyed celebration, of places and habits of the ibis, with peripheral human figures tentatively rediscovering 'things about themselves, and about the ibis'. Section 11 continues the celebration of places, and describes the almost accidental acquisition of memory and significance by children; the children are learning ancestral things (and communing with them through the act of eating the fruit) which will inform their sense of the world and of their country, and make it just a bit harder for them to become thoroughly alienated or effectively colonial. You might say they are absorbing the accidents of nationality. The very long twelfth section evokes place and season and the great rhythms of the day and the weather. Its central insight is the one about abandoned things 'thronged with spirits'. We will come back to this in a moment. Section 13, of course, is the poem's finale, and links the evoked region with the heavens, with what I call the Great Imagery of the stars. The region is *placed* in the universe, and the whole experience of the Holiday, the walkabout quest, is mapped and sealed for the people who now have to go back to their other life. The Southern Cross is evoked emblematically, at each end of the section, and is described in intimately colloquial terms echoing the loving intimacy of the Aboriginal treatment of the Evening Star in the Moon Bone Cycle and the vernacular ease and tang of the most characteristic white Australian style of speech.

Apart from quality, my poem cycle differs from its great model in two main ways. It is progressive, in a loose sort of way, while the Moon Bone Cycle is static and accretive, and it contains irony and social comment, though these are always presented in contexts which have the power to overcome or at least soften them. It would have been treason to the facts of modern Australian life if all conflict, all edginess, had been left out, and only a sugary picture of too-easy reconciliation allowed to remain. Again, there is a time element in my poem, because our white cultures *are* time cultures, and because one of the great secular religions of Australia is worship of the past and of that which has been made harmless and poignant with the passage of time. Abandoned things, whether in folk museums or compendia of obsolete slang, are thronged with spirits for us. Sadly, it is perhaps a measure of the acculturation of the Aborigines, a process in which black radicalism may be just another stage, that we now sentimentalize them in much the same way. For good and ill, one of the chief bearers of our new secular Shinto in recent years has been the conservationist movement. Great tributes have to be paid to that movement for, in particular, implanting the Aboriginal concept of the sacredness of the land and of one's native region in the minds of many Australians. This has come about largely as a by-product of the agitation for Aboriginal land rights – and has begun provoking some white country people to start thinking about *their* land rights, rights to live in places which have formed and continue to nurture their spirit. Where this is merely an attempt to trump the Aborigines, it is to be deplored, but it does point to the inequity of, as it were, releasing one section of our population from the ordinary laws of economics while letting the rest continue to suffer the effects of these. We need to think about the applicability of the principle to all of our people.

In a lecture given to the English Association at Sydney University on 25 May 1973, David Malouf writes:

> It is only through Caliban that we get this sense of the richness of the island, its tumbling fecundity. His capacity to name things, and by naming evoke them, is a different sort of magic from Prospero's but no less powerful and real. It might remind us of the extraordinary way our own Aborigines have possessed the land in their minds, through folkstories, taboos, song-cycles, and made it part of the very fabric of their living as we never can.

My contention is that of course 'we' can, and some of us do possess the land imaginatively in very much the Aboriginal way. We have recently been awed by the discovery that the Aborigines have been here for thirty or forty thousand years, or even longer, but I think too much is often made of this. Forty thousand years are not very different from a few hundred, if your culture has not, through genealogy, developed a sense of the progression of time and thus made history possible. Aboriginal 'history' is poetic, a matter of significant moments rather than of development. To make it historical in our sense requires an imposition of Western thinking.

In art, in my writing, my abiding interest is in integrations, in convergences. I want my poems to be more than just National Parks of sentimental preservation, useful as the National Parks are as holding operations in the modern age. What I am after is a spiritual change that would make them unnecessary. And I discern the best hope for it in convergence of the sort I've been talking about. In Australian civilization, I would contend, convergence between black and white is a fact, a subtle process, hard to discern often, and hard to produce evidence for. Just now, too, it lacks the force of fashion to drive it; the fashion is all for divisiveness now. Yet the Jindyworobak poets were on the right track, in a way; their concept of *environmental value*, of the slow moulding of all people within a continent or region towards the natural human form which that continent or region demands, that is a real process. Once or twice, perhaps more often, I have been able to capture a sense of that process in verse. From the earliest days, with few real exceptions I can think of (Thomas Keneally is partly one; Xavier Herbert is another), white Australian writers have written about Aborigines as figures *other* than themselves, as objects almost, figures to be described with perhaps very great sympathy, but figures existing over against the writer and his world. Identification with them has been sporadic, fashionable only during a particular period, and has lately been attempted mainly at the level of polemic, which can be exploitative, as well as pointlessly divisive. In particular, urban writing has tended to work over against almost *all* kinds of Australians who do not share a certain derivative 'educated' sensibility, and to use Aborigines as a stick to beat the Ockers with.

It is true that ease with Australian imagery has become much more noticeable in our poetry in the last few years. But it is not true to claim, as some do, that the whole question of acceptance of Australia by poets has been resolved and is now old hat. The attitudes, the orthodoxy, of alienation work too powerfully on us for that. It's what I was saying to Lionel Brockman in the Lake Country poem: you, as a primal embodiment of essential Australia, are right to reject people like me. The takeover smell, the gubba smell, is still strong on us, because modernist orthodoxy has changed art from being Culture (which is bad enough) to being *a* culture, an enclave of borrowed despairs over against our fellow Australians. I am deprived of my natural audience by the stain of association; for now, and perhaps all my life, I have to live with that and try not to let it distort my work.

I'm out to break that gubba-ism, though. I am grateful beyond measure to the makers and interpreters of traditional Aboriginal poetry and song for many things, not least for showing me a deeply familiar world in which art is not estranged, but is a vital source of health for all the members of a community, and even goes magically beyond the human community, ensuring proper treatment of the natural world by its dominant member-species. Aboriginal art has given me a resort of reference and native strength, a truly Australian base to draw on against the constant importation of Western decays and idiocies and class consciousness. If the lore-which-is-law has a weakness, it is in its too-rigid separation of the sexes, and in its secrecy, though that has clearly been a strength as well, in times of violent conquest. The parallelisms, the convergences here are fascinating, especially as regards separation of the sexes. This separation seems to have been particularly rigid in Central Australia: the Northern Aranda circumcision story may refer to a historic moment in the past in which the ritual separation was begun, or accentuated. In my region, spiritual adventures, usually under the cloak of alcohol, were a male preserve, while women were expected to preserve a certain fairly narrow Puritan respectability. Venturing was for men: women were supposed to embody stability. Among Aborigines in eastern Australia, women have often found solace in conversion to Christianity, while men, deprived of the flights and intricacies of their religious preserve, have suffered a crippling inner collapse – and it is the same with white men deprived by fashion of their military and work-ethic themes and scorned for their decency and lack of education. In times of conquest, or repudiation, it is possible that while women suffer more, men lose more.

With responsible scholars like Berndt, Strehlow and some others, one may be sure one is not reproducing anything which should not be published. Strehlow, in particular, was entrusted with the Aranda sacred verses in order that he might preserve them against the day when the old culture died out, at least in its old pure form. At his death, he still held large amounts of material which cannot and should not be released until those who own it in the traditional sense are dead. I gather some mainly pictorial material did get out improperly, through what looks like naiveté about the international syndication links of popular magazines; this was the unfortunate *Stern* case. The elders of many tribes have made at least tacit provision for the storage of important material in white archives, knowing that assimilation and acculturation are facts; in many places, few if any young men are found fit or willing to embark on the lifelong arduous disciplines of traditional ritual instruction.

It is to the credit of the Jindyworobak poets that they were the first white artists to try to make assimilation a two-way street. Convergence is a better word here, though; assimilation carries too deep a stain of conquest, of expecting the Aborigines to make all the accommodations while white people make none. The Jindies represent a creolizing impulse in our culture which may be constant, though faint just now and inhibited by a temporary ascendancy of separationist rhetorics. I suspect that creolization and separatism are complementary impulses which will persist in our society for centuries, each having its alternating periods of dominance. Perhaps ironically, the present phase of confrontation has led to an emphasis on and an enrichment of the idea of the sacred in Australia, at a time when religious concepts were supposed to be in decline. Even those interested in using the Aboriginal struggle as a stalking-horse against the wider social order were constrained to talk about sacred things, and keep alive a term they would otherwise wish to see disappear.

My guess is that creolizing convergences will have their next run when the Land Rights phase has obtained whatever proportion of its mostly quite moderate claims the practical politics of the nation allows it. It should be remembered, of course, that the Jindyworobaks were not solely concerned with the resources of Aboriginal culture; they sought recognition for all genuinely Australian traditions, including such suppressed ones as Barossa German. The movement did start in South Australia after all. In a way, they were our first multi-culturalists, long before we imported the Ethnic idea wholus-bolus from Canada and the United States. In much the same way, the Australia First movement some of them were peripherally involved with was arguably a forerunner, a generation early, of one very major strand of the anti-Vietnam campaign. With hindsight, it is possible to see both impulses as having implicit republican content. And of course some of the Jindies were out-and-out republicans.

My affinity with Aboriginal art and thought is only partly elective, and goes on into convergences I have yet to explore. The ground of integration, of convergence, is rocky and ill-mapped; sooner or later, I will have to give some blood for dancing there. What I hope I may have done so far is to promote, and revive, the use of Aboriginal themes and imagery in Australian poetry. Although mistakes and distortions are probably inevitable – and may indeed be fruitful in artistic terms – I hope I have got my borrowings mostly right, and done some justice to our greatest autochthonous tradition. It may be proper for me to close by quoting from Strehlow again, daringly, though I see myself mainly as a precursor; on page 729 of *Songs of Central Australia*, he writes:

It is my belief that when the strong web of future Australian verse comes to be woven, probably some of its strands will be found to be poetic threads spun on the Stone Age hair-spindles of Central Australia.

Of Phenicopters and Beccaficoes

The Pantropheon, or A History of Food and Its Preparation in Ancient Times, by Alexis Soyer (Paddington Press, 1977)

The thing which strikes modern people, when we think about the eating habits of the ancient world, is the number of foodstuffs familiar to us which were unknown to the ancients. Imagine a world with no potatoes. And no tea, or coffee, or cocoa, or oranges, or sugar, or cauliflowers, or capsicums, or even any pumpkins or spinach. And no peanuts or tobacco either. Imagine Italy without the tomato. Or summer without watermelons.

The Classical peoples did, of course, have pretty well our whole range of meats, fish and poultry, excluding the turkey, and most of the grains, fruits and spices we know, as well as many of our modern vegetables. Some familiar things were not used nearly as freely as we might use them. Garlic was known, for example, but despised as soldiers' food, just as the Greeks scorned beans as food for lawyers. The poor subsisted on pretty monotonous fare; gruel was the Roman staple in pre-Classical times, being replaced by bread comparatively late. Crowds at the gladiatorial games feasted on cooked peas, and soldiers conquered the known world on a basic diet of hard *buccellatum* biscuit, onions and watered vinegar.

The ancients were deficient in stimulants (or comparatively free of them, if that is your preference). Distilled grain spirits were a later Celtic invention, and beer was an aberration which the cultured Egyptians shared with the barbarian tribes of northern Europe. Apart from wine, usually served with water, or else mixed with honey and all manner of spices, the Greeks had only poetry and conversation, plus perhaps the odd bit of pederasty, to enliven their banquets, and the Romans had only these plus cruelty and licence. Unless we count cannabis seed, which was sometimes served fried as a dessert. The author of the *Pantrophaeon* is rather disgusted by this:

That hemp should be spun and made into ropes, well and good, but to regale oneself with it after dinner, when the stomach is overloaded with food, and hardly moved from its lethargic quietude by the appearance of the most provoking viands that art can invent – what depravity! What strange perversion of the most simple elements of gastronomy!

Perhaps the ancients knew something which Soyer didn't.

As readers will have guessed from this quotation, if the name of Alexis Soyer hadn't already put them on the alert, this is not a contemporary book, but a reprint of an 1853 treatise on the history of food and cuisine in ancient times.

Alexis Soyer was a talented, dashing, delightfully vain Frenchman who, as well as reigning supreme as the master chef of London's Reform Club, also organized food relief for the starving during the great Irish famines. With Florence Nightingale, he reorganized the catering system of military hospitals during the Crimean War. His grand breakfast for two thousand people at Gwydyr House in 1838 long remained a legend, as did his *banquet de luxe* for Ibrahim Pasha and a hundred and fifty guests on 1 July 1846. The breadth of his reading, and his wealth of Classical knowledge, are astounding. The ease of his High Victorian prose is a delight, too: though French by birth and training, he wrote this and most of his other books in English, and his style is almost entirely free of Gallicisms.

M. Soyer's history is craftsmanlike, in his own rather than the academic sense, and probably the better for it. He begins with a short account of ancient agriculture, then moves on through a detailed discussion of ingredients, to methods of preparation, preservation and cooking, to culminate in descriptions of meals, service, tables, eating habits and the like. At times, his writing has a delightful straight-faced quality, as when he recounts how shepherds used to cook eggs by whirling them around rapidly in their slings, the cooking being done by the heat of friction with the air.

Reading the book, one gets the impression that Roman banquets were in some ways rather like modern Chinese and South-East Asian ones. Courses consisted of dozens of dishes placed on the table together, with little concern for gradations, and many of the dishes served would probably seem to us a bit like the sweet-and-sour ones of Southern Chinese cuisine. Sugar ('honey of reeds') was a rare import from the East, used almost solely in medicine, but honey was apt to be used in almost everything, even the meat dishes.

Many dishes, too, may have tasted rather like those of South-East Asia, because of the Romans' fondness for *garum*, a condiment made of fermented fish and brine that sounds very like the *nuoc mam* sauce of Vietnam. *Garum* was likely to be added to almost anything, rather as some moderns add tomato sauce. In that age of no refrigeration, too, many foods came in pickled or preserved form. One great difference from East Asian cookery, of course, was the use made of milk and cheese. Butter, on the other hand, was a rarity pretty well confined to medical preparations.

The author has some hard things to say about the *nouveau riche* Romans' habit of scouring the world for rare and expensive delicacies – the fatty tongues of flamingoes, or phenicopters as he calls them, were a particular favourite – and he disapproves of their frequent gluttony. Of course, they only ate one main meal a day, usually in the evening, but after reading about some of their blowouts it comes as no surprise to learn that they went in for digestive salts. Food was eaten mainly with the fingers, one's own or those of slaves, though spoons were used for eggs and shellfish. Despite the breads and honey the ancients ate, it is clear from the recipes and menus given that the diet of even the richest Greeks and Romans was basically healthier than our own, lower on carbohydrates and higher in protein and roughage. If there is one fancy dish I would like to see resurrected, perhaps only once, from the days of Apicius and Macrobius, it would be the little fig-pecker birds, or beccaficoes, roasted and served in a jacket of fine sauce inside an egg.

Unlike some of his noble and mercantile patrons, Soyer seems to have had a real concern for the poor of his day. He does not fail to mention the horror of ancient slavery, when a magnate could fatten his conger eels for the table by throwing live slaves to them, and there is a very dry passage in the introduction to this book which still bears thinking about:

> The Greeks and Romans, egoists if ever there were any, supped for themselves and lived only to sup; our pleasures are ennobled by views more useful and more elevated. We often dine for the poor, and sometimes dance for the afflicted, the widow and the orphan.

Sydney Morning Herald, 3 December 1977

The Bonnie Disproportion

It is probable that something under one-tenth of all Australians are of predominantly Scottish extraction. I call these people the Scots Australians, though not all of them might approve of the title. In my own family, the term was always the older form 'Scotch'. John Kenneth Galbraith, in his delightful book about the Scots settlers in Ontario, *The Non-Potable Scotch*, reports the same usage, adding that 'Scots' was considered a bit precious there. It seems to be the preferred form nowadays, though, if only to distinguish the people from the whisky. In family contexts, ingrained habit will probably lead me to speak of the Scotch, and being Scotch, keeping Scots Australian for the pukka, generalizing parts of my treatise.

Apart from the tenth who are Scottish in the main line or lines of their ancestry, a great many other Australians, of course, would have a substantial Scottish admixture, whether they were conscious of it or not. This is where things get shaky. Given the facts of inter-marriage in a new country, separating out the different ethnic strands can be a task at once intricate and gross. Opting for one ethnic tradition, usually that of the father's line and the surname, tends to downgrade the female side of one's ancestry. If anything undercuts the present vogue for ethnic consciousness, especially amongst Old Australians (perhaps it wasn't primarily meant for us) it is the question of the slighted mothers. I've been a publicist for the ethnic thing myself, so it behoves me to say that.

The Scots, along with the Jews, have probably been the great ethnic success story in Australian history. Some Irish Australian friends of mine once demanded to know what the Scots, as compared with the Irish, had achieved in Australia. 'Well,' I replied, 'we own it.' The enormous number of Scots and Scottish descendants, in proportion to our share of the population, who have been leaders in commerce, in politics, in education, in military matters and in the pastoral industry is pretty well known, even in the absence of any really comprehensive and respectable study of the Scottish part in Australian history. Which is an amazing lack, when you think about it. Even though Australian politics has sometimes seemed a perpetual struggle between one Irish and two Scots parties, it has been the Irish who have attracted the historians and the explainers of our nation's culture. The Irish have been more visible, and more tragic, though there is a sadness at the heart of Scottish success which might yield much to a scholar prepared to probe deeply. And this sadness may also have a bit to do with my first surprising claim, namely, that another field in which we have been active and successful in a measure way out of proportion to our numbers is poetry. Just under one-tenth of Australia's population has so far produced between a fifth and a quarter of the country's poets. Ethnic satisfaction quite aside, this is a mystery, and a breach of stereotype, which I am concerned to understand. And it leads into other mysteries which are anything but comfortable.

Figures and numerical proportions, however approximate, are apt to seem coarsely managerial when applied to literary achievement, though there's also a dash of caste-snobbery in our resistance to statistics in the context of art. I think my figures are pretty reliable, though, and point in an interesting direction; I'd better say here how I arrived at them. The figure for the proportion of Australians having a predominantly Scottish background is derived from the Census question regarding religious affiliation. Until the mid-1970s, when the Uniting Church arose to muddy the picture, the main Christian denominations were still a fair guide to the ethnic background of most Australians. Catholics were rapidly diversifying, but Church of England was still a very reliable pointer to English origins, and Presbyterian overwhelmingly signified Scottish descent. As late as the Census of 1971, the last before the Uniting Church was formed, you could put together a pretty good estimate of the numbers of Scots Australians by taking the figure for Presbyterians, subtracting forty or fifty thousand from that to allow for Dutch, Swiss and Hungarian Calvinists, who tend to join the various Presbyterian churches here, and adding a much larger guesstimate number from the Not Stated to No Religion categories. The Scottish rationalist tradition, surviving in exile, ensures that there will be plenty of strong Calvinist atheists among the No Religion group.

It is harder to find a basis on which to attempt a decent guesstimate of Scots Australians who've followed less typical religious paths, the Scots Catholics (relatively few, in the earlier days of Scottish emigration, though the Catholic minority in Scotland itself now embraces nearly a quarter of the population) and Catholic converts, or those, usually Establishment Scots, who have become Anglican over the years, or those who have joined the smaller Protestant sects. I ended up awarding these less typical cases a purely aleatory figure of twenty thousand; I had to get my Romish self in somehow! Using the 1971 Census figures, the whole procedure gave a total somewhere between 1,200,000 and 1,300,000, in a population of just under thirteen million. I doubt the proportion will have shifted much since, though it is hard to see how even this sort of rough calculation will be possible in future times. In the absence of a specifically ethnic question in future Censuses, which for many reasons would be a thoroughly bad idea, we have probably lost our only possible index of Scots Australian numbers. Names, even when you know your Scottish Macs from your Irish ones, are infinitely less reliable; indeed, they have got so thoroughly mixed around in the English-speaking world as to be hopelessly misleading, unless you happen to know a bit about each person bearing a particular surname. This was the basis on which I was able to use surnames in my survey of more than a dozen anthologies of Australian poetry, the survey which confirmed my long-held suspicion that the proportion of Scots Australians among our poets was freakishly high. Knowing at least a little about most of the writers whose names I encountered in the various collections, I could make a reasonably informed guess about their major ethnic heritage. And in many cases, I knew a lot about it. I was also able to include cases where a Scottish ancestry was masked by an untypical name. Two such cases were Peter Kocan and Judith Wright. When Clan McGregor was proscribed and forbidden the use of its name, in the early seventeenth century, one branch took the name of Wright; Judith is actually a proud clanswoman of Rob Roy himself! In Peter's case, I knew he was a Douglas; the name Kocan was that of his stepfather. Eschewing, for once and gratefully, all considerations of poetic quality, I simply looked at the names included in each anthology, and worked out the ratio of Scots ethnics as against the total number of names included. The proportion sometimes even exceeded twenty-five per cent. In two successive numbers of Philip Roberts's *Poet's Choice* (1972 and 1973), nine out of thirty poets included had predominantly Scottish ancestry. And in Douglas Stewart's recension of *The Wide Brown Land*, the ratio was twenty out of seventy-seven. The two *Penguin Books of Australian Verse* gave more typical proportions, fifteen out of sixty in the first edition and twenty-one out of ninety-four in Harry Heseltine's revamped edition. The proportion fell slightly below one-fifth in Bernard Hickey's Italian-English bilingual collection, *Da Slessor a Dransfield*, which had ten Scots ethnics out of fifty-two

poets represented, but only fell markedly below it in Hall and Shap-
cott's *New Impulses in Australian Poetry*, where I could identify only
two definite Scots Australians in a line-up of twenty-two authors.
More recent collections of a modernist tendency generally yielded
much higher and more typical ratios.

I felt confident enough in doing my ethnic breakdown of the
various anthologies, because so far as I know no one had previously
thought of doing such a crazy thing. I was convinced that even
unconscious ethnic bias could be ruled out; to my knowledge the
polemical intents of even the most programmatic editors have never
exhibited an ethnic dimension. Not of precisely this sort, anyhow.
The proportion of Scottish descendants amongst our poets surprised
me at first by being even higher than I had guessed it would be, and
then by holding pretty constant all through this century; it was a
good deal lower among the balladists of the nineteenth century and
the early part of this one. In what was, I think, a very natural comparison to make, I found that the Irish ratio, high among the balladists and other poets of the last century, tailed off markedly around
Federation and has tended ever since to hover around one-half to
one-third of the Scots one. And this is in absolute terms; given the
very much greater proportion of Irish descendants in the overall
population, one would expect the contingent of Irish-descended
poets to exceed the Scots by a wide margin. The two peoples are
ancestrally linked by ties of blood and culture, though the linkages
are ancient and complex, and are sometimes overstated, but a contrast of the sort I discovered clearly points to a major dissimilarity,
not of native talent for heaven's sake, but perhaps of preferred cultural expression. I suspect that it may be significant that Irish Australian representation among the country's poets drops off at the period
when the Labor Party was starting to gather widespread support.
It is possible that the Labor movement, as well as their religion or
in place of it, absorbed the souls of Australian Irish folk in ways
for which our declining Calvinism and pragmatic mercantilist politics have offered no parallel. But it might be fruitful to examine
other differences between the two groups as well.

The great link between the Irish and the Scots is, of course, the
Gaelic language and culture, and in particular the common institution of the *fine* (pronounced, approximately *feen*-ey), the extended
clan family, which may yet prove the most durable legacy of the
Gaelic past. Both countries were Gaelic kingdoms in the remote
past, yet even when we look at all closely at this common fact, we
begin to see wide differences. While Ireland enters recorded history

as a country with a uniformly Gaelic culture, the space which gradually came to be known as Scotland was occupied, at the end of Roman rule in Britain, by at least three distinct peoples, the Britons of Strathclyde and the south who had known a slight degree of Roman domination, the Picts who had resisted Rome well enough to dissuade her from colonizing their (to Roman eyes) unattractive regions in the north, and the *Scotti* or Irish Gaels who had recently established themselves in the Western Highlands. With the Teutonic invasions, a fourth people were added to the mosaic, as the Kingdom of Northumbria conquered all the south-eastern zone between Hadrian's Wall and the Firth of Forth.

The Gaelic kingdom of Dalriada conquered and began to absorb the Picts in the ninth century, and out of this conquest there arose the first 'Scottish' kingdom, known as Alba, which remains the Gaelic name for Scotland to this day. It took Alba the best part of two hundred years to extend her sovereignty southwards to the present Anglo-Scottish border, and in the process she conquered the northern march of Northumbria whose Teutonic English language would eventually displace Gaelic as the dominant speech of the kingdom of Scots. There is evidence that Gaelic did penetrate for a time south of the Forth, and it did replace Welsh in the ancient British kingdom of Rheged, which became Ayrshire-Strathclyde, but the displacement of Gaelic by 'Inglis' at the royal court probably began around the time of King Malcolm III Canmore (*Ceann mór*, the big-headed) and his Saxon Queen Margaret, in the middle of the eleventh century. Alba had, however, imparted a strongly Gaelic 'set' to the whole society of the kingdom, not so much through language perhaps – though the echo of Gaelic is pervasive in Scots speech even today, if you have an ear for it – but rather through institutions and modes of behaviour. Among these, the most powerful and long lasting seems to have been *finechas*, the feeling of kindred. The gradual retreat of the Gaelic language after Malcolm's time did nothing to hinder a remarkable fusing together of the disparate peoples into a new people, the Scots, who have kept a strong identity all down the centuries since, despite linguistic and other cleavages.

The Scots probably learned earlier than the Irish to think of themselves as one people whether they spoke Gaelic or English; in Ireland, until the English conquest hotted up under the Tudors, the Irish had always managed to assimilate incomers, Vikings, Normans, Welshmen and the rest, to their own language and culture; thereafter, the language and culture gradually became, and long remained, the prime bastion of oppressed Irishness. Probably right up until the collapse of the language in the period of the great potato famines after 1848, the Irish-speaking majority accepted as their own only those who belonged to their clans and their religion, and who shared in some measure the cup of their suffering. The bardic keepers of the old tradition, whose order survived until the early eighteenth century, would not have regarded Catholicism or sympathy as sufficient credentials for admittance to the by-then-underground continuities of the native culture. Even possession of a native name would have been no advantage, on its own; having the name without the language and the poverty put one at least to some degree in the odium of a renegade, a Quisling, a climber of the oppressor's social ladder. What the *Gall*, or foreigners, chose to call Irish was not necessarily what the Gael regarded as worthy of the name. It is fairly clear that the dynamics of this resistance to the oppressor's order, to the world-picture of the prison guard and the privileged man, are still a factor in Australian life today, with a certain salty egalitarian tribalism replacing the old tests of religion and culture and serving as their equivalent. In Ireland itself, it is very clear that some people still apply cultural tests as to what constitutes 'true' Irishness, and are prepared to push the matter tragically far.

For many reasons, Scottish identity was never a contentious matter in any way or degree comparable with this. The Scottish nation was absorbed, in large measure, by the English; it was never the victim of brutal conquest (though that was tried several times in the Middle Ages) or centuries of merciless suppression. The dreadful harrying of the Gaelic Highlands after the Rising of 1745-46 is, of course, an exception, but the only one. Otherwise Scotland was incorporated, after the unfortunate union of crowns in 1603, through economic pressure and cultural preponderance. When surrender of her national sovereignty in 1707 gained Scotland relief from English economic blockade and admission to economic opportunity in the growing English empire, Scots were allowed to keep their Scottishness as a consolation prize. After all, it threatened nothing; apart from Calvinist missionary work, there was no exclusively Scottish sphere of activity beyond the Scottish borders. Success outside Scotland was on terms set by the Predominant Pairtner or the other host countries of the Scots diaspora.

It is impossible to say to what degree something like the Gaelic clan system existed amongst the different peoples of Scotland before the kingdom of Scots came into being. The Brythonic kingdoms, being Celtic, may have had something similar, but the Picts appear to have had a system of tribes, probably matrilineal and totemic; we will probably never know much about their organization and structure, though I think the persistence of certain recurring symbols in the heraldry of different groups of Scottish clans (the wildcat, the three stars and others) point to the origin of those clans from identifiable earlier tribes. The Northumbrians probably had nothing really comparable with the Gaelic system of *finechan* or kindreds. Quite early in Scottish history, however, we see the evolution outside the original area of Gaeldom of great territorial family groupings. The problem of powerful families was one which the Scottish kings never wholly solved. Some of them died trying. Well before the loss of sovereignty, lowland families in which Gaelic had probably never been spoken were behaving exactly like the Gaelic clans, and are fairly well justified nowadays in referring to themselves as clans in the Highland way; it isn't just modern hoopla invented by Sir Walter Scott. In the period of the Stewart kings (Stuart, the French spelling, is probably better reserved for the period of French exile and Jacobitism), we often encounter the term *interest* being used to refer to the territorial families, the Hamilton interest, the Huntly Gordon interest, the Atholl interest and so on. It should be remembered that, as late as 1746 in the Highlands and Islands, and generally earlier on, the chiefs of the local families, feudalized to some degree during the Middle Ages and later, possessed rights of judicature, of 'pit and gallows', over their tenants and subjects. The kingdom was structured as a nexus of powerful families, whose power waxed, shifted and waned with the onrush of history. The family motto of the Bruces, *Fuimus* (We Were), is an excellent pointer to the experience of one such family, which once held the crown, but afterwards dwindled to comparative unimportance.

The common Irish and Scottish institution of the *fine*, the extended clan family, antedates feudalism by at least a thousand years and probably more (the Old Celtic form of the word is *vinja*, and must have referred to something comparable) and has survived in a real if subterranean and often-ignored way into modern times. Feudalism is a coloration it bore for several centuries, but has now almost sloughed off. It gave the two countries a terrific decentralized resilience to invasion, as well as an inherent tendency to division and petty warfare; Ireland survived and defeated the Vikings largely because there was never one centre, one stronghold whose capture would bring the whole culture undone. If the *finechan* weakened the two countries as nations in our sense, they also provided a resilient second line of defence for them as cultures. Their strongholds, each the residence of the patriarchal chief who was seen as the descendant or 'Representer' of the perhaps legendary founder of the name, were centres of music, of poetry and storytelling, of style-setting innovation and the rituals of family unity. The chief's officers and tenants were his *clann*, a word which means nothing other than children, and consanguinity, real or theoretical, with him gave his subjects rights of appeal and criticism, often expressed most effectively in horatory song-poetry addressed to him by his bards. Chiefs were not by any means all-powerful, though their power tended to increase as the system became more feudalized. They were still subject, in the last resort, to the will of the clan, and there are cases of chiefs who were deposed or even killed by their clansfolk. John 'Handsome Iain' Macdonald of Keppoch (floruit *c.*1498) was deposed by his clan for handing over a relative to the vengeance of the Mackintoshes. His descendants were thereafter known as *sliochd a'bhràthar bu shine* (the line of the elder brother) and were the forebears of the fierce Jacobite satirist John Macdonald, known in Gaelic as Iain Lom. Some bards very likely were toadies to their chiefs, but their position carried a very large measure of traditional dignity and indeed sacrosanctity, which made it possible for bards of character to look two ways, and serve the people as well as the chief.

In 'Inglis' and Gaelic alike, the literature, that is poetry, which survived was preserved in family verse-books (*Duanairechan*), the greatest of these being the Bannatyne manuscript made in 1568 for the Stewart court. The tradition of manuscript books persisted in Scotland well into the era of printing, and was still dominant in the Highlands and Islands in the eighteenth century. As in Ireland, the bards and their more vernacular successors tended to be a conservative force, celebrating the lasting values of the society and the clan and keeping these ever before the eyes of the chief and his people. It is misleading to see these relationships in terms of modern polemic. This whole patriarchal power structure has long since vanished, but the essence of the *fine* system persists in clan societies and family associations found wherever the Scots and Irish have emigrated. These societies often appear rather sentimental and backward-looking, but there is something real contained in them, a sense of identity, of historic pride, of *finechas* or kindred transcending time and space. And transcending class, as well; as R.L. Stevenson wrote of a servant woman in 'Weir of Hermiston':

> ... she is not necessarily destitute of the pride of birth, but is ... a connection of her master's, and at least knows the legend of her

own family, and may count kinship with some illustrious dead. For that is the mark of the Scot of all classes: that he stands in an attitude to the past unthinkable to Englishmen, and remembers and cherishes the memory of his forebears, good or bad; and there burns alive in him a sense of identity with the dead even to the twentieth generation... The power of ancestry on the character is not limited to the inheritance of cells.

There is a modern version of Scottish history, not wholly disinterested, which would depict the country as inherently and fatefully divided as between the Gaelic north and the non-Gaelic Lowlands. What Stevenson is describing, however, is pure *fine*, though the family involved is the Elliots, a Border name of Norman origin.

Antic pride of family, however poorly informed, is a sort of dormant social principle we carry with us, one which has the potential of becoming real again in adapted forms whenever circumstances warrant it. I grew up in a place in which such a resuscitation of the system actually occurred, and in which the family nexus is still a moral and social reality existing and holding its own amongst other, competing systems of value. My experience may perhaps be anachronistic, in modern Australia, but it is far from unique. Many other country people, especially, could tell a similar story – and might well suspect that the very frequent downgrading or ignoring of the family-dynastic elements in our national life has something ideological in it.

Our family is Pictish in origin, one of a number of families stemming from the lowland area around the Moray Firth which have three stars as their prime heraldic charge; Brodie, Innes and Sutherland share this symbol with us. We may all once have been a single tribe distinguished from the Cat people (the term Clan Chattan still exists, though as a grouping of clans rather than a single family) or the Deer people by a tribal tattoo of stars; the Latin term *picti* means painted or tattooed, and we may have borne tattoo designs in much the same way as the Maori wear their *moko*. The name of our family is identical with that of the Firth, and its meaning is unknown but certainly pre-Indo-European. Scattered all over Scotland in the early Middle Ages, as a result of their resistance, the historian Ian Grimble believes, to the feudalizing of the Gaelo-Pictish north by Queen Margaret's descendants on the Scottish throne, the Moraymen or Murrays acquired territorial holdings from the Central Highlands clear down to the eastern Borders. Some of their local centres of power remained small, others grew in importance, until by the eighteenth century there were two Dukes of the name in Britain, Their Graces of Atholl and Mansfield; that is a piece of swank no other family in Britain can match. Except that Hanoverian one.

Sovereignties and titles probably meant something, but not too much, to the struggling farm people around Jedburgh, Hawick, Denholm and other small towns in the eastern Borders in the middle of the last century. The Murrays of the region were respected as a 'good' family, but their strict Calvinism and Covenanter traditions must have militated against respect for worldly pomps, and the aristocracy by that late stage were mostly Anglicized and infinitely remoter from their kinfolk than they had ever been under the old kingdom. What was probably of much greater interest to the Border Murrays was their ramified interconnections with the other local families, the Veitches, Turnbulls, Scotts, Beatties, Eastons and Rutherfords, to all of whom we're related. When John Murray, farmer at Camptown near Hawick, Roxboroughshire, died in 1845, his widow Isabella decided to send four of her eldest sons and their nineteen-year-old sister Agnes to New South Wales to see what prospects existed there for the family. To ease them into the new country, the boys had the promise of jobs with the Australian Agricultural Company on arrival; their mother's cousin George Easton occupied the post of Overseer of Free Men at Stroud. If all went well with this arrangement she would follow with the five younger boys. This first party accordingly embarked under sail in the *Castle Eden* in 1848, and my great-great-grandfather Hugh Scott Murray and his wife Margaret Beattie had their first child on the voyage. The child was my great-grandfather John Allan, Johnnie of Bunyah, born according to tradition in the middle of a great storm in the Bay of Biscay. He lived up to that beginning later on, though always with great geniality. Agnes married a Gaelic-speaker from Inverness named Paterson, and their descendants are to be found all over the Manning-Myall region today. The boys all quickly secured parcels of land along the upper reaches of the wild Manning River, and in 1851 their mother arrived with the rest of the brothers. The rich flats of the upper Manning have been the heartland of the family ever since, though it has put out offshoots into all the districts around; Johnnie and his wife, also named Isabella, moved out to Bunyah in 1870 and took up land there, as did Uncles Jimmie and Tom. Another brother, Veitch, was more venturesome, and travelled all the way north to the Atherton Tableland to found his dynasty. Until my own generation, though, most of the Murrays stayed around the Manning, and remained in close touch with each other and the other

Scots of the region, the Lobbans, Eastons, MacKinnons, MacCraes, Patersons, Cowans, Wrights, Breckinridges and others, that it was only the grandchildren of the first-comers who regularly spoke with an Australian rather than a Border accent.

Following a very ancient pattern embedded in their civilization, the Murrays installed themselves on separate farmsteads (land for selection was plentiful at a pound an acre, uncleared). These farms were worked by father, mother and all the children. Four years was the usual age for learning how to milk cows, and a child's day from then on began before sunrise with a backbreaking hour or two of milking, unless he was off on business with his father; my father, for instance, began helping his father to drove cattle to market at the age of seven, and was dealing in them on the latter's behalf at nine. Girls did their full share of the dairy work as well, and were excused only the heaviest and most dangerous jobs on the farms, grubbing stumps, ploughing, felling timber. Their household tasks of breadmaking and slinging the ponderous iron jam-pans and camp ovens on chains above the open fire were quite onerous enough, and unremitting.

The cultural life of these settlers had two main centres, the church (I never heard the form 'kirk' when I was a child) and the house party. The Murrays belonged to the strict non-conforming Free Presbyterian sect of Calvinism, which survives to this day in small pockets right along the east coast of Australia, from Geelong and St Kilda to Sydney and the northern rivers and thence up into Queensland. It is the true heir of the Covenants, this small church, still heavily predestinarian and given to an effortful plainness of observance intended as a rebuke to all papistical idolatry and opulence. Churches are utterly unadorned, and the only music allowed in them is unaccompanied singing of the Psalms; hymns are mere human songs, and an organ would be the devil's kist o' whistles. And yet the services have no silence in them either, no mystery, no awe; they are dry theological lectures interspersed with extempore prayers and the Psalms of David in Metre.

A severely Puritan style of life is enjoined upon followers of this tradition. My great-grandfather's first cousin, Sir James Murray, of the *Oxford English Dictionary*, never entered a theatre in his life. Neither did any of the early Australian Murrays, for the good reason that such temptations to loose living simply didn't exist on the northern rivers in their day. They went along, the men anyway and the less fanatical womenfolk, to any travelling amusement that did come their way. The Wee Free faith had a tendency to turn some of my forebears into bigots and one-upping hypocrites, eager to score points over you by displaying greater rectitude and rebuking your laxity. Some of my relations are still like that, and I fear that my detestation of that whole religious tradition began early. A chance copy of Darwin's *Origin of the Species* that fell into my hands when I was nine helped me to escape the mental atmosphere, and my religious travels eventually led me to Catholicism and the Sacraments. In a way, predestinarian Calvinism is a sort of disguised Islam nominally within the Christian fold. Only God matters, and Christ's sacrifice is really a vain thing, because election to glory, or damnation to everlasting death, have been settled for each soul from all eternity, and no action of vice or virtue can change that. No one can deserve anything of God; grace is a free gift. And yet I have known some Free Kirk Presbyterians who were gifted with real grace, despite their theology. Our minister, the late Mr Malcolm Ramsay, who had the charge of Taree and district for many years, was a gentle, scholarly, rather saintly man whose delight was to read some Greek every day; he preached erudite theological sermons to bush congregations, but was also on hand in our times of trouble. He was a good pastor. In Scotland in earlier times justification and the assurance of election became almost obsessive themes, bulking far larger than they had in Calvin's own writings. It is worth noting that in the Scottish Faust story, James Hogg's *Confessions of a Justified Sinner*, the devil does not have to tempt his victim at all; he merely appears to him in mufti and encourages him in his beliefs, to the point where he will commit patricide, matricide, any enormity. There was a terrific pull against this faith under the surface of my people's lives, but it left on many of them its marks of cruelty, moral snobbery, competitive holiness and wilful ignorance, the ignorance that dismisses all culture of the mind as worldly and unclean. In the absence of a Christian morality, we made do with pride plus something like what the Greeks called *Themis*, a sort of moral-aesthetic sense of propriety which is, I think, the true ancestress of the Right Thing and the Fair Go, and a close cousin of proportion. Enthusiasts in Australia make a bad tactical error when they offend against *Themis*. She is more ancient and more ruthless than they imagine.

The house parties in the old days tended to be weekend affairs, beginning on Friday (sometimes as early as Thursday) and ending God knew when the following week. My father remembers a pair of bearded elders striking matches at eleven of a summer's morning to determine if there were a frost; this was on the Tuesday or Wednesday after a big 'shivoo' as these affairs were sometimes called.

The word comes from *chez nous* 'at your place' – a modern Irish equivalent might be 'hooley', though that's often just a one-night party. I imagine the word is derived from *ceilidh*. The days were devoted to huge meals, picnics, horse sports and raising hell; the nights, except for the sabbath night, were for non-stop dancing to the piano, the fiddle, the accordion and occasionally the pipes. On the Sunday night, recitations and stories, and sometimes singing, were allowed. Many Australians have, away in the back of their memory, a feel for what is called in Gaelic *corra-cagailte*, which means a heart fire when it has burned down to glowing coals late at night, and the deepest stories and the oldest, most profound traditions are brought out amid spellbound silence. It was our lens, that hearth, for looking back down the experience of our people right to the fields and attitudes of the Heroic age. A shadowy blind man sits by the glow and begins to chant an intricate cross-weave of syllables, and the blood freezes on the brink of understanding. Your very bones know the tune, but what do the words say? You may spend your life trying to find out.

Of all the non-church values the Murrays instilled in their children, the greatest was the one called not freedom but *independence*. It went with the separate farms, the houses standing at a dignified distance from each other in the valleys and on the hills. It went with self-containment and discretion about private matters: 'Don't tell anyone how much you've got in the bank, boy. Don't let old mother So-and-so pump you: she wants to know the ins and outs of a mag's arse.' I still don't know what sort of a mag was meant. Independence went with making your own judgments about the worth of people and actions, and here moral snobbery was apt to raise its head. The key values were very much Burns's 'Sense and Worth o'er all the earth': good sense, integrity and a certain nobility of demeanour were valued; weakness, childishness and lack of basic solidity were despised. There are few things colder than a Scots eye turned upon footling behaviour – unintentionally footling, that is; intentional leg-pulling foolishness is well understood and appreciated – and few phrases are more withering than a Scot's laconic 'I hear you', meaning that what you've said is not worth a response. It was a shame culture, rather than a moral culture; in my childhood, I would have heard the word 'disgraceful' far more often than 'wicked'. A person could be good and still be an idiot, and the common phrase 'he's a good poor bastard' was anything but a recommendation. There was a large dash of family pride in the judgment of behaviour: 'Murrays don't do those sort of things. They're for them low-living people.'

A lot of this, I admit, persists in me; how could the son of Cecil Murray behave beneath his father's standard and shame the family? I was amused the other week when my eldest daughter was reported as saying airily at her school: 'Murrays *never* misspell words!' A lot of them in fact do, but she doesn't.

In small communities, surveillance is unceasing; I have often told the story of my two aunts who had telescopes to scan the district for signs of pregnancy or other evidence of carryings on. A few old women, and old men for that matter, took a delight in loosing a sudden volley of reproof on the young, to disconcert them and make them submissive. By the time you decided that the whole thing was just a farrago, you had lost the initiative and been made to feel bad – a necessary preliminary to making you pliable. This was the more vicious side of the leg-pulling, straight-faced style of humour our people favoured. By the time I came along, the old bush predilection for the practical joke had pretty nearly passed away – thank God! – but in earlier generations many of the family had devoted fiendish ingenuity to working up schemes for gulling each other and any innocents within reach. For economy of means, it would be hard to beat my cousin Veitch (Bunyah Veitch, that is, not Killawarra Veitch or Queensland Veitch) who once bestrode a stick and happily rode it down through Bunyah to visit my uncle Sam. After a merry day or two of whisky and Burns, Veitch returned home without his mount, and asked his serious-minded farmhand to go over to Sam's and retrieve it for him. Sam shared the man's concern when the horse was not to be found, and solicitously suggested directions in which it might have wandered; the hapless employee spent the whole day searching paddock after paddock on foot. Towards evening, Sam consented to come and help him search. 'God blast it, George, here he is still tied up to the fence where Veitch left him. I don't know what the boys can have been thinking of, to leave him without feed or water!' The man left Veitch's employ that same evening, at the top of his voice.

When I was a child, and to some extent still, the word 'Scotch' had two meanings amongst my people: we were Scotch, and anyone who was careful with their money and goods was Scotch. Outright meanness was condemned; a cousin of mine was nicknamed Gandhi, because he was said to be too mean to feed himself. A certain largeness of gesture, especially in matters of hospitality, was respected; my great-grandfather was famous for keeping open house at Bunyah, entertaining dozens of guests at a time. He was never considered foolish because of that; there was a proper nobility of attitude in what he did. Losing his homestead in card game, however, *was* excessive, and was hushed up fairly thoroughly; I only found out about it a few years ago, from an aged aunt who waxed loquacious late one night. Gift-giving was uncommon, and done, when it was done, with a certain perfunctoriness and lack of imagination, as a duty; a birthday would bring me several handkerchiefs, which would be passed on still wrapped to others having birthdays. I still have to be reminded to give presents; it was not a spontaneous thing with me – not that spontaneity was ever regarded as a virtue among Scots! Presents were mostly for children, and given at Christmas. That was expected, and my uncle who told his kids that Sandy Claus had been shot down by the Japanese and wouldn't be coming any more was considered a dreadful brute.

Some of the Murrays were co-operative souls, but it was far from unknown for others of them to charge their kinfolk money for helping out on the farm in emergencies; when important business obliged us to go away, we usually had to pay to have the cows milked. Conversely, I have often known relatives to offer money in return for a favour. That way, you buy off obligation and remain independent. Many of these things point backward, surely, to ancestral frugalities in a country that was rarely prosperous. And to something else: for our ancestors, opulence and high living were almost never a constant thing. They were part of *occasion*, of celebration and display. Few even among the clan nobles lived well all the time, and the poorer folk probably tasted fresh meat only once a year, when the surplus cattle were killed at the beginning of winter. Music, poetry and the other arts attained their full magnificence in the ambience of the *feast*. So did sports, so did dalliance. The dream reiterated in hundreds of the bardic elegies and eulogies which have survived is that of the ever-opulent house and the ever-generous chief; it was probably always more the ideal than the reality. In Australia, poor settlers from the Gaelic world often found themselves quite prosperous, and suffered a painful inner struggle between ingrained peasant frugality and the stereotypes of noble open-handedness imprinted for centuries on the deep mind of their culture. Generosity and concessiveness were more common in that culture than kindness. Not that kindness was rare; however, I have seen, and experienced, tremendous kindness there – often disguised as the dourest sort of concessiveness.

Although the Gaelic language, in both of its forms, contains literally dozens of endearments, my Lowland forebears were apt to seem emotionally parsimonious. They had been through, and were often still in, the centuries of Puritanism, and distrusted demonstrativeness. Nothing, in fact, was valued more highly than deep feeling, but a consequent vigilance about the genuineness of that feeling – and surely such vigilance is still all-pervading in Australia – led to a tendency to regard all true emotion as too deep for words. Intimacy too was often conveyed, in a way which has become endemic among Australians, by signals rather than words, by small things like not using the formal *please* and *thank you* with people close to you; those words are for strangers. There is a world of warm emotional shading in Australian gruffness, if people will look for it. Control was highly valued, and loose, excitable gestures were thought insincere, as well as undignified. My own abhorrence of twittering, kissing hostesses has probably chilled many a warm heart, but that, as the Californians say, is where I'm coming from. A Scotsman might reserve his feelings for twenty years and discharge them all in one tearing shriek of joyous self-immolation as he leaped amongst the enemy with his bayonet. I've heard that same death-howl in a Glasgow pub brawl that burst out into the street in front of me once. There is an element of the visionary in it, a decision to crash boots and all into vengeance or significance, and damn the cost. The stereotype of the Celtic hothead is not without foundation, and can be a danger to beware in oneself. It may underlie the very strong disapproval of argument and dissention instilled in my people as children. Any community has reason to fear Kamikaze gestures of rage that may arise out of ordinary bickering. I was brought up to fear 'rowing' and still find public disagreements exhausting and dangerous. Many of the older male Murrays of the Drinking generations went in for very loud choleric displays that terrorized their families.

One thing which 'Scotch' never meant among my people was whisky; that was called by its name, and assumed to be Scotch; Irish whisky was unknown, and no one would drink Australian. It was the drink for solemn occasions, particularly those with some ancestral connection; it was invariably part of Old Year's Night, for example – the term Hogmanay was never used by my people up home. It was also, for men, the gateway to a world of owlish intensity and yearned-for significance. They would go on benders together, in which they recited and discussed Bobby Burns and Scottish things in befuddled terms for nights on end. My father's generation tended to abhor this ritual, partly because they had been forced so often in childhood to witness it and clean up after it. It was more a thing of my grandfather's generation, and the source of endless stories. Like the time Sam, Veitch and Grandfather, on about the third night of a spree, enticed their abstemious and rather hen-pecked neighbour Joe Lynch down from his house to the road and coaxed him into a strathspey-and-reels contest. 'I'll whistle the tunes, Joe, and Sam here'll step you for a fiver.' They danced Joe for hours, slipping whisky and rum into him under his guard, until he collapsed on his hands and knees in the mud of the road. 'It's been terrible dry, Joe,' cried Grandfather through the drizzle: 'You're a good man, and we want you to pray for rain for us.' Joe prayed loudly and disjointedly until he collapsed into incoherence and passed out. With befuddled concern for his welfare, and a healthy fear of his wife's wrath, they then shifted him into the gutter and tied a hur-ricane lamp to him with his pyjama cord, so that no one would run over him. 'Must give the man a tail-light,' they agreed, and drove off to look for more entertainment. Joe's wife discovered her sleeping spouse the next morning, and the Murrays did not travel that road again for some months.

Wives, of course, like all women, were utterly excluded from the drinking ritual; their permitted intoxication was religion, and if they didn't choose to go in for that, they were certainly expected to be respectable and dependable. A drinking wife was, if anything, even lower than an unfaithful one. The shamanism of distilled liquors was resented by the wives, though most resigned themselves to it somehow, and resented even more by that generation's sons, as they saw their inheritance going into the pub till, while they sat outside in the car or the sulky waiting to drive Dad home. Each man's 'boys' were his labourers, often working for no wages beyond the promise that they would be given land and a 'start'.

I suppose what I have been describing is the common trap of ethnic consciousness. As the ancestral motherland recedes farther into the past, it becomes a dream, a fossilized style, a place of the wise dead. You have been taught to look to it for significance and depth, and yet it has become remote, a haunting tune recovered only in extremity, and then impossible to hold. My grandfather's generation was just at that distance from Scotland, in their lives. And they did not read, so they had no real way of refurbishing the fading image. Their grandparents probably had some grasp of the old Scots literary tradition, some familiarity, if only in an oral way, with the Border ballads and the great Scots poems, but the generation of drinkers up home had lost everything but Burns. They still under-stood, from childhood, the language of Burns' poems, though they did not really speak it or pass it on to their children. It is usually in the third generation that an immigrant group will suffer the wholesale loss of its language. After which the mind is apt to be haunted by the loom of words, a sense of a lost native idiom just below the horizon of the mind. Broad Scots – Lallans, if you like, surely a marvellous name for the language of the intoxicated – will produce this effect just as readily as Gaelic. Or German, or Arabic. I suspect that this phenomenon can, in odd cases, provoke the artistic urge in a person; there was a weird, undirected proto-poetry in the drinking Murrays' quest. And a hunger for cultural experience which their dour religion did not supply, any more than their bookless, almost schoolless region. Apart from the Bible, Scotland and the Bush were the only books they had, and neither was substantially on paper.

But we needn't become po-faced; I daresay the old fellows had a lot of fun, too. The family, both the majority still living on the lower north coast and the scattered members, is now well and truly over the hump of assimilation. Few definite traces of Scots custom or speech remain. We say 'plat' for 'plait', but that has become pretty well the standard Australian pronunciation. A trace of Scottish vowel quality remains when we pronounce words like 'rinse' as 'rense'. Farmers call their cows' udders 'elders', and the people of Bunyah say 'gen' or 'agen' where most Australians would say 'by the time that': 'Agen he gets here, I'll have the tractor fixed.' Similarly, I have an impression that people from my district used to be almost as likely to say 'I'll not' as 'I won't' – the Scots pattern and the English one competed there. A trace of Gaelic phonetics is to be heard among some elder people when they say 'srink' and 'sred', for 'shrink' and 'shred'; the *sr*-cluster is, I believe, disappearing now even in Gaelic. Customs are in a comparable decline. It is probably a generation since any bridegroom has had his feet ceremonially washed by a senior male relative on his wedding day, and only some older people still avoid sleeping with their feet to the east. Few people in my generation even remember to put the adjective 'poor' before the name of a dead person who was close to them; it was once almost an invariable title. Funerals are still the biggest social event in the region, though, and can easily draw crowds of four or five hundred. A week after I went to Kenneth Slessor's funeral in Sydney in 1971, which was attended by perhaps thirty people, I went to my cousin Hugh Murray's funeral at Krambach. Hughie, known in his lifetime as Johnnie Cope, drew eight hundred mourners to his internment. The wake is held afterwards, often at the pub or the club, and is called the send-off. The contrast to be drawn here, I suppose, is between overt, conscious survivals of custom and unnoticed cultural continuities. The strength is now almost entirely in the latter.

In the last two generations, explicit clan feeling and the Scottish link has been preserved mainly by women, but the sense of 'our lot' as a network of loyalty, of communications, of understanding and concern, that is common to all of us. In its Scottish and historical dimension, the *fine* is now a bit sentimentalized and bookish, but in its practical, local dimension it retains tremendous strength. Mine is the first generation to have enjoyed, or had a chance to enjoy, a decent formal education, and there has been keen understated rivalry between parents regarding the academic and worldly success of their children. All such successes are taken, however, as reflecting credit on the clan. And making up, in a sort of delegated way, for past deprivations and stunted lives. The clan gives you little encouragement to make your mark; after all, you should have enough gumption and independence to spur yourself along. It does, however, treasure and boast about your achievements when the world acknowledges them. So long as you haven't developed a swollen head; you are tested carefully and often on that score. You are reminded that of course any of the family would have done as well, if they'd been given the opportunity.

The clan – the word is used, usually jovially by menfolk, to refer not the historical worldwide *fine* of the Murrays, but specifically to our branch of the family – is a superb and invaluable retreat from the asperities and alienations of the outside world; that is probably its chief value for the scattered members. It is a warm, but not cloyingly warm, nexus of familiarity; within it, you can talk easily to women, and even to young girls who would otherwise tend to regard any male approach as an Approach.

For people who stay in their home region, this extended-family aspect is probably satisfying enough. Conscious exploration of the historical dimension is an extra, brought on in my case by culture shock of the city and the university. It is a powerful sheet anchor for a threatened identity, to possess a blood tie, not genealogical in the linear feudal way but ramified and tribal in the Gaelic way, with a quirky assortment of noble and sometimes poignant figures inhabiting distant centuries: the Jacobite general Lord George Murray, the Marquis of Tullibardine who raised the Stuart standard in Glenfinnan in 1745, Sir James of the OED, the Marquise de la Trémouille who held out against Cromwell in her castle when all the rest of the British Isles had fallen to him, Lady Macbeth, whose name was Gruoch and who was a Gaelo-Pictish heretrix married to Macbeth for dynastic reasons, the first Duke of Atholl, who voted against rhe Union in 1707 and was narrowly dissuaded from raising a revolt when it passed the Old Parliament, the Countess of Airlie who was raped by Malcolm Fraser's ancestor Simon Lovat Fraser while his pipers played loudly to drown her screams . . . save for one, a roll-call of magnificent losers. No vulgar success there to shame a man's romanticism. Lexicography and lost causes, rather; things infinitely more germane to poetry. We rescued the lady of Airlie, by the way, and punished Lovat. Not half as severely as the Hanoverians fifty years later, though, when having tried to play off both sides in the Forty-Five, he ended up on the wrong side and became, in his nineties, the last man in Britain to be hanged, drawn and quartered for high treason.

I have dilated on the inwardness of the *fine* and on my own experience, not merely as an indulgence, but also because my upbringing was perhaps more old-fashioned than that of many especially urban Scots Australians, and thus more in contrast with older social and psychological aspects of Scots settlement here. This has perforce meant that I have largely neglected the experience of wealthier and better-educated Scottish immigrants, people who rose fairly inevitably in colonial society because they brought with them the means of rising. I have also neglected those settlers, pastoral, mercantile or whatever who lacked education themselves but whose success, whether based on hard work or rapacity or luck, enabled them to buy position and education for their children and descendants. Scots did not typically come to the colonies as convicts, though some notable convicts were Scots; nor were they Catholic, so they were for the most part spared two heavy early disabilities. The four Scots universities and the excellent, relatively egalitarian Scottish secondary schools turned out a large number of well-educated people to whom Scotland itself offered no breadth of opportunity, but for whom the British Empire was a worldwide field for energy and enterprise. It is possible that the disproportion of Scots descendants among Australia's poets is merely a parallel case to the disproportionate numbers of them in, say, law or politics, and a result of nothing more than a high average of affluence and educational opportunity among Scots Australians in comparison with other ethnic groups here. It may be as mechanical as that, but I doubt it. I cannot think that the cool, individualistic Scottish version of the ancient Gaelic *fine* has had no effect – if only in promoting a sense of history in us and giving us a sense of more than ephemeral, rootless existence. Consciously developed as a personal myth, historical *finechas* can be almost as rich and strange as totemic descent from the original Platypus or the dreamtime Kangaroo. It can also be a valuable sheet anchor against a common modern tendency to downgrade all 'biological' ties in favour of economic ones. Some of this effort is thoroughly worthwhile, of course; the sooner racism, for example, disappears from the world, the better. But the campaign can go too far, and promote a form of society in which the individual is not so much autonomous as atomized and helpless, available to be recruited and disposed of at will.

A personal connection with history, even if only vaguely examined, must surely have given many Scots Australians a feeling of greater weight and confidence, helping them to offset the common colonial sensation of insubstantiality, of being somehow less real than one's coevals in the metropolitan centres. Then, too, there is the old, serious regard which Scots have paid to poetry, above all other branches of literature, compounded in the past of respect for poets and their work and a readiness to read and judge the work. I find that most Scots Australians have now dropped this latter readiness, though thankfully they have at least kept the respect. An example of unnoticed cultural continuity, that, but unfortunately a truncated continuity. A third possible cause of the Bonnie Disproportion might well be the long-surviving Scottish delight in philosophical and theological disputation, a delight by no means confined to the formally well educated; this may have led some into quandaries of the mind and spirit that only poetry could express and assuage. I have not examined all of my Scots Australian poets to see whether any commonality of style or tone or poetic concern exists amongst them, but if anyone did survey them in search of a common denominator, I'll bet they'd find it lay somewhat in the direction of philosophical concern, mixed with verbal quirkiness, a measure of humour and patches of backward-looking yearning for a light once seen and now extinguished. Its greatest fault would probably be respectability of a poetically conservative sort. It might also frequently exhibit a measure of pedantry; the self-educated lad o' parts is a well-known Scots intellectual figure. James Murray and Hugh MacDiarmid, himself a Murray on his mother's side, are two examples out of many. James Hogg and the quarryman geologist Hugh Miller are two more.

The self-made scholar and the idiosyncratic self-made artist are variants of the self-made man, and it is possibly here that Scots Australians differ most markedly from at least a very visible and articulate group of Irish Australians. Amongst the latter group, there is an historic distaste for the self-made man. And it is here that we step on to less genial ground, so let's talk about dragons. Amongst a number of dragons who live, Merlin-like, beneath the surface of Australian life, the green one and the blue one have a great deal in common, and yet they're often at loggerheads. The green one, having had a Catholic education, tends to be more familiar with concepts of charity and self-sacrifice for the group than does the Calvin-blue beast; the green dragon is also arguably more collectivist, and he has a different attitude to work. The blue dragon still clings to something of the old Puritan work ethic coupled with a severe blindness to the real sufferings of those who don't share that ethic, or who have 'failed' its requirements. Much modern-day work is mere employment, of course, and close to a ritual activity, but the blue dragon is apt to be deadly serious even about treadmill-running. And to punish those who won't run, as well as those who can't. The green dragon is serious about it all in a slightly different way; he will insist, often, that you run on the treadmill, and stay among the treadmill runners, as an act of *solidarity*, of sharing the common lot – even though he knows it's all a charade. Or he will let you step off the treadmill, but only on condition that you pretend you haven't really abandoned the ranks of the croppy boys for alien privilege. Now, since the blue dragon tends to win the politics in Australia, while the green one wins the culture, this can be a matter of some discomfort for sons of the blue dragon who are engaged in the arts. They can find themselves expected to be 'Characters', the permitted form of individualism in the Irish diaspora, rather than simply being themselves, and more oppressively they can find themselves subjected to demands for solidarity, for rhetorical attitudinizing and for hectic, often baseless hopes which have their ancestral roots in the tragic past of Ireland.

Much of the above may sound like a deposit of class warfare, and there's some validity in that view, though I think all class-based analyses of society tend to be simplistic; ethnically based studies of history may be a useful corrective for them, though these obviously don't tell the whole story either. By what could be seen as an accident, but which is really related to a national tragedy of their own, Scottish settlers were amongst the first Europeans in Australia to interpose themselves between the convicts and the keepers. And that meant we were apt to be co-opted, and despised, by both groups. We were not so much the first Australian middle class as the first Australian 'class' caught in the middle. It is undeniable, of course, that many Scots settlers here did, for reasons of moral snobbery, opportunism and the like, make common cause with the garrison gentry and the peculators. And some of the garrison gentry *were* Scots. We've been belaboured for all that. There is also a sense, though, in which we helped to *absorb* the garrison system and relegate it to the past; the first colonial ruler to see beyond the realities of the penal colony and begin the work of its relegation was, of course, the Gaelic speaker from Mull, Colonel Macquarie. In time, we helped to create new role models which a great many ex-convicts and Irish settlers were eager to follow – so far as long-lasting religious exclusivism on the part of Protestants here would permit. Many of our worst crimes, in this country, have been done in the name of religion. It has only really been possible to get something of a hearing for ideas of common Celtic identity since the loud static of the Reformation began to fade away. And of course in some places it hasn't been tuned out yet.

Parts of the style of Irish Australia are attractive to Scots Australians, stirring ancestral chords, but other parts of that style irritate us; this is something enthusiasts for the Celtic cause need to face squarely. It may be that some of the dissonance merely reflects the fact that our ancestral homeland is lost, while theirs is still a moral force to them, as it battles to save and restore itself. Their Jacobites won, in the end; ours lost. And this may be relevant to poetry, even among the descendants. Poetry has an enormous ancient prestige among both peoples, but in the Irish case, perhaps for the very reason that it was often the tough spine of an embattled civilization, Irish poetry even in English has never really developed the idiosyncratic, sometimes cross-grained venturesomeness of Scots, or the readiness to deal with new realities. For an Irish parallel to Hugh MacDiarmid, you would have to look to prose writers, perhaps pre-eminently to James Joyce. As descendants of a people which sold itself out, or was sold out, under pressure, we lack a Kathleen Ni Houlihán, the all-loving, all-demanding mother-muse who permits only endless variations on the one immemorial sad tune. If suffering narrowed and concentrated Irish poetry, grief and anger opened Scots poetry out. The Irish balladists of the last century in Australia, from Frank the Poet Macnamara onward, were after all composing in translated Gaelic metres on Irish themes only lightly disguised by an Antipodean decor; they are still singing the sorrows of Ireland. By contrast, the Scotsman Adam Lindsay Gordon, and Paterson and Will Ogilvie more confidently after him, could respond to and celebrate a new way of life, with new possibilities, new energies. Of course, they did tend to make that life into something of an idyll.

I must avoid any appearance of unkindness to the Irish; my father's mother came of the Wexford Paynes. We do share a great deal with them, especially a passion for talking with the dead. The difference, though, and this is the secret sadness at the heart of Scottish success, is that our dead shame us. When the Whigs, the merchants and the Calvinist extremists voted to end Scotland's sovereignty, something was lost for which worldly achievement could never quite compensate the thoughtful Scot. The gold standard of his identity was debased, the pattern-book of his people's distinctive evolution was torn apart, and the pages could never be bound up correctly again. The dead were truer men than the living, closer to the heart of something very simple that had been given away. Gaining access to England, he lost the old contact with Europe. Gaining access to the British Empire, he gained the whole world – at the Biblical cost.

An anonymous contemporary pasquil on the Treaty of Union and the unrepresentative magnates who acceded to it conveys some of the fury felt by Scots of all classes at the loss of their country:

> Our Duiks were deills, our Marquesses were mad,
> Our Earls were evills, our Viscounts yet more bad,
> Our Lords were villains, and our Barons knaves
>   Who with our boroughs did sell us for slaves.
>
> They sold the church, they sold the State and Nation,
> They sold their honour, name and reputation,
> They sold their birthright, peerages and places
>   And now they leave the House with angrie faces.

It was inevitable that, more than mercenary soldiers, Scotland would now also export her peasantry, her scholars, her ambitious money men, her anachronistic Gaelic clansmen, her men and women of action; Scotland would never again be a whole world, capable of containing all of her people and meeting their needs. And that is at least an illusion a nation has to create, in order to function as a nation and focus an evolving human distinctiveness. Scottishness was a wounded and partial thing which, for all the efforts of her vernacular poets, Allan Ramsay, Fergusson, Burns, right down to MacDiarmid and his school in our own time, could never turn enough of her people, at home or in exile, away from what they saw as the economic and social realities of the world. 'Reality' is a word with which Scots lacerate, or silence, their deeper selves. Poetry continued to be valued, if also often debased, because it was a thing connected with home and the values and unforgettable flavour of the lost nation;

it was a *Scottish* endeavour, in contrast with most of the endeavours of exile and of modern times, which were things accomplished, often superbly, in alien terms and on the basis of alien values. Perhaps it is because of its ambiguous and painful importance to the exiles of the past that poetry has carried over, by a sort of inertia, into the time of the unconscious cultural continuities. That, too, might help to explain the disproportion we have been discussing, and its surprising persistence.

Much of the foregoing illustrates, I think, the elusiveness, the danger, the attraction and the decadence of ethnic consciousness. I was heavily exposed to the Scottish side of my inheritance because, when my parents married, my mother moved into the rural world of the Murrays from her native Newcastle, and I was born and grew up there. I was always in much less constant contact with her people, their Cornish-English background and their world of coal mining and heavy engineering. And the contact was weakened still further by her death late in my childhood. She had one last tremendous effect on my life, however, as it were from the grave; her strong wish that I should have as good an education as possible was faithfully honoured, to the point where I was financed at university longer than bare exam results might have seemed to justify. I was enabled to gain a real education, almost in spite of the system, and to begin to find myself as a writer. This, in turn, made it possible for me to appreciate and value my rural Scots Australian world, since there was no danger I would be trapped in its narrowness. I have lived in Scotland for a period, and explored it at a level a bit deeper, I think, than the romantic; when I was there, though, just after the failure of the Devolution referendum in 1979, I found the haggisry and the tartan trade more distasteful than ever, since the emptiness of heart and the cynical 'realism' behind them had just been demonstrated. For all the tough, concentrated flavourfulness of style affected by many Scots, Edinburgh seemed more than ever the sham capital of a sham nation. And Whiggery did not seem to have changed its essence merely because it had adopted the intellectualizing fake-airiness and fanatical chic of Transatlantic culture. And yet, when all has been said, Scotland is still the only overseas country in which I have never felt foreign.

Back home, I am probably one of the last of our lot to have felt, in a real way, some of the terrible gravity of the past; that won't persist beyond my generation at all, I suspect. My elder children love the old home region, and much of the life there, but they have mostly grown up in the cities. Besides, in the four generations prior to their own, they have no less than nine ancestral nationalities, nine ethnic traditions. The Scottish one probably won't emerge more strongly for them from that Babel of faint voices than, say, the Hungarian one or the Swiss one. Their only real option is to be Australians. Being Murrays won't now impede them in that; a couple of generations ago, it might well have been both a help and a hindrance. Now, if they are interested, they can approach the matter of origins and ethnic background in a spirit of study and perhaps use such studies to correct what Tom Keneally would call 'Hanoverian' biases in the received thinking of our society. They are unlikely to suffer possession by the spirits of the restless dead.

Helix, 1/1980, and *Edinburgh Review*, May 1981 (shorter versions). Expanded version published Brennan Society Colloquium Papers, *Celts in Australia: Imagination & Identity*, 1981

Isaac Rosenberg

The Collected Works of Isaac Rosenberg: Poetry, Prose, Letters, Paintings and Drawings edited by Ian Parsons (Chatto and Windus, 1979)

There's a piece of perhaps hardboiled writers' folklore, borne out surprisingly often, that if you've managed to build and keep a reputation in your lifetime, it is bound to fade after your death and only start to rise again, if it ever does, some fifty or sixty years later. Fifty years, of course, is the period an author remains in copyright after his death, but it also seems to be approximately the turnover rate for literary sensibility, the time it takes for a dominant tone to pass into history and be seen objectively. Of couse, there are cases in which your period of obscurity will last much longer; John Donne was on the outer with critics for more than 250 years. And with poets who die young, especially those who die 'relevant' deaths, deaths related to the great concerns of their time, the pattern is apt to be rather different. Love, and the group loyalty of those who were in the battle with the dead one, play a part in such cases. Pity, sentiment, guilt, anger and their political derivatives can enter the picture too, and a reputation can grow up almost as a defiant substitute for the life the author was prevented from living out. In a tragic way, such a reputation can also be made into a substitute for the development which might have made him or her into a major writer. In the years since Isaac Rosenberg's death on the Western Front in April 1918, his reputation has grown steadily – and yet it too has undergone a sixty-year spurt. No less than three biographies appeared in 1975, and there have been recent efforts to put him up as the greatest of the lost English poets of the First World War. A Penguin anthology of the War poets, edited by Jon Silkin, gives Rosenberg pride of place over Owen, Sassoon, Blunden, Graves and all the rest. I think these efforts are misplaced, if honourable, and that they might well embarrass the man himself, if he could hear of them.

It is notable, though also prone to politicizing overemphasis, that

Rosenberg was almost alone among the significant English poets of the First World War in not being an officer. It meant that he lacked the secure, relatively comfortable background of the others, and that he suffered the full misery of barrack-room brutishness. At the front, his life was probably only marginally more miserable and inconducive to writing than theirs; it is hard to know what difference having some ascribed dignity and having none at all makes when all are in Hell together. It probably makes some, but Rosenberg never harps on the point. His real torment came before this. As an undersized man and a Jew to boot, he appears to have found his first months in the Army almost unendurable. Ian Parsons, who has sensitively edited this complete and probably definitive collection of Rosenberg's writings, recommends that the surviving letters be read through from start to finish, and it is a deeply moving experience. Almost the only time Rosenberg complains or approaches despair is during the period of his training in the so-called Bantam battalion of the Suffolk regiment, among down-and-outs, illiterates and ticket-of-leave men; the Bantam battalion consisted of men so small and weedy they would never have been accepted for the Army in less desperate times. The really tragic thing about Rosenberg's war service is, of course, that he only joined the Army because he was chronically broke; he wanted to help his family by allotting half his weekly seven shillings to them. Men in the AIF at the same period got five shillings a day. He hated war, though he seems to have accepted the current attitudes to Germany and the Kaiser fairly uncritically; he did at least one piece of Jingo versifying in 1914 ('The Dead Heroes') and a few more later on. He found himself drawn into the holocaust by sheer poverty, and several letters survive in which he can be seen resisting the temptation of dreadful but easily available 'employment'. The Rosenbergs, huddled in the slums of London's East End along with so many other Jewish refugees from the Russian empire, had never broken out of the cycle of destitution and dependence on their people's communal charities. In his efforts to make a living as a painter-poet (or was it poet-painter?), their son never broke the cycle either; it says a great deal for his courage and endurance that he tried, and a lot for Jewish community spirit and kindness to talent that money was found for his training at the Slade School of Art and for some of his later needs. A few of his letters, from the period before he joined up in October 1915, are clearly begging letters and duty letters to patrons, if you read between the lines; they are cheerful and dignified, however, never arrogant or cringing.

Probably the only good thing the war did for Rosenberg was that it resolved his indecision over whether to concentrate on painting or on poetry; poems can be scribbled with a pencil stub on scrap paper in a dugout, but painting under such conditions is impossible. A few small sketches survive from his war service, but all of his relatively few surviving paintings date from before he went into the Army. Several are reproduced in Ian Parsons' book, but I do not feel able to judge their worth; I know from experience that there's no such thing as a reproduction of a painting. The art critic Maurice de Sausmarez wrote of them that they had

> a quality that is intensely personal and suggests the probable direction of a later development. This quality is not easy to characterise, but includes a simplification that moves towards compression of experience rather than towards the schematic, a design which is not arbitrarily imposed as in some of Stanley Spencer's work, but is distilled and inseparable from the content. The symbol always retains the sensuousness of the original experience and he mistrusts an art that uses 'symbols of symbols'.

This is also a very good description of what is best in his poetry. To cite just one example, here is the second stanza of 'Midsummer Frost', a poem written in 1914 but revised several times before its publication in the following year:

> See, from the fire-fountained noon there creep
> Lazy yellow ardours towards pale evening,
> To thread dark and vain fire
> Over my unsens'd heart,
> Dead heart, no urgent summer can reach.
> Hidden as a root from air or a star from day;
> A frozen pool whereon mirth dances;
> Where the shining boys would fish.

Beneath all the fag-ends of a worn-out poetical diction, there is something alive in this, a genuine imagination finding terms for inner experience, re-creating it in images rather than in formulae. The image of the heart 'hidden as a root from air or a star from day' is pure Rosenberg, alive and infinitely more daring than the tame decorums of most contemporary Georgian poetry; it foreshadows the beautiful image, used in two of his poems written in 1917 ('Soldier: Twentieth Century' and 'Girl to Soldier on Leave') of a figure hidden like 'a word in the brain's ways'. As a whole, 'Midsummer Frost' is a failure; the first two stanzas are fascinating, with the real grip and involute strangeness of poetry, the rest of the poem loses tension, loses focus, loses itself in unresolved verbiage. As so often happens, the sense of a powerful, evolving style peters out almost as soon as it is created. The poet obviously detected this himself and wrestled with it; time after time, the useful notes which the editor supplies with very many of the poems and fragments record repeated rewritings, recastings, pleas for advice or comment from the half-dozen or more people to whom he would send his drafts and who served as his sounding-boards. In what is really quite a small output if we remember that he was writing seriously for twelve or thirteen years before his untimely death at the age of twenty-eight we see poem after poem marred by the scheme, the arbitrarily imposed design, the retreat into received sentiment, archaism, pallid atmospherics:

> Have we sailed and have we wandered,
> Still beyond, the hills are blue.
> Have we spent and have we squandered,
> What's before us still is new.

That is from 'Have We Sailed and Have We Wandered' (1914). It doesn't get better in the remaining two stanzas; the jingling rhyme and metre do all the poet's thinking for him. What is more heartening is the wide variety of attempted forms to be found in the same smallish output. There is even a small impressionist sketch from 1915 that has something of the vivid freshness of a Welsh englyn or a Japanese tanka:

> Green thoughts are
> Ice block on a barrow
> Gleaming in July.
> A little boy with bare feet
> And jewels at his nose stands by.

It is interesting to note that, apart from the very early and unsuccessful 'Ballad of Whitechapel', this is the only glimpse of East End life, perhaps of his own childhood, in Rosenberg's whole corpus.

It is also one of only seven or eight poems of Rosenberg's which I would consider complete, finished pieces. More even than most poets, he is a writer of starts, passages, middles, fragments, and more than most poets he has to be read in a spirit of retrieval, of sorting out the magical from the overcompressed, the off-key and the muddled. He has little sense of poetic logic, though he strove to master it. Even the best of his war poems, the four or five on which his reputation has grown, are shaky, with dead lines, patches of bathos and frequent tendencies to melodrama. In his most famous poem, 'Dead Man's Dump', there are passages like:

> . . . rusty stakes like sceptres old
> To stay the flood of brutish men
> Upon our brothers dear.

And there is the unfortunate description of the dead:

> They lie there huddled, friend and foeman,
> Man born of man, and born of woman,

which does seem rather hard on one side or the other. The whole conception of this poem, in my opinion, is essentially melodramatic; it is rescued only by precariously successful writing strung between some truly excellent bits, such as the well-known image of the death of soldiers:

> When the swift iron burning bee
> Drained the wild honey of their youth

or that other image of the war's stupendous charnel:

> Burnt black by strange decay,
> Their sinister faces lie
> The lid over each eye,
> The grass and coloured clay
> More motion have than they,
> Joined to the great sunk silences.

Melodrama of conception ruins several other poems of the war period altogether, poems such as 'In the Trenches', 'The Dying Soldier', 'In War', and disastrous bathos wrecks the mock-portentous 'The Immortals'. 'Break of Day in the Trenches' succeeds, shakily, because it attempts no very high flights, but really the only satisfyingly complete, all-of-a-piece war poems are two or three quite short ones, the successfully philosophical 'A Worm Fed on the Heart of Corinth', 'The Troop Ship' perhaps, though it is little more than an impression, and 'August 1914', which is worth quoting in full:

> What in our lives is burnt
> In the fire of this?
> The heart's dear granary?
> The much we shall miss?

Three lives hath one life –
Iron, honey, gold.
The gold, the honey gone –
Left is the hard and cold.

Iron are our lives
Molten right through our youth.
A burnt space through ripe fields,
A fair mouth's broken tooth.

I am a little worried by the youth / tooth rhyme; Rosenberg is far from immune to the bad habit of inserting a word, or writing a whole line, for the sake of a rhyme, but, in view of the quality of the rest of the poem and the marvellous image of the ripe fields, the last line can probably be allowed to pass muster. The famous 'Returning, We Hear the Larks' has a more serious weakness in its ending, an image about girl's hair which has not been properly worked out and integrated in the poem; we see that it is a Medusa image, but it has been left conventional and disjointed, not tautened into poetry. This is a great pity, because the conception of the poem is sound and original, and the balancing of joy and deadly threat summons up a vivid sense of a moment in the nightmare life of the trenches, a moment when an unexpected grace comes out of the natural world at dawn and seems to bless stumbling, tired men full of profound relief at still being alive.

Given the circumstances under which Rosenberg wrote his war poems, my strictures may seem harsh; I doubt I'd have done half as well, in his place. I also understand the problems of the slow-developing kind of poet, the poet who experiments widely in order to find his way. There is ample evidence, in the letters, that Rosenberg regarded it as essential to get poems and concepts down and fixed, even in an imperfect way; shaping and refining could come later, after the war. Writing to Laurence Binyon in autumn 1916, he says:

> I am determined that war, with all its powers for devastation, shall not master my poeting; that is, if I am lucky enough to come through all right, I will not leave a corner of my consciousness covered up, but saturate myself with the strange and extraordinary new conditions of life, and it will all refine itself into poetry later on.

Similarly, writing to Edward (later Sir Edward) Marsh in May 1917, he says:

I liked your criticism of "Dead mans dump". Mr Binyon has often sermonised lengthily over my working on two different principles in the same thing and I know how it spoils the unity of a poem. But if I couldn't before, I can now, I am sure, plead the absolute necessity of fixing an idea before it is lost, because of the situation it is conceived in.

It is legitimate, I suppose, to wonder how much faith Rosenberg thought he could invest in the prospect of a calm life after the war in which all of its horrors and depths could be refined into great art, and how much he was driven by the reality of terrible danger to get something down on paper, even if patchy and imperfect, something to stand against extinction. Like many of us, he was half in love with the big-poem-yet-to-be-written, and conscious of the provisional nature of nearly all actual poems. It takes time, perhaps a lifetime, to see what is lasting and timeless in one's own work and what isn't, to realize that the great project is *in there*, wound through the texture of what one has done. Rosenberg didn't have that sort of time; he died with youth's belief in an available future, profoundly shaken perhaps, but still necessary to his thinking about his art. If he is sometimes praised nowadays rather in the spirit of the process theory of poetry, the poem as a mimesis of disorder rather than a wrestling with it to discover deeper order, I think that is anachronistic and rather corrupt, an attempt to recruit him to modernist, revolutionary purposes he never espoused and probably never heard of. It is probable that, if he had survived, he would have become a very important poet indeed, perhaps more important than any of the other English poets of the war generation, but it is also likely that his unsureness and lack of an instinctive sense of poetic design would have plagued him for many more years. Despite everything, I do believe his best passages point to a distinctive power in him which might have allowed English poetry to renew itself in a native way through his development. This may be what attracts English critics and poets to his cause, a wish that English poetry had been able to cross over into the modern era in its own terms, without the alien and wrenching effects of Eliot's and Pound's Franco–American modernism, that powerful but suspect strain which English poets have aped and resisted ever since.

But this is a nostalgia for national prestige in art, and resentment at relegation: it's about the Empire. In the long run, Rosenberg might have made the transition to peace better than Wilfred Owen, and might have found more to say. His wide range of experimentation with different modes and subjects before the war suggests it. Compared with the classic, coherent war poems which Owen achieved, however, his look patchy and tentative, and we are forced into valuing potential above performance if we place him above Owen. I think it is more justifiable to see him as ultimately superior to the rest, even Graves. Given a longer run, I'm pretty sure he would have left Graves far behind.

Ian Parsons mourns the lost potential of Rosenberg, but does not stretch it into speculative polemic. He has the more modest purpose of showing that his subject should not be thought of simply as a poet of the war, but as one who achieved distinctive and lasting things in the prewar period, things quite different from and in advance of what most of his Georgian contemporaries were doing. There is some merit in this claim, in that he certainly *tried* many quite distinctive things, poems about a female godhead, about a dead and rotting god, about gigantic, quasi-Blakean figures, and there is the rather fervidly erotic 'Night', which reads like a tussle with a deep and potent anima. There are many traces of this figure in his other poems, and we could start what the Germans call *culture-historical* hares if we began to speculate on its significance. To grow too involved in a poet's half-realized or unrealized themes, though, is to court the academic preference for ideas above poetry, that ambitious vice which has been the curse of criticism in this century. In my opinion, the nearest thing to a satisfyingly worked-out poem from Rosenberg's pre-war period is the delicate 'In Half Delight of Shy Delight', in which the young girl is seen 'still plaiting her men-unruffled curls'

> She walks so delicately grave
> As lovely as her unroofed fancies
> Of love's far-linked dances
> In waters of soft night they lave
> Through measureless expanses.

That is the true dancing measure. For an Australian reader, the comparison with Shaw Neilson is probably irresistible. A slighter poem from the same period which achieves simplicity without slipping into trite tum-te tum is 'A Bird Trilling its Gay Heart Out'. Otherwise, we are once again left with fragments and retrievals.

From the letters, it is clear that Rosenberg carried with him into his war-time period a great many continuities and poetic interests from the past; he probably never thought of the war as his prime theme, in the way that Owen did. The letters show that he held on, naturally enough, to a lot of poetic coggage which he would have had to discard if he had survived; in particular, he remained interested in his huge, fragmentary and nearly unreadable 'Moses', a sort of historico-mythical verse play on which he worked for years. An extract from this, the 'Ah Kolue' speech, was the only poem of Rosenberg's which ever appeared in Marsh's annual *Georgian Poetry* anthology. It is hard to escape the feeling that, faithful as he was to his Jewish identity and heritage, the Hebrew tradition (got at second hand, since he did not read Hebrew) was never a very fruitful source for his poetry, though he dipped his bucket there many times, and was planning an epic or verse play on Judas Maccabaeus for the post-war period; a lot of his experience of war, and a lot of his thinking about it, was to have gone into this project. I have a feeling he would have met with a good deal of frustration, if he had lived to attempt this. The garment might not have fitted the body. His Hebraic poems always have a worked-up, costume-drama feel to them. He was, after all, a modern Jew, admittedly only a generation away from the *stetl*, but drawing nearly all of his cultural sustenance from English society and English art. His contribution, and it is a real and precious one, is to English poetry. His tragedy was part of a greater tragedy of Western man whose dimensions no one in his time could discern; he helped us to feel and imagine something of its inwardness. To that extent, he helped to bring our age into consciousness of itself.

Quadrant, March 1980, Reprinted in *Twentieth Century Literary Criticism* edited by Dennis Poupard (Gale Research Co., Detroit, 1984)

Notes on the Writing of a Novel Sequence

Quite literally I wrote *The Boys who Stole the Funeral* in order to find out what happened in it. I had the beginnings of a story, that is to say, a situation and some characters, and I wanted to see how it and they would develop. I'd written portraits, pieces of action, even crowd scenes, but never characters, and I was curious to discover how it felt to create figures who would stand up, move off and assume a life of their own. Oddly, perhaps, I never doubted that I could work this magic. What I didn't yet know was how imperious characters can become, how they will reject out of hand some line of action you propose for them, and take another. I also didn't know as yet how hard it would be to give them up at the end of the book and put them to sleep again. For more than a year after I'd finished *The Boys*, they kept popping back into my mind, wanting to move on into a further book and more adventures. Indeed, they haven't stopped yet.

At the outset, all I had was an incident in which two young men in Sydney steal an old country man's body from a suburban undertaker's and ferry it up the north coast for burial. This notion came to me in about July 1977. I knew that the old man was an ex-serviceman, probably a veteran of the First World War, and that he'd been something of a rolling stone in his lifetime, until he fetched up in his last years in a converted back shed belonging to some distant relations. I did not yet have a motivation for the theft of his body; all I knew was that the reasons for this had to be good ones, in no way frivolous. None of this was based on any actual incident; the truth of it, which I felt strongly, was wholly fictional. Knowing that the question of the boys' motive would find its own answer if I waited, I mused about the possible meanings of such a journey, and its relation to the serious value which is attached to funerals in the Australian rural culture from which I come; it's not unusual for a funeral Up Home to attract seven or eight hundred people wishing to pay their last respects. I thought, too, about the vital importance for many Aborigines of returning a person's remains to their particular spirit country so that their soul may be reincarnated when a pregnant woman passes nearby; the spirit of a person buried in a strange place is lost, dwindling away in homeless misery. And I worked on some formal problems I'll describe in a moment.

After a couple of months, the necessary breakthrough came. I was talking to a friend who serves on the New South Wales Prices Commission, and that body had just done a survey of the undertaking trade. 'How much would it cost,' I asked, 'to have an undertaker arrange a funeral in which the corpse had to be transported from Sydney up to such-and-such a place in the mountains behind the north coast?' An approximate figure was named, and I was delighted. I had my motivation! The old Digger's family, not considering that funerals warranted any very large expense, weren't prepared to honour his wishes and bury him in his native district. They wouldn't put up the money, so the one young relative who had been close to him in his last years would have to act decisively and fast, and go right outside everyone's conventions. Getting him back inside these when necessary would be a fascinating problem to solve further on in the story. First, though, there would be the theft, and the bizarre journey.

At around the same time, in about September 1977, I also solved the other problem which had been standing in my way, that of the form and structure of the book. I wanted to reclaim the narrative for poetry, to recapture ground which the senior literary form had begun losing to the novel as early as the end of the seventeenth century, and which it had decidedly lost to film and TV in the twentieth. But how to do it? Every time I started to write the story in continuous verse, with a single metre or a varied one, it broke down almost at once. Something was wrong, and I can't write anything until I've established some sort of formal base for it. If I were a Scottish piper, I would say that I need an *urlar* or base-tune before I can begin weaving variations. Need focuses receptivity, though, and the answer came through a glimpse of pattern, rather than through any verbal models. John Forbes lent me a book of sonnets by a New York poet whose name I'm afraid I've rather ungratefully forgotten, and while I was only mildly interested in the poems themselves, their arrangement on the book's pages, two on the left, two on the right, gave me a picture of the form and the density of verse I needed, and how to organize it, which is to say, really, how to *time* it. Also, I'd always liked the sonnet, and had written single ones and sequences. It had always seemed to me a very 'natural' form, concise enough to restrain sloppiness, roomy enough to accommodate almost any content. With its containment and its one or more internal *volte* or turns, it seemed an ideal conjunction of discipline and freedom. And there was nothing to prevent its serving as an analogue of a 'take' in film, or a scene on stage, or even as a short chapter or section of a chapter in a novel. It could be entire in itself, or it could serve as a unit in building up larger patterns, or be the means of cutting back and forth between different foci of action, and there was ample room within fourteen lines for both action and meditation ... The possibilities were not only adequate to my purpose, but inexhaustible. I tried a couple – and the story was away and running, moving at a rapid underlying speed but containing all the stillness, the timeless pointing quality which poetry reconciles with movement better than any other art can, which I knew my narrative also needed. It moved, but it didn't blur; everything could be in motion and yet *held*, in ways which tend to look artificial and literary in prose narratives. I found, too, that I could have amplitude without crowding but also without the heavy explanatory quality you get in all but the very best prose. I could have everything, in short, that the novel, the drama and the film could provide, without losing poetry. I just had to keep on discovering the potentials of the structure I'd set up.

A colleague of mine, a prose novelist, says that the best book is the one you chuckle over as you write it. I had a lot of that quiet, intense joy over the next fourteen months. I was freer than I'd ever been from the grey, conformingly non-conformist consensus tone of modern poetry whether it's written in Wigan or Wichita or Wollongong, and I was further than ever from acquiescence in its received class values, or from playing little timid variations on them within a permitted range. It was so damn good to be away from Modern Literature at last, and working deeper and deeper into a native voice, or voices. Writing *The Boys* was the best fun I've had from poetry, and I long to tackle a project of similar or even bigger dimensions again some day. For that, though, I have to wait till the right idea comes along. Using, essentially, the storytelling methods I unconsciously learned from my father in my childhood – Dad is a man whose culture is almost wholly oral and musical, and he is a truly gifted spinner of stories – I didn't plot *The Boys* in advance at all, but simply wrote it from the beginning to the end and then stopped. With the characters having plenty of say in my decisions, I constructed each scene, each moment, each departure pretty well as I came to it. I only remember a couple of occasions on which I had slightly to shift the placement of a sonnet, and only one (number

24) had to be discarded and rewritten differently. Of course, there were some passages which had to be refined painstakingly into shape, as for example when Clarrie Dunn is describing life in the trenches, before shifting abruptly to the story about the woman who gave him the white feather in Bond Street (Sonnet 52). It took a while to get the precise tone for his image of barbed wire 'like singed guts in the wind'. The white feather incident didn't have to be invented, however; that actually happened to one of my mother's brothers, a gunner on HMAS *Sydney*, when he was on shore leave in Melbourne after helping to sink the German raider *Emden*. Another device which came to me with a sense of inevitability and naturalness as soon as I started writing the story was that of giving each character a 'signature', some peculiarity of speech or punctuation or rhythm which would make it immediately clear who was speaking. Or thinking.

There is probably little more I can usefully tell about my motives and methods in respect of *The Boys*, at least in the absence of specific questioning, and it's probably not for me to enter too deeply into wider evaluations of it or commentary on it. One thing it isn't, I would claim, is any sort of Catholic thesis-novel. That would have been to reduce the eternal Church which is based on Divine revelation to something approaching what is pejoratively called Literature in the poem, which is to say, repeated attempts by man to force meaning on the world and seal it with literal human sacrifice. Experience, Catholic Christianity and what I discover by writing poems are my three prime guides to reality, and they guided me in the writing of *The Boys* as they guide all of my work. In the poem, the Church is not a cause, but a touchstone for judging causes, just as one's mind and spirit are touchstones for judging the Church. If there was any sort of meta-artistic concern in the book, it is probably for the despised and relegated country poor, the people I come from and belong to, and to whom I dedicate everything I may achieve. And I guess that, here, I don't finally mean only Australian country people, but all who have to put up with this world's Pilates and Pharisees.

Australasian Catholic Record, July 1981

Some Religious Stuff
I Know About Australia

Most people would agree, perhaps after some dispute about terminology, that something like a religious dimension exists in every human being. Some might want to call it a dimension of wonder, of quest, of value, of ultimate significance or the like. Some have denied its reality altogether, but I think the weight of human experience and, to beg a few questions perhaps, of perceived human behaviour is against them. Modern students of religion, and modern proponents of what we may call natural religious systems, tend to differ from upholders of at least some traditional religions in suggesting that religious activity arises from a human perception of phenomena, whether in the world at large or within the person. They think of it as a human response to the beauty, horror, mystery or incongruity of the world, or to some emotional need within us. The Christian and also I think the Jew and the Muslim, though their terminologies would be different, would rather assert that it is a response to the activity of God's Spirit working within us at a depth usually too great for direct sensory perception; it impinges on our consciousness most directly, perhaps, at the point we call the conscience, though some modern schools attempt to explain that away as internalized social conditioning and the like, and perhaps what we regard as our conscience may include some of that. The attempt, the wish really, to dispose of the divine element in conscience is interesting in another way, however. Christian theology teaches that the love of God, like the rejection of Him, arises from the will rather than the emotions. It is a decision of acceptance, of Assent, in Cardinal Newman's term. We choose to love God because He has touched us in some way; as Scripture says, 'we love Him because He first loved us'. And we can only come to an understanding of the real things of religion through our acceptance of the subtle, persistent lifelong offer of Itself which the Spirit makes to every human being.

In the second chapter of his first letter to the infant church in Corinth, St Paul says, in the Jerusalem Bible translation, 'an unspiritual person is one who does not accept anything of the Spirit of God: he sees it all as nonsense; it is beyond his understanding because it can only be understood by means of the Spirit. A spiritual man, on the other hand, is able to judge the value of everything, and his own value is not to be judged by other men.' This does not signify a haughty refusal to be judged, but merely points out that the person who lacks some share in the mind of God a acquired by accepting His Spirit can't accurately evaluate the insights (or, as an unfriendly critic might say, the claims to insight) of one who has such a share. The Spirit, we say, works upon and awakens to life something in us which is like Itself and may indeed be, or perhaps become, a part of Itself. Christ has told us that no one comes to God except through Him, and in past centuries many Christians have taken this to mean that no one who wasn't a Christian could be 'saved', that is, come to an adequate response to the activity of the Spirit working on their inmost life. A more modern understanding, though it isn't wholly modern, of this saying of Christ's would be that Christ is That through which such an adequate response happens, whether the person responding knows His name or not. St Paul's statement quoted above doesn't deny the possibility of degrees of acceptance of the Spirit; something that is little more than, or no more than, a vague yearning to 'make sense of it all' may be the beginnings of a spirituality we would have to recognize. Such early stages can be perilous, but perhaps not more so than later ones; the religious dimension in man is quite possibly the most dangerous thing on earth. A great deal of history, and perhaps pre-eminently a great deal in the terrible history of this century, supports such a contention. We cannot deny our inmost nature; as Christopher Koch says in his novel *The Year of Living Dangerously*: 'The spirit doesn't die, of course; it turns into a monster.'

Since the spiritual dimension universally exists in human beings, it has to be dealt with by them in some way or other; a sacramentally minded Christian would say that it has to be fed. It can be wrongly fed, though, with dreadful results for the world. God's Spirit may stir our soul and then not be allowed to enlighten it. In this chapter, I want to talk about some of the ways, 'natural' ways if you like, in which Australians attempt to feed it, apart from the means of mediation offered by the churches. Some of the responses I'll be describing are innocent and wholesome ones, others are less so. And some are quite simply frightful, if not usually as spectacularly so here as in some other countries. They may be the more insidious for that, insofar as our fairly orderly social polity protects us from their more obviously horrifying implications. They are thus less commonly recognized for what they are and so allowed to persist. An example of what I mean would be human sacrifice.

Wait on! Human sacrifice? Surely that's an archaic horror that survives only very marginally in a few Third World groups that anthropologists write about? Surely the holocausts of this century in what we call 'our' civilization can only be called human sacrifices in a very metaphoric sort of way? Surely there's a distinction to be made here between the literal and the metaphorical? My answer is, there may be, but I don't know of one watertight enough to prevent the blood from seeping through it. When I hear someone say, as I did yet again the other day, that this country needs a war to restore and cement its sense of community, I recognize that as a call to literal human sacrifice, to be performed for one of the classic archaic reasons. When I am told that thousands of Australian men died in the First World War so as to prove their country's worth to the world and make it 'come of age', I don't know whether that was in fact their motive (I strongly doubt it), but I see the assertion as one which makes their death into a post facto human sacrifice, and accepts it as such. And this despite not only the Enlightenment we used to praise as our deliverance from such archaic nonsenses, but also despite the much earlier action of Christ in consciously taking the whole deeply ancient human motif of sacrifice on Himself and as it were completing and sealing it, so that henceforth we might refer the whole complex impulse to His action and never again enact it literally on a living victim. The position of the Catholic and Orthodox sacrament of the Eucharist is interesting here, as lying midway between the literal and the metaphorical, as a sort of middle term which maintains a vital tension between the two; this is an essential feature of the sacramental dimension, I think. A much harder implication of Jesus' action, of course, is that sacrifice, including human sacrifice, is as it were wrong but not erroneous. It suggests that it is an inherent tendency in human behaviour, as universal as we observe, say, ritual to be. It could not be dismissed, as rationalism would later attempt to dismiss it; it had to be *resolved*, and the very act of its resolution then kept alive.

With the decline of traditional Christian observance, things formerly bound have a way of being loosed again on mankind; after the mass suicide of Jim Jones's followers in Guyana a couple of years ago, it is surely much harder than it may have seemed before to say that man evolves beyond highly developed religion. In perhaps a majority of cases, he falls out of it backwards, back down into archaic practices (none the less archaic for their modern veneer) and quandaries which had long since been resolved. In a poem I wrote a year or so ago, I put it this way, adding a codicil to something Chesterton once said: *Those who lose belief in God will not only believe in anything; they will bring blood offerings to it.*

Of course, not all quasi-religious practices in Australia or elsewhere are as dire as this. After the above long but necessary preface, let's look at a few, with headings to prevent my trying to say everything at once.

STRINE SHINTO

In the native religion of Japan, deity (*kami*), sometimes individualized into deities of a polytheistic sort, is held to be present in all sorts of existing objects, in certain mirrors, wells, rocks, swords, mountains, in special shrines and the like. These bearers of immanent divinity are called *shintai* ('god–bodies') or *mitamashiro* ('divine–soul–objects') and can even be living beings, such as the Emperor, and reverence is due to them. It appears to be a formalization, surviving surprisingly long in a developed form, of a pretty widespread early response of man to intimations of the Spirit's presence. In the West, Wordsworthian romanticism, the 'sense of something far more deeply interfused' in things is a modern analogue, and ancient analogues abound in the major and minor observances of the Greeks, Romans and others. Something similar is obviously also at work at times in Catholic and Orthodox veneration of icons, despite repeated warnings by the clergy that the spiritual realities are represented by the devotional object, not immanent in it. We, and God, put the value into the object; it isn't inherently in it.

Speaking metaphorically, but not perhaps entirely so, it is possible to say that every people has its own peculiar form of Shinto, not perhaps as developed as the Japanese form, but consisting in all those intimately familiar, common properties and distinctive features in which what is felt to be the spirit or soul of that people somehow resides. Australia is no exception here; we have our familiar landmarks, such as Ayers Rock, the Murray River, the Barrier Reef, Sydney's Bridge and Opera House, our distinctive animals, among which the kangaroo and the kookaburra carry perhaps the warmest freight of identification, gum-trees, sheep stations, even such products of man's genius as pavlova, distinctive idiom and Australian Rules football. Some of our venerated sites and objects have the National Trust as their priesthood, others have conservationists and park wardens to be their guardians and supervise their rites. In many country towns, as well as the war memorial, there will be a special shrine, often tended by old people and open only at erratic times, called the Folk Museum. This will contain the memorabilia of the community, mingling documents, portraits, and objects of real historical interest with quaint stuff which the museum has had to accept and display on what I call the O'Hennessy Principle: refuse some prized piece of junk offered by one of the O'Hennessys, or any other long-established local family, and the whole clan will become the enemy of your enterprise. A great deal of writing in our magazines and even more notably in the features pages of our newspapers consists of anxious sub-theological debate about the relative fitness of different sites, objects and even products to be counted among the Sacred Treasures of the nation, and this debate has grown ever more vociferous with the passage of the decades. War memorials rise, are devalued by many, are reinstated by some as at least acceptably campy, then genuinely begin to regain prestige; the terrace house is despised as a slum, then it is painted by Sali Herman, discovered as indigenous vernacular architecture and begins its long reign as an icon to be admired and possessed.

As in any late-colonial society, it is possible to be shamefaced or dismissive about any of the enshrined symbols of identity, and to miss the real love which they may half-covertly bear. In Australia, though, a couple of further developments occur. First, there is a broad general consensus about which symbols are to be treated seriously at pretty well all times – no one slings off about the Barrier Reef, and only a few subcultures now eschew a fundamental respect for Aboriginal things – and which of them may be more or less affectionately sent up. Second, a class of what we may call clown-icons has arisen whose rites are always and characteristically derisive: tomato sauce, the meat pie (though I've always thought that one something of a journalistic ring-in), blowflies, gladioli, exaggeratedly grim country cafés which close for lunch and regard sauce with the steak and eggs as a Christmas treat or an indulgence of the epicene, suburban respectabilities, early-model Holden cars – with varying degrees of good taste, Barry Humphries has made himself perhaps the high priest of the derision cult. This institution of the clown-icon is comparatively rare in other countries; I have struck analogues of it in the Celtic lands, especially Wales, but it is hard to imagine in, say, France or China. It may be more highly developed in Australia than anywhere else, and has a complexity and restraint often missing from, say, the rather indiscriminate nihilism of Goon Show-Monty Python humour. There is far less fatigue and angry despair at its heart, and less childishness.

The ability to laugh at venerated things, and at awesome and deadly things – remember the Anzac Book, and the infantrymen advancing into battle in North Africa singing 'We're off to see the Wizard, the wonderful Wizard of Oz' – may, in time, prove to be one of Australia's great gifts to mankind. It is, at bottom, a spiritual laughter, a mirth that puts tragedy, futility and vanity alike in their place. It was one of the things that led me back to Christianity, when I heard my Catholic friends making affectionate fun of sacred matters in their religion, intoning *Dominoes and biscuits*. It was something I had never encountered in the deeply puritan Free Kirk Presbyterianism of my childhood, except perhaps when my father slyly used the word 'religious' to mean glum, long-faced dreariness of demeanour. 'Righto, stop grinning now; look religious!' The rites of derision in our native Shinto only become ugly when they take on a flavour of class warfare, of putting the supposedly ignorant and boorish folk back in their place; this is what mars much of Humphries' work; perhaps he is not yet, even after many years of developing his art, fully aware of its priestly nature. I have sometimes been tempted to oversimplify the matter as follows: if America, then France and the other countries which followed her example of revolt against feudal hierarchy, are the bourgeois revolution, Australia is perhaps the proletarian evolution, and what develops from that fact may be more productive for mankind than what develops from the effort to suppress or disguise it. We began as the poor who were sent away, to England's South Sea Gulag, and our continent was settled largely by the poor who got away. Our immigration policies since the Second World War have, if not usually for altruistic reasons, tended to continue the pattern, importing the broken middle classes of Communised countries certainly, but importing in even greater numbers the town and village poor of Europe with a short-term view to using them as factory fodder. The more important effect of their coming, however, will probably be to enrich and further diversify Australia's vernacular culture; this is already happening. If one of the great marks of our vernacular culture is its wide and subtly ramified levity – I once wrote that we are most colonial when serious – that is because it has been fed by underground traditions of working people's irony and fantastical peasant wit that existed for centuries under the surface of respectable Upper culture abroad. Here these things emerge into the daylight and grow, and the clown-icon is one of their first fruits.

It is probable that many Australians now spend more of their spiritual energy on the quest for national and communal identity than on any other theme. This is not surprising, in a country just far enough in time from its initial settlement for the themes its people brought from their original homes to have faded and become unreal in the minds of their descendants. If it looks at times like the nationalism of older countries, I think that is a superficial view. A new people's efforts to find itself are, I think, a cleaner thing than aggrandizing National Interest, that idol for whom so many millions of human beings have been sacrificed in this century. Of course, any nation is a semi-criminal conspiracy – but there is a sense in which finding some new vision, or new style, some new tune for the world to enjoy and maybe whistle, is a necessary work of atonement for stealing a continent and living well from the theft. If we don't make something worthwhile for mankind out of our conquest here, we are little more than thieves living on spoils. If the churches have so far taken no great part in this work of atonement, that is perhaps natural and not wholly to be deplored; they supply the terms in which we can identify our situation, but their ministry is finally not local and particular so much as a corrective to the local and the particular. Christianity was brought into being out of a particular tradition through an act done 'for all men, so that sins might be forgiven'. It is universal in its intent, and our best, if not always effectual, defence against the idolatries of nationalism; this is perhaps not always remembered by denominations which hang up battle flags in their churches and take sides in wartime.

Christianity can co-exist with a good deal of Shinto, particularly perhaps a Shinto tempered by humour, because the two are about different spiritual concerns. The sort of Shinto I am talking about is almost obsessed by style, by manners, but it has nothing to say about Last Things. On the other hand, it does fit in, in a way which ought to interest Christians, with the oldest spiritual traditions existing in Australia in its celebration, now formal, now casually familiar, of special sites and objects and particularized animals held in emblematic, partially mythologized poses of contemplation. The Aborigines accorded this kind of veneration only to natural phenomena – they didn't, for example, venerate their spears or their digging sticks, and their *tjúrunga* were held by them to be not objects at all, but the actual bodies of the great creative ancestors – but

Australians of overseas ancestry have added human monuments of all sorts to the list of what a Catholic might call the 'sacramentals' of identity, while still reserving their most serious regard for the natural features of 'our' fragment of the primordial Gondwanaland continent. This convergence is suggestive, I think, and may be enormously productive. We have come to the sense, which the Aborigines had before us, that after all human frenzies and efforts there remains the great land. As George Johnston wrote, nothing human has yet happened in Australia which stands out above the continent itself. We know in our bones that the land is mightier than we are, and its vast indifference can drive us to frenzies of desecration and revenge. We know, deep down, that the land does not finally permit of imported attitudes that would make it simply a resource, a thing; it has broken too many of us who tried to make such attitudes fit it. Unlike North America, it is not a vaster repeat performance of primeval Europe, a new Northern Hemisphere continent with familiar soils and seasons into which a liberal variation on inherited European consciousness might be transplanted with prospects of vast success. It is something other, with different laws.

Another and perhaps by now related convergence arose initially from fortuity: the continent to which the rejects of Great Britain were sent turned out to be one in which the native people were egalitarian in their way of life to a degree beyond the imagination of privilege and even of earlier liberalism; it must have been of some effect, even if only a barely noticed one, on the colonists that the new land offered no ancient indigenous models of hierarchy at all. The solitary ego could be at once as vast as the horizon and as unimportant as a straw of windblown grass. Fences were a desperate spiritual necessity, and yet kept failing to hold. We still punish the Aborigines for the fear and temptation this sets up in us. It was an insult to all our notions of productive work and getting ahead, that they could be so seemingly destitute and yet at the same time lords of infinite space: 'The Natives are unfitted for anything,' cried an exasperated early commentator, 'except to be gentlemen.' In every generation, men especially have felt this temptation to drift away and camp out along the creeks forever. It was only by hiding from the continent, in homesteads and towns and cities, that the colonists could feel comfortable with their traditional, imported ways of life. God, in Australia, is a vast blue and pale-gold and red-brown land-scape, and his votaries wear ragged shorts and share his sense of humour. Space, like peace, is one of the great, poorly explored spiritual resources of Australia. In the huge spaces of the Outback, ordinary souls expand into splendid and often innocent grotesquerie which the cramping of urban surroundings might transmute into ugly, even dangerous forms. And it may be, in the end, that humour is the touchstone for the viability of any import here. I have thought at times that our patron should be St Philip Neri, for Australia really seems to be where God puts a sardonyx to the lips of Western man and teaches him to laugh wisely.

THE RALLIES

If the sort of vernacular Shinto I have been describing is partly a matter of looking afresh at old importations, as well as finding a sense of shared identification in phenomena we haven't always noticed or valued, most of the other rituals of heightened meaning I want to talk about in this segment are more recent imports. We didn't invent them, and our having them, as it were, second-hand weakens and exacerbates them at once, and may help to give them the sour, angry stridency some of them exhibit at times. They're things we joke about less, and a good deal of group or class identification lies behind whether we get a laugh or not.

There is an interesting, often noted but poorly explained significance in the fact that, while both have earlier antecedents, the two most notable mass ritual forms of recent times arose, or in the one case re-arose, in the early 1960s, spreading worldwide from a number of centres with extreme rapidity and practically in tandem; I refer of course to the pop or rock concert and the political rally or demonstration. It is also interesting that, with the coming of economic recession in the Western world, the latter form has once again declined and become fairly fitful, while the former continues unabated. Both command an intensity of involvement that is much stronger, or at least closer to the surface and more vehement, than almost any churchgoing. A fair few people who attend such manifestations also go to church, both here and, perhaps more commonly, in some other countries. Their demeanour in the two cases, however, tends to be quite different, because different ends are being served. And of course a good many who go to the modern mass rituals wouldn't be seen dead in a church. There is an evangelical analogue of such mass events in the revival meeting, a reality in some overseas countries, notably the United States, but never really acclimatized here. And there are equally clear analogues in the regimented yet fervent rallies of Hitler's Germany and other modern dictatorships.

If wildly different overt content, ranging from heavily amplified love songs to exhortations to crush Malaysia or slaughter the Jews, can elicit strikingly similar behaviour in crowds that listen and scream their approval, it is clearly not very useful to evaluate and argue about the messages that are being presented. Rallies, mass concerts and demonstrations have had a variety of effects running right across the moral spectrum from genocide to the preservation of irreplaceable buildings and helping to end the war in Vietnam. Their effects therefore aren't the essential point in the transaction either, though they may most certainly be evaluated by the rest of us, and credited where beneficial and resisted where evil. Such evaluation can never be done from within, however. At least not by participants.

The essential elements in what we may call the liturgy of a rally are probably three in number, the *enemy*, the *secret* and the *sharing group*. The enemy is necessary to give participants the delicious sense of being a beleaguered but heroic band; if he did not exist, he would have to be invented. With rock fans, an older person not absolutely in the groove soon realizes that he is not going to be allowed to understand and sympathize, and probably won't get any marks for trying, since the point of the thing is partly its psychodrama of rebellion against an outmoded and unjustly dominant adult world. The secret is the exciting new perspective on things which exalts the recipient and makes him or her significant, while still perhaps safely anonymous, and exalts at least the fantasies of the lowly by substituting for their lonely imaginings something far more vivid and imminent, something which they can take with them out into the dull world of bewilderment and dreary work, or dreary unemployment; when it begins to fade, the glorious picture can always be renewed at the next rally – or replaced by another one. Most important of all, though, is probably the sense of belonging to a group, to a 'generation', to the Circle, the Chosen Company, the In-Crowd, the supportive nexus empowered to judge, to demand compliance and to punish by exclusion. This is very close to the thing which can make soldiers fight on with magnificent courage when their cause is hopelessly lost and all belief in it has left them; loss of belief long before the end is sometimes the dark secret of victorious armies, too.

The dynamics of the group-mind are fraught with all sorts of strange paradoxes, one of which is a profound distortion of the sense of size: a mass movement which has captured a whole nation and converted a majority of its citizens to its world-view may still behave like an embattled band, while a handful of activists with no significant following may believe that they are the determining force in a nation's life and the wave of the future. In the atmosphere of a rally, almost any group of participants will see itself in both of these perspectives at the same time. The group and the mass rally are of course not quite the same thing – except that they are, so convergent are their attitudes and behaviour. We may say that the large rally is the core group writ large and diffuse, while the dedicated core group is the large rally distilled. Within the catchment of the large rally, there will usually be several smaller core groups who enjoy the special exaltation of being Inner, and it is very often these rather than the mass membership who will actually enact the works which the broader rally calls for, and perform, or make, the necessary sacrifices. Not all of those who roared *Sieg Heil* actually operated the gas chambers. I have heard activists in some of the dedicated core groups of the women's movement say that, to be one of their number rather than merely a supporter, it is indispensable to have had an abortion. To be fair, I have also heard members of the movement say that, while women lack self-determination in most areas of life, they will tend to have abortions to prove their power over at least this one central area, as well as to revenge themselves on a confining mystique.

One advantage which the rally and its core-group analogues have over Christian observances is that they deliver the goods, in a very immediate way. They produce the spiritual and emotional effects which people seek from them, in much the same way that technology delivers the devices and supplies we want from it. If, as some commentators have held, technology is magic which works, the rally and similar practices are magical and effectual in the same way. Occult practices, whose vogue has paralleled that of the rally very precisely, can be seen as retarded forms of engineering. The difficulty with all these things is, they only deliver what we think we want. The Spirit gives us what we need, and doesn't necessarily heed our petitions. God may not even rescue us from cruel death when we implore Him to. Being God, He can see both sides of death, as we cannot. This is hard to bear – but the alternative is to seek your spiritual supplies from sources which provide, in the end, only what cannot satisfy you, since what humans imagine to be their salvation can't logically be anything greater than the human measure. 'This world of appearances,' writes the Australian poet Robert Gray, 'is the Diamond.' True, perhaps – as a poet myself, I certainly think it is true – but it is not the Light. There is impressive power in what we can imagine, but no transcendence. There is great depth, sometimes, in our perception – but, again, no transcendence. Political commitment, art, drugs and the like may be effective for quasi-religious (actually magical) purposes such as establishing an identity for oneself, or acquiring protective prestige, and some of them may even mimic transcendence, but it is not the true otherness to which we are, as it were, keyed in the depths of our being. Without that transcendence which is the only coin the soul recognizes, you are left restless and unfulfilled, though clinging perhaps so fervently to the substitute you have found that, in order to crush down your unadmitted disappointment, you may be capable of any enormity that serves to exalt the supplier of your substitute and bind you to him. Pooling your strength with that of all those who depend on the same supplier, you may even change the world – but it remains the world. All you have done is to rearrange the pattern of joy and pain, bewilderment, disappointment and dominances. The hunger of the soul remains, even if we feed it on our very heart and mind and on the lives of millions of the innocent. The first of these is the essence of ideology, the second is its ultimate tendency.

Jesus Christ came out of a milieu similar to our own, in that it contained millenarian hopes and a tradition of political-eschatological rallies aimed at throwing off an oppressive foreign-dominated establishment. Superficially, some of the events of His ministry on earth look like rallies, and it is likely that many of those who flocked to Him intended them to be. He differed from modern demagogues, however, in not giving the people what they thought they wanted, even in an impressively 'improved' version. Not being the creature of His audience, as every demagogue finally is, He gave them difficult truths, valid for all time and all peoples, when all they wanted was a hero-king who would drive out the Romans, restore the local glories of their small nation – and maybe give them a taste of the joys of empire in their turn. If He had yielded to that demand, He could have been a success in the world's terms, and eventually just another name in the history books. Instead, we all know what happened; David Campbell has a poem in which Christ is crucified because of His failure to be the creature of the crowds: 'We played you music and you would not dance.' It is a strange, urgent, but queerly equivocal poem, oddly unlike most of David's work, but these days I find myself asking in the case of most poets: Show me his or her Strange poem, the one (or maybe more than one) that is unlike the rest. That's likely to be the genuinely contemplative one as distinct from the competent or professional ones, and so may be the one in which the Spirit peeped forth.

In comparison with the core groups and cells of modern movements, there is no doubt that Christian churches, in the West particularly, often fail to provide that sense of warm mutual support and reinforcement they must once have provided. And there is often a canting, constrained quality about these things when we do provide them, what the Canadian novelist Robertson Davies calls the 'unreal, stricken quality of religion'. In an age when self-consciousness often sees itself in terms of its problems, we can seem all too ready to leave a lot to the individual dealings of the soul with God. The care of church members for one another, like the priesthood of all Christian believers, tends to be almost entirely delegated away – or, if it isn't, the sort of caring control and surveillance a community provides is often resented. Why did a person come to the city, it not to escape from that cloying hometown stuff and find some excitement in independence?

Elias Canetti remarks, in his book *Crowds and Power*, on the very great distrust of the Catholic Church for crowd phenomena, and its concern to slow such phenomena down into a measured, uneruptive ritual; he calls us a 'slow crowd'. This is an interesting view, and true as far as it goes. Unlike groups for which excitement and ecstasy are the point, the purpose of Catholic ceremonial is slowly and solemnly to construct a bridge between the ordinary and the spiritual realms, so that life and strength may flow from God to us. It is also meant to bridge over our inner divisions, so that health and power may flow across these too. Unlike art, this ceremonial does not rely on freshness or novelty to attain its effect; the familiar itself becomes the ever-new as we enter more deeply into it. The efficacy of the whole process depends not at all on the passionate noise of our desires and yearnings, but on the receptive quality of our stillness. It has emotional results, and emotive meaning, but at heart it is not a matter of emotion, which would be just another source of 'noise' blanking out receptivity. In the Free Church service of my childhood, with its emphasis on the sermon, there wasn't enough receptive silence; there was no sense of ceremony deepened to the point where human activity briefly fell away and God was present. Not the God we theorize and chatter about, but God, the incommensurable, the Strange, speaking health to our soul in rapt silence, as we take Communion with Him.

THE SUPERMARKET AND THE COMMON DISH

With the decline of the normative position of Christianity in the West, we now live in a sort of spiritual supermarket, full of competing systems and brand names. This is partly the result of higher education, of course, and the technology of the paperback book, but that is not to sneer at it: it is also a visible manifestation of need, and quest, and even of pilgrimage. Christianity in the West may, by now, be almost the religion to which people characteristically *return*, after trying many other options. And we should never forget that the paperback pilgrim, like the follower of the rallies, is very often a person of large spiritual gifts which are in desperate need of expression. The supermarket situation is also in part a result of the twentieth century's anthropological revolution; the cultures of mankind are now on display to the literate and TV-watching Westerner as they never were in any previous age. The rhetoric of decolonization in the Third World has flowed back to us and quite properly shaken our old superiorities. As the traditional societies enter upon their Industrial Revolutions, the cities and universities of the West are becoming a kind of cultural museum in which the loved monuments of everyone's tribal or agrarian past are stored, handled and misunderstood. It is natural that people bored with their own traditions, or angry with them, should draw upon this museum and take up alien systems which can never threaten them, because they can never really enter them. I have known several Australians and British and American 'Buddhists' whose real motivation for being so was patently a fear of commitment, of being hurt again by family or other attachments. It was a way of sanctifying indifference and solipsism, of being religious without belief – and sometimes of being aggressive without being frank about it. We have seen a lot of that sort of thing in Christianity, too, in competitive holiness and pious bullying, so it's not hard to recognize a variant form. But that form issues in numbness and loss of the ability to love. It is a lumpen aristocracy, one which reduces everything to a single snobbish level of indulged illusion. How sad: the peasants believe, in their unenlightenment, that they are hungry.

So far as I can judge, from a lot of experience in the milieu, there's nothing very distinctive about supermarket spirituality in Australia, apart perhaps from a natural interest in Aboriginal tradition and the greater difficulty of fitting cyclic pagan systems to a place where the seasons are both back to front and subtle, and where nature often forgets to be effectively cyclic for years at a time. This is very bad news for the more innocent dabblers in witchcraft, who claim to be interested in reviving an allegedly universal primordial religion of the Stone Age (for which there is no good anthropological or archaeological evidence; ancient religions, so far as we know much about most of them, seem always to have been very varied and by no means always tuned to the cycles of nature). It will probably confine them to the towns and piped water. The main danger they're in is that of being drawn into the flesh markets of that high-society Satanism which seems to pop up in our country from time to time, and which may well be related to the excruciations of a tiny old-money caste driven to Gnosticism and worse by the shameless success here of the Lower Orders. The loathing of 'ordinary' Australians and all their works evinced by some of our privileged folk is very striking, and an important corollary of egalitarian aspirations.

We have said that Australia is perhaps the proletarian evolution. This is more a matter of manners and style than one of politics, and political parties which try to reflect or exploit it often end up baffled. This is the thing which tends to make privilege, 'high' culture and some of the groups we have been discussing defensive, self-conscious and, at times, strident. It helps to accentuate in them that modern tendency to constant prickliness and social anger which, perhaps paradoxically, they now share with self-conscious defenders of 'traditional' values. Since the early 1960s and the rise of the universities, we have seen a process not so much of heavy Americanization (the Californication of Australia, as someone has called it) in our country as of the ultimate democratization of formerly aristocratic attitudes. If the people who tend to sympathize with the rallies and the spiritual supermarket, but who also value education and social concern, can be termed an emergent class in our society, different from but ultimately convergent with older colonial privileged groups, it is possible to see the religious preferences of that class as humanist, with some embroidery of occult or Oriental borrowings and a tendency to be anti-Christian. Over against this new class, the religious tendency of what may be called majority Australia may best be described as Residual Christian, with side servings of such themes as stoicism, luck, heroism in the strict sense of survival through the memory of one's supreme achievements in approved fields, plus pieties of various kinds, for example towards the extended family, among country people especially, or towards dead comrades, among ex-servicemen. In majority Australia, chivalry, in the sense not of equivocal gestures towards women, but in the more central sense of the thousand-year effort to Christianize and civilize raw pride and Lawrentian swagger, still carries force. So, lamentably, does a measure of racism, and the sad shamanism of alcohol, as beautifully and sympathetically described in David Ireland's novel *The Glass Canoe*. On the other hand, majority Australia has produced, along with most other things we think of as distinctively Australian, the two human figures which we tend to recognize as peculiarly our own, the Battler, who may be man or woman, and the Larrikin, who has tended to be male. Because of denominational strife in the past, there are sanctions in majority Australia against too-visible display of religious differences. Piety is very often suspected of hypocrisy, and it is usually bad form to 'talk religion', unless one is a cleric and doing so, as it were, professionally. But if Australians are reluctant to talk religion, they are often eager to talk spirituality for hours on end, so long as sect is kept out of it and no attempts at recruiting are made. Some folk in remoter parts of the continent rarely talk about anything but spiritual concerns, in cloudy, sometimes confused, sometimes penetrating terms of their own.

Many people in majority Australia are of course practising Christians, but even among these, perhaps as a result of the centuries of Puritanism, there is a tendency to confuse morality with standards of behaviour, and to run a shame culture rather than a moral one. The downgrading of guilt and the coercive use of shame, of course, are also features of the new class; there is some intersection between the two groups here. If both classes are capable, at times, of a peculiarly cold-eyed, contemptuous authoritarianism, it is perhaps instructive to remember that the first white Australians weren't all convicts; some were warders and guards, and quite a few played both roles at different times. Common to both classes, too, is a great deal of Cargo Cult acquisitiveness and something of a consumer attitude to life and values, though the objects sought are different and class-determined. The important new class newspaper the *National Times* is practically a consumer guide, to approved attitudes, books, wines, indignations, causes and even eccentricities, and the earlier *Nation Review* performed the same service in its time, though arguably with more tolerance of variety, and perhaps more innocence, being less tightly market-researched.

Although we may regret – and I suggest that Christians should logically also oppose – the divisiveness of class, it is futile to pretend it isn't there. Just compare the attention and respect given to people in, say, a public hospital when they speak Broad, without educated vocabulary to alleviate the impression, and that which they obtain by speaking Flash convincingly. The much-decried apathy of Australians is often a misnomer for sensible imperturbability. If we were to seek a common denominator for majority Australia, it would not lie so much, I think, in her widespread and almost instinctive rejection of the rallies (I well remember the man who described Woodstock to me as 'the Nuremberg of Peace and Love'), nor in its disdain for spiritual chatter, pretensions to being free from guilt and evil by one's own mere say-so and the like (the brutal term used here is *bullshit*), so much as in her harsh rejection of those somehow privileged to escape the common lot. This is a very negative way of putting what is a deeply proletarian feature, one encountered in the older societies as well but perhaps more powerful and noticeable here. Seeing it in a more positive light, I would be inclined to use a term I invented in a verse novel I wrote a few years back, and call it the ritual of the Common Dish, that vessel of common human sufferings, joys, disappointments, tragedies and bare sufficiencies from which most people have to eat in this world, and from which some choose to eat in order to keep faith with them. This dish is the opposite of the medieval Grail, which was a vessel attained only by a spiritual élite. To refuse the common ration, or to fail to recognize and respect it, earns one the contempt and rejection of battlers and all who live under the laws of necessity. It is a harsher vessel than the Christian chalice, and not identical with it, except perhaps for the saints, but I believe it lies close to the heart of Australian consciousness, and can never be safely ignored. It is the fountainhead of much of the conformity so often deplored in our society, and much of the art of living in Australia consists in judging, continually and if possible gracefully, just what distance we may wander from the common table and how often to come back.

A NOTE TO CO-RELIGIONISTS

For many historical and other reasons, some of them Australian and our own fault, Christianity is no longer On Top in Australia, though the great majority of Australians continue to believe in God. Others writing in this book (*The Shape of Belief*) will have gone into the modalities of this more effectively than I could do. All I have to add are some personal impressions. The first of these is that the experience is probably a salutary one for us. The time for ecclesiolatry, the worship of the visible church instead of God, is past. We're no longer free to indulge our bad habits of boring people, bullying them and backing up respectability; we're no longer in a position to call on the law to do for us what we should be doing by inspiration and example; we're no longer in a position to push second-rate thinking and an outworn picture of the cosmos, where God is Up, we are in the middle and Hell is Down; we're no longer free to indulge the internecine warfare of denominations that has so harmed God's cause on earth for the past four centuries; finally, we're not going to be universally accepted as a spiritual élite, so we'd better get on with being what our Founder told us to be, which is the salt of the earth, the baking soda in the loaf of mankind. Salt and baking soda aren't privileged substances, but they're pretty essential ones.

The second of my impressions is that, while our vision is no longer the dominant one, and may never have been, neither is any other at the moment. There is as yet no other vision abroad in our society which commands the same authority as ours does, the same sense of being the bottom line, the great reserve to be called on in times of real need. Many of the themes of the rallies are necessary problem-solving and little more, and much in the spiritual supermarket is fair-weather stuff, adjuncts to a prosperity which may now be vanishing. Unbelief, once a daring and rather aristocratic gesture, must by now have exhausted most of its glamour; it is certainly no longer exclusive, or particularly rebellious. Much the same could be said of sexual indulgence, pornography and the like. Having by now surely lost most of its flavour of forbidden fruit, sexual licence has to justify itself in terms of whatever real satisfaction it can give; its utility as a bait to draw people out of traditional ways and beliefs, and if possible into new allegiances, must by now also be wearing thin. The reaction against Victorian values has now lasted longer than Queen Victoria's reign. And it will be difficult, at the very least, for the cult of unremitting youthfulness and physical beauty to survive in the era of ageing populations which it has helped to produce. By now, liberal humanism is as badly fragmented by dissension as our witness ever was, and its fiercest adherents are often covertly uneasy at its lack of gentleness, its readiness to force the facts and its desolate this-worldliness. What misery, to be forced to be Interesting all the time or face cold relegation. What horror, to know one will be obsolete and Irrelevant sooner or later, before the arrival of unending death. The style of unrelenting adulthood forces people on to the thorns of tragic complexity, to face the strange intractability of the world, mobile but irremovable Shadow on all things, and often when people who subscribe to it relax for a moment, their eyes are seen to contain an almost desperate appeal: please prove us wrong, make us believe there is more to it than this, show us your God and that Grace you talk about. We are more widely judged on our own best terms than we think, and more insistently expected to be the keepers of the dimension of depth than we find comfortable. We will be punished if we do try to live up to what we profess, but we will be punished much worse if we don't, because so many of our enemies are relying on us. If we say God and Christ and stand by what we've said, we don't stand alone, but we do have to expect some splinters in our shoulders. We should not, I suggest, be tempted to see ourselves as a team that has to win for God; He is not helpless – and anyway His idea of a win is the Cross, which may be the place where the truly irresoluble contradictions, by which our life in this world is torn but also perhaps powered, meet and get the only resolution they *can* obtain, that is, a living continuous one, which we've agreed to take part in after all.

It is possible, if we must think in terms of doing rather than being, of *actio* rather than the equally potent *passio*, the Passion of the heart of our tradition, that the most urgent tasks facing our faith at this juncture have not got to do so much with the reconversion of the disaffected (Christ said that He came to minister to the sick, not the healthy, and most of the disaffected would probably consider themselves healthy), as with the reconciliation of Black and White Australia and improving the contents of the Common Dish from which Third World people, including our own few such, have to eat. That, and some positive fostering of the contemplative life in a country which has not widely valued it hitherto, except in the figure of the bush hermit, who has tended not to be a specifically Christian type here. We need to strengthen our intellectual presence in this society, while always remembering that a modicum of true vision, or a truly holy life, is more to the point and more effectual as witness than any amount of combative argument. It might not be amiss to point out though, that a good deal of talk about religious decline is in fact incantatory, an interested prophecy constantly reiterated by those who *want* religion to decline. Disentangling the facts from the ill-will is an unstated purpose of this essay. Sentencing by assumption is a familiar tactic of some secularist groups. There are other practical tasks, of course, which concern some of us, if not all. If, for example, we are concerned about abortion, as some of us are, perhaps it is time not merely to combat it, but to offer, without being at all superior about it, to take the threatened babies into our own families and care for them for as long as their parents don't want them or can't look after them. For this and a hundred other purposes, it is most important for us simply to *be* here, to serve and receive the desperate if they come to us, and pray for them whether they come or not. Or simply to be here keeping faith, which is given to us to keep.

Movements which Christ initiated are still dominant forces in the life of the world. To cite just one instance, I think that the Kingdom of God, which is not solely of this world, *is* slowly coming closer to being more clearly figured in this world, in part through the steady push towards human equality in many countries, and I say that in the teeth of all the great crimes which have been committed in the name of that evolution. God works through His enemies as well as His friends – because in the security of His Godhead he possesses the unutterable nobility of full freedom and can choose not to have any enemies. He offers to share that freedom with us, since without Him we could neither attain it nor dream it. Those who can handle something like that degree of freedom we sometimes call saints, when we recognize them in our midst, but God doesn't intend that they should remain forever alone in their sainthood; they are meant to be models and forerunners for us all. And it is probable that there are a great many whom only He knows to be saints, hiding their status from most eyes, including perhaps especially their own. We who are not saints are caught up, not by God but by the logic of our choosing to delay sainthood, in a combat we keep thinking is new (or even Modern) because of the novel shapes and pressures it keeps presenting, a physiognomic struggle between those who somehow accept grace and those who bear the distorting strain of trying to block it off, to act without it or against it. This, I think, rather than the usual superficial divisions between Right and Left, Black and White, religious and irreligious etc., is where the real lines are drawn. By that very grace, though, no one is irremovably fixed in his position. And we should remember that it is often hard to know which side of the line we, let alone others, are standing on at a given moment. Religious practice does, or should, develop the ability in us to discern our own position, at the same time as it makes us wary of judging the positions of others. But when I come to meditate on topics such as grace, I don't finally trust myself to talk about them in prose. For the important stuff, I need the help of my own medium of poetry, which can say more things. Here is how I talked about grace in a poem called *Equanimity*, which opens in the world of Sydney suburbia and goes on:

> Fire-prone place-names apart
> there is only love; there are no Arcadias.
> Whatever its variants of meat-cuisine, worship, divorce,
> human order has at heart
> an equanimity. Quite different from inertia, it's a place

where the churchman's not defensive, the indignant aren't on the
    qui vive,
the loser has lost interest, the accountant is truant to remorse,
where the farmer has done enough struggling-to-survive
for one day, and the artist rests from theory –
where all are, in short, off the high comparative horse
of their identity.
Almost beneath notice, as attainable as gravity, it is
a continuous recovering moment. Pity the high madness
that misses it continually, ranging without rest between
assertion and unconsciousness,
the sort that makes hell seem a height of evolution.
Through the peace beneath effort
(even within effort: quiet air between the bars of our attention)
comes unpurchased lifelong plenishment;
Christ spoke to people most often on this level
especially when they chattered about kingship and the Romans;
all holiness speaks from it.

From the otherworld of action and media, this
interleaved continuing plane is hard to focus:
we are looking into the light –
it makes some smile, some grimace.
More natural to look at the birds about the street, their life
that is greedy, pinched, courageous and prudential
as any on these bricked tree-mingled miles of settlement,
to watch the unceasing on-off
grace that attends their nearly every movement,
the crimson parrot has it, alighting, tips, and recovers it,
the same grace moveless in the shapes of trees
and complex in our selves and fellow walkers; we see it's indivisible
and scarcely willed. That it lights us from the incommensurable
we sometimes glimpse, from being trapped in the point
(bird minds and ours are so pointedly visual):
a field all foreground, and equally all background,
like a painting of equality. Of infinite detailed extent
like God's attention. Where nothing is diminished by perspective.

Written as a chapter for *The Shape of Belief*, edited by Dorothy
Harris, Doug Hynd and David Millikan (Lancer Books, 1982). First
published by permission in *The Review*, Melbourne, 1982

Eric Rolls and the Golden Disobedience

Among a host of lesser and sometimes quite justifiable omissions from the recent *Oxford History of Australian Literature*, the really surprising one was the fourth wheel of our literary wagon, non-fiction prose. In its place there was a very exhaustive bibliography queerly out of whack with the rest of the book, with long entries listing the works of writers barely mentioned in the text and often no entries at all for writers treated at length. My view of the importance of non-fiction prose is echoed, ironically, in the apology for its absence given by the editor, Professor Leonie Kramer, in a prefatory note to the *Oxford History*: 'Our most difficult decision was to omit a section on non-fictional prose. Documentary writing, memoirs, essays, diaries, letters and general prose have a special importance in Australian literary history, because of their quality and their influence upon other literary forms. But in the space available we could not have included this material without serious distortion.' Perhaps the space available should have been expanded or transcended, or the distribution of elements within it rearranged. I gather that in a future edition, possibly even the second one, the omission will be put right. Space could be made by cutting the bibliography back to its General component, and perhaps publishing a revised bibliography-by-authors as a supplement. I suggest this partly because I do think bibliographies important, and partly because I don't like to see anyone's hard work go for nothing.

Non-fiction prose, though, is pretty clearly a vital part of our whole tradition, and is now perhaps the sector of Australian literature where specifically Australian themes, tones, concerns and even identity are most freely allowed to persist. There, we are even permitted to learn about the past and have continuity with it, without charges of 'bush epic' and 'costume drama'. We are permitted to recall and draw on non-fashionable vernaculars, and to examine things for their interest rather than their relevance. In matters of style and tone, there is less pressure to appear always in cord jeans and Adidas shoes, and less pressure towards what I call display prose, the sort which calls attention to itself constantly and with more or less subtlety, wearing its maguey-fibre shirt with a knowing flair. In the absence of such constraint, non-fiction prose may occasionally develop modes and strategies of its own, drawing on native elements and, I believe, creating possibilities for fiction, poetry, the drama and even film. A book which does this, I think, is Eric Rolls' regional-ecological history *A Million Wild Acres*, and I would like to look at its manner, over and above its matter, though the two are finally impossible to separate. It seems to me at once to represent and to extend a tenuously surviving native tradition, and to do things which could be extremely fruitful for fiction writers, poets and others to examine. In its manner as much as in its matter, though the effect is more spectacular there, it is a deeply disobedient book.

Because most scientific and scholarly writing in Australia has tended to be technical and constrained by professional disciplines, with no points given within those for literary excellence, non-fiction writing in this country favours Australiana and matters of Australian rather than universal significance. When we think of Australian non-fiction classics, these are mostly books about our country and its people; Dakin and Banfield and Mary Gilmore are names which come to mind, as do Geoffrey Blainey and Manning Clark, Bill Gammage and C.E.W. Bean, Gavin Souter and Germaine Greer (the last-named partly escapes the Australiana net, though her *The Female Eunuch* does stand as a distinguished cousin to a host of routine excoriations of Australian life and culture, the various Godzones and Australian Stupors). Other names which would have to be added to the list would be Francis Ratcliffe and Rachel Henning, T.G.H. Strehlow and the Berndts, Robin Boyd and Hal Porter – the list keeps lengthening in the mind, approaching Legion and dizzying us with its dance towards and away from and across the borders of classification. A lot of our poetry, for instance, has a strong element of non-fiction about it, and much of the tone of prose works that grapple with the realities of a new, strange continent. In the fields of polemic especially, but also elsewhere, we may begin to wonder just where the borders of fiction, poetry and non-fiction lie. That, of course, is a whole field of study in itself, and its results may tend to undermine our categories altogether. For my purposes here, it merely demonstrates the risky artificiality, the unreality even, of leaving non-fiction writing out of consideration. How can you write at length about Hal Porter's novels and merely glance at his auto-biographical writings, without distorting your whole account of the man's achievement? How can you look only at Mary Gilmore's poetry, and short-change her greatest achievement in the *Old Days Old Ways* books?

While not failing to credit Professor Kramer's reasons for leaving non-fiction out, there are emphases in the *Oxford History* which militate against its giving a full account of a literary field strong, as we have said, on Australiana and matters of national concern. The *Oxford History*, following Patrick White's strictures against 'dun-coloured' journalistic fiction of the sort once prevalent here – authors such as Katharine Susannah Prichard, Kylie Tennant, Frank Hardy, the Palmers and others have a pretty thin time in Dr Adrian Mitchell's long essay on Australian fiction – is ruled by European-style criteria of High Art rather than any wish to register all local outcroppings of literary significance, though it puzzlingly fails to compare approved Australian works with their overseas coevals, and so operates in something of a vacuum as regards its own criteria. The *Oxford History* is concerned to oppose a test of high literary quality, not as promised but as actually achieved, to any and all prescriptive or extra-literary programmes. And I think this is perfectly proper. I have often inveighed against the corruption of our poetry anthologies, all of which select their contents on grounds which include many considerations other than poetic excellence. The *Oxford History*, though, is particularly opposed to the legend of the 1890s and to prescriptive views of Australian literature and culture derived from that legend, and here we may be justified in suspecting the presence of the demon Politics. It would of course be contrary to all decent pluralism to object to a High Tory history of Australian literature – and I don't think the *Oxford History* is such, at least not in its Poetry and Drama sections – but it is also fair to say that our whole culture owes an immense debt to the older Left traditions. I freely acknowledge my own debt. Without such books as Russel Ward's *Australian Legend*, or Manifold's *Who Wrote the Ballads*, I would not be the writer I am. Without major default, no single ideology 'owns' any important subject matter.

Non-fiction prose pretty obviously has as great a potential for moulding and changing opinion as any other branch of literature, and nowadays when the other branches do effect changes in our sensibility or world view it is with the strong help of non-fiction writing. How much of the revolutionary effect of modernism in, say, poetry arose from the texts themselves, and how much from the commentaries and the early proselytizing critics, men such as I.A. Richards and F.R. Leavis? To cite a case in which non-fiction prose had far-reaching efforts in Australia, C.E.W. Bean's decision to write the history of the First AIF from the standpoint of the ordinary soldier arguably set our whole basic attitude to Australia's part in that war and those to follow, and largely determined the form our commemorations would take in the long run, in spite of official overlays of Empire sentiment. Where other countries' traditions in military history had always stressed the generals and leaders, ours would be unique in its emphasis on the citizen soldier, or the citizen-as-soldier, and would even do less than justice to our one really great commander, Sir John Monash, a general of international significance. It would be interesting to trace which of the great themes and images of our imaginative literature, the Explorer, the Voyager, the Inner Emptiness, the Alienness of the Bush and so on, arose from non-fiction sources and which were created by poets and novelists. I do not know the answer in any particular case; I suspect that the alleged alienness of the bush had mainly poetic origins powerfully reinforced by D.H. Lawrence on his visit in the 1920s. But even with this one I suspect there would have been antecedent reportage by diarists and writers of descriptive prose in colonial times. The same may even be true of Mateship, which we think of as a great 'folk' discovery of the short-story writers and poets of the eighties and nineties of last century.

If non-fiction writing is powerful in establishing views which gradually become accepted reality, it is arguably even more powerful than imaginative literature in overturning such orthodoxies. Imaginative literature is unique in its power to give to materials that vivid life which we may call poetry; it has no unique power to make discoveries, though it probably makes some, and certainly deepens and consolidates many. When it goes against an accepted view, however, it lacks the sober documentary force to sway tough-minded and 'realistic' spirits, or deeply committed ones. It may delight them and weaken them, but it will not usually convince them on its own. And yet it is possibly poetry which does in the end convince and convert, conferring reality on successive constructs – but that is as likely to be the 'poetry' of a remembered distillation of non-fiction prose as the actual poetry of verse or imaginative prose. I think poetry is the principle which controls reality, and I doubt there is any more final truth, but when I say that I use the term poetry in its widest sense. We are ruled, and sometimes martyred, by successive large loose 'poems' which become the governing paradigms of our world.

It is a commonplace, of course, that poetry can even drive out personal experience. I grew up near and often in the great forests of the New South Wales lower north coast; our house was less than two miles from the edge of the Myall State Forest, and four more large State forests lay within the ambit of my childhood; my father had been a bullock driver and timber-getter in those forests before he married and started dairyfarming – and yet even I was almost seduced by the myth of the alien bush, as I began learning to write poetry. A received sensibility almost had me subscribing to its agenda, in spite of my awareness that the bush wasn't alien to me at all, but a deeply loved vastness containing danger and heavy work, but also possessing a blessedly interminable quality which was and is almost my mind's model of contemplation. It was years, though, before I had a character in a verse novel discover that 'the bush is sensible; it'll kill you, but it's – decent'.

The part of the bush I grew up in is first mentioned in Eric Rolls' book on page 70, as he describes the surveys carried out by Henry Dangar to find suitable country for the newly formed Australian Agricultural Company:

> The one area left that seemed likely to contain the company's grant lay between Port Stephens and the Manning River. In February 1826 Henry Dangar made a thorough reconnaissance. And he found good land. There is beautiful cattle country around Stroud, Dungog, Gloucester and Taree. Further east, though it was obviously not the rich farm land that Dangar would choose for himself, there was fair open grass land. It was not the wooded tangle of today.

The poor grassland country down around the Myall Lakes, now all under eucalypts and red-barked angophoras and great tracts of paperbark forest standing in rushy grass on white clay soils (where the AMP Society has not bulldozed the bush to put in super-phosphate pasture for its cattle), was deemed suitable for fine-wool sheep, and the world of the local Aborigines was destroyed to accommodate them. Within a few years, footrot and the soils' deficiencies in copper and cobalt, defects unknown to nineteenth-century science, had wiped the sheep out. And with the Aborigines no longer there to burn the country over continuously, the lonely Myall Lakes scrublands we know today, with their tremendous wealth of wildflowers, began to cover the grassland over. Back in the hills I come from, north-west of there, the rainforest which had always withstood the Aborigines' fires in moist gullies began to expand as the settlers and cedar-getters usurped the black people, then retreated again before the white man's axes and crosscut saws. The scattered clumps of sclerophyll forest, never large or dense in Aboriginal times, began to surge outward, spreading down off the ridges to cover the valley flats which had carried only a few trees to the hectare in pre-European days. When my father was a young man, he and his brothers could ride everywhere in 'the State', as they called the vast forest reserve near their home, seeking the giant timber trees that stood among the younger spindlier growth. As my father told me recently, 'You hardly had to make roads for the bullocks then. You could see through the bush for hundreds of yards.' Now, you could barely get a horse through most parts of the Myall State Forest, among the vines and wattle thickets and dense stands of young trees which flourish there after eighty or ninety years of mill logging and sleeper cutting. And if modern use by trucks and tractors has not kept them open, it is a job even to find the bullock roads of forty years ago. Fifty years ago, my father and his brothers happened on a promising quartz reef in a clear gully, and the assays were promising. I remember seeing the shaft when I was a child, but when Dad and I went to find it again a few years ago, we couldn't even identify the right gully, among the masses of lopped heads of trees and surging second growth. The bush out there would be far too thick to go possuming in now, as Dad and his brothers and cousins used to do on moonlit nights. Their great-grandfathers had learned from the Aborigines how to 'moon' possums, perhaps even while they were still working for the Australian Agricultural Company at Stroud.

It is Eric Rolls' controversial and perhaps revolutionary contention that the forests of Australia as we know them are no more than a hundred to a hundred and thirty years old. Apart from the tracts and patches of rainforest that follow the eastern face of the Dividing Range from far north Queensland down almost to Victoria, and a few large pockets of sclerophyll forest mainly in areas of high rainfall, he contends that Australia bore the appearance in pre-European times of a vast parkland kept open and well grassed by constant burning off. It was a *paysage humanisé* and *moralisé* which the Aborigines had maintained for untold centuries; the wilderness we now value and try to protect came with us, the invaders. It came in our heads, and it gradually rose out of the ground to meet us. As Rolls writes (page 400):

> Those who value our forests and wish to preserve them declare, as in this extract from *Save Colong Bulletin*, November 1976, "More than half the forest in eastern Australia – the dry sclerophyll and savannah woodland – has disappeared since European settlement."

Hugh Tyndale-Biscoe of the Society for Social Responsibility in Science (ACT) irresponsibly exclaimed in *The Sydney Morning Herald* of 18 September 1978 "there is no equivalent in Britain to our great primeval forests." Over and over one finds similar statements in modern writings. What forests? How many trees make a forest?

"Everywhere we have an open woodland," wrote Charles Darwin on his 1836 visit. "Nowhere are there any dense forests like those of North America," explained *Chambers Information for the People* in an article on "Emigration to Australia" written in 1841. Such statements are made over and over in early writings. De Beuzeville was aware of them. He reasserted them in his *Australian Trees for Australian Planting*. "Even along the... gullies and the contiguous streams," he quoted, "the country resembled the 'woodlier parts of a deerpark in England.'" In the seventy-two forests declared in New South Wales in 1879 the tree count of those assessed varied from two and a half mature trees to the hectare inland to eighty on the tablelands and coast. The Forestry Commission in experimental plots in the Yerrinan section of the Pilliga forest found that sixty-year-old White Cypress Pines thinned in 1940 to two hundred to the hectare produced the best timber over the next thirty years, but, if thinned to six hundred to the hectare, they produced the most timber. Nowhere, in a search lasting months, did I find reference to former stands of timber as thick as those modern thinned stands.

The author goes on to describe, in the same passage, the few stands of relatively heavy timber which existed at the time of settlement, places such as the future Nundle Forest Reserve first sighted by Oxley, where a density of a hundred and fifty mature stringy barks per hectare as assessed in 1879 was enough to form a canopy and permit the growth of large tree ferns which do not grow in direct sunlight, and the mountain ash gullies of Victoria. He also refers to the large jarrah and karri forests of south-western Western Australia, though he doesn't add to his case by mentioning the frequent references to expansion of those forests since settlement. On visits to Western Australia, I have read many accounts of those forests which state, how truly I don't know, that places where giant trees now grow in profusion were wheatlands a century ago. After pointing out that the great eucalyptus growth on the Dividing Range and on every little hill in central western New South Wales, the Bimble Box swaths in the west of that State, the long forests of river red gum on the western drainage and the coolabah forests found on plains subject to flooding are all post-settlement growths, he candidly details the destruction of much of our rainforests and the idiotic overexploitation of *Toona australis*, the red cedar which, apart from Tasmania's Huon pine, is Australia's only truly long-lived tree, living for upwards of two thousand years but tragically hard to regenerate artificially. Even the cedar grew only sparsely in its brushes; good stands averaged one great tree to the hectare. Modern timber-getters have learned the hard way to be secretive about the odd red cedar they know of in the forests, often passing the location of such trees on to their children as a sort of inheritance, or at least waiting many years before felling the big solitary treasure trove they have been saving up. When such a log comes in to a city mill, it is an event; I remember the arrival of a red cedar log at the Asquith mill in Sydney a few years ago, a middle-sized stick taken from private land on the northern rivers which earned its owner eleven hundred dollars after cartage. A decent-sized red cedar log nowadays can easily fetch five or six thousand dollars at auction. In case conservationists may worry that he is undermining their cause, Rolls goes on to point out that while there are now more trees in Australia than at settlement, just as there are more kangaroos, this does not make proper care of our forests less important. 'Our forests are vulnerable,' he writes. 'Their concentration puts both plants and animals at risk. They are the packed containers of so much that has gone from the rest of the country.' And he describes the shortcomings of many of our forestry authorities, with their ignorance of soils and their persistent temptations to monoculture. One man up our way hated the sterile plantations of slash pine (*Pinus elliotii*) north of Tea Gardens so much that he waited over twenty years, then, in a searing drought-stricken summer, put a match to them and wiped out half the stand in a fire which must have been an orgy of expensively fragrant destruction. Rolls describes right and wrong ways to conduct the woodchip industry, which he regards as sound and necessary, and deplores the sneaky, servile way in which several State governments have sold off forest resources in secret deals.

Except for the rainforest Aborigines of north Queensland, I have never heard of any groups of Aboriginal people who habitually lived in thick forest, nor have I ever read any legends which had a good word to say for it. In my home region, people who spoke the various dialects of Kattangal used to enter the thick brushes along the Manning River each year to bring down flying foxes for food, but stories from the region tell of cannibal spirits (*dooligarl*) which inhabited the riverine forest, so we may imagine the hunters did not hang about in there when they had got their quota. There are legends, not mentioned by Rolls, which describe the permanent destruction of forests by fire – the Rubuntja fire-ancestor legend from Central Australia is an example – and stories of the gradual widening of the sky as ancient forests disappeared; these may go back thousands of years and describe a process which began as Australia became drier. Forest does not provide good hunting ground for nomads equipped with long spears and throwing weapons. Spears would catch and break in thick bush, and boomerangs would be lost in it. Similarly, animals would have too much cover, and get out of sight too quickly when startled. Fire, we know, was regularly used by Aborigines to flush out and drive game, and the green feed which came up quickly after burning attracted grazing animals. Rolls is not alone in citing numerous early European references to Aboriginal fires seen burning in places from Tasmania to Cape York; in his *Triumph of the Nomads*, Geoffrey Blainey devotes a whole chapter, titled 'Australia, a Burning Continent', to the fire-husbandry practised by the first Australians. We are becoming familiar with this concept now, and coming to appreciate the unique adaptation to fire of dominant floral and faunal communities in this country. Most people, for instance, must by now have heard of the leaf-regenerating epicormic buds in eucalypts, and be aware of the many plants whose seeds only open when a fire cracks their hard coverings. And country people know the way birds will gather as soon as smoke begins to rise from a paddock, butcherbirds, kestrels, satin birds and kookaburras appearing as if from nowhere and dodging through the smoke to catch grasshoppers, lizards and other small animals driven from cover by the flames. It would be fascinating to know how far back they learned to do this, and know the answer to the various chicken-and-egg questions which the unique fire ecology of Australia poses for evolutionary theory.

Rolls' general theory of the Australian forests is anchored in the particular story of one forest, the Pilliga (from Kamilaroi *peelaka*, a spearhead), which lies beyond the Dividing Range in New South Wales and extends from Narrabri in the north to Coonabarabran in the south. Its eastern extremity is close to the village of Baan Baa and in the west it peters out around the small town of Baradine. It is characterized by a mixture of eucalypts, acacias and callitris trees, usually known by the collective name cypress pine, and is enormously rich in birds, animals and flowering plants. Rolls writes (page 1):

When John Oxley saw it in 1818 there was little forest there as the word is used now. The meaning of forest has grown with the forests. "Brush" he called it in small areas, "a very thick brush of cypress trees and small shrubs." "Scrub" he called the stunted growth on the dry ridges, "mere scrub". Most of it, about 800,000 hectares, was a "forest" of huge iron-barks and big white-barked cypress pines, three or four of them only to the hectare.

We would not now call it forest. "But it is open grassland" we would say in bewilderment. "One would scarcely have to clear it to cultivate it.". . . What Oxley saw he did not like. "Forbidding . . . miserable. . ." he said, "a sandy desert. . ." Oxley was using the term "desert" in the sense of deserted, not dry. It was a decidedly wet desert in August 1818.

Slowly, with a leisurely accretion of detail from sources that range from printed books to previously unread family diaries and Lands Department archives, Rolls tells the story of how European animals, plants and humans spread northwards on each side of the Dividing Range and took over this belt of sandy country. It is not purely human history, but ecological history he gives us, showing how the real explorers were as likely to be escaped cattle and introduced grasses as men. By the time the hard men of the infant colony and their convict slaves arrived to take up new country, cattle had usually preceded them and begun compacting the ancient spongy soils with their hoofs, driving out the native ground-plants with the chemical and light-occluding properties of their huge droppings. He is unsparing of the rapacious human landtakers, but will not take the easy course of repudiating them. As he writes (pages 11-12):

The tormented community generated its own men. Some hard gobbets indeed were thrown up. Those attracted later as settlers were the same type – capable, adventurous, and extraordinarily adaptable, difficult, crude, vigorous, dishonest, selfish, violent. They differed only in the extent to which each of these qualities was developed. Some were more violent than others, some less adaptable. They developed Australia.

If these men had remained in Britain they would have had no influence on their times. Society would have restrained them. In Australia they moved outside the law. It is no use wishing they were different. To do so is to dispense with our culture. No other men could have done what they did. Australia might have been abandoned as a British settlement.

If it had been abandoned, of course, the bush cattle and introduced plants and Mr Brumby's horses would still have gone on spreading. And since in a world rapidly heading towards being crowded, no large area of even marginally exploitable land could expect to go on supporting only a beautifully adapted small population of hunter-gatherers, some other nation or nations would have invaded Australia and brought destruction to the world of the Aborigines. Rolls does not theorize or agonize about the morality of the invasion, but he also does not seek to evade its ruthless violence. We are given a sense of that curious meshing of warfare and accommodation which commonly comes about on frontiers:

> From the beginning of settlement there was an astonishingly close relationship with the Aborigines. It was rare for a white man to be killed by unknowns. When a shepherd in a lonely hut was speared, if he saw the man who threw it, he knew him by a name. And, when stockmen rode out to shoot Aborigines in retaliation, they counted the dead by name. But the names they called them were cursory and degrading: Bobby, Saturday, Sunday, King Billy. Most Europeans could not be bothered learning to pronounce Aboriginal words and in choosing names for Aboriginal acquaintances they took less trouble than teamsters in naming their work bullocks.

There are black people still alive in northern Australia who bear such names. From time to time, casual killings and small massacres turned to pitched battle. On Boorambil station in 1827 or 1828 – we may call it a station, though the term didn't originate till 1836 – a large force of Kamilaroi tribesmen attacked white stockmen sheltering in a well-built hut with rifle slots in the walls. It is possible that the Kamilaroi had issued a formal challenge to meet and fight on a stipulated day, but the handful of white men did not come out and line up to meet their challengers in the honourable traditional way. When spears and boomerangs thrown against the walls in derision did not bring them out, the black soldiers stormed the hut and tried to unroof it. They kept attacking for hours, and perhaps as many as two hundred were shot, most of the young men of the tribe. This battle is known from two slightly differing accounts, one handwritten by William Gardner, one in a book published by the bushranger Martin Cash.

The story of the Pilliga forest is one of advance, disappointment and retreat by pastoralists and then by small farmers. It is possible that we have never had so penetrating a study of the realities of settlement before; certainly I do not know of one which interrelates the human and non-human dimensions so intimately. Also, and it is a country man's point, Rolls realizes that more of Australia's history took place outside the law than within it, and more attempt was made to hide than to record it. He has a knack, born of sympathy and human knowledge, for detecting the outlines of concealed knavery even a century old. History is not just the propaganda of dominant groups, but also the public record of approved classes of human beings, and there is a way in which country people in Australia are apt to miss out on their due by being neither acceptably Upper nor recognizably proletarian, and their wary reticences compound this still further. Given rapid changes of ownership of runs, by chicanery, bad luck, disease, opportunism or poor judgment of country, and changes in government policy such as John Robertson's Selection Acts of the 1860s, few were able to amass large stable fortunes. Dynasty and great wealth are features of many parts of the New World of European settlement, but are far less important in Australia, and the difference sets us off from many apparently comparable societies. The ecological result in the Pilliga was that neglected runs and failed selections went under surging masses of gum and cypress pine seedlings by the 1870s. Cypress pines came up ten thousand to the hectare, and soon there was no room for grass to grow. Foxes and competition for grass destroyed the rat-kangaroos which had previously kept the seedlings nibbled down, and the disappearance of the Aborigines meant that burning off was no longer regular and cyclic. Happening occasionally, sometimes as a result of lightning strike or accident, fires had the opposite of their historic effect: they now induced the appearance of millions of seedlings. The blue-green *peelaka* spearheads of cypress pine trees filled up the country. Rabbits, arriving soon after the first great spurts of growth, tended to keep the forest in check to some extent, until myxomatosis in the fifties of this century wiped the rabbits out, and bush fires in the same decade were followed by soaking rains. After the fifties, the Forestry Department, which had assumed that milling in the Pilliga would eventually cut the timber out, began to think in terms of sustained yield from the region. And unless the periodic threat of a new international airport in the Pilliga 'scrub' becomes a reality – let us hope Rolls' book makes that less likely – the area may at last have reached some sort of natural balance of human and non-human life. Not that such balances last forever.

Reading and re-reading *A Million Wild Acres* with all the delight of one who knows he has at last got hold of a book that is in no way alien to him (I begin to understand the sheer relief of a black Australian who has at last obtained a book written by one of his own people and not by whites) I was struck by the almost pointillist way in which he writes history. The book has historical sequence, and is arranged in chapters, but its logic is really accretive, made up of strings of vivid, minute fact which often curl around in intricate knottings of digression. Patches of timeless life are shot through with patches of sequential narrative, and vice versa. In the chapter on bird life in the Pilliga, we suddenly get a thread of human history and a fascinating needle of speculation. After telling us about the feeding habits of many of the birds in the forest, and their reliance on pollen and nectar from flowers, he writes (pages 390-1):

> This extensive pollen feeding helps to explain the pollination of Australian plants. Anyone, scientist or layman, asked today "What is the principal pollinator of native flowers?" would answer "The Honey bee". The honey bee was brought out with as much care as the first rabbits – Gregory Blaxland's hive travelled in his cabin – and spread with settlement. In many districts it has been principal pollinator for no more than a hundred years. One wonders whether more efficient pollination allowed the heavy growth of modern forests. Could the honeyeaters and lorikeets or the little (native) *Trigona* bees have coped with thousands of hectares of massed flowers or millions of extra solitary bees found enough holes or dug enough burrows to store their individual honey pots?

Historical sequence in the book shifts constantly from the drily economic to the personal, and report is charged with reminiscence. For instance, on pages 181-2 we read:

> Thomas G.G. Dangar married Catherine MacKenzie, daughter of the man who grew wheat so early at Wangen. He built a good home on Bullerawa. No one in the north built mansions costing a hundred thousand pounds sterling like Thomas Chirnside or Sir William Clarke and several others in the Western District of Victoria. But whereas homes on most northern runs were valued at about two hundred pounds, the home on Bullerawa was valued at two thousand.
>
> By the river he built huts to house twenty-five ex-convict workmen who had grown too old to work. He supplied a cook who called them to meals by ringing a big brass bell. Thomas Dangar later donated the old bell to the Pilliga school.
>
> W.C. Cormie, the son of David Cormie who was manager

for Thomas Dangar, used to watch the old men bathing naked in the Namoi when he was a child. The cat o' nine tails had so scarred their backs they seemed to be covered in scales not skin.

The events described belong to the seventies of last century, and on the same page we revisit the sprouting acacia and cypress pine seedlings now beginning to take advantage of the depletion of cattle numbers by drought, and also of runholders' attempts to destroy spear grass and wire grass by burning. In that decade, stock routes are invented and gazetted, and sawmilling begins in the Pilliga for the first time, at Narrabri on its northern fringe. As elsewhere in the book, everything is in motion yet held in a sort of dynamic tableau, measuring some thousands of square miles by about 160 years. In contradistinction to most European art since the Middle Ages, there is little sense of foreground and background, that perspective of heroic agents acting out their drama before a series of sketched-in theatre flats, the Renaissance schema by which the aristocratic principle was able to triumph over an older Christian 'field' (the sense of Everyman, or Piers Plowman's Field Full of Folk) in which prominence was reserved for supernatural figures. In Rolls' presentation, things human and non-human are all happening interrelatedly, and the humans barely stand out. Through a fusion of vernacular elements with fine-grained natural observation, and a constant movement of back-reference, he breaks through sequential time not to timelessness but to a sort of enlarged spiritual present in which no life is suppressed. We feel that the myriad activity of the book's 'field' does not cease when we move our gaze through it and over it. Of all art, it reminds me distantly of Pollock; perhaps *Blue Poles*, which I take to be as much as anything a painting of equality, was an appropriate purchase for an Australian Government to make. It also reminds me of just a few Australian works, Boyd's Breughelesque paintings such as *The Mining Town*, with their myriad active figures mostly held below the high horizon line, or Geoffrey Lehmann's vernacular-meditative *Ross's Poems*. It is perhaps a nascent New World form of vision, struggling to emerge from under successive impositions of neo-aristocratic style derived from abroad. When I look at a piece of art which mimes community or commonality in something like this way, it gives me an obscure sense of homecoming I rarely get from, say, the theatre, with its dominant and subordinate characters, its conflict and its merely human interactions. This may admittedly be a preference drawn from poetry, in which the rocks, the trees and the animals are as important as the human figures and all things can be taken as referring to the human anyway without stressing the point.

In the laconic, discursive and yet economical pace of its narrative, and in its dry tone, Rolls' *Million Wild Acres* reminds me at times of the Sagas, particularly I suppose the Icelandic *Landnamabók* or Book of Settlements. And yet there are differences. Rolls' book presents a complex system greater than any of the agents in it, but does not call it fate, or indeed refer it to any metaphysic. It has a much larger quotient of meditation than a saga story, but it is usually a meditation based on elegaic and unobtrusively intense scrutiny of detail, as in the beautiful brief accounts of older country lore, of bells and bullockies' commands and the way to oil seasoned pine planks. And, as the sagas only occasionally do, he treats his human and non-human agents pretty much on a par. This par we may call ecological consciousness, and see it as a new form of a very ancient sense of the interrelatedness of all things. A way of expressing this which we find in surviving fables and fairytales is to make the animals and even the trees talk. Rolls' animal figures do not talk, and so don't offend modern rationalist expectations, but he shows us their lives in vignettes which capture their unidealized behaviour, sometimes in situations we have imposed on them. An irritated sow in a sty bites off the penis of an importunate boar, a homosexual steer provides relief for young rig bulls. Any kind of aristocratic sensibility is liable to scorn such things as mere peasant anecdote, fearful perhaps of being itself caught in a web of laconic storytelling which might deflate prominent or highly polished humans and reduce them to a memorable feature here, a perhaps devastating recollection there. The Reverend Samuel Marsden, for example, merits less sympathy than that possibly happy steer, and gets no more space. Rolls merely writes of Marsden hauling a miller before him one Sunday morning and fining him because his mill was desecrating the Sabbath. Marsden's own mill turned throughout the hearing. Or there is the picture of 'sedate, scientific and religious' Lieutenant Dawes, of the Royal Marines, tramping through the hills in the year after settlement with his bags for collecting soil samples and his habit of quizzing the Aborigines about Noah and the Flood. The Aborigines had certainly heard of a flood, and Dawes was delighted. Anecdote, which is of course not exclusively a bush or a peasant thing, has some threatening relativities about it, and can be merciless in an equable way which gives power to the powerless. It is a music of equality.

The anecdote of course, based as it is on interest and selection of detail, may carry tyrannical potentials of its own. A lot depends on the breadth of the group it appeals to, and the complicity it seeks. We need to ask whether, in a given case, anecdotes and details are being selected in order to impose a world view or reflect one. Are we looking at the familiar journalistic trick of selecting details and presenting them blandly in order to shift our perceptions towards a view which the writer is covertly pushing – always telling stories that make religion seem foolish, for example – or are we looking at an attempt to mime the balanced complexity of reality according to something like a common view held by a broad range of society? Of course one may do a lot to change a common view by adopting a common tone: that is a familiar post-1890s strategy in Australia. I think Australian readers have already come to see Rolls' book as genuinely representing a broad rather than a sectional sensibility, however, and existing on a plane we instantly recognize as common Australian property rather than the atmosphere of an élite. I have heard conservationists growl at Rolls, and call him 'that old fraud', but I can't see how he damages their cause; he may, indeed, have burnt off a derivative form of ecological consciousness and let one more truly adapted to Australia spring up. He gives an originally imported notion the 'sound' of common acceptance, partly by freeing it from overtones of a mandarin desire to reform and civilize us. And so there is no strain of intimidation in our assent to his book.

The ruling literary culture of our time exhorts us to many disobediences. Very many of these are fraudulent or by now worn out, but there is a disobedience I value and call the golden one – and that is disobedience of the dominant literary sensibility itself. It is often wise, in the New World, to write literature as it were against the grain of Literature, because then you avoid the resistance which literary claims very often provoke, perhaps at a deep level, in the minds of readers whom Literature as usually understood in late-colonial societies often seems to threaten with relegation if they resist its assumptions. We have grown used in recent years to highly mannered forms of prose fiction, many of them derived in this country from Patrick White's method of dabbling small exacerbated qualifications of extreme sensitivity over narrative and character alike in ways which constantly threaten to snub us if we do not render abashed assent. Few writers, perhaps, have followed White's other trick of inverting ordinary snobbery and transposing it into mystical election, but a myriad of other transformations and inversions of snobbery are around, to the point where the marks and shibboleths of enlightenment and competitive modernity have become a study as intricate as the quarterings of European heraldry encountered by Voltaire's Candide. Canny writers such as Frank Moorhouse, of course, can get away with holocausts of damaging exposure of fashionable circles by remembering always to have their narrators do approved things and seem to reflect the reigning sensibility. But even playing tricks on a divisive and alienating mandarin tradition is not the same as discovering new styles and departures in art, and perhaps freeing it to reflect more of reality than a received sensibility allows. In its steady 'middle' voice, Rolls' narrative seems to be attempting nothing less than a complete account of its large subject. The whole truth, with no let-outs of polemic or withheld sympathy or portentousness or even of the chic brilliances which often disguise hollowness of vision. In its very different tone, and in a context of half-personal documentary rather than fiction, Rolls' enterprise may be seen as Proustian. But only tangentially, because in achieving his effect of completeness Rolls has done something which the aristocratic literary traditions of Europe make hard even to conceive: he has penetrated to the condition of the best 'primitive' art. In painting, the term *primitive* refers to art executed by people without formal training; in literature, where it is much rarer as a genuine and productive thing, we may take it as meaning unaware of the received sensibility. This is quite different from Latin American 'Magic' Realism, currently rather fashionable in Australia and elsewhere, which is a sophisticated appropriation of some primitive techniques. The hollowness of Magic Realism lies in the way it affects to love the People, but really considers their life too boring on its own, and so heightens it with implausible surreal incident and fantasy. In six and a half years as acting editor of a poetry magazine, I only twice encountered work of quality produced by genuine primitive poets; these were Carmen Blomfield, of Armidale, whose strange, utterly individual and yet deeply communal poem 'Lament for Kangaroo Flat' I published in *Poetry Australia*, and Allan Jurd, of Lismore, whose poems had a tumbling fecundity of observation and an oddness of imaginative angle which cannot be faked. Rolls' own early 'Sheaf Tosser' poems had a comparable 'primitive' quality which impressed many good judges who could see beyond the roughnesses and repetitions. It now seems that this essence in his early poems has stayed alive in Rolls and kept him from conformities, so that he might consummate it three decades later in a prose masterpiece.

Claims have been made that Rolls' *Million Wild Acres* will be seen as one of the great books about Australia, rivalling *Voss, Such is Life* or *Capricornia* as the 'ultimate statement about national experience'.

The book has a larger scope, perhaps, than any of those, but I am unsure of the precise meaning of that term 'ultimate statement'. Rolls' history probably contains as much poetry, in the wide sense, as any of them, without their dimensions of fiction, and none of its poetry consists in 'purple' writing. Interestingly, two of the three books named draw upon vernacular elements of our culture, and use yarning as an element of their construction. *Such is Life* at once creates and celebrates a new 'Australian' sensibility based on conscious exaggeration of the actualities of the itinerant workers' yarn; while pretending to be a structured novel it is actually a meandering picaresque entertainment that flows rather like the Murray River, with infinite bends and lagoons of minor incident and newly sprouted forests of comic meditation. In this latter regard, *Capricornia* is fairly similar, with emblematic characters who undergo much disaster but little development.

Rolls' book is more classically 'laconic' in its tone than either novel, and proves just how long a laconic performance can go on without tiring the reader or ceasing to be laconic. The only part of the book which did drag a little for me was in the early chapters minutely detailing the spread of settlement north and west from Port Jackson. Those were the chapters which, dealing with times beyond living memory, were most affected by documentary history, and closest to merely sequential narrative. Later in the book, human characters could emerge in a way which owes little either to literary fiction or to historical writing. Figures of timber-getters and rabbiters, Forestry officials and farmers are then simply named, with perhaps a word or two of designation when we first meet them, and are thereafter apt to re-emerge in an apparently casual way when needed to tell a story or anchor a statement of fact. They appear with the sudden naturalness of old friends mentioned in a fireside yarn, and reveal themselves while contributing to the flavour of the narration. Writing about the great bushfire of 1951, for example, Rolls allows a number of figures to play their small parts and vanish again (page 305):

> Initially some of the firefighters were not worth feeding. With so little equipment they saw no point in risking their lives for a bit of scrub. They played cards and let it burn. A young sleeper cutter, not mentally normal, could not resist lighting a few extra fires. Others risked their lives trying to cut breaks with the little graders. Noel Worland worked the first sixty-three hours without sleep. Ned Edwards spent thirteen days and nights at the fire, his brother, Roy, eighteen.

Arthur Ruttley was sent up to take charge. He organised big bulldozers from coastal forests, five new graders from Sydney, water tankers from the RAAF. He flew in a plane load of forestry students to get experience. He recruited local volunteers and enough cooks to feed several hundred men. He kept everybody working. They put out the fire in three weeks.

Noel Worland watched the forest for further outbreaks from a De Soutter aeroplane flown by Dick Burt of Baradine. The high wings were made of plywood and they drummed as the plane came in to land. The noise got louder and louder till at touchdown it seemed the plane must disintegrate. Dick Burt's cattle dog rode with Noel on the back seat and licked his face while he was spotting. Each time he pushed it away it growled venomously.

Every individual figure in that passage, except the unfortunate sleeper cutter who is perhaps still alive and anyway better unnamed, has the dignity of his name; there is no recourse to the lazy (or superior) passive voice: bulldozers *were organized*, five graders *were got* from Sydney etc., and no reliance on periphrases such as 'one man spent thirteen days and nights at the fire'. The difference, though apparently small, is the difference between democracy and aristocracy, or between community and élite culture. Naming implies respect. And by naming a great many of his human figures, Rolls almost paradoxically gives them as great an individuality as the birds, flowers, creeks and cattle breeds of his narrative. Not all European-style writing about milieux which combine nature and the human dimension bothers to do as much.

It is possible that the sobriety of Rolls' book and a few like it reflect more exactly than any past fiction the temper of vernacular Australia. Attempts to work from the vernacular tradition in creating imaginative fiction have tended to result in a laboured flatness, as in much of Prichard, arty falsity and inflation, as in Patrick White's *Tree of Man*, in arch rumbustiousness and grotesquerie, as in David Foster's *Moonlight* and a hundred lesser novels, or honourable eccentricity, as in Furphy and Herbert. Only one recent novel based on vernacular life which has made me prick up my ears in the way I always hope will happen is David Ireland's *Glass Canoe*, which does contain suggestive shapes and captures of rhythm. Rolls' 'field' method of telling history and depicting a milieu all at once may suggest new possibilities, however, to writers of fiction. It is even possible that the novel, as a form we have adopted from elsewhere, may not be the best or only form which extended prose fiction here requires. Its heavy emphasis on the human, on character and the development of character, may tend to lead us into repeated misrepresentation of our world. Man and his classes and disputes may not be *important* enough, here, to sustain such a form. So many of our novels are portentous in their essence, piling up sensibility and brilliance on themes which cannot quite bear them, trying to exclude space in order to attain intensity. And the novel's inbuilt bias towards the individual may be fatally at odds with the communal basis of much of our life, though truly developed individuals are, I think, rare in our fiction; disguised humours and types, the Intellectual, the Bushman, the Liberated Woman, so often take their place and fatally short-change real individuality. This parallels (feeds, feeds off) a deadly habit of self-stylizing we may always have gone in for, in preference to developing full selfhood. Again, there is something anti-ecological about the novel: in its assigning all of agency to humans, it may be seen as a product of the overhumanised landscapes of the old world. Rolls himself repudiates the distinction between fiction and non-fiction, holding that it rests upon a confusion of the concepts of *imagination* and *fantasy*, or as the eighteenth century termed them, fancy and wit. Real things are *imagined*, in live writing, that is, they are deeply understood and made into images that touch the mind, whether the context is historical or projected.

It is good to have Rolls' great book in a time when so much of our literature seems in the first generation of widespread tertiary education to have become urgently mandarin, obsessed with the markers of consumer Style. It is hard to make unwelcome caveats when a culture long taught to despise itself achieves a tentative self-confidence and goes all out to capture the talismans of 'high' culture, in this case Style and highly visible Sophistication. Style here, though, has tended to stylize its subjects, and sophistication of the sorts we have been exhorted to admire tends to issue in gestures of conformity with currently received literary values, over against the life very many of our people lead. We may construct beguiling networks of artistry, but in the back of many Australian minds there is often a suppressed dismay even in the midst of admiration, a feeling that some more essential network is being short-changed, dismissed unjustly, not got right. Our fiction is long on exhortation, on revision, on a habitual social scorn we have been three-quarters persuaded to endorse, but somehow it so often estranges us from something in us which goes on wanting to be represented, to be spoken in its true words. And so, almost behind the back of our learned proprieties, we welcome time and again books of non-fiction, books which articulate even some part of our deep experience as a people, and speak to us in a level, balanced, undecorated voice we 'hear' as our own. To cut through alienation by simply ignoring the received sensibilities which produce it is a form of what I call the Golden Disobedience, and that disobedience seems at the moment to be available to non-fiction writers in greater measure than to other writers of literary texts. Poets may come next as writers to whom the Golden Disobedience is available. Novelists and play-wrights, with honourable exceptions, seem to come a poor third. Rolls sidesteps all the received literary manners, and tells 'people's' history in a way which belongs to them rather than to most these days who would speak of The People. And in doing so he creates a great work of art in which a central native tradition is renewed, altered and immeasurably deepened.

Quadrant, December 1982

On Being Subject Matter

If I sometimes boast that I was Subject Matter at my university before I graduated, that is partly a rueful admission of the inordinate time I took in graduating. I entered Sydney University in 1957, stayed there, educating myself and avoiding employment, until the early sixties, and then came back in 1969 to complete the two courses I had left hanging when I ceased going to lectures in 1960. I never got a mark above bare Pass, and my degree of Bachelor of Arts was probably the least distinguished the university ever conferred. I do think, though, that in my case the degree should be called Bachelor of Arts Studies; I am demonstrably married to my art, and it is only towards academic studies that I behave like a bachelor. I have understandably never put the letters BA after my name but I might be tempted to append my true distinction, the degree of Subject Matter. Les A. Murray Sub.Mat. It is a degree at once distinguished and democratic. In anthropology, sociology, medicine and many other fields, every single human being holds it.

Of course, I would only have been Subject Matter in a very minor way before 1969. It should be remembered that regular courses in Australian literature, especially undergraduate courses, are an innovation. When I drifted out of university in 1962, they were available only, I gather, at the Universities of Toulouse and Leningrad. In Australia, Brian Elliott had pioneered Australian courses at Adelaide and plans were well advanced for a Chair of Australian Literature at Sydney. There may have been other developments in a similar direction elsewhere of which I am not aware. I do know that, in the university as in high school, my generation was never exposed to Australian authors. We had, unknowingly, said goodbye to those in primary school when we finished Dorothea Mackellar's *My Country* and went beyond the excellent, varied old New South Wales *Schools Magazine*.

Poetry, though Scots Australians of my grandfather's generation venerated a limited range of it, was for us a remote and unreal form of writing which referred to the seasons and flora and class-ecology

184

of an archipelago off the north-west coast of Europe, and seemed to deal in sentiments mostly quite unacceptable to boys of the future Third AIF. At least, it seemed sissy on the surface and that was enough for us; we could not be coaxed or driven to look deeper, and most teachers then had too little conviction about – or even understanding of – poetry to force it on us.

It was an option they nearly always allowed us to evade, often not even trying to teach it: 'You won't do the poetry question, so I won't waste my time taking you through it.' I almost managed to get right through high school without any serious engagement with poetry. I had read *The Rime of the Ancient Mariner* with some fascination in fourth year; also I had read *Paradise Lost* – indeed, all of Milton – in a single long weekend sometime in my teens, but that was for the science-fiction. I remember being irritated by the wordy, cumbrous manner of the story's telling; the poetry stuff seemed to make it stiff and preachy. In the end, I enjoyed *Samson Agonistes* more. That was a yarn I had enjoyed in the Bible, about a God-favoured Big Bloke who tore the gates off towns and slew enemies wholesale, and ended up as one prepared to pull the factory down rather than work. But I am getting ahead of my story.

I can scarcely have been Subject Matter earlier than the year 1966 because it was only in 1965 that Geoff Lehmann and I published a joint first book, called *The Ilex Tree*, thus giving readers some sort of very early conspectus of our work. We would both thereafter have been mentioned in odd lectures – indeed, we were told this was happening – and part of the impetus for this may have come from a favourable, possibly overgenerous, review of the book by Kenneth Slessor in the *Daily Telegraph*. That, and perhaps the kind review we were given by Roy Fuller in the *London Magazine*. We deserved some such rewards, perhaps: ANU Press, emphasizing its great magnanimity and daring in taking on a pair of young unknowns, had offered us a contract under which we received no royalties. And we were green enough to agree to it.

My work was in its infancy in *The Ilex Tree*, of course, and it is probably surprising that the first Honours thesis on it was written only five years later, by Dianne Ailwood in 1970. This was published in *Southerly* (3/1971). There have been a fair few since, some submitted to universities cosmically remote from my native Bunyah. It gave me special pleasure to hear the brilliant young Teresa Altamore, of Sans Souci and Calabria, formally defend her thesis on Aboriginal art and my debt to it in Ca' Foscari, the University of Venice's palazzo on the Grand Canal, one morning in 1979; it was an excellent piece of work and deservedly got her a *Magna Cum Laude*.

Without any flippancy, I am grateful to all of those who have chosen to study my work. Partly because of their numbers, I imagine, the Tasmanian education authorities began setting it for study in schools in 1978 and those in my home State followed suit in 1979. This showed considerable magnanimity since I had never been a fashionable writer and had been known to say hard things in print about educators.

Many of the hard things I wrote about educators arose from a campaign to upgrade Federal Government patronage of the arts which began in 1969 with a policy paper I wrote for the Labor Party. In this paper and in an expanded article published in the *Australian Quarterly* in 1972, I pointed out the extreme discrepancy between the wages and conditions of educators and the often-desperate, hand-to-mouth existence of the living authors and artists they taught about. My case for expanded patronage was based on the injustice of treating middlemen handsomely while leaving the primary pro-ducers to suffer in irrelevant outside jobs or actual penury. This may have been the last major contribution of genuine old-style Country Party thinking to Australian public life. Many educators were slow to recognize the obligation they incurred by commenting on living authors' texts, and few admit it with any candour even now.

In 1971, desperate for a job of any sort (though also heartsick at the prospect of having one and so losing most of my real working time), I approached Professor Leonie Kramer, of Sydney, and asked her to use her influence to get me some sort of employment around my old university. Not an exalted academic post, of course: research assistant, translator, even trolley-pusher in Fisher Library would do. She refused to help me and I wrote her an intemperate letter demand-ing that she remove all of my work from the university's Australian literature courses.

Professor Kramer's reaction was to call in the university's lawyers to determine whether I had the right to bar my work from study in this way and, when they concluded that I didn't, she issued a memo to her department ordering that study of it should continue. About fifteen months later, the new Literature Board came into existence, and has since been able to alleviate the lot of many more writers than the old Commonwealth Literary Fund was able to – though the central problem is still far from being solved.

By no means all of my dealings with universities have been unhappy. In late years, I have been Writer-in-Residence at the Uni-versities of New England, Stirling, Newcastle and New South

Wales for a term each, and have spent the odd week at a few other tertiary institutions in much the same capacity.

Writerships in Residence are a rather mixed blessing for writers and probably a rather uncomfortable graft within the academic body corporate. They have – or are hoped to have – some public relations value for the institution (Behold, we are patrons of the arts!) and possibly also represent a channel through which unadmitted conscience money can flow, but they draw upon English departments the envy of other scholars competing for scarce funds – 'Here we are, desperate for a new gas chromatograph, and you waste university money on some hairy scribbler who's not even an academic.'

Students' reactions to the writer on campus vary quite unpredictably, but there is always an initial period in which you see very little of them. Those who come along for a talk, at least at first, are usually mature age students or people with only a peripheral connection with the place; young students suss you out for a while before they put in a tentative appearance. And when they do come, the men especially are apt to be highly tentative and defensive until you gain their trust. And that goes double for members of university writers' clubs. At Stirling, I spent two months in seclusion from all but the friendly staff – then, in my final month, a caucus decision seemed to have been taken in my favour, and I found myself yarning with dozens of Scots and English students in the department and the university watering holes alike.

I usually learn a lot from my conversations when I'm at a university; I've always liked learning things by word of mouth. People in English departments like to fill gaps in my literary education – 'Thank you for showing me this Ben Jonson chap: boy, he can write!' – and I gain wondrous knowledge and often wondrous vocabulary from professionals in other fields, though some scientists aren't entirely happy to see the sacred terms of their specialty used like recycled Roman tombstones in the construction of baroque works of art.

There are odd points of discomfort in some residencies. It can be slightly sticky to meet an academic critic who has been busily extracting prose meanings from one's verse in order to refute them and prove that one is a snake-oil doctor, but hypocrite affability will usually defuse that situation. A much worse pitfall, though, and one which the writer may not see at all until he or she has tumbled into it, is caused by the sad envy of those academics who are failed writers and know it. One may earn their savage public wrath merely by existing and writing well – and one may suspect nothing until the lightning crackles out of a clear sky into a critical journal. There is a tiny minority in English departments (writers often exaggerate its size) who will never feel truly compensated by their regular wage and lush conditions.

Writers who become Subject Matter differ widely in their response to the fact, especially in the degree to which they are prepared to assist students. Some, understandably valuing an often hard-won privacy, decline to make any statements at all about their work; some will give interviews and the odd public address but will avoid the distractions of anything like stumping the country and visiting schools and universities. Judith Wright has increasingly eschewed personal statements, and Patrick White has never made public comments about his writing. And this is perfectly proper. Such people allow their work to speak for itself. Students of geography don't expect a mountain to come into their classroom and explain itself. It simply exists and lets its investigators make their observations and hypotheses, which in turn are replaced by different observations and different hypotheses. Other writers, perhaps more foolishly obliging, perhaps less confident, make themselves more available to those who would or must study them.

I don't accuse Tom Keneally of foolishness or lack of confidence, but I know that one year he hired Sydney Town Hall and addressed a vast concourse of school students who were studying a novel of his. Others – and perhaps Tom, too – have talked to students on radio or television, as I have done, and taken opportunities to present themselves and their work in university and college seminars. Given the ambiguous modern entanglement of literature with education, these are forms of publication, and the presence of the author in the flesh can give a fillip of reality to literary studies without which those may never come alive for some students. Particularly for the conscript sort. And there is also, for some of us, the subversive hope of using the institutional set-up to reach and fire potential readers, as it were, over the system's head or behind its back.

The dangers of ego-tripping are of course patent, but there is arguably some value, for other writers as well as oneself, in bearing live witness to the reality and the craft of writing. Without this, many students may go on believing, perhaps only unconsciously, that the whole business of creating literature is somehow remote and a matter of no more than dry intellectual calculation. Or they may be seduced by stereotypes, by some image of trendily disreputable ravers or elegantly asthenic figures with long hair and Parisian berets. And who has ever seen a real poet who looked like that?

My friend Wayne Hooper, who is in adult education, once told me the most educative thing I ever did was to enter a classroom. Stereotypes crumbled to dust at my diffident Clydesdale approach. If only the students knew it, the outward cheerfulness of that approach masked an inner quaking familiar to all fat people with memories of the sort of treatment they endured as fat adolescents in schoolyards long ago. For early training in sensitivity and a balanced view of the nobility of humankind there's nothing like it, but merely crossing a schoolyard, even today, can fill me with muscle-tightening horror. Perhaps an element in my readiness to address school students was a delight in repeatedly facing down a personal demon.

One doesn't, I think, make up one's mind all at once about what one's attitude to making public appearances is going to be. To a considerable extent, one can drift into it. Friends who are teachers invite their friend the writer along to talk to their students. Institutions offer a trip and, usually, a fee – though this isn't an invariable rule: my old school didn't. They also provide a crowd whom they may see as students but whom the writer sees as an audience. Balancing the reading with the teaching, the show business with the education, is one of the strains but also one of the arts of this new field of performance.

The writer must learn the techniques of satisfying both educators and students without currying favour with either. Seeking to play upon tensions he may imagine to be present between teachers and taught is shoddy and self-defeating, and I was never tempted to try it. The tension is not always there and, even when it is, teachers and taught are involved with each other, while the visiting writer is at best a guest, at worst a transient freak show, but always an outsider in the situation. He must never be defensive, but he should not appear unduly assertive, either, and eccentricity only invites the reactions which have kept artists on the margins of life ever since the renegade Plato put us there. I have always found a sort of egalitarian honesty the best approach, partly because I don't have to fake it.

Without sacrificing or glossing over the fact that you are only interested in art of the highest standard – for theories which hold that all people are artists, all attempts at art are valid and of equal dignity, etc., are fraudulent, desolating nonsense and most people of all ages know it – show yourself prepared to talk to young people and their teachers as intelligent people worthy to be told the fascinating ins and outs of a great and ancient profession to which you are wholly committed. And you will usually gain their trust.

Being friendly without unction and genuine without any little lies hidden about you will get you a hearing and often beneficially change students' perceptions of art itself. This simple recipe may not, of course, be enough when facing doctrinaire groups, but those are not usually encountered in schools or in adult education. They are by no means the rule even in universities, though there the danger of tripping over passionately held theories and shibboleths is notoriously greater. And it is of little use going near venues where the audience has gathered partly to see controversy and fireworks among the artists, rather than art. Unless they have changed a great deal since I gave up attending them, major arts festivals in this country are pretty nearly impossible. Would David Oistrakh take his violin to parliament? And expect ears coarsened by dissension, rhetoric and the noise of competing egos to hear his more delicate nuances? He might beguile them momentarily but at the risk of damaging his instrument and his touch and possibly suffering gross insult to boot.

One further rule I always observe, with groups of all ages, is to prepare nothing in advance. If you are really master of your material – and certainly you should be if the subject is yourself and your own work – you can afford to speak impromptu. That way, you have room to interest and surprise yourself and make discoveries even about things you have discussed dozens of times before. If I developed a spiel, I would disgust and bore myself even possibly before I bored the audience. I am grateful to many students for discoveries they have made or helped me to make about my poems. Any performer – and that is what probably a majority of poets have to be today, at least part-time – is nervous about scenes where the audience is allowed to talk back, but that is the nature of the new education-based variants of the public reading and I have gained benefit from the fact.

As with any performance, there is always at least some 'edge' in facing a class. You quickly learn to size up the potentials. In a school, if all the boys are down the back and all the girls in the front seats you know you are going to have to work hard, because the boys will be inclined to resist you. If there are several teachers in the room and they're all sitting up at the front – or even merely sitting together – all will probably be well. The prospects are grim if they are standing around the walls like warders with invisible truncheons in their hands. Standing teachers are an ominous sign. Even more so if the male ones (it's usually the male ones) wear expressions which suggest that they'd really rather be in the pub, or that they didn't know what to do with their lives but there was this teachers' college scholarship offering.

The size of a class is surprisingly unimportant, though intimacy and real exchanges are naturally more likely if it is small. I have had successful sessions, though, with groups of four or five hundred, good rapport while I was speaking and during question-and-answer sessions. You need to be able to see the whole group without constantly turning your head. Curved seating or any kind of wrap-around arrangement plays hell with essential eye contact and other physical cues. Standing to face a class is all right, I suppose, but I usually find it more relaxing, more informal and less suggestive of domination, if I can sit – preferably on a desk or table, so as to gain a little height from which to project my voice.

When you go to a school to address students you enter the class-room as a privileged visitor, often as a welcome diversion from the normal grind, and you are the beneficiary of class control and good behaviour established for you by teachers. None of this will make your visit a success if you bore or disappoint the students, but you do owe the teachers the loyalty of not undermining them with what you tell their students. Teachers bear the long burden of repeating things until they are understood and assimilated, and the misery of never getting through to some at least of their pupils. They can be forgiven if their day-in-day-out performances lack the pizzazz of your single hour or so; they lack the authority you have as the Horse's Mouth. Teachers sometimes have a bumper sticker on their cars which goes: 'If you can read this, thank a teacher.' In my case, I learned to read at home when I was four and didn't enter a school or meet a teacher till I was nine. But it was a teacher who opened my eyes to poetry just before I left school, to such effect that I was set on the course of life I would follow. In class, students will often seek opinions and interpretations from the distinguished visitor which will contradict what their teachers have told them. Often you will not know exactly when this is going on but it pays to be cautious about it. I do warn students against common errors in dealing with poetry – against the still-widespread habit of looking for symbolism in everything, for example. As Freud said, a cigar is sometimes just a cigar. And the subject of a poem or of an image in a poem is frequently more important as itself than as a pointer to something else.

Poetry makes things real, restoring their life and our perception of it, and the ways in which things in a poem refer to the wider world aren't usually as simple as the ordinary school notion of symbolism would suggest: the knack of reading on several levels at once isn't hard to suggest, though, and is usually picked up readily by senior students. I also warn them, as good teachers do, that there is no one Great Golden Interpretation that will get them through their exams. If they want something of that sort, as many sadly do, I give them several. As they warm to me, they will often give me theirs – which I often can exhort them to trust... 'Yes, the poem will bear that reading. What is in the poem supports it. It's good. Now, I've sometimes thought this, too...' When that starts to happen, what may have seemed an onerous and artificial exercise begins to be fun as students catch on and begin to trust their own perceptions.

Shockingly to some, I even admit that I don't really mind analysis of my poems. A good poem, I tell them, should be indestructible and should recover its mystery and resonance as soon as analysis stops. It should be alive and inexhaustible, able to wait when you tire of it and come up fresh and vibrant when you return to it, even years later.

I ask students who don't like school not to take their revenge on poetry just because they first met it in school. I regret that poetry has to be any part of the grading and relegating mechanism which our educations so pervasively is, but I tell kids that poetry has to be part of education because it is the very point of education, as exam-passing is not. There was a point in my own schooldays before which I had not 'got' poetry, and before that illumination it was impossible to convey anything to me about it, beyond the most basic rote material and surface fact. After I had twigged, however, everything about the subject would henceforth follow, and I needed no more guidance from teachers. The next help I would need would come from colleagues. I think this moment of illumination is a key thing, perhaps in any field of study, and I always hope to be the one who can somehow cause it to happen or start happening in the students I speak to. In nearly any class, of course, there will be some to whom it has happened already, and those students are easy to spot.

I am not a teacher, and my time with any class is necessarily very brief and concentrated. Giving as little heed as practicable to age or grade or presumptions about my hearers' intelligence, I pay kids and adults alike the compliment of telling them the best I know in one large heap they can sort out for themselves when I am gone. They rarely seem to mind my being very demanding on their powers of assimilation. I tell them how I wrote particular poems, those on their course if their courses are structured around the study of set poems, and surprise some by revealing how imperfectly I usually understand a poem when I first write it; all I have to know is that it is 'right', that it is achieved and has its own life. I might never have thought deeply and, as it were, interpretatively about particular poems if I had not been asked to talk about them to classes of students. Students usually find it illuminating to be told the nodal points, the initial images, thoughts, etc., from which particular poems grow.

I usually tell them a bit about the literary life, about publication, magazines, the book trade and such like and frequently underline the distinction between vocation and employment with the hope that the two will not have to be distinct in their own lives. In all of my talks, I stress the idea of literature as a profession rather than as a mere adjunct to education. I often gently correct prevailing critical misconceptions, such as the belief that Murray hates the city and loves only the bush, and tell them about the relatively few core concerns any writer has – the topics to which he or she will perennially return, as it were, on a spiral of development; moving away from them for a while and then coming back to them with a fresh insight at a later and maybe higher stage of evolving wisdom. Whenever things flag, I read another poem or two – always including some not on their course.

In trying, as it were in one hit, to counter the widespread neglect and disdain of poetry students encounter outside the educational national park in which it shelters and is vivisected these days, I suppose I try at once to normalize it and show how special it is. To do this, I have somehow to separate in the minds of my listeners the ideas of excellence on the one hand and snobbish superiority on the other. Our education does, for complex historical reasons, tend to fuse those ideas together, and the worst obstacle I continually encounter is the dispirited self-regulation of students and teachers alike in all but the poshest places. This curse is marginally more prevalent, I find, in the country than in the city – though poorer urban areas are as rife with it as any bush town. If there is one quasi-political (but really spiritual) line that I try to push it is opposition to mandarinism and all other forms of consumer hierarchy, opposition to the notion that anything good can be somehow 'too good' for some people or 'over the heads' of a majority.

As I have said, the interaction I have with classes of all ages is usually good. Disruptive behaviour and attempts to stir the distinguished guest are rare. Out of probably hundreds of schools I have visited, I only remember one in which a class rejected me, telling me quite frankly that they hated poetry and would never read it again as soon as they escaped from school. I still smart from that defeat, even though the class was only a dozen pupils strong. I simply failed to click with them, and can't help thinking it must have been my fault. More or less subtle attempts at disconcerting or exploiting the speaker occur very occasionally, as once in a girls' school outside Sydney, where one member of the class tried, in the midst of a discussion of vernacular culture and the like, to get me to comment about the parliamentarian Ian Sinclair, then under investigation for possible misconduct. Of course I sidestepped the trap, since I knew nothing of Mr Sinclair and since the case was both *sub judice* and quite irrelevant to what we'd been discussing. It turned out, of course, that Mr Sinclair's daughter was a member of the same class. The teacher told me this afterwards, and I'm afraid I described the other girl as a little bitch. Really gormless questions from students are quite rare, and when they come I do my level best to rescue the questioner from embarrassment, by desperately finding some deep point of interest in his query or by almost any other means to hand. I have been a lifelong asker of stupid questions myself, and anyway can't bear to see people laughed at. The only such questioner I remember being unable to rescue from ridicule was the poor boy in one class who asked about my poem 'The Widower in the Country', 'Was his wife dead?' I simply could not, off the cuff, do better than reply sadly, 'That's how you get to be a widower.' Adult classes, of course, contain people with more experience and more ability to talk about it, and sessions with those often become thoroughly enjoyable conversations. Talking about my poem 'The Burning Truck', in which boys who have been hanging around the streets discontentedly go running after the apparently miraculous vehicle that burns but is not consumed and won't stop, a lady who had been through the Blitz in England snorted decisively in one of my classes 'Hmpf! Creatures like that creep into their holes like rats at the first sign of an air raid; you'd never get them back into the streets to follow a burning truck or anything else!' I protested mildly that such things could happen in fiction, surely, and that there were many literal and less literal Burning Trucks people commonly chased after in our time if they were bored with ordinary life, but she was unconvinced. The word 'canaille' burned too hotly in her mind.

I did have a consultative say, over duck casserole in a French restaurant, in the choice of my poems to be set for the New South Wales Higher School Certificate in 1979-80, but I neither had nor wanted any part in marking exams on them. Indeed, I have only ever seen three or four of what must have been thousands of school essays on my work; one, by a boy at Pennant Hills High School in Sydney who had previously preferred the bush ballads to any modern verse, struck me as truly excellent. He said things about my poem 'An Absolutely Ordinary Rainbow' which seemed accurate and which interested me from an artistic point of view. And that is what an artist wants from critics, even more than praise. Approval without real understanding can be a desolating experience. I have had a very good run from the critics, by and large, and have no scores to settle, but the reviews and essays I value and remember are those in which the quality of response answered in some way to the labour, the illumination and the delight which went into writing the poem or poems under discussion. I remember, for example, the illumination that came to me from an essay in which Harry Heseltine pointed out that 'An Absolutely Ordinary Rainbow' was written from the point of view of the crowd rather than the weeping man who stands at its centre, and that perhaps to side, as it were, with the crowd rather than the central figure might be an Australian characteristic. That helped me with my thinking on many Australian things afterwards. Some less helpful forms of criticism are at least amusing. There is that magnanimity, for example, which allows you a triumph but fills the chariot with slaves who whisper dire things in your ear: *You are the last of your line. You will run out of themes. All glory is fleeting.* Or the mild Tiptoe method, for minds eaten out by brilliance and the hard labour of spending the seventies finding some saving virtue in rubbish; such minds have usually lost all recollection of simplicity, and cannot bear to see the obvious. I remember one senior academic who successively asked David Malouf and me what we thought James Dickey had meant by a reference to cattle 'feeding together in the night of the hammer'. When we both told him, quite independently, that it primarily referred to the way cattle are sold by the knock of an auctioneer's hammer and taken to be slaughtered with a hammer-blow to the head at the abattoir, he was amazed. Surely some deeper interpretation was called for. Coarser forms include Fishnet (or Dragnet) criticism, which sees all things in terms of schools, and the Secular Rosary style, which is obsessed with decades.

The least helpful sort of criticism is the kind I call Inquisitorial, which presumes to investigate one's work in terms of an ideology or programme alien to it. Even where this isn't a cloak for ordinary rivalry and jealous ambition, it can tempt people to falsify the work in order to attack it. Tactics used include what I call the Targeting method of criticism, in which epithets are suggested or actually applied to a writer – *conservative, Establishment, reactionary, decadent, Jewish-cosmopolitan* etc.: the inventories of totalitarianism are long and the items remarkably interchangeable – in order to get him or her despised and harassed by activists and fellow travellers who need not look at the evidence for themselves, and may indeed not dare to. A variant tactic is to drop the target author in the path of an oncoming fashion or Cause. A related technique is the Chain of Presumption, which pretends that the writer's whole range of opinions can be deduced from a specimen position he is seen to hold, or perhaps merely to express: if he believes A, or F, he must also believe B, C, D, E and G. To dislike nudity on the beach is to support racial oppression in South Africa. Application of these methods can already, in Australia, get writers barred from particular magazines, can cause favourable reviews and indeed all reviews of their work to be suppressed, can cost them school and university settings and government funding, can get them defamed and insulted in public, and can provoke professional sanctions against other writers who speak well of them in print. All of these things have happened here. As with so much of criticism, the story which is told is less interesting than the one which might be. The main merit of all such criticism lies in displaying to the public the real implications of the ideologies espoused, and what life would be like for artists and people generally if they came to power. Such criticism is the case law, epitomised in advance, of prospective police systems. More subtly deadening, though, are the effects of the received literary sensibility, that pool of assumptions and habits of feelings of the literary-intellectual caste out of which all the ideologies ultimately flow. It is my old enemy, the RLS. It hates my religion, it disdains and patronizes my people, it yearns after aristocracy, it marinades its every word in contempt. If it could, it would make all art its prisoner. I tend to judge the worth of writers and critics alike by the distance they maintain between themselves and the RLS. At the same time, I know that the entrance to literature for most people leads through that sensibility. As we begin learning to write, we assimilate it like tribespeople learning a culture-language, one in which the warmest, most native and homely things cannot be expressed. We have to wrestle with it if we wish to tell any but its prescribed versions of the truth, and it pulls at us like a strange gravitational force, trying to think for us, to snub us out of our most distinctive insights, to proscribe unapproved subject matter, to control and harness unpredictable delight. However extolled, no work written in conformity with the RLS can be better than second rate, and if you are interested in attempting to write supremely well you have to essay a freedom beyond its reach. The joyful surprise there is that such freedom can restore you to the community of a broad readership.

The great secret weapon against the RLS, against Literature with a capital L, is that impenetrable mystery the reading public. Because the RLS cannot fathom or reliably conquer that, it affects to disdain it, and even ascribes class characteristics to it intended to evoke disdain. The dreaded Bourgeois, the unspeakable Mid-Victorian, the despised Housewife. I suspect, though, that the reading public is very much terra incognita, poorly explored and inadequately mapped by anyone. I find it continually surprising. It may in the end be purely a matter of individuals, of myriad singularity, for which all descriptions involving collectivity are inappropriate. The most surprising people, if we give any credence at all to stereotypes, turn out to be readers of literary books – and sometimes of the *Women's Weekly, Bugs Bunny* and the *Proceedings of the Australian Institute of Engineers* too, all in the one day. I have had letters from readers of poetry as diverse as station cooks, surgeons and banana growers. An old lady on a train, one of the 'Geriatric' caste so despised by today's Lawrentians, may be seen deeply immersed in T.S. Eliot. A floorwalker from David Jones, his carnation of office still in his buttonhole, may be seen deep in Dostoevsky in his luncheon break. I have seen these phenomena, and had letters from their like. No one even knows what causes people to buy books. We can investigate *who* buys books, but on the matter of which books or why we can only speculate. The Literature Board early in its life, around 1973 or '74, conducted a large study on the matter and arrived at no firm conclusions. Even the effect of reviews remained unknown. Reviewing and advertising must have some effect, we think, and yet we don't know for certain. Scores of books of verse published in the seventies and extravagantly praised by friendly critics ended up on the remainder tables, having sold twenty to fifty copies in eight or ten years. On the other hand, Kevin Hart's collection *Lines of the Hand*, which was practically sent to Coventry by reviewers, has sold extremely well. Readers seem somehow to have sniffed out its quality in the few bookshops which carried it.

Many publishers, including my own, rely on reviews as free advertising, and yet there seems to be some evidence that advertising as such is more effective. Roger McDonald's excellent *1915* really had quite a lacklustre time with the reviewers when it came out; few praised it unequivocally. On the other hand, it had energetic backing from its publishers, the University of Queensland Press, with large ads for months on end in all the leading publications. It became the book of the moment. People were made conscious of it, to the point where they would look for it, pick it up, dip in – and I have a suspicion, which I can't prove, that the crucial things happen at that point of dipping in. All I can really describe is an almost simultaneous complex of things which happen when I pick up a book in a bookshop. My eye runs over the print, sampling it here and there, inviting it to continue and focus the impulse which made me pick it up, looking for whatever may connect with my interest or surprise me by extending its range; I even seem to feel my nostrils constrict as I search for the book's tone, its flavour, its likely relations with reality (by which I don't mean just the everyday kind), as well as the quality of its argument, which doesn't have to be high, the quality of its humanity and its quotient of literary devices. All sorts of subliminal, half-physical things are probably also happening, more or less as they happen when we encounter a new person and discover what our attitude to him is. This process of sussing out a book happens in a quick lucid blur, rapidly forgotten if the book fails to grab me, and is really, beyond all reviews of puffery, the chance the book gets. I am probably a quite impure sample, though; after all, I am in the business of writing and publishing books. All the same, I don't think my practices have altered very much since long before I became a writer as well as a reader. The main evolution that has brought in its train is a growing ability to see through Literature to – literature. And to that much-scorned quality of *enjoyment* which may be what other, non-writing readers even more ruthlessly seek from books.

If the Unknown Reader is our best defence against the RLS, it is pleasing to know that in this country, for reasons we can only speculate about, poetry enjoys a much larger readership in proportion to population than in most Western countries. The normal print run of a new book of verse, a slim volume in trade parlance, is the same here as in West Germany, a country with four times our population. When I told people in the United Kingdom about the sales figures our best-known poets attain, figures which I know for most of them from trade sources, they were incredulous. No poet in Britain, not even the most celebrated, could match them. 'So what's the strength,' asked my clansman Glen Murray, editor of the Scots Nationalist magazine *Cencrastus*, 'of this legend about Australia as an uncultured land of illiterate philistines?' 'It is bullshit,' I replied, answering his smile with one of my own. In this late-colonial country, so patronized and excoriated by its ruling literary sensibility, we not only have a better poetry book market than most other Western nations, but our poets often sell better than all but a very few of our novelists.

Having said these things, though, and having praised the Unknown Reader as one of the safeguards of my artistic freedom, I have to pay tribute for my sales also to people driven to read me by the fierce giant Curriculum. As Subject Matter, I have to realize that some of my readership at least is conscripted. I apologize to all conscripts, and fervently hope they find my work such that I can be forgiven. Teachers tell me that they like teaching my work because students seem to enjoy it. I can't imagine they all enjoy it; I have too much faith in human differences to believe that. So long as those who dislike it dislike it on its merits, rather than for any thought-police reasons, I'm pretty well satisfied.

As well as the financial benefits which start to accrue visibly, if not copiously, when one passes from the degree of Subject Matter to that of Set Author, there is this final satisfaction which one has almost from the beginning, even before one is properly accredited as an Occasional Topic. With one's first reviews, there is the thought that, while society may treat writers and other artists as bachelors' children in the matter of worldly rewards, our profession must have some high importance, since it is subject to public scrutiny of a sort granted to no other. It is hard to imagine regular published reviews of barristers, for example, or cardiac surgeons. Think of it: 'With his move to the cardiac field, Mr Brodribb-Cleaver appears to have left behind the timid bourgeois formalism of his earlier appendicectomies and acquired an almost daredevil attack in his incisions. His suturing is as sensitive and finely considered as ever, but his bypass work shows a new insolence, and he brought a neo-*tachiste* profundity to our perception of the mitral valve. With the appearance of this superb stylist, Australian heart surgery has come of age.'

Bulletin Literary Supplement, Easter 1983

The Import of Seasons

Does Australia really have seasons? And does it have four of them? These questions have been asked seriously, and not only by visitors from the Northern Hemisphere. Over much of our continent, the seasonal changes that occur are less marked than in many of the Old World countries from which the ancestors of most of our people came. It took Europeans a long time to discern and come to terms with the patterns of the Australian year, and in the process two things happened: they became Australians, and they changed the ancient pattern with their importations. The four traditional seasons of the northern world are themselves perhaps the greatest and most significant cultural import the continent has seen, and only recently have we thought about the match they make with the primordial (perhaps we should say Aboriginal) climatic facts of Australia.

To visitors and new settlers from the northern world, Australia can be bewildering. It has the usual strangeness of lands below the Equator: the sun and moon travel anti-clockwise, the man in the moon is upside down, the Milky Way is more brilliant and many of the constellations quite unfamiliar. Added to all this is the specific oddity of the Great South Land, where native trees do not shed their leaves *en masse* in autumn, but may shed their bark in spring, where flowers often have no petals and rivers no water, where furred animals may lay eggs and barbed wire is homely and peaceful. But even to native-born Australians, for whom these things are part of reality's basic orientation, much of the subtlety of the seasonal pattern can be obscure. In the milder southern parts of the continent, it can often seem that the seasons comprise essentially summer and non-summer. A reign of heat, flies, snakes, beach culture and burgeoning growth is followed by a cooler time in which the discomforts disappear and both beachgoing and burgeoning tail off. And there is that bit of sniffling chill right in the middle. Over much of the dry inland a similar pattern is registered: a burning torrid season is followed by a pleasant season of brilliant skies and comfortable travel. In the tropic north, the great divisions of the year are conventionally called the Wet and the Dry. To those who work close to the weather, though, to farmers, graziers, gardeners and those who observe nature, it is obvious that the four-season pattern does fit Australia, with interesting gaps and reversals. It becomes the more obvious the farther south we travel. There are also four seasons in the tropic north, at least four say many people who live there, though they are not the traditional ones of our language. And alongside the four great face-cards of the year, there are also jokers bearing the sun's fiery image and the likeness of a wise serpent.

The four traditional seasons, Spring, Summer, Autumn and Winter, are suit cards first painted in the northern world before recorded history began. They are ancient human constructs, made out of observation and poetry, agricultural experience and human festivity, sacrificial myth and mankind's need for regularities. They stem from what has been called the Neolithic Revolution, the shift from nomadic hunting and gathering to settled farming. And they stem very largely from latitudes in which there was and is a marked annual cycle of death and rebirth in nature. The four-season pattern was developed, independently it would appear, in several parts of the northern world; in China, in Central Asia, in northern and southern Europe, in the colder Middle East, in North America before European settlement there. The four seasons are a cultural fact of the first importance, intricately bound up with the history of the calendar, with the zodiac, with astronomy, with religion and with art. They pervade the earliest poetry we know, and have remained a constant theme of poets.

In one half of the Western tradition which Australia inherits, nature is described in its seasonal aspects before it is described whole. The second-earliest poet in our classical tradition is Hesiod the Boeotian, who differs from his shadowy near-contemporary Homer in singing of the cyclic life of man under the power of the seasons and the gods. Homer subordinates non-human nature to a delineation of human heroism and dignity under divine intervention, but Hesiod's emphases may well reflect an older view, or a competing one. They are emphases of peace, of continuity and common life, where Homer's are aristocratic and warlike. What is background for Homer is foreground for Hesiod, and the ambiguity of background and foreground is not yet resolved nearly 3,000 years later. Can peace and order make a foreground, or must it be conflict and strife? Much poetry, painting and music lean the one way, most of drama and film lean the other. During the writing of this book, I have been haunted by the fear that survivors picking over the ruins of some future disaster may find a tattered copy, pick it up and read it in tears, saying 'Yes, that was the old peaceful Australia; that was the Lucky Country, before we blew it!' The four seasons are, in a way, a mantra we recite against disaster and its stoppage of time.

In the other half of the Western tradition, the Judaeo-Christian stream, the seasons, like rain and heat, toil and cold and hunger and the terror of death, are facts of a new, desolate perception of Creation which man begins to have as a result of sin. We embark, as soon as we attain full human freedom, on a course of evolution through suffering and blood, assuaged and tormented by glimpses of another order of life in loving accord with God. At a certain point, God becomes incarnate among us as a human being of that other, sinless order, and has power over the elements, over our sicknesses, even over death. Through his own sacrificial death, undergone and then reversed, he completes and ends the reign of blood sacrifice, making it obsolete, and makes himself our bridge between history and the eternal order. Historically, first in the Middle East and Europe, then in most of the rest of the world, this tradition has put a stop to the ugly blood rituals and human immolations which once attended the changes of the year, and has made the seasons an innocent natural succession. Traces of dark ancient ritual persist in some modern seasonal observances, but few of these have been imported into Australia in any real way. We are not slaves to the seasons, because of a victory won for us many centuries ago elsewhere.

There is of course a dimension of natural events and processes which is not bound to the cycle of the year. It includes earthquake and tidal waves, drought and flood, volcanism and such slow, continuous changes as the shifting of sea level and alterations in the global weather pattern. Australia is comparatively free of the more cataclysmic of these effects, though obviously subject to gradual planetary changes. Only a few million years ago, the lower Murray valley was under an arm of the sea, and the long stabilized sandhills of the desert inland are angled to ancient north-west winds which formed them and now no longer blow. Our continent is particularly subject to one great natural phenomenon which does not fit the yearly cycle, but may mute it into near-irrelevance over vast areas for years at a time: this is drought, the balefully recurrent super-season of the fiery sun which has been working on a formerly well-watered continent for twelve or fifteen thousand years, drying much of it into a delicate aridity in which fire becomes part of the weather, to be managed well by Aboriginal Australians and rather less effectively by more recent settlers.

Bushfires fit into the imported seasonal cycle fairly neatly, but drought is a condition which may affect and alter any of the seasons, thinning them and turning them into ghosts. Native plants and animals have mechanisms and habits to cope with drought, and to take advantage of the release which drought-breaking rain and flood eventually bring. This is the domain of the Rainbow Snake, that wise kindly serpent mentioned earlier, and of the petrichlor cycle.

In tropical Australia, and in an extent of temperate Australia that is now hard to delimit precisely, the mythical Rainbow Snake was, and in a few places still is, the most revered of all totemic ancestors. She was believed to be the mother creatrix who ruled over the fertility of all life. She lived in waterholes, in and around which snakes are most often to be found, and her shape was repeated in the winding of creeks and riverbeds. As a bogey to frighten the uninitiated, she was called the Bunyip. She appeared as a rainbow in the sky, or as rainbow hues in spray and falling water. The thunder was her voice and the lightning her flickering tongue. Animals and men went inside her body and were reborn, in the flesh or in the new spirit of initiation. When rain fell and her rainbow was seen, the delicate dryland plants knew to bloom and set seed, or to sprout from the earth, the birds knew to mate and lay their eggs, and the estivating frog knew to come up out of its chamber in the clay and pour its eggs into the full waterholes. All of life was switched on, after a timeless suspension, and reproduced itself quickly while things were propitious. Zebra finches are the fastest to respond; they can begin building a nest within two days of a storm. Bustards, banded plovers, diamond doves and budgerigars are also quick off the mark. Waterbirds wait until rising water in their swamps confirms that food will be plentiful; their sexual response is keyed to the rising water level, which may be fed by rains hundreds of miles away. Grey teal can pair, become sexually mature and lay eggs within fourteen days of a rise, and their response can occur at any season of the year. The return of water, from the sky or from upstream, constitutes a season in itself, half in and half outside the cyclic calendar of the white man.

In the mid-1960s, Drs Joy Bear and Richard Thomas of the CSIRO discovered that the characteristic smell of rain on dry earth, one of the truly poignant scents of Australia, was caused by a yellow oil which they could distil from rocks and soil. They termed this oil petrichlor, 'essence of stone', and were of the opinion that it came originally from plants. It seems that the oils which plants exude as protection from the desiccating sun, and which hang in a dusty blue haze over dryland forests worldwide, eventually fall back to earth to be stored in rocks and soil: some of this oil may penetrate deeply into the earth's crust and go towards the formation of petroleum. Heavy rain releases some of it from the earth's surface to wash down into swamps and streams, where it triggers the reproductive activity of fish and other aquatic animals and thus starts the cycle of life after a drought. A fraction of this oil rising from the earth provides the smell we notice, an odour to which many animals are probably keyed. Even rising humidity may release enough to alert keen-nosed dryland creatures that rain is on the way. Petrichlor may thus be one of the chief agents of the Rainbow Serpent, as well as a still potent fragrance from the Dreamtime.

Flaunt, Scunge and Death-Freckles

Above all things for many Australians, summer means the beach. It may well be the thing for which we are best known in the wider world: a huge innocuous nation-state mad on swimming, and blessed with great beaches. A sea-bathing rather than a seafaring nation. That strip of sand fifty to two hundred metres wide is a whole world, with tribes and subcultures. It is a capital location of the Kingdom of Flaunt, which is more powerful than civil governments, and exists pre-eminently in the summer time. That kingdom has its aristocracies and its hangers on, its castes and scavengers, and everyone knows how he must behave to enter it. To oppose it is to lose, and to ignore it is to be relegated to the margins of life. Or so it is believed in the Kingdom of Flaunt. In fact, the margins are very roomy, and receive nearly everyone in the end, when they leave the constantly appraising, status-conscious Kingdom, in which civilization and Christmas alike barely retain their reality.

The beach is a billion-dollar industry, supporting manufactures, services and several hundred towns. It is dotted with classic types. There is the rod fisherman, seen at dawn and dusk in his T-shirt and khaki shorts, casting for tailer in the surf. There are the muscled biscuit-coloured lifesavers talking in laconic graffiti around their coiled reel, wearing their chinstrapped cloth skull caps like a sect: red and yellow quarters for Patrol, club colours for Competition. There are the slim bulging people, not invariably young, who rarely enter the water, but come mostly for the display and the sexual meat market of pickups and sidelong checkings out. There are the athletes and health-conscious runners swinging along with rhythmic far-spaced splashes at the edge of the wavewash. There are the surfers, surging and bobbing in the waves. There are the unclassifiable swimmers and beachgoers of every shade from pimply white to mahogany, many with dabs of white on their noses, like a species of waterhens. A faint miasma of lotions and sun-block rises from the scene, and there is always a dog or two racing about loosely, barking at the speeding wash. A few people will be wearing sunglasses; the rest will be narrow-eyed in the tremendous glare, the skin around their eyes puckered with furrows and wrinkles. 'You'll never be a real Aussie,' the girls at her first school told my European wife when she was a teenager, 'you haven't got laughter lines around your eyes!' In the intense light, grains in the beach may catch and dazzle with incandescent power, and objects may lose their outlines, heading towards a buzzing abstract quality. Patches of reality exist only where there is shade. The abstraction has a hint of null gravity, and the patches of visible detail may seem boring to the point of annoyance. They anchor us to the mundane, against what may be the mystic beginnings of death by heatstroke. The time is midday, and will remain so for hours.

At the edges of the scene, children and adults are moving over cracked floors of rock, peering into pools, perhaps collecting shells in a bucket or a cloth hat. Live things move and settle in the pools, smails, anemones, green sea squirts confusingly called cunjevoi, a name also applied to the huge-leaved poisonous lilies of the wet forest which are carrying their large heads of fruit in fleshy buff lanterns at this season; down in the pools, too, there is the harmless brown octopus which few will touch for fear that it may prove to be the blue-ringed octopus which carries a deadly hypodermic dart. Tiny crabs scatter like spilled pennies through the rocks. From time to time, a tall open-sided van will park next to the beach, selling gelati or Mr Whippy ice cream. Somewhere on the beach or just behind it there will be a wooden tower with a bell and a thick white bell rope, or a more substantial watchtower with PA system. The lifesavers will squint at the sea continually, their eyes tuned to a raised hand or a jutting dorsal fin. Overhead, if it is an important city beach, a light plane or a helicopter will be winding around in long sweeps, similarly keeping watch for the first shark. Let one be seen, and the bell will clang urgently, the PA system will boom mighty words, and people will explode out of the water, shouting and shrieking, then crowd at the tide-line looking for a welter of blood on the waves' surface or the last thrashings of a hideous fight. It does not happen often; years pass between fatalities. But it is possible to be eaten alive within metres of the beach and one's family, and few who go to the beach fail to give the matter a passing thought.

The Australian beach culture as we know it goes back, perhaps surprisingly, only to the beginning of the twentieth century. And even that makes it an old one. On very many of the world's warmer coasts, little or no sea bathing is done even now, except perhaps in pockets of Westernizing development. The only truly ancient surfing culture I know of is the Polynesian. Body surfing as such was introduced to Australia around 1900 by a Polynesian gardener's assistant named Tommy Tana, and board surfing got its start with an exhibition held by the Hawaiian Duke Kahanamokau at Freshwater Beach in 1915. At Manly in 1902 the local newspaper proprietor W.H. Goocher openly defied the law which prohibited bathing in the sea during daylight hours. When the authorities failed to respond, people began flocking to the beach in a rush that has never abated. Lifesaving was well established by 1910. In many periods, the bronzed volunteer lifesaver has shared a place with the bronzed Anzac and the sunburnt bushman (for some reason, bushmen are never bronzed) in the gallery of Australian stock images, and there are signs that he is undergoing a slight revival now, after being unfashionable in the sixties and seventies. By the 1950s, lifesavers had rescued over 100,000 people from difficulties in the ocean; the figure must have more than doubled by now, given the increase in population. The surf lifesaving movement has been a lasting and very major humanitarian effort.

Two other figures typical of the ocean fringe during summer, but less bound to that one season, are the surfboard rider and the skindiver. More proprietorial about the sea, they are also apt to be more devoted to it and more respectful of its ways. They often taken themselves more seriously too, and much writing about the surfing life in particular is cloyingly sub-mystical and Serious. The flippered followers of Jacques Cousteau are likely to prefer a more scientific atmosphere, compound of wetsuits, demand valves, marine biology and a somewhat overdone tolerance of sharks. The surfer or Waxhead style bears a nimbus of sexual folklore and special idiom (Let's chuck the plank in the Sandman and cruise down to Cronulla; if the waves are ratshit we can check out the Jebbie tarts) but at its heart it is almost solipsist, interested only in infinite variations of the one solitary, speeding, sliding experience. The skill with which a good board rider walks and winds his or her way along a speeding wall of water, bending in and out under curling silvery roofs of crest, approaches the musical both in its intensity and its utterly useless purity. After a great ride, as after a great violin solo, nothing remains but a powerful impression – and the next performance. Which is embarked on at once, and then again, as long as the light and the waves are good. In the great compound world of the beach, board surfers are a visible but often rather aloof element, appearing and disappearing at behests different from those of the crowd.

Summer is also the time of still-water sports. We have mentioned the liba–liba houseboats of the lower Murray river, and sung of the water skiers in verse. A very beautiful and very recent sport is windsurfing. Beyond the obvious fact that it consists in standing on a surfboard and making it go fast with the aid of a hooped sail fitted to a light mast resembling a fishing rod, I don't understand the matter at all. But it makes a handsome show on a wide reach of water, with all the many-coloured sails standing up like quills, before a gust knocks half of them over. At the same time, the near ocean and every harbour, bay and estuary where humans live zings with powerboats and carries its drift of tall triangular sails. This is also the season of the swimming pool, the riverbank with sandy reach, of the farm dam and the old swimming hole down the creek. And all of them take their toll of drowned children. Of the 300-odd people who die by drowning each year in Australia, the largest proportion are small children who perish in private swimming pools. Still water and inland fresh water account for more Australians than the ocean. The other typical summer accident that befalls swimmers comes from diving into shallow water and breaking one's neck. Some drownings are a result of this, but more typically it ends in paraplegia. Each year, the wheelchair claims more victims than sharks, stone fish, sea wasps or all the other sea monsters combined. Years pass without a fatality from the sea monsters, but incautious dives into unknown water are second only to car accidents as a cause of paraplegia and quadriplegia. What became of that big strapping nephew of yours, Jim? Oh, he's painting Christmas cards with his forehead now, poor bastard. If that sounds harsh, it is meant to: it is a warning.

I should not give the impression that inland swimming is all hideous mishaps. For many, and amongst them myself, it is *the* way to enjoy water. The deep pressure of current moving between basalt boulders in a mountain headwater, or floating in the shade of willows and acmena trees above the causeway that divides fresh from salt in a coastal river, these are the pleasures of an alternative aquatic society which includes most country people and many others of pale Celtic skin. Best of all the arcana of this society perhaps, is the shocking cold of a pool under a high waterfall, and going in past the whizzing curtain of the falls to dream in a room behind the world. For many inland children, there is the squealing joy of a high bank buttered with mud for bodies to slide down, or a rope knotted in a red-gum branch above a deep hole, for children and teenagers to catch and swing away out, before dropping with a huge splash into dusty bottle green. For country town kids, this sort of swimming may win out for years, despite good advice and parental worry, over the shadeless municipal baths and their crinkling compound of chlorine and urine set at one side of the little Memorial Park of camphor laurel and kurrajong trees.

The season of jampacked caravans in beachside parks, of sunburnt right elbows denoting the driver and sunburnt left elbows denoting the passengers, of sandy towels under beachside shacks and children protestingly hosing their feet before coming inside, is also a season when formal and even casual clothing gives way to Scunge. A useful portmanteau word denoting what Americans would call funk or grunge and British people would call grot. Scunge when it refers to clothes need not connote dirt. Summer scunge is often quite clean, in a leached-out sunfaded sort of way. Unlike student scunge and artistic scunge, which is often carefully composed and full of socio-political signals (a better word for this is *tat*), summer scunge is an ultimate dismissal of ambition in favour of comfort and climatic adaptation. Formless shorts, bare feet, towelling hats and loose poncho-like shirts are true summer scunge. Rubber thongs, an Australian adaptation of Japanese wooden *geta* sandals, can never be much more than scunge. Surfers' board shorts and jeans cut off short with scissors are summer scunge, as are old swimsuits worn all day whether swimming or doing the housework. Ancient gardening trousers worn with a pyjama top are even closer to the ideal. Football shorts and athletic singlets may be scunge or costume or working clothes, depending on who is wearing them to do what. Tracksuits carry a suspicion of athletic ambition and discipline foreign to true scunge, but may pass if worn untidily enough by people who obviously never take exercise. A tracksuit top worn with a bikini bottom or ten-year-old hot pants is real scunge, as are ancient house dresses and chenille dressing-gowns worn all day. Old men sitting outside inner-city terrace houses on a summer evening in white singlets and antique suit pants may or may not see themselves as wearing scunge. Jeans of any notable tightness or most sweaters worn next to the skin are a bit suspect. So are sarongs and Indian cotton wraps (travel tat, solidarity-with-the-Third-World tat) or any allusions to special tribal costume, such as motorcycle gang colours. Those are all tainted with Flaunt, and the essence of scunge is a holiday from that kingdom, as from work and all the weighty attributes of identity. As far as possible, scunge makes you invisible to the world and to yourself.

Scunge is not, of course, confined to the season of fly screens and citronella. In warmer places, it may slap-slap on rubber thongs through the length of the year. With a modification or two, the addition of boots perhaps, it can enter the workplace, at least the farming or the labouring workplace. Or that of, say, university fieldwork. A white boiler suit can be a man's holiday scunge at home and his working rig at the garage. For more commercial, white-collar occupations, though, scunge is not permitted. There, we are in the middle to late stages of an evolution which has brought men, with initial great slowness, from dark serge suits and wing collars worn even in the tropics to a summer rig which Australians have been able to pass off as national dress. One Australian visitor to Chicago succeeded in getting service at the poshest of the city's hotels under the National Costume rule while wearing white shirt, shorts, tie, long socks and polished shoes. This outfit, with its half naval, half golfing air, is an attractive transitional style, still resisted in staid circles and still in the process of development. The colours are no longer invariably white, if they ever were (when South Australia's Premier Don Dunstan wore the outfit to Parliament in the early seventies, his shorts were pink) and the tie and long socks are under siege. Indeed, the Army has officially dropped the tie from its version of tropical rig. The tie is under siege everywhere, but is yet to give way completely. While it is worn in Parliament and the senior levels of the Public Service, it will hold out in the world of business too. Policemen in the southern States have finally shed it, at least for summer wear; they are still not allowed shorts, though. Their dignity and authority are held to require long trousers and boots. Policewomen are better off, in their tailored skirts. In general, women's clothing has made much greater progress towards climatic sanity in Australia than has men's. The obligatory stockings, hats and gloves of a generation ago have been swept away in all but the most exclusive circles. It is only in men's clothing, though, that the country has developed something approaching distinctive costume. Not National Costume strictly: the time for that has probably passed, and the peasantry from which national and regional dress usually arises has scarcely been allowed to develop here.

Men in Australia have the tropical rig already described, and out-back variants of it involving Army slouch hats or cloth giggle hats and lots of khaki; this was for a while known as the Harry Butler style, after a conservationist who made a hit on television. There is an attractive style of safari suits, but that seems to have stalled in the world of journalism and leftish politics. Major union leaders are often seen in it. And we have a style, originating in the nineteenth century, which bespeaks the squatter, the drover and the Pitt Street farmer alike. This is sometimes called the Fat Cattle style. It includes moleskin or gabardine trousers often, jeans less often, elastic-sided boots always, carved or braided leather belts frequently, sometimes worn with a leather watch case or pocketknife holster, low-crowned broad brimmed felt hat mostly, though it is proverbial that the wider the brim, the smaller the wearer's landholding will be. Stockmen and drovers often wear an Army hat, or an American Western number with high crown. The wealthy, rural-professional or Sloane version of this outfit will usually add a checked vyella shirt with woollen tie and tweed jacket. A khaki working shirt or T-shirt and a leather jacket or checked woollen Canadian jacket connote the drover and the stationhand, though they are often worn by truckies, farmers and rural machinery operators too. Aboriginal stockmen and rodeo competitors of all races favour gorgeously coloured and embroidered Western shirts of American pattern, and all who actually ride horses are apt to affect high-heeled elastic-sided boots, over which they trip when drunk in town. Although elements of this style point towards the American West on the one hand and the English counties on the other, at heart it is an Australian style. For one thing, it is older than all but the Spanish elements of American Western garb, which have influenced it least: it comes down from the pioneer squatter period of Australian settlement, which was going strong more than a generation before the Mexican War of 1848 opened the American West to English-speaking ranchers and pioneers. The elastic-sided boots and moleskin pants have their origins in the British cavalry, the shape of the hats comes down from Naval straw hats and cabbagetree hats of very early Sydney Town. It is an all-seasons style, not exclusively a summer one. It is surprisingly cool and comfortable in the heat, though. Stockmen say that the white moleskins 'turn' the sun's heat, and the elastic panels of the boots allow the feet to breathe. They breathed more effectively and pungently a few decades ago, when most bush workers wore them without socks. Many still do in the far outback, where general stores still carry tins of proprietary corn plasters.

If summer is the great forcing house of Australian clothing styles – and one of the justifications for outright public nudity, though that is still pretty well restricted to camps and designated beaches surrounded by binoculars and slow yachts – it is also the testing time for Australian skins. A true English rose complexion is uncommon north of Melbourne, and Australian women spend large amounts on skin emollients in an often fruitless battle against the ageing effects of the sun. People often yearn for a balance of irreconcilables, fine, soft youthful skin *and* a deep tan, season about or all at once. A rapid progression towards leathery wrinkled hide is the demon which stalks this aspiration, but a far crueller demon also lurks on its path. Australia has the world's highest incidence of skin cancer. On farmer's hands and the bare-skin skullcaps of the bald, the soldered patches of incipient cancer are often seen, and referred to by some as 'death freckles'. By the end of the century, it is expected by medical science that melanoma will be the most common form of cancer in Australia. The crab lies in wait for our Northern European complexions, and may be an evolutionary mechanism. Pale skins may be decadent here, and my own guess is that, by immigration and selection, we will eventually be a brown-skinned people. Right from birth. Some Aboriginal elders have always held that the white man would eventually go away.

Snow Gums

On the June long weekend, up in the ski resorts, clergymen are called in for the annual Blessing of the Snow, a pleasant custom originating in Austria and Bavaria. In some years, drought years particularly, they are constrained to bless the distant or future prospect of snow, for none may have fallen as yet. Many millions of dollars in investment capital depend on its coming soon, for snow sports are big business with a luxury image. Cars stream up into the high country from nearby Canberra, from Sydney and Melbourne and cities farther afield, pausing en route to fit chains to their tyres for the final climb over snowdrifts and slush. Buses collect passengers from Cooma airport for the haul up to Perisher or Guthega or Thredbo, or clatter with skis and ski stocks as they head out of Melbourne for Mt Buffalo or Mt Hotham. An ambience of coffee and Black Forest cake, of Porsches and glühwein and expensive knitwear has almost buried the older traditions of the high country, but not all of the skiers and ski-lodge habitues are wealthy, or even particularly Social. Many are immigrants of quite modest means who came to Australia from the traditional snow-sports countries twenty or thirty years ago. Some are veterans of the polyglot gangs who built the Snowy Mountains Hydroelectric complex in the fifties and sixties.

Among the older traditions of the high country is the town of Nimmitabel, freezing Nimmitabel, out among the rocky plains of the Monaro tableland. A passenger off the Cobb and Co coach once took a room at the town's hotel, and being a reader of books he called for a candle to read by. Unhappily, when he closed his book and tried to blow the candle out, the flame had frozen solid. Looking at this spearpoint of rigid light, he realized that he'd never be able to sleep for its glow in the room, so he hung his coat over it to darken it. During the night, the warmth of the coat thawed the flame, and set first the coat and then the hotel ablaze. All that was found of the man were some buttons. The story is told in a ballad by E.J. Brady, and I believe it; I've been to Nimmitabel. Not far away is the small town of Delegate, which was an early favourite among sites being considered for the Federal Capital early this century. It is said that Delegate dropped out of contention quite abruptly when members of the Parliamentary committee investigating possible sites happened to visit there on a typical winter's day. The birthplace of skiing in Australia was up at Kiandra, in the Snowy Mountains. Miners wintering up there during the short-lived gold rush of 1859–61 amused themselves by making skis and holding competitions, the first recorded in the world. Kiandra Ski Club is certainly one of the oldest existence anywhere. Another very old ski club is Kosciusko Alpine, which dates back to the 1890s. Skiing was a fairly minor sport, however, until the influx of European migrants after World War II. Australia is unlikely ever to host the Winter Olympics: New Zealand may yet do so, since her mountains are higher and provide steeper slopes with more reliable falls of dry powder snow. 'Good old wet Aussie snow,' as the international skiing buffs say sadly. As one of the very few places in the Southern Hemisphere with developed facilities for winter sports, however, Australia is an important venue for instructors and others wanting to ski in the months of the northern summer.

Away from the winter-sport venues, snow falls on the highest parts of the Dividing Range as far north, in some years, as the Granite Belt of southern Queensland, where that State's apples and stone fruits are produced. It may fall and lie for a day or two on the higher parts of the Stirling Ranges in Western Australia, and on the Mt Lofty ranges outside Adelaide. It may cover more than half of Tasmania, and will almost certainly mantle Mt Wellington and the other mountains around Hobart. The suburb of Ferntree on the slopes of Mount Wellington will usually be snowed in more than once in a typical winter, and snow sometimes falls, lightly and briefly, in the city itself. Even more than in Melbourne, a city which rather prides itself on its changeable weather ('Come to Melbourne and see all the seasons in one day!'), winter in Hobart is an evanescent time of clouds melting to sunshine, then darkening to rain that turns to sleet. The light changes from minute to minute, now jewelling, now obscuring the great estuary on which the city is built. The eye of the Derwent estuary, the Channel, looks southward towards Antarctica and the whaling grounds of more than a century ago, and catches freezing winds to funnel into the city along main streets laid out north-south as if to catch them. These are the winds which don't blow in summer, not even to help contestants in the Sydney-Hobart yacht race in their final struggle to the finishing line in front of Constitution Dock.

It is sometimes said that snow falls in Canberra every thirteen years, and records show this to be approximately right. Snow is visible from the city every year, appearing first on Mount Franklin and then investing the Brindabella Range of which that mountain is a part. Often, it will come in closer to the city, whitening the tops of nearby hills among the logs and scanty upland gums. In 1965, when we lived there, the winter fog which lends looming magic to large denuded Northern Hemisphere trees and closes Canberra's airport on many days between May and September lifted a few feet to show the whole city transformed by a ghostly carpet which seemed to draw the city's scattered design together and complete it. One remembered that Walter Burley Griffin had been accustomed to winter effects, and may unconsciously have provided for them when he designed Canberra. Every other family quickly made a snowman for the front lawn, and children took their opportunity to have snowball fights or simply to tumble around in the deeper patches. By evening, the snowmen were decrepit, and the miraculous carpet was turning to slush. That was the freak year in which snowfalls were recorded in places which had never seen snow in European times. Upland farmers close to the tropic of Capricorn in Queensland awoke to find their familiar paddocks made strange by a widespread rising light they would never see there again in their lifetimes.

Away from the fashionable snowfields, the mountains and high plateaux of Australia which carry snow in winter have a gaunt, secretive loneliness better known to foxes, brumby horses and native animals than to most humans. Snow lies in the twisted snowgum and bluegum forests and is marked only by the cuneiform marks of a crow's feet. Down under the still white, a rotted log will contain perhaps a sleeping carpet snake, or a prickly roll of sleeping echidnas. Bees huddle in their tree-hollow hives, feeding on summer honey and termites keep their nests at 25°C to 30°C inside by metabolic activity. Dirty yellow icicles hang under the banks of gullies and under the edge of rotting tankstands. Ice hides in sphagnum swamps, and sheathes tussocks and low trees in the Falls country. Clear ice clings all down the black basalt bosses and outcrops of waterfall gorges, where a niggardly stream of meltwater just manages to keep going in anticipation of the next rain's thundering perpendicular jets. Snow lies on the Barrington Tops, at the western edge of my home country, hiding the matted fine-haired native grass but not penetrating the dense stands of evergreen Antarctic beech where the fern trees shelter. In summer, those stands of ancient nothofagus, the beeches of the southern world whose fossilized leaves are found beneath the ice in Antarctica, have a smell of cold and decay like European forests, but their leaves are leathery and hard. They speak of the lost continent of Gondwanaland, mother of India, Africa, Australia, Madagascar and South America, where some scientists believe plants may first have learned to flower, tens of millions of years ago.

In this and more southerly high country, it is the old secret winter of the bushrangers' hideouts, the brooding hibernation of Ned Kelly. Up there are the caves and almost vanished huts where the robbers waited out the long nights, and their friends rode up to bring supplies and play cards by the light of a tallow candle or a boulder fireplace. It is the winter of Thunderbolt and Captain Moonlight, of the close-mouthed mountain pubs and the bushrangers' telegraphs. It is the winter of the cattle duffers, whose work still goes on by truck and secret mountain cattle-yard. Up there are the memories of Jimmy Governor, the part-Aboriginal farm labourer driven to murderous revenge by the slights of farmers and country women, and of his brother Joe; these were the last men in the British world to be placed under the medieval ban of outlawry. Up there are tiny remote villages like Nowendoc, which come alive for a day or two each year at the time of the annual rodeo, when men in Western shirts and with many reset bones arrive by way of a network few city dwellers follow. The nodal points of that network may lie a thousand miles farther north, in the backblocks of Queensland.

Up there, too, in the tablelands of northern New South Wales, there is the ghost of the long-dreamed-of State of New England, of which Armidale was to have been the capital. A distinctive region of Australia with its own atmosphere and traditions, New England and its nearby coast dreamed of freedom from the draining hegemony of Sydney, the great metropolis which contains nearly three-quarters of the population and all the government of its host State. When the matter was finally pushed to a referendum in 1967, however, the Sydney government cunningly included Newcastle and its hinterland in the referendum area. These historically had no interest in New England separatism, and so the move to separate was defeated, despite a yes vote of over ninety per cent in many of the northern tablelands areas. Now the ghost State lies moribund in the north, with its separate university and its handsome Teachers College building, built on parliamentary lines in the late twenties in order to house the new State government whenever separation was achieved. If we had escaped, other regions of Australia would probably have followed us into Statehood, breaking up the old British colonial borders of the present States and ending their sixfold over-centralization.

The wintry uplands of Australia are an amalgam of wealth and deep poverty, of large pastoral properties, orchards, and small farms whose hungry cattle are often turned out into the State forests in winter to forage for their survival. They contain the residues of an old struggle between pastoralism and smallholding, made all the more complex by absentee ownership of many properties. They hold a lore less expansive than that of the inland, but also less explored and familiar. The eastern foothills and remote gorges are a sort of inner outback which has never come fully into focus in the public mind, especially not in this century. Last century, it had the bushrangers and the police to bring a sort of glamour. People were aware of prospectors panning for gold along the mountain creeks, and of the stupendous scenery. We were more mountain-minded then, before we turned away to the surf beaches and to the romance of thirst and drovers and woolsheds. The decline of interest in horsemanship and fine horses as the automobile came in took away our imagery of the wild broken country where the great feats of riding occurred. And so the mountains are more remote now, in many ways, than they were a century ago. They are flown over, or driven around, or driven through rarely and quickly on the way to somewhere else. Their imagery survives most pervasively, perhaps, in genre paintings of abandoned farm buildings – but even those nowadays often have a Drysdale gauntness and an ochreous tone, relating to a frontier much farther out. The remembered childhood place beside a creek in the hills is displaced, for the grandchildren who don't themselves remember it, into barer imagined spaces derived from more recent art. We have almost forgotten the possum-skin rug. The lyrebird which nests in winter in the forested gorges, the scrub turkey, the rifle bird, the mopoke owl, all of these have to an extent become bygones. They were once commonplaces of Australia, along with fern trees, silver-mounted emu eggs and the lights of Cobb and Co ascending a flinty range.

Human isolation in a remote valley or behind a forested range may accentuate the tendency of large and small holdings alike to become kingdoms with their own laws. The quietly spoken people who meet and yarn on the post office corner in a mountain town are often laconically ceremonious, because they are lords over space, with places to fall back on. They and those they talk with are powers and potentates, able to obstruct each other badly if offended. They possess dangerous mutual knowledge and deeply shared measures of worth. They hardly ever see their lives presented at all, let alone accurately, in books or newspapers, on TV or film, but they wouldn't expect to, and the concealment can be welcome. The bush is instinctively close-mouthed, because so many have had to work both sides of the law to survive. Sometimes the closeness is cheerfully voluble, as persiflage conceals the dangerous information the outsider seems to be after. But many who live in pine-girt brick bungalows or the unpainted timber houses with their heat-wasting outside chimneys of flattened sheet iron are implacably remote. Like most bush people, they have wrestled with an angel.

The Cross and the Cool Island

The Doubleman by C.J. Koch (Chatto and Windus, 1985)

We first meet Richard Miller, the bearer of C.J. Koch's magnificent new novel, as a twelve-year-old boy heaving himself on a single crutch up the steepest street in Hobart towards St Augustine's College and the violent rages of Brother Kinsella. On this frosty morning in the early 1950s, he will have an encounter with the mysterious Man in the Lane, before whom he must not for his very life show any wavering or submission. It is at once a completely believable childhood encounter and something immemorially fateful, a testing which must be withstood.

I call Miller the bearer of Koch's story because he is at once its narrator and a principal character. As some character must always be in a novel, he is our representative. He is an only son, whose father has died in the war. His wasted left leg is the result of a childhood brush with infantile paralysis, as polio was called in the days before Salk vaccine. This has acted as a second birth, delivering him into the sadly privileged world of the marred, and turning his imagination away into a private world of fairytale and cardboard theatres; he is a precocious expert in the art of such Victorian and Edwardian illustrators as Rackham, Dulac and Simmons, full of a longing fascination with the Otherland of faery. In a subtly modulated metaphor which runs throughout the novel and is one of its main themes, illuminating both the characters and the late-colonial realities of Australia, he is a denizen of the kingdom of Second Hand.

The man in the lane, he will learn a few years later, is Clive Broderick, Madrid-trained master of the classical guitar, who works in a basement office in a city bookshop and instructs Miller's cousin Brian Brady in music. Little by little, Broderick introduces Miller to the doctrines of Gnostic dualism. Contained, icy and mysterious to the last, this man is the doubleman of the novel's title, the shadowy watcher who scorns Christian values and offers initiation into power to souls whom he chooses. Even after his death he will recur in

219

dreams and in conversations, and so play a part in the action.

Miller soon acquires a doubleman of his own in Broderick's young disciple Darcy Burr, who encourages him in his fascination with the otherworld. Burr sings in pubs with Brady and lives in Sandy Lovejoy's tunnel-like secondhand shop in tatty Harrigan Street; here, he introduces the cousins to seances and further rudiments of Broderick's teaching, and the three cement an uneasy relationship which will work itself out disastrously long after they have left Tasmania for the beckoning mainland.

Seven years pass. Miller has become a producer for the national broadcasting service in Sydney. He has shaken off a sterilizing sexual obsession and married; he is happy, and both his life and his career seem serenely upward bound. Yet both contain elements of second-hand: he is a producer, for example, and no longer the radio actor he started out to be. A degree of living through others remains with him, and will endanger him. When Brady and Burr reappear in his life, they have served their time on the country and western circuit, and are hungry for major success on the then-nascent folk music scene. Miller's Estonian-born wife Katrin joins them to form a folk group called the Rymers, specializing in British ballads of faery and the supernatural as well as more conventional material. In that purist stage of the early folk revival, they are a pioneer electric folk group, with traces of the Beatles and of Pentangle.

Miller is their producer, who will help them to national acclaim on television; Burr sees to that. For his part, Burr is the group's brilliant arranger, devoured by ambition for world fame, beyond the narrow confines of Australia. To keep Miller on side, he plays upon his old fascination with the occult, and leads him on into the dawning world of drugs and visionary trips. But as Burr's ambition grows, it also spreads, in Manson-like directions which trouble the others. And Miller himself begins to be an obstacle. It would be wrong to reveal the book's ending, but it is fair to say that there is a collapse, and a death which does not cause the collapse but rises logically from it. The smash itself is more interesting, however, and more unexpected than any ordinary tragic dénouement. It is one of the most daring feats that any Australian writer has ever pulled off. To realize just how daring it is may take more than one reading.

The novel is a major one and Koch's best yet, a speedy, compact work of very mature art from a master novelist. It is no occult thriller, but at once a modern psychological novel and a timeless fairytale. No one handles the dimension of dream more artfully, and yet so completely eschews the cheap tricks of surrealism. No one has written better about cool, remote Tasmania and its strange dual nature. No one has written better about Kings Cross, either. And no one, I imagine, will ever again capture from first hand that period of the early 1960s when the Cross was a tense amalgam of so many fading and rising influences in Australian life. The drama that plays itself out in that special quarter of Sydney, in the lush fringes of Elizabeth Bay, in the broadcasting studios of William Street and the bleary perpetual midnight of the Hasty Tasty café, is of a piece with events that convulsed the whole Western world in those years. The book's climactic year is 1966, the double six, that time when older shared values were eclipsed, when strange new spiritual leaders began to appear, and myth and fairytale burst forth to capture popular culture.

It is a time for illusions and hectic dreams, and each of the main figures in the book is prey to illusion in some way. 'All enthralment,' the narrator points out in a key passage, 'is an arrested past: the prolonged, perverse childhood from which some souls never escape.' If the doppelgänger and the life of second-hand are leading themes, illusion is an absolutely central one. And that, as much as anything, is what causes the downfall of Burr's dream. Because illusion perennially carries with it a complementary principle of boredom. To put that in another way, it cannot escape the soil from which it rises.

In an age of progress, of excitement and the hunger for constant stimulation, illusion flourishes, but everything is alike under the threat of relegation, of becoming tedious. In the age of belief, the concept of boredom hardly existed outside the Latin language, and the Church taught its clergy that tedium was sinful in its nature, part of the sin of despair. Which in turn arises from the refusal to love. This, we realize, is the terrible gift of Broderick to his disciple Darcy Burr, and the heart of that insistent élitism so typical of the occult. His master has used an aristocratic sophistication to purge him of love.

The Narrow-columned Middle Ground

19th Century Australian Poetry

1

In 1897, exasperated by snooty reviews from the scholar poets of his day, Henry Lawson wrote a furious rejoinder entitled 'To My Cultured Critics', Here are some lines from that poem:

> My cultured friends! you have come too late
>   With your bypath nicely graded;
> I've fought thus far on my track of Fate,
>   And I'll follow the rest unaided.
>
> Must I be stopped by a college gate
>   On the track of Life encroaching?
> Be dumb to Love, and be dumb to Hate,
>   For the lack of a pedant's coaching?
>
> You grope for Truth in a language dead –
>   In the dust 'neath tower and steeple!
> What do you know of the tracks we tread,
>   And what of the living people?

and it concludes:

> Must I turn aside from my destined way
>   For a task your Joss would find me?
> I come with strength of the living day,
>   And with half the world behind me;
> I leave you alone in your cultured halls
>   To drivel and croak and cavil:
> Till your voices go farther than college walls,
>   Keep out of the tracks we travel!

His fury was understandable: the high-art poetry of Australia's first hundred years was a pretty thin crop, and didn't stack up into

222

any very lofty eminence from which to patronize a vigorous 'folk' poet whose acclaim amongst his people was growing by leaps and bounds. Also, the labour movement which Lawson represented was emerging powerfully all over the world, carrying with it ideas of an authentic popular art, of poetry written to reflect the life and supposed aspirations of working people, over against the hermetic pedantry of élites. In the long run, though, as we know, what Lawson confidently saw as the wave of the future would run largely into the sand. In poetry first of all, and generally much later on, the labour movement would move relentlessly up-market. With the emergence of Norman Lindsay's Vision group in the early 1920s and the rise from there of poets such as Kenneth Slessor and R.D. Fitzgerald, the vernacular schools of Australian verse would increasingly be lumped together and dismissed as anachronistic bush balladeers, droning on futilely in outback pubs and shearers' quarters. A more sophisticated poetry would take centre stage, and even quite genuine vernacular elements would be adapted to its tone and range.

Lawson's cry of rage regrettably did much to crystallize a division in sensibility that has afflicted our culture during all of this century. More pertinent to our purpose here, the gentrification he was resisting helped to blind us to a healthily varied, idiosyncratic poetic scene that went before it. We tend nowadays to look back at nineteenth-century Australian verse with a squint caused by a great split. We see a series of struggling, under-appreciated literary poets trying to adapt a Northern European language and the fag ends of a classical tradition to a strange new continent we imagine we know infinitely more about now, or else we see a succession of hard-bitten but basically heroic folk balladeers eschewing the effete and capturing the real life of a vast oppressed underclass. The picture isn't always presented this crudely, but it can come perilously close to that, and variously refined versions of the same view are extremely pervasive. They amount to a received shorthand view of the facts – and of course such a picture suits highbrow and lowbrow alike, reinforcing their pet attitudes.

The facts, however, are more varied and intractable, and shot through with a good deal less of simplistic class division. That very division, perhaps surprisingly, only hardens towards the end of the nineteenth century, and is arguably more rigid in our own. There were, of course, carry-over Augustan versifiers like Judge Barron Field writing for a tiny circle of cultivated readers, and poets of a late Romantic cast writing for the many but mostly reaching only a few of the educated, and there were convict poems and songs which the authorities sought with varying success to proscribe; a very significant underground career of this sort which only really came to light again in the 1970s was that of Frank the Poet MacNamara, easily the most important and quite likely the most seminal poet of the first half of the nineteenth century here. Between these boundary cases, though, from the end of the first quarter of the nineteenth century up until the first quarter of our own, there was an enormous mass of verse published in newspapers and likely to be read by high and low alike. The intellectually exclusive little magazines which would carry literary modernism still lay far in the future, prefigured only by the expensive, self-published books of upper-class versifiers; most of the highbrow and highly literary verse of the day first appeared in newspapers along with the topical rhymes, and often the same poets wrote both. Many of the earlier ballads had their first appearance not in the mystical mouth of the Folk, but in some metropolitan or country town newspaper. We remember the *Bulletin*, but we forget all the others, even though Adam Lindsay Gordon was a star of the *Border Watch*, in Mount Gambier, and the witty, experimental W.T. Goodge featured not only in the *Bulletin* but also in the newspapers of his native town, Orange, in New South Wales. Henry Lawson himself was apt to publish widely, from the *Manly Daily* to the *Gardening Times*, and by no means confined himself to the *Bulletin*.

Again, there were goldfields poets who made a very decent living singing their verses on the vaudeville stage, poets such as Charles Thatcher, who reigned supreme on the stage of the Shamrock Hotel in Bendigo in the 1850s and early 1860s. There were street singers such as the famous 'Blind Billy' Huntingdon, of Sydney, and the lyricists of the thousands of popular reciters and songbooks which proliferated in that age of the piano and the fireside singsong. The weight of nineteenth-century Australian poetry, though, is in the newspapers. One unconventional scholar-poet who saw this clearly and realized something of its importance before others did so was Geoffrey Lehmann; his insights arose from a close study of several decades of the *Bulletin* in search of fresh material for his idiosyncratic anthology of Australian comic verse, published a dozen years ago. Now the search has begun on the other papers and magazines of the era, but as yet we are far from having fully combed their back files to rediscover all the nuggets that may still lie buried there amongst the tons of ephemera.

Between us and that tradition, there lies another shift of sensibility which the English critic Stephen Pile recently described very well in the *Sunday Times*:

Englishmen first started blushing in the proximity of verse between 1890 and 1910. We must blame the pre-Raphaelites, Swinburne, Rossetti and Co. At this time we developed our national image of the poet as a vague, hypersensitive, unpunctual, sexually ambiguous drip who is always in love, drunk, drugged to the eyeballs and perpetually unable to cope with the world.

Emerging even earlier from Murger's *La Bohème* and the lice-ridden wingroots of Baudelaire's Albatross, this stereotype probably reached Australia around the same time, though it took quite a while to silence the last reciter doing his stuff at a remote bush dance, and the sturdy upholders of bush balladry still apply it only to highbrow authors, never to their own beloved Banjo Paterson or Keith Garvey. They would be mad, as well as libellous, if they did. Back beyond that stereotype, though, the position and if you like the application of poetry is quite different. To a degree, it formed part of journalism, or could. Stylish, highly educated figures such as Robert Lowe, the later Viscount Sherbrooke, did not hesitate to publish racy ballads about current events; other public figures such as Sir Henry Parkes did the same, less well but voluminously. Verse was far less self-conscious, far less likely to be on its intellectual best behaviour than it usually is today. The whole 'middle' range of poetry escaped arty strictures by being classed as 'light' verse, in which live colloquial language was allowed. Here is Lowe, in one of his ironic 'Songs of the Squatters', extolling up-country life to a prospective bride:

> Our brave bridal bower
>   Is built not of stones,
> Though, like old Doubting Castle,
>   'Tis paved with bones,
> The bones of the sheep
>   On whose flesh I have fed,
> Where thy thin satin slipper
>   Unshrinking may tread,
> For the dogs have all polished
>   Them clean with their teeth,
> And they're better, believe me,
>   Than what lies beneath.
> My door has no hinge,
>   And the window no pane,
> They let out the smoke,
>   But they let in the rain;
> The frying-pan serves us

For table and dish,
And the tin pot of tea stands
    Still filled for your wish;
The sugar is brown,
    The milk is all done,
But the stick it is stirred with
    Is better than none.
The stockmen will swear,
    And the shepherds won't sing,
But a dog's a companion
    Enough for a king.
So fear not, fair lady,
    Your desolate way,
Your clothes will arrive
    In three months with my dray.
Then mount, lady, mount, to the wilderness fly,
My stores are laid in, and my shearing is nigh,
And our steeds, that through Sydney exultingly wheel,
Must graze in a week on the banks of the Peel.

The eye is keen and unsparing here as the mock-heroic parody, and the poem clearly reflects a long-lived Australian attitude that still gives rise to surreal-satirical events such as the annual boat race in the dry bed of the Todd River at Alice Springs. Less satirical but with every bit as close an attention to detail as 'A Hot Day in Sydney', published in the *Sydney Gazette*, in January 1829 and signed Q. Newspaper poets often signed their work with no more than a cryptic initial or two, or a pseudonym, and most of these are now quite impenetrable. Here is an extract from the poem:

You rise in disgust from the table,
    And, with your umbrella unfurl'd,
You toddle, as well as you're able,
    To the haunts of the mercantile world.

But whether you sit in your office,
    Or stroll to the market and shops,
To bargain for sugars or coffees,
    For snuff, or tobacco, or hops; –

You still are by no means forgetting
    The torments inflicted by heat –
For still you are puffing and sweating,
    And longing for some cool retreat.

You wash in Cologn's cooling water, –
  You swallow some brisk ginger-beer –
You say to some kind neighbour's daughter,
  'O give me some swizzle, my dear!'

You go to luncheon at BAX'S
  And call for cool jellies and buns –
But hotter and hotter it waxes, –
  The jelly to liquid soon runs; –

His dainties are only a pester,
  And so you withdraw from his shop; –
Loud rages the fiery North-wester,
  As back to your office you pop.

The streets are with dust so beclouded,
  You cannot see over the way;
The town is so perfectly shrouded,
  You scarcely believe it is day.

From the same year, though, and the same paper, we have the glowing satisfaction of some emancipist or free-settler farmer who has made a go of farming in the new country. The following is an extract from his poem 'Hey, Boys! Up Go We!':

When maize stands more than ten feet high,
And bursting cobs a yard or more,
On every rood ten bushels lie,
And each brings dollars three in store;
When pigs with dismal accents roar,
The sharpening steel and knife to see,
And pork keeps hunger from my door,
Why then, 'tis, 'Hey, boys! up go we!'

When wheat is standing thick and strong,
On brushy hill, and flooded dale;
And yellow ridges wave along,
As swells or falls the alternate gale;
When bursting barns and stacks prevail,
From fresh or flood no harm can be,
When grass hides heifer's head and tail,
Why then, 'tis 'Hey, boys! up go we!'

★ ★ ★

> When woodmen cut their mazy wood,
> And stately gums and cedars fall,
> And groaning teams the fencers load,
> And jocund herds their lambkins call;
> When trees are split with wedge and maul,
> And rising cots the settlers see,
> And acres cleared give joy to all,
> Why then, 'tis 'Hey, boys! up go we!'

Less exultant are the sentiments of an Irish convict who may for all we know have been an assignee on that happy man's farm. Again the poem is from that same year, 1829, and this time the signature is simply M. It is likely to be a fictional portrait, or at least one drawn by a writer who is no longer a serving convict, as it is hard to imagine a lag being allowed to send poetry to the papers – hard, but perhaps not impossible. There is a pathos about the poem which strikes through the almost bardic-school formality of the diction and the armament of Irish references, so common in early convict and bushranger songs. The poem is titled 'The Exile of Erin', and here are the first two stanzas:

> O! farewell, my country – my kindred – my lover;
> Each morning and evening is sacred to you,
> While I toil the long day, without shelter or cover,
> And fell the tall gums, the black-butted and blue.
> Full often I think of and talk of thee, Erin –
> Thy heath-covered mountains are fresh in my view,
> Thy glens, lakes, and rivers, Loch-Con and Kilkerran,
> While chained to the soil on the Plains of Emu.
>
> The ironbark, wattle, and gum-trees extending
> Their shades, under which rests the shy kangaroo,
> May be felled by the bless'd who have hope o'er them
>   bending,
> To cheer their rude toil, though far exiled from you.
> But, alas! without hope, peace, or honour to grace me,
> Each feeling was crushed in the bud as it grew,
> Whilst '*never*' is stamped on the chains that embrace me,
> And endless my thrall on the Plains of Emu.

On to subject of convictism, the nineteenth-century newspaper verse I have seen is apt to be cautious and jocular; we will hear darker and more unsparing notes sounded when we come to the oral tradition on the second of these programmes. Newspaper verse excels at genre paintings of civilian life, often rather in the manner of S.T. Gill, the famous pen-and-wash artist of the goldfields, and its great virtue is in its liveliness and its untroubled solution to the problems of language in which so many more ambitious literary poets bogged down. Here, from the *Hamilton Spectator* of 15 February 1865, is a rapid sketch of the desperate poverty suffered by thousands of itinerant rural workers, well before the Wallaby Track was seen as a road of old romance:

> Married and single travel about,
> The married with children on the route,
> The single carry their horse-collar swags,
> There's new chums, too, with carpet bags,
> Carpet bags and swallow-tailed coats,
> Hair on the face, just like the goats,
> Bell topper tiles the worse for wear,
> And under their coats their legs are bare.
>
> 'The Feeding Track', M.K.

A 'tile' is nineteenth-century slang for a hat. Countering the vague modern notion that nineteenth-century popular verse, folk and literary ballads and the like, concentrated on the bush and neglected the life of the rapidly growing cities, many examples could be cited, but an especially vivid one is 'The Wail of the Waiter', this time by a named author – the novelist and newspaper columnist Marcus Clarke; it appeared, I think, in the Melbourne *Argus* in the 1880s:

> All day long, at Scott's or Menzies', I await the gorging crowd,
> Panting, penned within a pantry, with the blowflies humming loud.
> There at seven in the morning do I count my daily cash,
> While the home-returning reveller calls for 'soda and a dash'.
> And the weary hansom-cabbies set the blinking squatters down,
> Who, all night, in savage freedom, have been 'knocking round the town'.
> Soon the breakfast gong resounding bids the festive meal begin,
> And, with appetites like demons, come the gentle public in.
> 'Toast and butter!' 'Eggs and coffee!' 'Waiter, mutton chops for four!'
> 'Flatheads!' 'Ham!' 'Beef!' 'Where's the mustard?' 'Steak and onions!' 'Shut the door!'

Here sits Bandicoot, the broker, eating in a desperate hurry,
Scowling at his left-hand neighbour, Cornstalk from the
    Upper Murray,
Who with brandy-nose empurpled, and with blue lips cracked
    and dry,
In incipient delirium shoves the eggspoon in his eye.
'Bloater paste!' 'Some *tender* steak, sir?' 'Here, *confound* you,
    where's my chop?'
'Waiter!' 'Yessir!' '*Waiter*!' 'Yessir!!' – running till I'm fit to
    drop.
Then at lunch time – fearful crisis! In by shoals the gorgers
    pour,
Gobbling, crunching, swilling, munching – ten times hungrier
    than before.
'Glass of porter!' '*Ale* for me, John!' 'Where's my stick?' 'And
    where's my *hat*!'
'Oxtail soup!' '*I* asked for curry!' 'Cold boiled beef, and cut
    it fat!'
'Irish stew!' 'Some pickled cabbage!' 'What, no *beans*?' 'Bring
    me some pork!'
'Soup, sir?' 'Yes. You grinning idiot, can I eat it with a FORK?'
'Take care, waiter!' 'Beg your pardon.' 'Curse you, have you
    two left legs?'
'I asked for *bread* an hour ago, sir!' 'Now then, have you *laid*
    those eggs?'
  'Sherry!' 'No, I called for *beer* – of all the fools I ever saw!'
'Waiter!' 'Yessir!' 'WAITER!!' 'Here, sir!' 'Damme, sir, this
    steak is RAW!'

Thus amid this hideous Babel do I live the livelong day,
While my memory is going, and my hair is turning grey.
All my soul is slowly melting, all my brain is softening fast,
And I know that I'll be taken to the Yarra Bend at last.
For at night from fitful slumbers I awaken with a start,
Murmuring of steak and onions, babbling of apple-tart.
While to me the Poet's cloudland a gigantic kitchen seems,
And those mislaid table-napkins haunt me even in my dreams
Is this right? – Ye sages tell me! – Does a man live but to eat?
Is there nothing worth enjoying but one's miserable meat?
Is the mightiest task of Genius but to swallow buttered beans,
And has Man but been created to demolish pork and greens?
Is there no *unfed* Hereafter, where the round of chewing stops?

Is the atmosphere of heaven clammy with perpetual chops?
Do the friends of Mr Naylor sup on spirit-reared cow-heel?
Can the great Alexis Soyer really say 'Soyez tranquille?'
Or must I bring spirit beefsteak grilled in spirit regions hotter
For the spirit delectation of some spiritual squatter?
Shall I in a spirit kitchen hear the spirit blowflies humming,
Calming spiritual stomachs with a spiritual 'Coming!'?
Shall – but this is idle chatter, I have got my work to do.
'WAITER!!' 'Yessir.' 'Wake up, stupid! Biled calves' feet for
    Number Two!'

A rollicking scene, as newspaper verse often painted them, this nonetheless has its darker echoes of overwork and harassed exhaustion. Humour was often the sugar coating on pills of bitter and incisive observation. In W.T. Goodge, though, we come to a different sort of mind, intellectual without a trace of snobbery, fascinated by the mysteries of poetic pacing and movement, appreciative of paradox. Here he is on the contradictions that abounded in the fervid oratory which preceded Federation in 1901; we almost hear the speakers ranting and bubbling over in their impassioned addresses:

Let us sing of Federation
   ('T is the theme of every cult)
And the joyful expectation
   Of its ultimate result.
'T will confirm the jubilation
Of protection's expectation,
And the quick consolidation
Of free trade with every nation;
And teetotal legislation
Will achieve its consummation
And increase our concentration
On the art of bibulation
We shall drink to desperation,
And be quite the soberest nation
We'll be desperately loyal
Unto everything that's royal,
And be ultra-democratic
In a matter most emphatic.
We'll be prosperous and easeful,
And pre-eminently peaceful,
And we'll take our proper station
As a military nation!

> We shall show the throne affection,
> Also sever the connection,
> And the bonds will get no fainter
> And we'll also cut the painter.
> We'll proclaim with lute and tabor
> The millennium of labour,
> And we'll bow before the gammon
> Of plutocracy and Mammon.
> We'll adopt all fads and fictions
> And their mass of contradictions
> If all hopes are consummated
> When Australia's federated;
> For the Federation speeches
> This one solid moral teach us –
> That a pile of paradoxes are expected to result!

What I have termed newspaper verse, partly as a contrast with the literary magazine verse of our time, and partly because it *was* published in the more plentiful, less cartelized and thus more genuinely independent newspapers of the last century, and only occasionally collected in books later on, represents a colloquial, middle-voice poetry that catches a great deal of ordinary human experience and shares it in an unfussed way with a broad range of people well before rising ideologies turned the idea of people's art into an ideal to be venerated and sought. Another surprising claim that can be made for it is made by the English poet and critic Hugo Williams, writing in the *New Statesman* (6 March 1987):

> ... the country's 19th and 20th century poets, who were expressing themselves in vivid speaking language and addressing real-life experience in a way that was not attempted by the more hide-bound British mainstream and American academics until much more recently, if then. Unencumbered by fashions of formality, obscurity and experimentation, Australians seem to have been writing relaxed modern stuff for years ... here at last is the alternative version of literary history in which poetry is written out of feeling, experience and fascination for the way things look and feel, instead of nightmare, lit crit and blind ambition ... this impressive archive [the *New Oxford Book of Australian Verse*] offers an answer to all those who have looked in vain for a plausible alternative route from the Romantics to the present day.

This does ignore some important figures in England and America, notably Kipling, who lived in both and did influence our later literary balladists, but I am fascinated by the idea, by no means ridiculous, of modern poetry existing in Australia well before modernism. Since it may shock some who do not think Australian literature has ever been innovative, I thought it better to let an outside observer make this claim rather than making it myself. In the next programme, we will deal with the more oral sides of our supposedly oral tradition, and then exhibit the features of some of our early literary poets. Some of the best of those prove to be women, a fact that can be traced because their work was generally signed, while newspaper verse, as we have seen, was often pseudonymous or anonymous.

2

In the nineteenth century, as in previous ages, the sharp distinction we make between poetry and song would have seemed strange. So would our copyright-minded attitude towards tunes. In the last century, it was almost a mark of a tune's genuine popularity that people kept putting new sets of words to it. Poems published in colonial newspapers often carried a note as to the air the verses were to be sung to, and the next time the poem appeared might well be in a cheaply produced paper volume entitled something like *The New Universal Fireside Minstrel*, full of what we'd call pirated material and selling for one and sixpence. Poems, like tunes, quickly became public property, and the idea of royalties and repeat payments lay well in the future. It can still work like that, around the folk circuit and the edges of the country music world, whatever protestations you may hear to the contrary. It is as well to keep these things in mind when looking at all but the most pukka nineteenth-century verse.

One of the most successful goldfields troubadours, a man we'd nowadays call a performance poet, was a Kentish music-hall trouper who migrated to Victoria in the early 1850s and made a good living for many years singing his verse in the theatres of the day; we have lost all record of most such performers, but Charles Thatcher is remembered because he published a book of his songs in Melbourne in 1864, before going on to try his luck on the fields of New Zealand's South Island, where he died in 1868. Thatcher's topical verse is lively, full of sharp social observation and good humour, and he was a much-loved figure around the Shamrock Hotel in Bendigo. Here is a sample of his work called 'Taking the Census', supposed to be sung to an air called 'Miser's Man', which I've never heard but which must have been well known in his day:

When the census is taken, of course,
    All the elderly females are furious,
They don't like to tell their real age,
    For gov'ment they say is too curious:
I got hold of a chap that went round,
    For I wanted to twig their rum capers,
So I tipped him a crown on the sly
    To let me look over his papers.

There's that elderly dame, Mother Baggs,
    Has marked down her age twenty-seven,
Although she's possessed of five kids,
    The eldest of which is eleven;
Miss Fluffen says she's thirty-two,
    But to tell such a story is naughty,
She's a regular frumpish old maid,
    And if she's a year old she's forty.

There's another thing struck me as queer,
    As the papers I sat overhauling,
Beneath occupation, thinks I,
    I'll soon find out each person's calling;
But the first I looked at made me grin,
    My wash'woman, old Mother Archer,
Beneath occupation I found
    Had described herself as a clear starcher.

The chemist's assistant up here,
    When his paper I happened to see, sirs,
'Pon my honour had the vile cheek
    To mark after his name M.D., sirs,
And Bolus, that wretched old quack,
    Whom folks here regard with suspicion,
When his paper I looked at, I found
    He'd put himself down a physician!

Here's a *barberous* custom you'll say,
    No less than three diff'rent hairdressers,
In the papers which they have filled up
    Have described themselves all as *professors*;
In Heidelberg district I find
    My bounceable friend, Harry Potter,

In the paper that he has sent in,
    Tries to make us believe he's a squatter.

My friend said he called on two girls,
    Who are noted for cutting rum capers,
They live in an elegant crib,
    And he knocked at the door for their papers;
They handed him what he required,
    He read, but exclaimed with vexation,
'The instructions you haven't fulfilled –
    'You've not put down your occupation.'

'Well, Poll, that's a good 'un,' says one,
    And both of them burst out a-laughing,
But the young man exclaimed precious quick
    'I can't stay all day while you're chaffing';
'Occupation' says she, with a scream,
    (Her laughter was pretty near killing her),
'*Poll, I'm blowed if I knows what you are,*
    But, young man, shove me down as a milliner.'

It is often quite difficult to say whether an Australian song is a 'genuine' folksong, in the purist sense of a song transmitted orally and not coming from, say, a printed source or from the music-hall stage. One can be pretty sure about some, as we shall see, but Australia's foundations lie well within the newspaper age, and an insatiable thirst for items of interest meant that all sorts of productions made their appearances – perhaps not their first appearances – in colonial newspapers; obscenity was out, but pretty sharp comment on nearly anything else seems to have been allowed, though naturally this varied with the tone and editorial prejudices of the paper. Henry Lawson's savage rubbishing of Queen Victoria, unthinkable in almost any other part of the Empire in her Jubilee year of 1897, found a suitably republican venue in the *Bulletin*. The following tart verses about the socially superior jackaroo, to be sung to the air of 'The Wearing of the Green', made their first appearance in Banjo Paterson's invaluable collection *Old Bush Songs*, published in Sydney in 1905, and though they are clearly a good deal earlier than that, it is not known whether they had had any previous appearances in print:

If you want a situation, I'll just tell you the plan
To get on to a station, I am just your very man.

Pack up the old portmanteau, and label it Paroo
With a name aristocratic – Jimmy Sago, Jackaroo.

When you get on to the station, of small things you'll make a
        fuss,
And in speaking of the station, mind, it's we, and ours, and us.
Boast of your grand connections and your rich relations, too,
And your own great expectations, Jimmy Sago, Jackaroo.

They will send you out on horseback, the boundaries to ride;
But run down a marsupial and rob him of his hide,
His scalp will fetch a shilling and his hide another two,
Which will help to fill your pockets, Jimmy Sago, Jackaroo.
Yes, to fill your empty pockets, Jimmy Sago, Jackaroo.

When the boss wants information, on the men you'll do a
        sneak,
And don a paper collar on your fifteen bob a week.
Then at the lamb-marking a boss they'll make of you.
Now that's the way to get on, Jimmy Sago, Jackaroo.

A squatter in the future I've no doubt you may be,
But if the banks once get you, they'll put you up a tree.
To see you humping bluey, I know, would never do,
'Twould mean good-bye to our newchum, Jimmy Sago,
        Jackaroo.
Yes, good-bye to our newchum, Jimmy Sago, Jackaroo.

Older still, perhaps, to judge by terms such as 'master' and 'servant' and from the fact that washing sheep before shearing them
barely survived the 1860s, is this anonymous song, 'The Sheep
Washer's Lament', from Queensland. It is perhaps a direct forerunner of the red-hot Labor balladry of the 1890s.

When I first took the western tracks, many years ago,
No master then stood up so high, no servant bowed so low,
But now the squatters, puffed with pride, do treat us with
        disdain,
Lament with me the bygone days that will not come again.
I had a pair of ponies once, to bear me on my road.
I earned a decent cheque at times, and blued it like a lord.
But lonely now, I hump my drum, in sunshine and in rain,
Lamenting on those bygone days that will not come again.

Let bushmen all in unity, combine with heart and hand,
Till bloody cringing poverty is driven from our land
Let never Queensland come to know the tyrant's ball and chain
And washers all in times to come their vanished rights regain.

It's not that 'folk' poets necessarily *want* to be anonymous, of course; it's just that in the spontaneous informalities of oral transmission, names are apt to be forgotten. And if a poem first appeared in a local newspaper over a pseudonym or an initial or two, there really isn't much provenance to hold on to anyway. Again, for the modern busker and the earlier street balladeer, the urgent thing is survival, not scholarly attribution. We have no idea whether Blind Billy Huntingdon, who flourished, if that is what one does on kerbsides and windy corners, in Sydney during the 1860s and 1870s, actually composed his famous signature tune 'Ten Thousand Miles Away', but it was the centrepiece of his stock in trade. Here it is, spoken rather than sung: listeners will be familiar with the tune from such television series as *Rush*, which often comes back in non-ratings periods:

Then blow ye winds, high-ho! A-roving I will go.
I'll stay no more on England's shore, so let the music play,
For I'm off by the morning train across the raging main,
I'm on the lay for my own true love, ten thousand miles away.

Sing oh! for a brave and gallant barque, with a brisk and lively
     breeze,
For a little crew, and a captain too, to carry me o'er the seas,
To carry me o'er the seas, my boys, to my true love as I say,
For she's taken a trip on a government ship ten thousand miles
     away.

My true love she was handsome, my true love she was young,
Her eyes were blue as the violets, and silver was her tongue,
Oh silver was her tongue, my boys, and while I sing this lay,
She's doing the grand in a distant land ten thousand miles
     away.

Then blow ye winds, high-ho! When last I saw my Meg
She'd a government band around her hand and a band upon
     her leg.
'Adieu!' says she, 'Today I can no longer stay,
For I'm taking a trip on a government ship ten thousand miles
     away.'

> Oh! Blow ye winds, high-ho! A-roving we will go!
> We'll stay no more on England's shore, we'll cross the raging
>   main.
> Across the raging main! We'll gó by the morning train!
> Where the whales and the sharks are playing their larks, ten
>   thousand miles away.

There is an echo of real cant language in that, in expressions such as 'on the lay' and the old Sydney Cove euphemisms that use the word 'government' instead of 'penal' or 'convict'. The slight air of sending up convict themes, though, helps to date the song to an era after the gold rushes. Too much sending up of convict things might still have given offence to many in New South Wales even as late as that, so it is done gently. All the same, the song lacks the biting anger of the many real convict songs, a class of compositions which hardly ever got into the newspapers and are pretty reliably part of an oral tradition. In a biographical and critical study published only in 1976, the folklorists Rex Whelan and John Meredith made a strong case for that whole tradition's having come from one man, a famous but till then shadowy figure called Frank the Poet MacNamara. If Whelan and Meredith are right in their detective work, this Irishman is the author of such seminal ballads as 'The Wild Colonial Boy' and the 'Seizure of the Cyprus Brig', ancestors of other defiant convict and bushranger ballads from later in the nineteenth century and an influential strain in Australian tradition right down to our own times – and at the same time is the author of several convict poems not meant to be sung, which constitute pretty well our entire corpus of convict verse, and put firmly in the shade nearly all more genteel poetry written in this country until at least well on in the middle of the century. Perhaps the greatest of Frank the Poet's work is 'A Convict's Tour to Hell', in which he consigns all of his immediate and even remote oppressors to a kind of folk Inferno where the Devil is kindly and considerate to those who have already suffered their Hell while alive. It is a masterpiece of inversion, and of the ancient Flash culture's theme of freedom through comic misrule. Here is a section from the poem:

> He louder knocked and louder still
> When the Devil came, pray what's your will?
> Alas cried the Poet I've come to dwell
> With you and share your fate in Hell
> Says Satan that can't be, I'm sure
> For I detest and hate the poor
> And none shall in my kingdom stand

Except the grandees of the land.
But Frank I think you are going astray
For convicts never come this way
But soar to Heaven in droves and legions
A place so called in the upper regions
So Frank I think with an empty purse
You shall go further and fare worse
Well cried the Poet since 'tis so
One thing of you I'd like to know
As I'm at present in no hurry
Have you one here called Captain Murray?
Yes Murray is within this place
Would you said Satan see his face?
May God forbid that I should view him
For on board the *Phoenix Hulk* I knew him
Who is that Sir in yonder blaze
Who on fire and brimstone seems to graze?
'Tis Captain Logan of Moreton Bay
And Williams who was killed the other day
He was overseer at Grosse Farm
And done poor convicts no little harm
Cook who discovered New South Wales
And he that first invented gaols
Are both tied to a fiery stake
Which stands in yonder boiling lake
Hark do you hear this dreadful yelling
It issues from Doctor Wardell's dwelling
And all those fiery seats and chairs
Are fitted up for Dukes and Mayors
And nobles of Judicial orders
Barristers, Lawyers and Recorders
Here I beheld legions of traitors
Hangmen gaolers and flagellators
Commandants, Constables and Spies
Informers and Overseers likewise
In flames of brimstone they were toiling
And lakes of sulpher round them boiling
Hell did resound with their fierce yelling
Alas how dismal was their dwelling

If Hugo Williams is right in his daring assertion that Australian poetry attained a relaxed modernity long before the rise of literary modernism, it was a collective achievement rather than a breakthrough achieved by a few large poetic figures. It may indeed be more accurate to see our tradition before Slessor, or anyway before the early part of this century, as a poetry of poems rather than of poets and poetic careers. Newspaper verse very often shares with folk poetry a haziness about attribution, but too great a concentration on poetic careers and poetic development, in the modern lit. crit. way, can obscure much that doesn't easily fit that model of looking at things, and may have misrepresented our tradition in the past. When we come to look at the literary poets of the past, of course, we do encounter people who for the most part were interested in having poetic careers, so the lit. crit. model works for them, and by that very fact may exaggerate their relative importance. Until very recently, it was customary to print their work and that of the anonymous or hazy figures lumped together as folk poets in separate anthologies! It was a social divide, like the rope which used to be strung across Wagga Town Hall in Mary Gilmore's childhood, to divide genteel dancers from proletarian ones at the annual Show Ball. If we ever have divided anthologies again, one wonders which side Frank the Poet will have to be assigned to, now that his career is known with fair certainty. He used to appear exclusively on the commoners' side.

The social-divide model of Australian verse has also, I think, obscured a lot of the cross-fertilization which took place. Genteel and literary poets were more prone to publish, indeed mostly self-publish, their work in individual volumes, and some published only in that form, but all but the most fastidious tended to put some at least of their poems into the great common pool of the newspapers, as well as the magazines of the day. Much of Charles Harpur's work was strongly engaged in the controversies of his time, and Kendall was similarly keen to reach his full potential public; both were capable of shredding a shonky politician in verses devoid of bosky dells or liquid bellbirds, and what we may term their poems in oils often had newspaper or magazine exposure as well as their pen-and-wash ones. An obvious case of cross-fertilization, and a complex one if we were to go into it deeply, is the so-called literary ballad, conventionally said to begin with Adam Lindsay Gordon in the 1880s, and still drawn upon with variations and inversions to this day. Indeed, so popular do the classic literary ballads of Henry Lawson and A.B. Paterson remain that reissued volumes of those authors still command enormous sales in our own time; they have become icons of Australian-ness, read as much for reasons of national identity as for their poetic merit.

The quintessential case of this is surely 'Waltzing Matilda', which is probably too well-known worldwide to need quotation here. Instead, it may be of interest to give the original version, as written by Paterson to the old tune 'Craigielea' on a visit to Dagworth Station, near Winton in Queensland, in 1895.

> Once there was a swagman, camped on a billabong,
> Under the shade of a coolibah tree;
> And he said, as he looked at the old billy boiling,
> 'Who'll come a-waltzing Matilda with me?'
> 'Who'll come a-waltzing Matilda, my darling,
> Who'll come a-waltzing Matilda with me –
> Waltzing Matilda, leading a water bag,
> Who'll come a-waltzing Matilda with me?'
>
> Down came a jumbuck to drink at the billabong,
> Up jumped the swagman and grabbed him with glee;
> And he said, as he put him away in his tucker bag,
> 'Oh! You'll come a-waltzing Matilda with me.'
>
> Down came the squatter riding his thoroughbred,
> Down came policeman one, two, three;
> 'Whose is the monkey you've got in your tucker bag?'
> 'Oh! You'll come a-waltzing Matilda with me.'
>
> Up jumped the swagman and dived in the water hole,
> Drowning himself by the coolibah tree;
> And his ghost says at night, as you ride down the billabong,
> 'Who'll come a waltzing Matilda with me?'

The version that is sung nowadays is a rearrangement carried out by M. and W. Cowan early this century. It seems to have been the Cowans who turned one policeman, with the cap number 123, into three separate troopers.

Many of the literary ballads actually belong to the early years of this century rather than to the nineteenth century, but that is barely relevant, as the tone and attitudes of last century can be seen as dominant at least up until the First World War, and many poetic careers which began in the actual nineteenth century retained its mindset to their end. Mary Gilmore, in my opinion a better poet than we have lately believed, lived far into the twentieth century, but she was never transformed by it. She retained the old century's pride and dash, its aristocratic socialism and its love of noble gestures, its stern stoicism and what we mistakenly see as its sentimentality. I *like* Dame Mary, but we will come back to her.

Since the classic literary ballads, 'The Man from Snowy River', 'Faces in the Street' and dozens more, are so well known to Australian listeners, I will illustrate the literary ballad with a less well-known example by the Tasmanian poet Marie E.J. Pitt. It has the heroic backward-looking note to be found in so many of those poems, and is entitled 'The West Coasters'. It commemorates a rainy island part of Australia very different from the inland slopes and plains beloved of men on horseback:

> Australia sings her Over-land,
>   From Murray back to Bourke,
> Her three-mile tracks, her sun and sand,
>   Her men that do the work;
> But here's to them, fill high the glass,
>   Who breasted drifting snow,
> Tramping through the button-grass...
>   Forty years ago!
>
> From Emu Bay to Williamsford,
>   From Strahan to Dundas,
> Through horizontal scrub they bored,
>   And quaking black morass.
> Old Bischoff saw their camp-fires pass,
>   Mount Lyell saw them grow;
> Tramping through the button-grass...
>   Forty years ago!
>
> The bleak winds flayed them as they strode,
>   The black frosts bit them sore,
> But still The Road, The Open Road
>   Went singing on before;
> And with them went a lightsome lass,
>   Adventure, face aglow,
> Tramping through the button-grass...
>   Forty years ago!
>
> Where red their leaping camp-fires roared
>   To forest legions thinned,
> The Axe flung, like a levin sword,
>   Her challenge down the wind.

> They slew the pine and sassafras,
>   The myrtle host laid low,
> Tramping through the button-grass...
>   Forty years ago!
>
> From out their dreams the cities rose
>   As yet from hill-heads gray
> The first red flush of morning grows
>   Into the lord of day.
> So here's to them! fill high the glass!
>   'The West Coast Esquimaux'
> Tramping through the button-grass...
>   Forty years ago!

It tends to be characteristic of those we have termed the newspaper poets that they accept their Australian environment wholeheartedly, or with only a light irony, right from the start. The balladeers are slower to settle into distinctively Australian landscapes and atmospheres, and the literary poets publishing in self-financed, slim volumes rather than in the vulgar press are slowest of all to acclimatize. Newspaper poets and balladeers alike tend to concentrate on the human and the social; nature is background, its asperities often no more than the obstacles that confirm courage or confer martyrdom upon it. What the popular poets did pioneer, in step with or even substantially ahead of poets elsewhere in the English-speaking world, was the use of vernacular language and the securing of effects by means of working people's idiom rather than high, poeticizing diction. This example comes from the early 1870s, and seems to be by Anonymous:

> The crows kept flyin' up, boys,
> The crows kept flyin' up.
> The dog he seen and whimpered, boys,
> Though he was but a pup.
>
> The lost was found, we bought him round,
> And took him from the place,
> While the ants was swarmin' on the ground
> And the crows was sayin' grace.

That was the period when poets, as much as or perhaps even more truly than political theorists, were inventing the proletariat, which for a long time many would confuse with Australia. It was natural that this mistake should be made, because our evolving culture first found a recognizable identity for itself in shirtsleeve terms and manners. Popular verse chimed with this and developed it, as both a national character and a political hope, and one of the results of this was our lasting tendency to tell ourselves lies about class, even to the point of pretending our society is free of caste and from inversions of it. In the long run, the literary ballad style would set as hard as concrete, and tend to prevent the expression of new social phenomena, especially among city people. Everything would be referred backwards, to the tone and idiom of the late nineteenth and early twentieth centuries, the decades of the early Labor movement. The band would play 'Waltzing Matilda', on and on as the world changed, while the coming of literary modernism would rout the newspaper versifiers by removing poetry from the old popular readership it had enjoyed for just on a century.

A last straggler of this nineteenth-century tradition, writing on twentieth-century phenomena in the spirit of a braver, perhaps simpler but at all events more resilient era, was Henry 'Hawkeye' Edwards, of Cundletown on my part of the New South Wales north coast. A bootmaker and advocate of Henry George's single tax theories, he flourished over a huge time span, from 1870 to the 1930s, and if his frequent topical verses in the local newspapers never reached very great heights, he was typical even in that of hundreds of his kind. And yet he captured much of ordinary life. Here is part of a poem of his from the year 1930, but full of social carryovers from the previous century; it is titled 'Selling that Wireless Set':

> Mother! she sold her wireless set –
> Sold it the other day;
> Took whatever old price she'd get,
> Or what the cove could pay.

> It told of markets, weather and wet –
> Babe's bedtime stories too;
> Granny, that couldn't read, would sit,
> And hear the programme through.

> And Dad would growl at the price of pigs,
> And the rate for poddy calves,
> And Sirs would hear about all the jigs –
> They never do things by halves.

All went well till the 'Second Test'.
(Our night is English day);
Then ev'ry stiff became a guest
To hear it – Hip, Hooray.

They'd smoke and spit, and wait and yarn,
The blessed night all through.
You'd think our home was Coogan's barn
With air tobacco blue!

Most of the mob were unemploy'd –
Some of them drew the dole –
But that sort never get annoy'd
While others pay the toll.

Hobble-de-hoys were there past twelve;
Old grey-hairs until four;
Next day they'll hardly dig and delve,
Who will settle their score?

Fags and matches! Matches and fags!
Following ev'ry test,
Country's credit is all to rags –
Production's going West.

Taxes piling, and piling more,
Till threadbare togs are worn;
The greatest theme is Bradman's score,
Till cock-crow in the morn.

Jazz of a city fills the gaps,
And the names of missing friends;
But not one man says 'So long chaps' –
Till the fight for Ashes ends

Mother put up her wireless set
In Taree pumpkin sales,
And says what news her home-fires get,
Can all come in the mails.

To the very end, and especially towards the end of its era, the newspaper poem tended to differ from the bush ballad in staying contemporary rather than backward-looking, critical rather than nostalgic, less inclined to rely on statuesque received attitudes and situations. It never fell prey to nationalist sanctification.

Despite their comparative invisibility to all but a tiny readership in the colonies or At Home, it fell to the more literary poets to wrestle with the really quite enormous difficulties of adapting a northern European language and its established poetic diction to the non-human and pre-European realities of the new country. There were thousands of failed attempts, poems so choked with outworn poetic tropes and phrases that nothing alive struggles to the surface, and all we have is a costive effort to Make A Poem in respectable terms. One way to get past these difficulties was with the aid of intense, almost scientific precision, aided by mimesis of natural sound. A poet well equipped to come at the problem this way was the science-minded adoptive Tasmanian Louisa Anne Meredith, the first person, so far as I know, ever to be granted a pension by a colonial government for her services to science, literature and art; this happened at the early date of 1870. Here is her poem 'Tasmanian Scenes':

Flowers in legions bloomed around in forest, scrub, and
      marsh,
Dropping soft petals o'er the brook, or on rocky ridges harsh,
Nestling in crevices and chinks, like jewels in the mine,
Or peering out with merry eyes into the noonday shine.

There grew the 'helmets' green, like elfin knights together;
Some wore their armour plain, some with a flaunting feather.
And caladenias quaint, with hoods and fringes rare,
Couched by old mossy trees 'midst delicate maiden-hair;
Acres of peaty swamps glowed purple with the shimmer
Of gay rush-lilies; and in dells where the forest-shades fell
      dimmer –
In deep, green, silent glens, – silent, except the fall
Of tinkling streams that made a monotone most musical –
The feathery fern trees dwelt, with palmy crests outspread,
Close interweaved and overlapp'd in canopies o'erhead;
Upborne on massy columns whence taper ribs upspring
And leafy traceries flow from their mazy clustering,
While round each pillar, wreaths of polish'd verdure cling
With long and shining fronds, in graceful garlands, drooping
Adown and down, till into the spray of the tiny cascade they're
      stooping.

But the rill goes wimpling on, round island rocks all mossy,
By groves of fragrant sassafras, and myrtles dark and glossy,
'Neath bridges of great fallen trunks, under whose dark
    shadows slipping,
It whirls to the deep and silent pool where the miner-birds
    are dipping;
And parrots skimming to and fro thro' a sunny gleam
    together,
Are bright, as though the sun had set a rainbow in each feather!

The struggle to naturalize our language and adapt it to the literary needs of Australia has been a long one, and continues to a degree even today. It has arguably seemed at times to stunt fantasy here; fictive and faery lands are less needed, because the Australian continent itself is our great object of meditation. This parallels our fascination with prose and photography dealing with Australiana of all sorts: at times ours can seem largely a non-fiction poetry. The great task, poetic as much as colloquial, of naming the creatures is as yet unfinished here, at least in English. As the poet Mark O'Connor has pointed out, hundreds of species of plants and fishes and humbler creatures have as yet only their Greco-Latin scientific names. Charles Harpur was one of the many who struggled with these problems, early and nobly, just as he struggled to make poetry itself, in its full range, a respected and natural part of civilized life in a frontier society just emerging from the odium of being a penal colony. One of his legacies to us is the national or anyway sporting colours of green and gold: gold for sun, sand and the dry grass of summer, green for the evergreen forest that doesn't shed its leaves in autumn. Not all of his protean effort is taken up, though, with literary or civic struggle, and it is dangerous ever to see Australian poetry too rigidly in terms of any one of its major themes. The following poem is quite outside the range we have been discussing, and belongs to the genre of the still-life, in which colonial painters such as William Buelow Gould also achieved some lovely and successful works. Harpur's poem is entitled 'A Basket of Summer Fruit':

First see those ample melons – brindled o'er
With mingled green and brown is all the rind;
For they are ripe, and mealy at the core,
And saturate with the nectar of their kind.

And here their fellows of the marsh are set,
Covering their sweetness with a crumpled skin;

Pomegranates next, flame-red without, and yet
With vegetable crystals stored within.

Then mark these brilliant oranges, of which
A by-gone Poet fancifully said,
Their unplucked globes the orchard did enrich
Like golden lamps in a green night of shade.

With these are lemons that are even more
Golden than they, and which adorn our Rhyme,
As did rough pendants of barbaric ore
Some pillared temple of the olden time.

And here are peaches with their ruddy cheeks
And ripe transparency. Here nectarines bloom,
All mottled as with discontinuous streaks,
And spread a fruity fragrance through the room.

With these are cherries mellow to the stone;
Into such ripeness hath summer nursed them,
The velvet pressure of the tongue alone
Against the palate were enough to burst them.

Here too are plums, like edible rubies glowing –
The language of lush summer's Eden theme:
Even through the skin how temptingly keeps showing
Their juicy comfort, a rich-clouded gleam!

Here too are figs, pears, apples (plucked in haste
Our summer treat judiciously to vary)
With apricots, so exquisite in taste,
And yellow as the breast of a canary.

And luscious strawberries all faceted
With glittering lobes – and all the lovelier seen
In contrast with the loquat's duller red,
And vulgar gooseberry's unlustrous green.

And lastly, bunches of rich blooded grapes
Whose vineyard bloom even yet about them clings,
Though ever in the handling it escapes
Like the fine down upon a moth's bright wings.

Each kind is piled in order in the Basket,
Which we might well imagine now to be
Transmuted into a great golden casket
Entreasuring Pomona's jewelry.

I don't really understand the term Post-Modernism, but it is used to describe the period we are in now. If it signifies a greater freedom of poetics open to us now that the struggles of modernism are well and truly over, then we're in a position now even to appreciate the sometimes accidental felicities of the old poetical style and its clotted impasto, as well as the unstraining life of topical newspaper verse. I well remember Kenneth Slessor's adamant scorn for the literary balladists and indeed all nineteenth-century Australian verse. Perhaps it is only now that a complete view of our older poetic heritage is even possible. As we have seen even in this short conspectus, the inherited poetical diction of last century didn't always spoil poems; sometimes, as in Mary Gilmore's 'The Harvesters', a discreet measure of it even helps a poem to attain the unpretentious, monumental quality it was seeking. Here is the poem:

In from the fields they come
To stand about the well, and, drinking, say,
'The tin gives taste!' taking in turn
The dipper from each other's hands,
The dregs out-flung as each one finishes;
Then as the water in the oil-drum bucket lowers,
They tip that out, to draw a fresher, cooler draught.

And as the windlass slowly turns they talk of other days,
Of quaichs and noggins made of oak; of oak
Grown black with age, and on through generations
And old houses handed down to children's children,
Till at last, in scattered families, they are lost to ken.
'Yet even so the dipper tastes the best!' they say.
Then having drunk, and sluiced their hands and faces,
Talk veers to fields and folk in childhood known,
And names are heard of men and women long since dead,
Or gone because the spirit of adventure
Lured them from familiar scenes to strange and far.
Of these old names, some will have been so long unheard
Not all remember them. And yet a word its vision brings,
And memory, wakened and eager, lifts anew
The fallen thread, until it seems the past is all about them

Where they group, and in two worlds they stand –
A world that was, a world in making now.

Then in sudden hush the voices cease,
The supper horn blows clear, and, from community
Where all were one, each man withdraws his mind
As men will drop a rope in haulage held,
And, individuals in a sea of time,
In separateness they turn, and to the cook-house go.

Finally, of course, it needs to be remembered that the point of looking at the poetry of the past is not the history or the sociology or the national development it may be alleged to reveal; the point is the poetry itself, and the life it contains. No poem is free of all conditioning by the time and the milieu in which it was made, but still we rightly treasure the ways in which good poems transcend these things, to attain a timeless inexhaustibility.

Nearly all the poems I have presented or excerpted in these two programmes are important parts of our literary heritage, and I think all have a value beyond their time and place. I want to end, though, with what I consider a jewel of a poem, by Mary Gilmore, that at once crystallizes the nineteenth-century theme of the death of little children – a piercing sorrow few parents in those days seem to have escaped – and stands as a small masterpiece on the subject, equalled in my own reading only by the Roman poet Martial's superb elegy for the little girl Erotion. Mary Gilmore's poem is titled 'The Little Shoes that Died':

These are the little shoes that died.
    We could not keep her still,
But all day long her busy feet
    Danced to her eager will.

Leaving the body's loving warmth,
    The spirit ran outside;
Then from the shoes they slipped her feet,
    And the little shoes died.

Broadcast by ABC 'Radio Helicon' programme, July 1986.

Embodiment and Incarnation

Notes on preparing an anthology of Australian religious verse

In 1984 I was approached by David Lovell of what was then Dove Communications in Melbourne to compile and edit an anthology of Australian religious poetry. 'Do you want an anthology of Australian Catholic poetry?' I asked, seeking at once to clarify and to delimit the job I was being asked to do. 'No,' was the reply, 'not just Catholic.' I then asked whether they'd like a book of Australian Christian poetry, thinking that that might at least have manageable limits, and knowing that no full-scale, high-quality anthology of Christian verse written in this country was on the market at the time; I couldn't really recall one from the past either. Again, though, the reply was no. What was wanted was a wider survey, embracing religious poetry from all traditions and none. 'Ah,' I sighed, 'you mean you want me to do the *hard* one?' I knew immediately, and had really known since the conversation began, that such a book was needed. Indeed, under the influence of R.S. Thomas's *Penguin Book of Religious Verse*, which had drawn upon the corpus of British poetry, I had even toyed at times with the idea of just such a book based on our own material. I may even have mentioned this idea to people, including Father Edmund Campion, the member of the Dove Board of Directors who, I gather, had instigated David's call to me. So I had quite possibly made the yoke that was being gently laid on my back, and I guess my questions were in part the wrigglings of a man trying to get out of, or at least reduce, a heavy task he really knows he should undertake.

I must say the timing of the request was uniquely opportune. I had just embarked on my reading for another anthology, the *New Oxford Book of Australian Verse*, a huge job which would involve my examining the whole corpus of English-language poetry written in Australia since European settlement, plus all accessible translations of Aboriginal song verse. Reading for another anthology at the same time would be a very small extra burden, and greatly preferable to doing the whole large survey twice at different times! It would be no trouble to photocopy likely poems for both anthologies at the same time and put them into two separate cardboard boxes for subsequent winnowing. In the end, my reading for the religious verse anthology went on for a few months after I had finished that for the Oxford book; some poems were sent to me by individuals, and I was able to track down more in publications outside the usual literary ambit. Readers of both anthologies may have noticed a degree of overlap between the two, however, and now they know how it came about. I really don't think the overlap means very much, beyond the mechanical circumstances that brought it about; I would have been scanning the same corpus of published sources whether I did so twice or just once, and the spirit in which I did both jobs was, allowing for the different objects of the two collections, essentially the same. Poetry is my work, my field and I think my vocation, the prime channel through which I ever achieve (or am given) any apprehension of ultimate and divine things. I'm fairly zealous in its defence and in its service, and I think it presents us with some highly important insights about the very nature of religion itself. Indeed I think that religions are themselves large poems, but I will come back to a discussion of that later in this paper.

Not all poetry is religious, of course. My first task, after settling the point that the book was to be essentially a survey, was to set up criteria by which poems would be admitted to the collection or excluded from it. I decided to keep these loose, in the sense that they would include a measure of instinct, of intuition and sympathy as well as a framework of intellectual clarity. I would not make strict intellectual definition central, because I don't think it ever finally is so in the most important realms of life. I would, rather, make poetry itself central and decisive, because I believe, perhaps controversially, that this is a truer reflection of reality. No poem would be included if it lacked poetic quality. Some lowering of poetic wattage might be allowed in cases where nothing else was available to represent a theme or a tradition in our religious verse, but nothing wholly lacking a spark of poetry would be put in just for representation's sake. To do that would be to betray poetry itself and to belittle the thing represented. As I wrote in the foreword, this was to be an anthology of poetry, not a source-book of religious sociology or a pious book of spiritual golden thoughts for all. In the same foreword, I went on to write:

> Most of the religious traditions existing in Australia are represented in this book, though there are bound to be a few gaps. No attempt

has been made to ration representation in accordance with respective numbers of adherents. The religious configuration of the Australian literary world is apt, in all periods, to be different from that of the wider population, and talent is not shared out evenly among human groupings anyway. Also, and obviously, the religion of artists is quite often art itself; a poet's intense spiritual experience is apt to be bound up with writing poems. Art is anciently a part of religious activity, and is surely still at least continuous with it. I have only been a bit restrictive in respect of two broad poetic types: vague poetical pantheism of the automatic sort, and the more vapid kinds of devotional verse of whatever tradition. Anything more distinctive or specific is likely to have been represented, and the same goes for anything more strictly mystical or contemplative, in the proper sense of those words. I have regarded as coming within the ambit of this book any verse dealing with material commonly regarded as religious – this is partly why the book opens with bells, bishops and church buildings, things that anyone might vaguely summon up when starting to think about the religious dimension – as well as any verse that seemed to me to evince some real engagement with the numinous. And this includes negative engagement, which is not to be confused with rejection.

Books of poetry which actually give primacy to the poetry in them are quite rare in our age, and I was compiling two of them that year. Most anthologies nowadays use a good deal, often a great deal, of managerial prose to marshal and discipline the poetry they are presenting, rather as if it were a primitive and rather dangerous force they were obliged to keep under control – and sometimes to harness for useful work, such as refining the souls of future office workers and grading their minds' quality in public exams. Poetry as a zoo animal, as an educative workhorse, as a fuel for political Molotov cocktailas, as grist to an academic or therapeutic mill – these are some of the secret functions which the very design of most modern anthologies would have our ancient art serve, often while pretending to be its protectors, preserving it like a frail endangered species in a paper Wildlife Reserve. I had decided very firmly to do all I could to counter these received views. My two anthologies would carry as little managing prose as possible, so as to leave more room for poetry, but more importantly, so as to give it its freedom and let it have its effect, without all the guide rails of commentary to which many readers will cling if they are provided. I would not even trammel my books with biographical data on the poets; other books contain those, and can be looked up. In the case of the religious verse anthology, I even eschewed poets' dates of birth (and death if things had gone that far with them) so as to exclude the relativizing effects of an historical view. All the historical orientation I thought relevant went instead into the Foreword, and consisted pretty much in the observation that it was striking how much of the decent religious poetry of this country dated from the period since the Second World War; this is where the preponderance lay, and I left readers to mull over possible reasons why. I hesitate to give my opinion even now, though it is hard to resist the speculation that a decline in religious certainty has provoked an upsurge in searching and questioning – and a decline in an older sort of anti-religious hectoring, which required a firm opponent to batter against. Things have arguably gone too far for that now, and the near-total divorce of the State from any underlying religious ethic has produced not 'freedom' but a terrifying void against which comfortable old Enlightenment audacities are meaningless. It is generations since being an agnostic involved any daring, and atheism tends to put one into coercive rather than generous company. More seriously, whether one believes in the soul or not, neither of these positions feeds it; we feel its hunger as a matter of experience, and have nothing to feed it on but our own selves. At bottom, we cannot build a satisfying vision of life upon agnostic or atheist foundations, because we can't get our dreams to believe in them.

I could not, of course, attain utter purity in my rebellion against presuming to manage poetry. For one thing, the mass of material I had gathered had to be put into the book in some sort of order, for another thing there was the special case of Aboriginal verse. I was determined that the latter be presented as far as possible on the same terms as the rest, since it had been selected on the same terms of poetic impact, but in a few cases I relented and, in order to orient readers completely unfamiliar with Aboriginal culture, left in the notes supplied by those, usually anthropologists, who first translated particular song-texts. The fact that the Aboriginal poems were all really translations, from another culture if not from another language as well, gave them a claim to some privileges. In ordering the book as a whole, I resorted to loose, unlabelled groupings based on primary or apparent subject matter, always ruefully conscious that even to say what a poem is about is to limit its life and begin to constrict it in a web of prose. And of course the timeless Aboriginal song-texts with their utterly different relationship to subject matter tended to cut across the constellations of common concern traceable in the English-language poems.

Critical reaction to the anthology when it came out was mostly generous and favourable. Some said, rightly, that I had over-represented myself: I simply hadn't noticed that, as I put the book together. Some people regretted the absence of favourite poems, and I am sorry myself about some of my omissions. In particular, I am ashamed that I forgot to seek out the work of Fr Peter Steele, the Melbourne Jesuit poet; no collection of his came my way during the long months of reading for the anthology, but I did know of his work and even put a poem of his into the *New Oxford Book*. I should perhaps have had just a little more of Fr Hartigan ('John O'Brien') on an older style of Catholic family devotions, because he gives us perhaps our best window on those, and really conveys their sweetness in ways that are only occasionally cloying to modern tastes. I fight hard against being a prisoner of the sensibility of my own time, or of any time, but that is one case where I failed in my fight. I should have been more diligent, too, in my search for Australian hymns. Those are difficult poetic territory because only some of them work on the page, without their proper dimension of music. They belong to the realm of song, which most kinds of poetry have been drawing away from for centuries in order to be a pure and not a composite art form. The music of most of the poetry written in the last few centuries is verbal and gestural, bound up in the sounds of words and the ordering of breath which the structures of written verse are designed to bring about; it is also frequently present in the logic of a poem. All of this would usually be merely impeded by an overt musical accompaniment – and to call the musical side of song an accompaniment is to denigrate its importance, in the majority of cases. Song really is pretty much a separate art, and I am less confident when I get into it. Some critics, in fact quite a few, spoke of the preponderance of Catholic material in the book, which may be so, but I claim in reply that this reflects the situation I was examining; I'm pretty sure I didn't over-represent Catholic material in relation to what exists in print in our literature. In fact, I was on my guard against this danger, and this possibility of bias in myself. It was amusing that some who complained of my neglecting identifiably Protestant material weren't any longer practising members of their original denominations: loyalty outlives commitment, it seems, or may be meant to serve as a residue from which commitment may re-grow. A few were forgivably disoriented by the lack of signposting in the book, and quite a few were puzzled at some of the inclusions, wondering how this or that poem could be regarded as 'religious' at all.

No one, so far as I can recall, went into detail as to which poems troubled them in this way, and though I have told a few inquirers privately why I put in particular poems, it would violate the spirit of the book if I were to go into public defences of particular inclusions, particularly if I were merely guessing which poems to defend. I merely claim, therefore, that I had my reasons in each case, and I leave it to individual meditation to wrestle with apparently puzzling cases.

Of all the reviews, I think the one which understood best of all what I had been trying to do was that published in the Anglican (or anyway Anglican-based) *Eremos Newsletter* (No. 18, February 1987) by my fellow poet John Foulcher. Under the title 'Poetry as Divining Rod', John wrote that his very uncertainty as to why much of what he read in the book was strictly speaking 'religious' came to seem the key to understanding it. He goes on to say:

> On one level, this lack of apparent structure looks decidedly perverse – when I read an anthology, I like to dabble a bit, read a few favourite poems and the like, rather than reading the entire thing right through. I suspect most people approach poetry in the same way. Yet Murray forces us to actually read the book as a whole in much the same way as we would read a novel – a long picaresque outing written from the viewpoint of many disparate characters. Ultimately, this dumping of the reader into a virtual sea of poetry turns out to be one of the book's major strengths. You don't drown in it, as you thought you would, but you're buoyed by the constant interplay between the earthy and the mystical, between despair and hope, cynicism and faith. And when it's all over, you find you're still breathing, but you're immersed in that basic question Murray begs throughout: just what is 'religion'?... It comes as no surprise then, to find work by many of Australia's greatest writers here, many who would not call themselves religious, and who certainly would not call themselves Christian. But the book implies that the poet and the theologian can cover the same ground, they just approach it from different angles. I like this approach, as it forces truth to be separated from dogma and self-interest, it returns God to the wordless, and then tries to find words for Him.

A Catholic might have added here that forcing truth to be separate from dogma for a moment is done in order to allow it to recover its freshness, its poetry. I assent to the dogmas of the Church, but I was compiling an anthology of work by authors who might or might not assent to them for readers who similarly might or might not, and I had to be fair to all equally. Dogmas, too, quickly and inescapably approach the condition of prose, though they are ultimately grounded in a sublime poetry. The Popes are the administrators, we should remember, of a great ever-living poem – and perhaps no poem in the anthology shows a more sympathetic awareness of that, or describes it better, than the superficially risqué 'Pope Alexander VI' by my old colleague Geoffrey Lehmann, who often presents himself as a fierce anti-Catholic. Again, my making the poetic dimension and experience paramount in the book's design arose partly from a realization that in an age of seemingly hopeless religious fragmentation, poetry itself is one of the few channels of spiritual life all may still have in common. Indeed it may be the only one. And given Literature Board fellowships, few and brief as they are, it may indeed be our only established church. Each person may be caught up in the large 'poem' of his or her beliefs, or involved with fragments of several such, but poetry itself remains as an available universal value. I was sorry that one poet whose work would have yielded many worthwhile inclusions in the anthology misunderstood this, and refused to be represented because he did not want to be seen as a religious poet. It was no part of my intention to present anyone as that, or to pigeonhole them in any way. As John Foulcher goes on to say, after commenting on some adverse reaction to his own work by a Sydney Christian arts group:

> I think such people wouldn't like Murray's anthology: in the long run they're probably not interested in poetry. Nor, perhaps, are they interested in religion. They seem to be interested in order, in neatness, and that's precisely what Murray refuses to provide. In the book's final poems – the most metaphysical of all, concerned with the 'Spirit' or 'Presence' of God in the world – we are left with a sense of yearning, of longing. And if anything unites the poems in the anthology, it is precisely that sense. On that level, poets are basically a religious lot, and religious people have a lot of poetry inside them.

The problem John encountered with those straitly devout people seems to have been that they disapproved of his using poetry as a key to the subconscious bringing into the open our greatest fears and doubts as well as our great joys. Anxiety and despair come through that door to the light of day, and poetry is not always the obediently reassuring, inspirational thing some want it to be. To expect it to be so is to ask it to be subservient to laws not its own, and this is a very effective way of killing it off, because for its very life it has to dare the great depths. So does religion, in exactly the same way, if it is not to be merely a neurotic refuge from life. No one exactly said so, but it may have been a shock to some readers to see the likeness of their own religious commitment in strange mirrors, in poems dealing with such religion-substitutes as drugs, doctrinaire politics or the obsessive nationalist heart-searching we go on with in Australia, the sort of domestic Shinto with which we revere every fragment of national distinctiveness, sometimes in rites made of searing ridicule. All these aspects of our religious conscious- ness are reflected in the book, as are the authentic spiritual insights of atheists and the stinging criticisms of anti-religious polemic. Most importantly, authentic spiritual experience is present everywhere, from moments of illumination to whole passages of positive and negative mystical encounter. An example of the latter would be Lex Banning's 'Apocalypse in Springtime', with its profound evocation of a sense of nothingness that deepens and deepens but oddly does not seem to include the observer who experiences it. A positive parallel to it would be Kenneth Mackenzie's 'Two Trinities', in which a man realizes his distance from all his earthly attachments and finds himself ready to accept his soul's invitation to accompany it on its journey. Other examples of this same theme can be found in the anthology, along with many other sets of experience which can be discussed only in terms provided by religion. As a sort of lowest common denominator, there's even a small clump of ghostly poems, involving the universal human experience of the delicious shudder, or *grue* as my old master Rudolph Otto called it, borrowing a word from the Scots. Here, though, I must stop itemizing the book's contents or I will start to sound like a publisher's representa- tive out to push it.

The point I am making, of couse, is that the book is filled with experiences and concerned with experience, because it is founded upon a single experience with which all those reported in its pages are congruent. This is the poetic experience, the thing poets and their readers share, and the thing we all seek from poetry. This, as I have said elsewhere, is an experience as primary and distinctive as sex or the enjoyment of food. It is the verbally based version of the aesthetic experience, that which transfixes us in the presence of a great painting or sculpture, or enraptures us in music. It seems, at bottom, to be an experience of wholeness. If a poem is real, it is inexhaustible; it cannot be summarized or transposed into other words. Something intrinsic in it inhibits us from doing so, and makes us feel silly and frustrated if we try. It is marked by a strange simultaneity of stillness and racing excitement. Our mind wants to hurry on and have more and more of it, but at the same time it is held by an awe which yearns to prolong the moment and experience it as timeless. We only half-notice, consciously, that our breathing has tightened and altered, submitting to commands from beyond ourselves. It shifts in and out of this sympathetic obedience as the experience oscillates within us, coming and going in its successive small peaks of intensity. We may say that the poem is dancing us to its rhythm, even as we sit apparently still, reading it. It is, discreetly, borrowing our body to embody itself. We speak of being struck by an image or a phrase – 'I came to that place in the poem,' as a friend said to me once, 'and clunk! my mind turned inside out, quite painlessly. "Huh?" I said, and read that bit again, and it happened again, precisely there, and I couldn't explain it to myself.' Where this sort of thing begins to happen in series we are as it were watching someone on a tightrope, and so caught up in the skill, the danger, the whole shimmering alternation of grace and teetering in the performance that we are really on the tightrope ourselves, in sympathy, exhilarated, dreading that their fall would be ours. It can seem, fuzzily and in ways we would be hard put to explain, that a great deal is involved in the success of such a walk, and that a fall would be momentous. These mechanisms operate even with poetry of lesser intensity, though we can become disgusted if we sense that the tightrope is too close to the ground, or that the walker is not walking for mankind, for us.

The poetic experience is not, of course, confined to verse; it can arise from properly tuned prose, too, and can affect us whether we receive it through listening or reading. Where it is at all intense, we find it enthralling but quickly exhausting. We want more of it, or we want it again, but we also need frequent rests from it. And if we resist this need for rests, the experience itself will fluctuate. We can have it repeatedly, and each time timelessly, but we can't have it steadily. We are as it were not yet permitted to live there. And yet it is itself a quietly perpetual thing, this ordinary ecstasy: it is kept for us in a finite vessel, the poem, which we can return to whenever we want to have the same experience again. Each time we return, the poem is the same, and yet fresh intimations of significance are likely to arise from it. It is, as St Thomas said, *radiant*. And we can grow in relation to it, perhaps over our whole lifetime, if it is a favourite poem. It is complete, finite, yet inexhaustible. Analysis cannot touch this reality, because it is a different order of discourse lacking the mysterious integration of what it examines. Nothing equally complete or economical is available to describe it. Each interpretation we put upon the poem will wear out in time, and come to seem inadequate, but the standing event of the poem will remain, exhausting our attempts to contain or defuse it. The only way in which commentary can defuse a poem is by inhibiting our surrender to it; we are taught strategies of intellectualizing about it, of comparing and classifying it, all the myriad ways of forestalling our looking attentively at it in itself. This can sometimes seem the nervous purpose of literary education, to protect society from poetry. This impulse is not wholly unwise, as we shall see, though it is crucially wrong at its heart, because it protects us against the wrong sort of poetry.

Human beings have two main modes of consciousness, one that is characteristic of waking life, one we call dreaming. The former is said by psychologists and physiologists to be the province of the 'new' part of the brain, the recently evolved forebrain, the latter relates to the older, limbic levels of the brain, sometimes called the reptilian brain. We now know from sleep studies that we need to experience both, and that we grow distressed if we are prevented from dreaming. Our dreams can invade the daylight realm of our life, and that is psychosis. In normal life, we experience a substratum of dream mentation running along just below our waking consciousness and seeping through it here and there. This is reverie, or daydreaming, and if it is too markedly out of kilter with our daylight thinking, we find ourselves agitated and under stress. As we have known since Freud and other early psychoanalysts, neither of our two lives is wholly subordinate to the other – or, if it is, we are likely to be more or less severely ill. Harmony between our two modes of life promotes health, and it is my belief that aesthetic experience is the supreme case of harmony between them. To be real, a poem has to be at once truly thought and truly dreamed, and the fusion between the two represents incipient wholeness of thinking and of life. A poem, or any work of art, enacts this wholeness and draws us into it, so as to promote and refresh our own. We find the atmosphere of this fusion intensely attractive, and may even become addicted to it; this is the Good Addiction, which the other kinds merely point to and parody, and we can judge them by Jesus's test of examining their fruits.

What attracts us to art and poetry is probably, first of all, the signals it sends out that here the secret world is present; to put that another way we are drawn by the bloom of dream life that the work bears. If the work is too drily intellectual and forebrainish, we apprehend it as arid and not really worth the trouble, or else shallow. If it is too indulgently dreamy, we may gulp it greedily in search of sustenance, but finally find it arbitrary and unsatisfying, and if it is contrived to look dreamier than it really is, we will react to that, too, more or less quickly depending on the strength of our need for dream-sustenance. In the long run, our unconscious will persuade us of the fraud, and reject it before we are aware the rejection has happened. This is frequently the fate of all but the best surrealist art, which apes dream mentation in order to invoke it. The danger though, always, is that our need of the good, true harmony which the best art evokes and nourishes may be so great that we will fool ourselves as to the quality of what seems to be supplying it, or a sufficient measure of it. And since the fusion of dream life and waking consciousness, of dream and reason if you prefer, lies at the very wellsprings of human endeavour, extending far beyond anything we can recognize as art, it behoves us to be fussy about the nature and sources of the inner equilibrium between the two which we attain. The artist Francisco Goya wisely observed that the sleep of reason produces monsters, and we have redoubled evidence for that in this century. The monsters are generated in part because the sovereignty of daylight reason we have extolled over the past few centuries is an illusion, based on the delusion that we can ever fully wake up, and the further delusion that perpetual rational wakefulness would even be bearable. Our very evolution, I submit, doesn't tend that way, but towards a wholeness of which art is the model.

I have been convinced for several years that the fusion of our two modes of life is a prime datum of human life and action. Everything we make, beyond the immediately utilitarian and the trivial, and perhaps much of that, too, comes of combinations of vision and reasoning. The thing has to make daylight sense, and have some sort of rationale, but it must also feel right, have the right sort of vibes as we say, and be acceptable to the contemplation of reverie. As we all know, work done without any vision, any sense of consonance with our deeper life, approaches the condition of drudgery, just as bad products or bad buildings lack a certain enlivening charm. Bad products, like bad poems, lean too far one way or the other: they look too calculated and possibly inhuman, or too banal, or else they look bizarre, flimsy and idiosyncratic to no purpose. A bad marriage may be too cool and emotionally arid or too painstakingly thought-through and fair-minded, or too designing; on the other hand, it may be too intensely romantic, a sort of *folie à deux* which can't handle the asperities and practicalities of the outside world, or it may be bedevilled by the personal kinks and nightmares the partners bring to it. I am necessarily describing these imbalances in the biased language of daylight consciousness because we are speaking here in verbal language, not the dream-world's language of feelings, atmospheres and symbols. It is a moot point whether the dream has any verbal language of its own; how many actual words or phrases do we remember from our dreams? A few, perhaps, and we may have a sense that speech was present in some of our nightly visits to the personal other-world. In waking life, pretty clearly, dream mentation may charge words, or bend them, or inspire them to be uttered, but it doesn't reason or explain *in* words. Indeed, while we may say that dream is the explanation for a lot of things, it itself never explains! It evokes, and moves, and conveys, and suggests, and it can do more of that with, say, one poignant memory from childhood (which of course it may also edit) than it could achieve with many closely reasoned paragraphs.

It follows from all we've been saying that the systems, ideologies, religions and other loyalties by which we live our lives are also fusions of the sort I've been describing. Freud's poem, Marx's poem, the poem of the Enlightenment, Buddha's poem, Jesus's poem. Just as surely as the smaller poem-constructs of our private lives, the personal quasi-poems which may constitute our 'image' or 'role' – the tough Australian bushie, the no-nonsense business executive – these larger poems make sense both to reason and to the unconscious world of our fears, needs and aspirations. Or each does so for a great many people. I may find, say, the poem of science too cerebral and too poorly integrated on its dream side (though it does have its own mythologies and legends, such as the theme of Galileo's persecution), but for some it serves as the poem of their lives, and they may find Catholicism, as they understand it, to be aberrant to reason in some way, or distorted in what Germans might call its dreamwork, lacking warrant from the unconscious for some of its claims. A lot of such judgments of course are based on perceptions of atmosphere and 'feel', whether or not these are rationalized afterwards. And it is surely true that a religion, with an explicit space for and vocabulary for the non-rational side of things, will be better equipped to understand and work with poetic fusions than can any tradition which explicitly or implicitly relegates the dream side, and so doesn't comprehend its own origins and nature.

Here, perhaps, I should mention two terms I have started using and which may be useful. I call properly integrated poetic discourse Wholespeak, while discourses based on the supposed primacy or indeed exclusive sovereignty of daylight reason I call Narrowspeak. The former embraces all good poetry including that of religion, the latter embraces most of the administrative discourse by which the world is ruled from day to day, as well as most of criticism. The two are obviously not commensurate, and it was also for this reason that I tried to reduce the proportion of Narrowspeak in my book of religious verse to a minimum. We have come, over the last few centuries, to think that we live in a prose universe, with prose as the norm of all discourse. This is a cause, or a consequence, of the decline in belief in creation (*poesis*). In fact, descriptive prose doesn't answer to our own inner nature, and so cannot describe the cosmos adequately.

Narrowspeak made to look like poetry but not truly dreamed (we are all guilty of this at times) is enormously common in modern times, and constitutes a majority of the verse published in literary journals everywhere, but in the absence of true or sufficient consonance with the dimension of dream it can only appeal on the basis of whatever intellectual interest it manages to generate. The aesthetic of interest is characteristic of a spiritually starved period, and among its features is an insistent appeal to excitement, to innovation, to relevance or to some group alignment or other. Real poetry has its own authority and needs make no such appeals. Works obedient to the aesthetic of interest I term *poesies*, and of course strains of poesy, in this sense, are often found even in real poems. There, though, the true fusion that also occurs justifies and redeems them. A further and final point to make about Narrowspeak is that while it lacks the true simultaneity of fusion in its own right, it is always in the service of some large 'poem' or other (Marxism, Rationalism, Science, Christianity, Islam) at one or more removes; it is a secondary and derived thing, a servant. Which is not necessarily to denigrate it. It has its essential and complex place in the world, just so long as we don't consider it primary. Part of its function is to protect us against the strain and fallout of Wholespeak and to help integrate this into the web of ordinary life. Narrowspeak can't be all bad, or I wouldn't be writing this essay in it, or mostly in it!

As we saw earlier, there is a third partner in the integration which is art, and that is the body. If we allow this to have the two obvious meanings which join in the term embodiment, it refers at once to the materials in which a work is realized, and to its somatic effect upon the beholder. This latter effect, felt in the ghostly sympathy of breath and pulse and muscle, is particularly central to poetry, but not limited to that sphere. In the face of strong examples of other art forms, we speak of being brought up short, of having our breath taken away, of being made to shiver, of being knocked sideways, being rocked on our heels. Experience of my own reactions tells me that these are more than merely metaphors. Music will often cause us to tap our foot or beat time with our hands, and we have all felt the tense slight participation of our muscles in the action of a gripping film or play. Religion, by more than analogy, has both ritual and spontaneous movements built into many of its observances; one thinks of the set bowings and upraisings of the Mass, or the rocking (called *davinen*) of Orthodox Jews at prayer, or of Miriam dancing before the Ark of the Covenant. And there is the full surrender of dropping to one's knees before God or before a great painting; if you think that is confined to more emotional cultures than our own, I cite the case of staid Calvinist and post-Calvinist Dutch people falling to their knees a few years ago when Rembrandt's *The Night Watch* was carried past them for re-hanging in the Rijksmuseum. Beauty and the identity-poem of patriotism had combined to overwhelm them. At a far extreme, beyond the familiar lump in our throat when we are deeply moved, there is the exaltation, common to hysteria and ultimate joy, of laughing and crying at once. That is a very special momentary kingdom in which only truth is possible, and we reach it only at the end of our tether. Within the processes of creating art, in turn, there is a world, better understood and described in some arts than others, of gesture and bodily participation. In some of the arts, for example ballet, this may constitute most of the means by which fusion is attained. In poetry, it is at least a quarter and probably a third of the story, especially if we add to the orchestration of breath and cadence the whole lore, far better understood on the unconscious than the conscious level, of affective sound and what we call mimesis, which is the transposition of natural sensations into words: a jack-plane lisps over a plank, a nun walks on her prayer, from underwater the troubled floor of the world becomes a remote and beautiful sun-bewildered ceiling. All these things produce tiny pauses in the mind, stop time, and echo right down into bodily aspects of our life. In their own sphere away from rhythm, they are a borderland music of arrests and releases, and not one which can easily be scored, or played purely by calculation.

Such is the embodiment and bodily echo of art, but what of those poetic moments which do not issue in art? They seek embodiment, too. Ferdinand Porsche's poems came out as cars, Henri Dunant's emerged as the Red Cross, those of Fred Burley took the form of ladies' foundation garments. Hitler's poems took concrete, steel and possibly forty million human lives to find expression. Karl Marx's poem, as variously augmented and re-expressed, shared with Hitler's a liking for such lines as leather top coats, merciless secret police and eager communal mind control, but has also issued in stanzas of improved rights for working men and women, in good folklore studies and in health care, along with such stanzas as the Gulags and the starvation of the Ukraine, though the latter may have been a composite stanza with lines borrowed from the older poem of Mother Russia. What is very clear is that poem fusions which do not find embodiment in art, and rejoice our bodies through that, may find more terrible embodiments and take our bodies from us altogether into the bargain. A poem-fusion seeking its embodiment outside art may well be the most dangerous thing on earth, and we need all the thickets of existing art and other, realized poem-fusions to hide among when one of these comes looking for its human materials. In a verse novel I wrote some years ago, I contrasted my religion with some other allegiances by saying: 'The true God gives his flesh. Idols demand yours off you.' A poem which stays within the realm of literature completes the trinity of forebrain consciousness, dream wisdom and bodily sympathy – of reason, dream and the dance, really – without needing to embody itself in actual suffering or action, and without the need to demand blood sacrifice from us. It is thus like Christ's Crucifixion, both effectual and vicarious. And yet criticism seems keener to police such poems than to grapple with the non-literary ones that come seeking embodiment, and warn us about them. Even this might well be futile, though; only a poem can fight a poem. A completed poem, of the literary kind, needs no commentary beyond perhaps the elucidation of unfamiliar words. The appropriate response is meditation, conducted on the level to which it raises us, and this may or may not be written down.

Aesthetics has three legs, as we have seen; religion has a fourth one, the Divine. To fusion we must now add the dimension which theology calls infusion. God can reach us through any of the modes of our life, through our dream consciousness, through our waking intellect, though that is much more capable of resisting Him, and through the vegetative life of our body, in which He may be most constantly present. He seems to reach us most easily in our wholeness, or at the opposite extreme in our disintegration; where we are most resistant to Him is in the middle range of premature and temporary self-integration. An example of the Divine reaching us when we had not sought it is given in Judith Wright's poem 'Grace', which I placed near the very end of the anthology:

> Living is dailiness, a simple bread
> that's worth the eating. But I have known a wine,
> a drunkenness that can't be spoken or sung
> without betraying it. Far past Yours or Mine,
> even past Ours, it has nothing at all to say;
> it slants a sudden laser through common day.
>
> It seems to have nothing to do with things at all,
> requires another element or dimension.
> Not contemplation brings it; it merely happens,
> past expectation and beyond intention,
> takes over the depth of flesh, the inward eye,
> is there, then vanishes. Does not live or die.

It is certainly true that contemplation doesn't bring this sort of authentic infusion, though it often invites it and may find the invitation answered. No form of prayer commands God, and it is possible that our seeking Him, as distinct from His seeking us, has its natural terminus in the Crucifixion, which showed us what we would do to God if we could get our hands on Him. We need not be shocked at this. He told us He would die so that sins might be forgiven, and it was surely necessary for us to discharge our fury at much of the world's workings on Him who had made it, and seemingly made it the ambiguous place it is. The existence of consequences, and of our freedom, necessarily involve great anguish which the space of our lives does not provide room enough to redeem, and our bewildered anger at this has to go somewhere before we can attain the sort of purified wholeness which can give and receive pardon. The Crucifixion is also the end of any self-righteous notion we may have of ourselves as innocent victims of a bad cosmic set-up, which helps to explain our eagerness, to shift the blame for it on to the Jews, the Roman Army, Pilate, anyone who was there at that point in history. But I digress, a little, into matters I only apprehend and which no one fully understands, since they are inexhaustible. I would certainly never trust anything I could fully understand.

If we are suspicious of our dreaming side as a channel of the Divine, guessing that it can be a realm of demons and delusions as well, and know that our intellective side is fatally well equipped to resist Him, and if, finally, we find it hard to do more than dimly sense His presence in our bodily frame (we sadly know that its homeostasis, its health, are temporary things), we are left with the plane of integrations between all three, that is, the plane of inspiration and prophecy as well as of beauty, as the most trustworthy area for interactions with Him. How many of the poems in my anthology do or do not contain instances of inspiration, in the true narrow sense of the word, it would be presumptuous of anyone to say. Most such interactions, though, are apt to be as brief in their intensity as our experiences of art; timeless while they last, but brief in time, and harder to recover than passages of art because they leave no exterior deposit. If there is anywhere in us a sort of embassy of such wholeness, it may be what we call our conscience – which some, at times to avoid the Christian theology of it, prefer to call their integrity. In my experience, conscience shares with art an ability to be instantaneously and convincingly there and a total resistance to untruth (you can't lie in art, any more than in prayers), and it has an eloquence both in and beyond words, and a stern logic that operates without any need of them, seemingly at the level of design – we speak of artistic conscience, and mean a firmer inner monitor which threatens to dissipate the essential effect of a work if we try to flout or evade it, say by leaving something in we know shouldn't be there, or by getting an image near enough to right, instead of right-plus. In some ways, I would go close to saying that the conscience resembles a permanent poem of ourselves that we carry within ourselves, though not one which claims our attention unless we try to circumvent it or some external influence challenges it. It is in no way subservient to interest, in either of the ordinary meanings of that word. It differs most signally from art, of course, in not bearing any aura of the rare and special, and in having no power or need to communicate itself to others. You can claim things on its behalf, but you can only display its effects through what you make or do; you can't directly show your conscience to another. In Christian terms, this hiddenness, this deep intimacy of presence, signalizes a resemblance between conscience and God the Father, rather than God the Son.

In that unique Divine embodiment for which we reserve the term Incarnation, Jesus lives from the first in a wholeness no mortal artist can sustain; he lives on the level of poetry, and thus shows us the way to that quality of life which he calls the Kingdom. This Kingdom is Jesus's own poem, and He embodies it fully, while revealing it as an aspect of God's poem. He never speaks in abstractions; there seems to be no Narrowspeak in Him. He speaks to the elements with the authority of a director, and of the wild lilies out in the paddocks with the just appreciation of one who respects them and their making and knows their real worth; we may say that He puts Solomon's man-made glories, and ours, in their place with the calmly ruthless judgment of an artist comparing two pieces of work. His words constantly go beyond the expected, and dazzle us with their quality of paradox, and of discovery; every 'line' is better than you expected, and deeper, and truer. His cures most often have no paraphernalia, and seem to come as directions spoken with authority, as by an author to a character. Sometimes they seem to cost Him strain and grief, but for reasons we can't fathom, rather as if they involved the body of the text which we can't see because we're in it. Human wholeness is always good, in His sight, but not so the premature integration which thinks of itself as human wisdom and lacks interaction with the Divine. 'You think as man thinks,' He says, 'not as God thinks,' or again, 'Blessed are you, Simon Peter, for flesh and blood have not revealed it to you, but my Father who is in Heaven.' And He also speaks with calmly terrible knowledge of the future, which being within time is also partly subject to human freedom and human device; clearly, the great work is also in part committed into the hands of its characters. When He speaks of laws, it is never in the one-dimensional terms of legal Narrowspeak. He transposes them into their full poetic value. Just as a work of art must never merely obey its own rules, but always excel them within its obedience, He gives the Law its more tremendous dimensions, showing it in the way it exists in the Kingdom, or, to put that another way, He consistently shows us the Law as it is when raised to the power of love and grace. And He refers his message always to the vision of children, to that integral and naturally poetic vision we all have before reason, the dream and the dance drift apart in us and our perceptions flatten. Like any great poem, that of Jesus is inexhaustible, and not all the books in the world could contain a sufficient meditation on it. Meditation would not be enough, anyway; this is meant to be not merely a poem we can appreciate and gain spiritual strength from, but one we can join. By sharing in our tragedy to the full, embodying it all the way to its tragic end and then re-assuming His own embodiment beyond it, He confirms better hopes, even for our bodies, than we had dared to hold on the basis of our health and our dreams alone. And He leaves his own incarnation behind, in a way that at once goes beyond metaphor and, surprise of surprises, confirms that even our most primitive, dream-impelled rituals of taking on the power of a god or an awe-some animal by eating it were in their way good, because they were on the right track. Or else, if we insist on human autonomy in the matter, they were a poem we arrived at repeatedly in different cultures worldwide and He took the poem, sanctified it and made it both harmless and salutary for all time to come. The impulse need never again be savage, for it is redeemed, and transposed into a life-giving thing like the calm eating of ordinary food! The very fact of eating is redeemed, since we are at last feeding upon what can afford to be eaten and not on what can't. The way to our true potential, we are shown, lies not through the rationalizations of the fore-brain, which imagines itself bodiless or exploits its embodiment, but through integration of all the dimensions of our life, each of which is good and holy, with the Divine.

The 1986 Aquinas lecture, first published by the Aquinas Library, Brisbane, reprinted by the Eremos Institute, Sydney, January 1987

A Music of Indirection

The Haw Lantern, by Seamus Heaney (Faber and Faber, 1987)

Seamus Heaney is deservedly the most celebrated Irish poet since Yeats, and one of the three or four most renowned poets in English today. He is also one of the most guarded of poets, and has sometimes been chided for not taking up declarative positions. He comes, though, from Ulster, where declared positions have caused such woeful human suffering, and where a deep guardedness once common to all of native Ireland retains its necessary force. Alec Hope's 'noble candid speech, in which all things worth saying may be said' was never really an option for tenantry, servant girls and itinerant labourers living under a bitterly sectarian foreign ruler. The old habits of obliquity and sotto-voce irony die hard, even among descendants living on the far side of the planet. As Heaney himself, and his mother before him, said in an early poem: 'Whatever you say, say nothing.' It can be raised to the condition of a poetic, almost, this wily slave-talk, and can be a potent way to woo delicate truths, in connections where even to say the truth is better wooed than forced or raped is to say too much. Again, for a dairy farmer's son from County Derry, the tradition of a language adopted from the ruler a few generations ago and seamlessly altered to fit native patterns of thinking and all the wealth of intimate native understandings is prime protection when one is obliged, as poets are these days, to move in exalted intellectualizing worlds where social control is exercised with whip-flicks of fashion and deployments of such terms as *naïve* or *second-rate*. In the light of history, which none of us are above, there is never enough good reason for people who write assertive, daylight style to denigrate those, civil libertarians in Eastern Europe say, or Christians anywhere now, who have learned the music of indirection. The congruence of that music with delicacy is a happy extra.

The contemporary realities of Ulster are not to the fore in Heaney's latest book of poems, but they are present. To cross into his ancestral heartland, the poet has to pass what one poem calls 'The Frontier of Writing', where quite literal rifles and machine guns cover him as he made to halt in his car:

> and everything is pure interrogation
> until a rifle motions and you move
> with guarded unconcerned acceleration –

* * *

> past armour-plated vehicles, out between
> the posted soldiers flowing and receding
> like tree shadows into the polished windscreen.

Again, some of the elements that underlie the modern civil war are present, though they aren't dominant, in the sequence called 'Clearances', a dedicatory poem and eight sonnets in memory of the poet's mother, who died in 1984. The first of the sonnets treats of an incident that happened to his maternal great-grandmother a century ago, and which his mother's death has now made fully his, an inheritance as real as silver or Victorian lace:

> She's crouched low in the trap
> Running the gauntlet that first Sunday
> Down the brae to Mass at a panicked gallop.
> He whips on through the town to cries of 'Lundy!'

I only learned the term *Lundy* last year, from Gerald Dawe, another fine Ulster poet; it's an Orange term for a turncoat, or for one who marries a Catholic and 'turns' for them, as used to be said in sectarian circles even in Australia. Much more in these poems, however, is very movingly taken up with the intimacy of mother and son:

> When all the others were away at Mass
> I was all hers as we peeled potatoes.
> They broke the silence, let fall by one
> Like solder weeping off the soldering iron...

There is a great and rueful delicacy, as well as another angle on discretion of language, in a sonnet which treats of the worldwide modern problem of preserving one's dignity before an educated offspring, pronouncing 'learned' words wrongly to signal areas in which one fears to be humiliated, and the impasse faced by the son who chooses to use the old familiar home pronunciations so as not to be estranged, or estranging. In another of the sonnets, in fact more than one, there are intimations of life beyond death, done now in genre, now in momentary images. And in a sonnet with the central image of mother and son folding sheets together, there is an oddly familiar reference to the two as resembling the letters x and o.

These are perhaps the most moving pieces in a short but varied and quite experimental collection. The letter-shapes may echo some themes of the first poem in the book, called 'Alphabets', which moves fascinatingly from a child's learning to read and write to a whole civilization learning and re-shaping its letters, then shifts almost imperceptibly back to the child again. There are the familiar Heaney deployments of vivid couplets, that manner of his which admirers and parodists seem readiest to imitate. One in this book is a vivid portrait of the Irish revolutionary Wolfe Tone affecting epaulettes and a cockade, 'out of my element among small farmers', and another poem-in-couplets called 'The Spoonbait' which is too oblique for me to get any sense out of it. There are poems of observation done seemingly for the sheer recaptured life of it, such as an obvious childhood memory called 'The Milk Factory', that begins: 'Scuts of froth swirled from the discharge pipe.' A master-class, that one line, in how little of a thing, in this case a rabbit's tail, it takes to make a beautiful, memorable image. The fascinating 'A Daylight Art', addressed to the Scottish poet Norman MacCaig, explores a moment in the life of Socrates which, if it hadn't happened on the last day of the philosopher's life, might have altered the course of Western thought and helped to balance the voracity of its abstraction. There is also an accomplished translation of a passage from Beowulf, and a christening-present poem from 1972, the patterned warmth of which can make much else in the book seem just a touch too oblique, too coolly proofed against the hyper-sophisticated criticisms the poet might fear now.

The only gauge of another poet's work I have used for a long time now is how often and how intensely in a poem or a book of theirs do they provide that unmistakeable quiet, riveting experience we call the poetic emotion. As might confidently be expected, much in *The Haw Lantern* (though not the title poem itself) grips me in the authentic way. My only reservation is that this happens least in the poems where Heaney is essaying something of a new departure, the semi-allegorical poems such as 'From the Republic of Conscience' and a couple of others with titles starting with the word 'From'. I find these intriguing rather than exciting, well-reasoned often, but lacking a dimension of dance to move our body-mind in a necessary sympathy with them. And this is true, too, of a poem called 'The Mud Vision', which struck me when I first read it in a magazine some while ago, but which I realize now had only excited my interest. It now seems full of what fashionable theoreticians call *écriture*, rather than a piece with a truly dreamed core sufficient to suffuse it with poetry. But this and much else in the book represents a fine poet's eminently legitimate casting around for ever new ways of coming at poetry, at reinventing it, as we have constantly to do. And the book as a whole is well worth getting, for the very moving in memoriam poems and six or seven other achieved pieces. Worth getting, that is, if you are not put off by what seems to me a horrendous price of just on thirty dollars for a hardback volume of only fifty-one pages; that's a savage test of how much one truly loves poetry, and Heaney's poetry in particular.

Filming a Poem

C.J. Dennis's verse narrative *Songs of a Sentimental Bloke*, with a glossary 'for the Thoroughly Genteel', was published by Angus & Robertson of Sydney in 1915. It sold extraordinarily well, even for a country in which large sales for poetry have not been rare. Seven thousand copies were sold in the first two months, sixty-six thousand in less than eighteen months. And this does not include considerable sales in the United Kingdom, Canada and the United States. Australian and New Zealand readers were enchanted to see an inventive colloquial language that was familiar and native, even if they did not themselves speak quite that way, and by the comic tension between harsh street argot and tender sentiment. The Bloke is indeed sentimental, and most seemed to find him lovable in ways which gratified national and class feelings alike. Though less often read nowadays, the book's magic persisted almost into our own day. A volume of Dennis's selected verse issued in 1950 and containing a choice of the 1915 Songs was still able to sell forty-five thousand copies by 1958, and remains in print even now. Sequels, especially *The Moods of Ginger Mick*, using characters introduced in the initial sequence, were equally popular. If Pauwels and Bergier are correct in their suggestive derivation of the term Gothic from *argot* (*art Gothique: argotique*), the Sentimental Bloke is a very interesting attempt at an Australian Gothic edifice, made from local materials in a time of strong and still fairly new national aspiration.

It was natural that such a well-loved narrative should appeal to the modestly flourishing Australian film industry of the day. Raymond Longford, who had been directing features since making his debut with *A Maori Maid's Love* and *The Bushwhackers*, both made in 1909, was introduced to the Bloke by J.D. Williams, the flamboyant American showman who had introduced the idea of continuous picture shows to Australia early in the century. Longford liked the story, and so did his partner and leading actress Lottie Lyell. She was certain it would prove a great success on the screen, and favoured it particularly because it lacked a murder of any sort.

Backing proved hard to find, however, and it was not until 1917 or early 1918 that Longford found a backer in the Adelaide company Southern Cross Feature Films, for which he had just made *The Woman Suffers*. Pre-production on the Bloke began in the middle of 1918, and the screenplay was written by Longford himself in association with Lottie Lyell. We may assume that Lyell had a good deal to do with the art direction, wardrobe and choice of locations. Personally and professionally, the relationship between Longford and Lyell was both deep and artistically fruitful, and Longford's career never really recovered from the tragedy of her early death from tuberculosis in 1925, when she was only thirty-four years old. The film of the Sentimental Bloke displays the restrained profundity of her art as an actress, in the intelligence which guides her every look and gesture and the depth of meaning which she could convey with her eyes alone. The contemporary magazine *The Triad* commented:

> Doreen in the book charms us so little that we often feel like throwing things at her, but the little Australian girl who plays Doreen on the film is so sprightly and honest, so womanly and so sweet, so unaffectedly Australian and human, that we find ourselves really believing in Doreen, and that is a great miracle.

Cloying though we may find these epithets now, the judgment is accurate. It is a signal fault in a narrative whose deepest trajectory is surely the encounter between a tough masculine culture developed in the woman-starved Australian colonies and the reality of the feminine, that where Dennis's Doreen is not wooden she is bossy or snippish, and scarcely develops any independent life beyond the worship lavished on her by the Bloke.

The harmony which the film develops between the characters and their gritty world was carefully nurtured by Longford and Lyell. Cast and crew alike immersed themselves in the milieu, reading and re-reading the verses, talking street language among themselves, frequenting the pubs and laneways of Sydney's inner suburbs and going on adventures with barrowmen and rabbit sellers. Though the Bloke's career had been set in Melbourne, Longford himself decided to move the action to Sydney. The street argot was the same, at least as regards everything except the preferred football code, and Longford said later that he made Bourke Street, Darlinghurst rather than Bourke Street, Melbourne his inspirational location 'for the very good reason that I know it, as indeed I ought to, for I was practically raised there, and spent most of my impressionable years in the precincts of the old gaol'. Longford's father had been a gaol official. The grim old sandstone prison later became the city's leading art school, and the suburb of Darlinghurst, or Darlo as it is affectionately known, had undergone a good deal of gentrifying change, while managing to remain perhaps the leading red-light district of Sydney. A poignant touch early in the film is the close resemblance between the old colonial sandstone terrace houses of Darlinghurst and the cells of the prison in which the Bloke is confined for 'stoushin' Johns' (beating up policemen). The grimy rubbed stone walls and square-cut doorways are identical, reminding us of the very genesis of Sydney as Britain's vaster Devil's Island; incarceration and gaols determined the atmosphere and the architecture of our beginnings. Nothing in younger, more genteelly founded Melbourne could have made this connection so effectively, nor is it made in Dennis's verse.

Casting Lottie Lyell as Doreen had been natural and immediate, but it took several weeks and much weary sitting in city and suburban theatres before Longford chanced upon a burly vaudevillian named Arthur Tauchert. Here was the right combination of broad vivacity and expressive ordinariness, of authentic Australianness and diffident force. Born in 1881 and veteran of a fairly marginal stage career, Tauchert had previously appeared in a short comedy film, *Charlie at the Sydney Show*, a pseudo-Chaplin piece directed by John Gavin in 1916, but *The Sentimental Bloke* was the peak of his career. Unlike Gilbert Emery, who played Ginger Mick and went on to become a character actor in Hollywood, Tauchert was never really successful in any other role. He played the Bloke again in two subsequent films, *Ginger Mick* (1920) and *The Dinkum Bloke* (1923), both directed by Longford. Although he had a number of other film roles in the Twenties and appeared in the first Australian talkie, *Showgirl's Luck* in 1931, the public identified him exclusively with the Bloke. He made a living at times from stage appearances reading C.J. Dennis's verse, before dying in 1933 after a long illness. Australian director (*The Picture Show Man, Caddie*) and film scholar Joan Long says of his performance in *The Sentimental Bloke* that:

> Tauchert's Bloke faces the world with a blend of aggressiveness and bewilderment, of swagger and shyness, of resentment that life should be dishing it out to him, yet readiness to meet whatever comes. Despite his urge to stoush cops and beat up his rival lover, he remains innocent and vulnerable. The verses on the screen seem the very expression of his inner thoughts.

Shooting of the film was beset by official restrictions. The State government prohibited any filming in its prisons, and forbade actors to wear police uniforms. Longford and Lyell had to resort to subterfuge. They obtained the co-operation of Commonwealth dockside officials, who agreed to appear as policemen and to provide an old watch-house in neighbouring Woolloomooloo to serve as a prison. The Sydney city council, by contrast, refused permission even to film a brief scene of the Bloke sitting on a park bench in the Botanical Gardens; Longford went ahead and shot the scene there anyway. The interiors were shot in the open at Wonderland City, in the beachside·suburb of Bondi, and the orchard which served as the Bloke's berry farm was at Hornsby, then on the outskirts of Sydney; the farmlands there have long since vanished under suburban development. The whole production was completed within its budget of £2,000. It was ready for private screening in Adelaide by November 1918, though problems with distribution companies delayed its release until October of the following year.

From the moment of its opening to a packed house in Melbourne Town Hall on 4 October 1919 the Bloke was a runaway success. It was also immediately recognized as a classic film. Writing in the *Picture Show* magazine on 25 October, the critic H.K. Carhall called it not only Australia's greatest screen classic, but also Australia's *first* screen classic. English reviews were equally favourable. In the London trade paper *Bioscope* on 23 September 1920, a commentator wrote:

> Acted quietly and naturally by players who perfectly embody the types they represent, the film has extraordinary charm. By its rich, shrewd humour and its simple humanity, it will certainly make as powerful an appeal to every class of audience as the famous British film classic *My Old Dutch*, with which it has been aptly compared.

The film made large amounts of money in Britain and Australia, and continued to appear in re-runs for several years. On the other hand, it never achieved a release in America. Distributors there found the language of the intertitles incomprehensible, and attempts to rewrite them in American slang were not a success. The natural consonance between British and Australian street language, both deriving in part from the underworld Flash Language of the eighteenth century East End slums, was missing in America, whose slang had become differentiated earlier and developed its own idiosyncrasis. Argot and attitude alike were irreconcilable, or were alleged to be by the guardians of America's own film industry. Also, the actors in the Australian film were said to look too ordinary; their faces didn't bear the standard marks of filmic glamour as it was beginning to be developed in Hollywood, and they were not svelte. It is perhaps a measure of the later collapse of Australian filmmaking in the face of American competition, that of the 160 or so films made here during the silent era, a bare thirty survive. Despite its huge success, only a single chance copy of *The Sentimental Bloke* came to light in 1955, after a fire in the vaults of the Commonwealth Department of Information in Melbourne. And even this might have crumbled away in the back sheds of the National Library had it not been copied on to modern film stock by enthusiasts and given repeated screenings by film societies.

Before its release, one of the first private screenings of *The Sentimental Bloke* took place in Melbourne before C.J. Dennis himself. He had kept a wary distance from the production, and came to the screening with sheepish reluctance, hoping not to be recognized. What he saw astonished and delighted him. He said later:

> I am amazed at the fidelity with which the written work has been produced as a visual narrative. At best, I expected to see a burlesque, at worse, a fiasco. Instead of that I came away almost believing in miracles... The difficulties which I thought would arise have all been admirably swept away.

Clarence Michael James Dennis was born in rural South Australia in 1876, the son of an Irish sea captain who had become a publican managing hotels in a series of small towns on the dusty, sun-bitten fringes of settlement north of Adelaide. Prim, pious maiden aunts in the village of Mintaro, to whom the boy was sent to get an education, insisted on dressing him in hot, stiff suits, making him into a figure of foppish ridicule among the ribald bush children of the neighbourhood. He was forced to play mostly with girls. The critic A.R. Chisholm suspects that this experience may have seared his soul, and given him his lifelong literary interest in creating tough guys. Whether this is true or not, it is interesting to add that Dennis's macho figures, larrikins as they are known in Australian parlance, are very often tamed and 'sivilised', as Huckleberry Finn would have spelled the word, by small, determined women. Dennis's women are almost all described as 'little', though admittedly the phrase was a commonplace in his day.

Most of Dennis's youth, and the first half of his adult life, were spent 'knocking around' south-eastern Australia, making a living at various jobs, including repeated spells of journalism and newspaper versifying. Unmarried in his late thirties, he was more or less derelict when he retired first to a tent and then to a timberworker's abandoned house in the mountains east of Melbourne. The first sections of what would become the Sentimental Bloke were written under the shadows of looming depression. In fact, the opening Song is probably as much a self-portrait as it is an introduction to the Bloke:

> The world's got me snouted jist a treat;
> Crool Forchin's dirty left 'as smote me soul;
> An' all them joys o' life I 'eld so sweet
> Is up the pole
> For, as the poit sez, me 'eart 'as got
> The pip wiv yearnin' for – I dunno wot.

> (The world has got me baffled and dead beat;
> Cruel Fortune's dirty left has slammed my soul;
> And all those joys of life I held so sweet
> Are up the pole
> For, as the poet says, my heart has got
> The blues with yearning for – I don't know what.)

★ ★ ★

> I've lorst me former joy in gittin' shick,
> Or 'eading browns; I 'aven't got the 'eart
> To word a tom; an', square an' all, I'm sick
> Of that cheap tart
> 'Oo chucks 'er carkis at a feller's 'ead
> An' mauls 'im... Ar! I wisht that I wus dead!

> (I've lost my former joy in getting drunk
> Or tossing pennies; I haven't got the heart
> To chat a girl up, and tell the truth, I'm sick
> Of that cheap tart
> Who throws her carcase at a fellow's head
> And paws him... Arrh! I wish that I was dead!)

The Bloke longs for a truer, more exalted love:

> Somethin' or someone – I don't rightly know;
> But, seems to me, I'm kind er lookin' for
> A tart I knoo a 'undred years ago,
> Or, maybe, more.
> Wot's this I've 'eard them call that thing?... Geewhizz
> Me ideal bit o' skirt! That's wot it is!

> (Something or someone – I don't rightly know
> But, it seems to me I'm kind of looking for
> A girl I knew a hundred years ago,
> Or, maybe more.
> What have I heard them call that thing? Geewhizz!
> My ideal woman! That is what it is!)

His hopes of finding her, though, seem doomed by his lowly status:

> I've watched 'em walkin' in the gardings 'ere –
> Cliners from orfices an' shops an' such;
> The sorter skirts I dursn't come too near,
> Or dare to touch.
> An' when I see the kind er looks they carst...
> Gorstrooth! Wot is the *use* o' me, I arst?

> (I've watched them walking in the gardens here –
> Young girls from offices and shops and such;
> The sort of girls I daren't come too near,
> Or dare to touch.
> And when I see the looks they turn on me...
> God's truth! I ask, what is the *use* of me?)

It is springtime, and the frustration is so acute that:

> If this 'ere dilly feelin' doesn't stop
> I'll lose me block an' stoush some flamin' cop!)

> (If this here crazy feeling doesn't stop
> I'll lose my head and knock down some damn cop!)

In Dennis's own case, the astonishing success of his verse narrative
utterly changed his fortunes. In an age when marriage was held to
be proof of responsible maturity, he himself married in 1917, and
lived on very happily in the cool forested hill country he had come
to love. When some of his later verse, outside the ambit of the Bloke
and Doreen, failed to make a hit with the public, Dennis put his
talent for deft rhyming at the service of the Melbourne *Herald*, and
for more than a decade turned out daily pieces of occasional verse
for the paper. He even borrowed the idea from Osbert Sitwell of
turning out 'verse portraits' of people on commission and offered
to furnish his 'verse snapshots' on a mass production basis. He died
in 1938, and is buried in Box Hill cemetery, in suburban Melbourne.

The successive Songs in which the narrative of the Bloke and
Doreen is told are set pieces having approximately ten to twenty
stanzas each; the opening 'Spring Song' which I quoted above is of

rather less than average length, at eleven stanzas. The number of lines to a stanza varies from Song to Song; some are quatrains, some sestets, a few are octets, though a sestet rhymed ababcc is the preferred measure. Very often, the stanzas have quite strong closure, so that the narrative does not speed along like a train, but is continually summed up and then recommenced, like the sea. Dennis relies on his idiom and the ready-made imagery embedded in it to do much of the work of his poem, and such new imagery as he introduces is usually there for easy comic surprise rather than to provide real ornament or poetic reflection. Constantly, we are expected to smile at the incongruity of tender images and romantic poeticisms in the mouth of a larrikin, rather than to be delighted by any fresh observation of life. Where the action moves along reasonably fast, the verse carries our interest effectively, but when the Bloke pauses to meditate, or to indulge a comic set piece such as the embarrassing trope of 'The Stoush o' Day', where Night and Day are boxers and in perpetual contest, the effect can be exasperating. The joke of his argot, and of trying to push it beyond its normal range, then wears thin and can seem condescending. And yet at bottom it is a serious joke, and obviously reflected something quite crucial that was happening in Australian society at the time it was written.

The Bloke is easy to criticize from the standpoint of a modern sensibility, but really it is hardly a modern poem at all, and I mean that in a sense which goes beyond the modernism which was just beginning to come into English poetry at the time it was written. The Bloke lives somewhere between folk balladry and popular comic theatre, though it avoids farce. It has the habit, common to folk balladry, of concentrating on the stanza, rather than the overall design of a poem, and of savouring its situations at length through the accumulation of stanzas, each of which will vary the expression of much the same situation or mood. All the matter that is contained in the first Song, for example, is expressed adequately in the twenty-six lines I have quoted above, and yet the Song runs to sixty-six lines. A traditional audience, such as the Australian public at the time still very largely was, likes to be lulled as much as excited or hurried along, and enjoys variations. Australian balladry, both of the folk sort and the later literary ballads, typically moves at a leisurely pace and dwells lovingly on its material, though some of the ballads of the earlier part of the nineteenth century have a genuine spareness and economy. Dennis's public was trained to a poetry, usually presented in the form of recitations, which a modern reader finds exasperatingly overlong – but which really shows a more egalitarian solicitude, being designed to give pleasure to more people than just the sharpest wits in the audience, who can assimilate things at lightning speed. Length, in a poetry designed for recitation, is the equivalent of re-reading on the page, and only seems a fault when it is seen in print on the page. On the other hand, all but the very best such poetry will typically exhibit elaboration rather than development or the unfolding of nuance, and Dennis's Songs are very often guilty of this. Their slowings-down do not bring in the enrichment of poetry, and the substratum of dream we now expect poetry to have at all times and to touch fairly often is hard to detect, though the substratum of bodily gesture is there. We can often sense the Bloke wriggling inside his clothes, flexing half-baffled muscles. The Bloke strains after a fullness of life, and thus a poetry, that he senses to exist beyond his social limitations – but he can occasionally resent poetry, too, as in the Song called 'The Play', where he recognizes it as a sort of gold leaf laid upon sordidness to give it an acceptability not accorded to his class:

> Wot's in a name? Wot's in a string o' words?
> They scraps in ole Verona wiv the'r swords,
> An' never give a bloke a stray dog's chance,
> An' that's Romance.
> But when they deals it out wiv bricks an' boots
> In Little Lon, they're low, degraded broots.

> (What's in a name? What's in a string of words?
> They fight in old Verona with their swords,
> And never give a man a stray dog's chance,
> And that's Romance.
> But when they dish it out with bricks and boots
> In Little Lonsdale Street, they're low, degraded brutes.)

Poetry also embarrasses him in *Romeo and Juliet* because it transgresses the tough, emotional parsimony of his world and expresses fully the very emotions he is half-ashamed of feeling but desperately wants to express.

Ever since George Orwell in the 1930s denounced the use of comic 'uneducated' spellings to represent low-class speech, they have been repugnant to many readers, being seen as a form of ridicule of the poor. They were the currency of poor people's theatre, though, and did provide earlier poets with a means of exploring the possibilities of working-class language and making poetry of previously buried life. Kipling, who was almost certainly one of Dennis's models for the narrative of the Bloke, celebrated much of that life, from the viewpoints of soldiers, engineers and other tradesfolk, in a real and mostly uncondescending way, while using the old vaudeville 'dialect' spellings. And there were plenty of models in Australian balladry too, poems which used especially the argot of itinerant rural workers. One day, Dennis's spellings may be a source of information about Australian pronunciation in the early twentieth century, but for the moment we can still 'hear' his accent as a perfectly native if slightly outdated variant of our own. The main feature that has largely vanished is the long *o* in such words as 'lost' or 'office', indicated by his spelling of these as 'lorst' and 'orfis'. In Dennis's time, the Australian dialect of English was even more uniform over the whole continent than it is today.

C.J. Dennis has been called the Robert Burns of Australia, for his use of dialect in the Bloke narratives, but the identification is misleading. Burns, who was enormously popular in Australia before and during Dennis's lifetime, wrote in a dialect of Scots, but not for comic effect. Where he had a comic purpose, his language was not the *means* of his comedy, as the inner city argot of Dennis's narrative always is. Dennis's language is built upon the ordinary Australian dialect of his time, but carries a heavy overlay of argot, and it is the argot which is always highlighted, as if to concur with snobbish views of Australian dialect as being nothing but a low, vicious slang speech. The distinction I make here is very important. While a dialect is a variant pronunciation or even a variant language, in which a wide range of things can be said and in which some distinctive things can *only* be said, an argot is a drama. An argot belongs to a milieu rather than a region, and rehearses the identity and rituals of the milieu. It enforces a certain set of attitudes and habits of mind, and though it may allow a vast range of inventive elaboration, at bottom it is a story which the group continually tells itself about itself, over against other stories. Seen in another way, it is perhaps the only wholly open-ended, collectively created *poem*. The 'poem' or drama of the Bloke's argot is that of the larrikin. This is a purely Australian term for a human type not confined to Australia, though we fondly take some of his features to be distinctively our own. A larrikin, originally always male, was a figure of the slums, tough, breezy, street-wise, adaptable, not exactly a criminal but acquainted with crime, not exactly a hoodlum either, but having some of the same menacing dash. The term was also, but less often, applied to comparable if slightly more innocent types from the country, worldly only within their own world and naïve elsewhere. A good modern example of this variant larrikin is *Crocodile Dundee*, while Barry Humphries' Bazza Mackenzie is a larrikin of the 1950s from the newly affluent suburbs. At his most vicious, the original nineteenth-century larrikin might be a member of one of the 'pushes', or street-gangs, which went in for vandalism, mugging and savage fights with rival gangs. The original push-ites, descendants of convicts and sailors in the squalor of our early cities, are well described in Henry Lawson's scatalogical ballad *The Bastard from the Bush*:

> As the shades of night were falling over city, town and bush
> From a slum in Bludgers' Alley slunk the Leader of the Push.
> He scowled towards the north and he scowled towards the south,
> Then crooked his little finger in the corner of his mouth,
> And with a long, low whistle woke the echoes of The Rocks
> And a dozen ghouls came sloping round the corner of the blocks.
>
> They saw nought to rouse their anger; yet the oath that each
>   one swore
> Was less fit for publication than the one that went before;
> For they spoke the gutter language with the easy flow that
>   comes
> Only to the men whose children know the brothels and the
>   slums.
> Then they spat in turn, and halted, and the one that came
>   behind
> Spitting fiercely on the footpath called on God to strike him
>   blind.
>
> Let me first describe the leader, bottle-shouldered, pale and thin;
> He was just the perfect model of a Sydney larrikin.
> His hat was most suggestive of the place where Pushes live,
> With a gallows-tilt that no one, but a larrikin, can give;
> And a coat, a little shorter than the fashion might require,
> Revealed his arse and bollocks – all the lower part entire.

This poem, which pits the push-ites against an equally formidable coeval of theirs from the frontier, has passed into the folk idiom and bred several variant texts, some of which attain to a true rococo of cursing and violence. Among men, it may be the best-known poem in Australia; every man in the country seems able to quote snatches of it, in one or other of its forms, though it was only finally printed in a mainstream anthology (by me) a couple of years ago. Interestingly, no one knows the origins of the word larrikin. It sounds Irish, but is not found in dictionaries of Irish Gaelic or Irish English. A folk etymology derives it from the older English slang word 'larking' (playing about). An Irish-born constable in Sydney is supposed to have told a magistrate that: 'The boys was just larr-ikin' about,' which is how larking sounded in his pronunciation. Folk etymologies are notoriously unreliable, but that one may be correct, and there is no better-founded theory.

The larrikin was a distillation of a hard, clannish, poverty-stricken world by which the more comfortable classes in colonial society sometimes felt menaced. By the time we get to the Bloke, however, written perhaps twenty years after Lawson's ballad, the image has softened considerably. No one in the broader society need feel menaced by the Bloke or his mates. They do not belong to a push, but to a click (clique) of drinking and gambling acquaintances. All through the twentieth century, as his older world has faded, the larrikin has been undergoing a process of gentrification rather like that which has overtaken the poor suburbs in which he used to flourish. In the Sentimental Bloke, we watch him coming to terms with a still limited but richer world of genteel domesticity and regular work. People who enjoyed reading the Bloke narratives were in effect laughing at an earlier model of themselves, and the strains of their own transformation were softened by the comedy. What happened to the Bloke is what happened to most Australian men, at least before the 1960s. Since then, the larrikin style has been gentrified much further, beyond the modest domestic happiness attained by the Bloke. It has become something of an élite style, affected by women as well as men, and may inform the social behaviour of students, artists, journalists, businessmen, even Prime Ministers. The use of a very salty Australian accent and vocabulary inter-larded with learned and literary terms is one manifestation of the style. Like blue jeans, it moderates the inegalitarianism of higher education. The larrikin has almost become an Australian variant of the arrived Bohemian, a style now dominant in much of the West, or at least present as an alternative élite.

As a partial, and maybe partly conscious, attempt at a national myth, or even as a fluke in that line, the verse narrative of the bloke has probably had its day. This is not a matter of language, however: almost all of the Bloke's argot is instantly comprehensible to present-day Australians, even though nearly every actual word in it has been replaced, sometimes several times over. A girl has long ceased to be a 'donah' (from Spanish doña), a 'cliner' (from the German or Yiddish *Kleine*), or a 'tom'; she is scarcely even any longer a 'sheila', the Irish-derived word which replaced all those. Nor does anyone speak of 'doing his gilt' (wasting his money, from the German *geld*) getting 'shick' (drunk, from Hebrew by way of Yiddish). We do still get 'crook' (ill), but we no longer feel 'bonzer' (marvellous). While things no longer go 'cronk' (badly) for us, we're still apt to 'skite' (boast, from Scots) when they go well. Even in Dennis's own time, fewer people were saying 'ribuck' (origin unknown) when they meant okay, all right, no worries or, with a rising inflection, riiight! This is an affectionate museum of language, and I must stop indulging my pleasure in conducting a guided tour, even under the guise of helping non-Australian cineastes with those intertitles! What is crucial is that our attitudes to class are altering rapidly now, and making us sentimental in new ways. The poem of the Bloke belongs to a period that has ended, and is not timeless in the way a classic must be. On the other hand, I think the film is a classic, because it raises a rather one-dimensional piece of broad comedy to the lasting status of true comedy, and it accomplishes this through an editing job which it does on the original in order to transcend it.

I am a film-goer rather than a film scholar, but it is my impression that very few poems get filmed. Aside from box office considerations, a non-narrative poem is one of the most integral and complete things on earth. Like a painting, there is nothing more you can do with it, except maybe ruin it. A film may take off from a poem, but if it tries to elaborate or restate it, the result is apt to be embarrassing. With a good narrative poem, too, the riches are already there, and will resist further elaboration or interpretation. An exception I can think of is the recent French film *Perceval le Gallois*, which utterly charmed my wife and me on its very brief run in Sydney. We were delighted by the beautifully spoken poetry of Chrétien de Troyes text, which my wife understood rather better than I did, and by the stately tableaux of the action; it was as if there had been a mediaeval film industry, working perfectly well long before the invention of pedantic perspective. To a large degree, perhaps, the film was a *reading* of the poetry, rather than a reinterpretation of it in visual terms, but the deliciously stylized visual side of it charmed us. In the film of the Bloke, a much inferior poem allows the film-maker much greater latitude. The dimension of language, and thus the one-dimensional argot joke, is necessarily confined to the intertitles. The film replaces the lines of the poem with visual and gestural 'lines' of its own. And these are more varied, sharper and more delicate. In their greater breadth of reference, and their greater freedom from the same endless joke, they are better lines, and more genuinely poetic. They capture the vivid sense of contemporary life which the poem might have caught had it not been trapped in its situation and its argot. Once the poem is stripped back to a series of epitomes, it becomes a reflection of just one of the sensibilities in the film. The other characters are free to express their own sensibilities in their actions, their expressios, the whole rhythm of their living on the screen. The poem, in its new filmic rescension, is in the hands of a better poet, who is able to absorb its qualities and transmute them, rather as Baudelaire absorbed and enriched Edgar Allan Poe.

In his work of transmutation, Longford is of course helped by contemporary visual references. It is fascinating to look at the incidentals of a past era, at the feathered hats and rabbit sellers' carts and short bumfreezer jackets. It is quite poignant, in the scenes at the theatre, to notice a number of men wearing a baggy uniform of the First AIF, the expeditionary army most of whose members were still fighting fiercely in northern France when production began on the film. Some of these men, casually caught by the camera, would have been wounded returnees from a war in which the fictional Ginger Mick had already been killed. Contemporary audiences would have noted at once: 'There's Mick. He dies in the next book, you know.' By dying in action at the Dardanelles, Ginger Mick represents the other large process of history which happened to the larrikins, and which was seen by Dennis and many more as vindicating their underlying human quality.

The sequence at the theatre must have been one of the hardest tests for the discipline which Longford and Lyell brought to their version of the Bloke. In the verse narrative, the Song which describes this is one of the longest and most replete with action, but also one which carries us to the queasiest margins of embarrassment. As we have seen, there is justice in the Bloke's reductive view of *Romeo and Juliet*, but there is also an underlying flavour of a small poet tilting crudely at a great one, trying to cut Shakespeare down to size in a way at once democratic and ridiculous. There is also a frisson of older push brutality in the Bloke's exhortation to 'put in the boot', that is, kick the dying Tybalt as he lies on the ground. Longford manages the elements of the scene marvellously, through pacing, through the intensity of the Bloke's involvement with the play, and through the complexity of Doreen's attention, now entranced by the play, now defensive about what her beau may think of it, now frankly appalled and apprehensive about his enthusiasm. The intent straining forward of the two figures conveys more and more as the scene progresses. At the same time, Longford gives us an historic glimpse of long outmoded theatrical styles, and wittily contrasts the naturalism of his own art with the heavy melodrama which dominated most contemporary silent films.

Time and again, Longford and Lyell use their naturalism to convey a greater affection for the characters than the Songs and their argot-joke would allow. Naturalism permits them to avoid the seductions of stereotype and broad caricature. For example, the first visit of the Bloke to his future mother-in-law might easily have been a comic turn about mothers-in-law and grotesqueries of shabby-genteel etiquette. Any flavour of that is left for the intertitles, where the Bloke learns what indeed is 'in a name'. The scene on the screen becomes one of rather moving distress, grading into sympathy and growing human affection despite the obvious misery of the Bloke's tight shoes and choking collar. Any resentment he feels at the respectability which challenges him but is also his destination is taken out on the 'stror 'at coot' (straw hat fellow):

> I took a derry on the stror 'at coot
> First time I seen 'im dodgin' round Doreen,
> 'im wiv 'is giddy tie and Yankee suit,
> Forever yappin' like a tork machine.
>
> (I took a dislike to the straw hat coot
> The first time I saw him making up to Doreen,
> He with his giddy tie and American suit,
> Forever chattering like a gramophone.)

In the language of the time, the coot is a 'masher', of Doreen's own precariously maintained class or higher, and thus seems a real threat. Considering the looming threat of the American film, too, Longford may have enjoyed giving so American-flavoured a figure a firm elbow in the ribs, but here I may be reading things into the film.

In its closing scenes, a gentility which is beginning to chafe the Bloke, as witness his fall from grace through a night on the town with the boys, is deflected in a very Australian way. Through a warmly realized, thoroughly believable *deus ex machina*, an uncle from the country, the Bloke and Doreen are enabled to step sideways into an Australian dream which has been potent, and disliked by our élites, since at least the 1850s. They are given a small freehold farm, away from the constraints of the city and, by implication, of class itself. Some critics have disapproved of this, almost as an evasion of politics, but it is central to Australian experience, this encounter with the land. Robert Hughes and others before him have pointed out that it was this encounter which absorbed and assuaged the agony of our convict beginnings. Displaced Europeans became Australian, some say, by meeting and wrestling with the remote beauty and difficult strangeness of the new continent. Possessed of an unreliable climate that includes drought, flood and fire among its armaments, the bush can be an all-absorbing opponent and an hypnotic environment at once, reducing individuals to insignificance at the same time as it lends them a strangely anonymous heroic stature. The poet Peter Porter has written that Americans dream of Utopia, while Australians dream of Arcadia, and there is a lot of truth in the distinction. There is also much that is delusive in our Arcadias, unless they are supported, like the *dacha* of the Russians, by money from elsewhere. Real farmers avoid Arcadian fantasies; they are canny Boeotians. Or else they do not survive as farmers. In their move to the (by implication) more natural, wholesome world of the countryside, the Bloke and Doreen travel a very well-trodden Australian path, though we are not shown the slow heartbreak that path can lead to. Some of the soldiers we saw in the theatre sequence were to learn about all that, as they failed on too-small farms provided them after the First World War by the Soldier Settlement Schemes. Longford does, however, follow Dennis in showing us one of the genuine terrors of bush life, that of living a long way from medical help. Thousands have died of that, in the past. Much more importantly in the film's own terms, the brusqueness of the Bloke's exclusion from the mysteries of childbirth, and his permitted peek at his baby son, complete his introduction to the power and mystique of women. He is now, as in the poem, fully transformed and capable of dedicating his life in an adult way. The terms in which he does so even confirm his sentimentality! But they also confirm the message Dennis tried to convey, that of the rough ordinary Bloke's underlying decency. The end of the film also redeems his language, which he has not modified or repudiated.

Notes to accompany the special screening of *The Sentimental Bloke* at the International Film Festival, Cannes 1987

Wheatish and Auspicious

Novelist Chris Koch and I travelled to India in the service of Australian literature. We were there to speak and be questioned, at seminars on the subject, and were greatly impressed to find that scholars and fellow authors travelled from all quarters of that large country to attend.

As in many parts of the world, interest in Australian art and literature seems to be growing almost insatiably – rather to the surprise of people who grew up in this country in the recent era of the Cultural Cringe. Sadly, penetration of Australian books into India is likely to be impeded by brute economics. A slim volume of verse costing $10 here would cost around what an Indian pays from a vastly lower salary for a large hardback. Unless our books can be published in India on some sort of generous licence arrangement, reading and study of Australian authors is likely to be restricted. But I'm getting ahead of my subject.

Two weeks in a country as strange, as varied, and as fascinating as India does not make one an expert, especially if it is one's first visit. It does produce some vivid impressions, though, and the freshness of one's view doesn't have time to grow dulled. I seemed to be learning things all the time. As we drove from Indira Gandhi Airport to the Australian High Commission in Delhi, where we were to stay during our week in that city, I noticed a man riding along a suburban street on a white horse.

'That,' said the driver, Mr Dutt Singh, 'is a man who rents out his horse to the bridegrooms. A groom has to ride the last three or four hundred metres to his wedding feast, so as to arrive as a prince.' Apparently quite a decent living can be made, in this land of teeming small scale enterprise, from owning a white horse, for it can be hired out many times a day. We were to learn more about Indian marriage customs from reading the bride and groom advertisements in the Sunday edition of the national newspaper *The Hindu*. The finest specifications of caste and sub-caste were set out, and a premium was set on having a fair skin, often described as 'wheatish'. That seemed to be at least as important as a BA degree, or having a secure job with real prospects. Only a very few ads declared caste to be no bar, and fewer still among the prospective grooms announced that widows or divorcees would be considered. It was good to see that a few did make that daringly modern allowance, in a land where arranged marriages are the rule.

Like many Westerners heading for India for the first time, I experienced a deal of apprehension about the horrors of poverty I might see, and the guilts I might have to feel. It was a real happiness, as well as a relief, to come across no real starvation in the two cities we visited, and to meet only a few out-and-out beggars. I was as helpless with these as most Westerners are, since they lie too far back in our own history for us to have any memory of dealing with them.

The streets were thronged instead with men and little boys, keen to sell you anything from a packet of combs to a guided tour – 'No charge, Sahib: I am government guide!' And this was true ten times over around any spot of likely tourist interest. Experienced travellers in Asia will find this boringly familiar, of course, but this was my first time in Asia. Chris Koch, who knows Asia well, was amused by my transformation, within a fortnight, from gullibility to brusque reserve, but I bore an extra burden he did not share. I am large of frame and girth, and these are qualities Indians consider auspicious; throngs were apt to form of men and youths eager to speak to me or shake my hand, for luck. Indian screen idols are generally beefier than their Western counterparts, and I was sometimes asked: 'You – make film, eh?' Mixed in with all the offers of goods and services there is a great deal of simple friendliness on Indian streets, and an unabashed readiness to find entertainment there.

Against heavy odds, the Indian economy seems to work. The threat of horrifying unemployment and starvation which a huge population poses, is met in various ways. One is apparent over-employment. At any roadside cold drinks shop there will be one young man to fish the frosty bottle of Campa-Cola out of the cooler, another to fetch it, another to pull the cap off, another, probably the boss, to take your money. Any clothes shop will tend to have a boy at the door to draw you out of the passing throng and conduct you inside, and another will be on hand to fetch hot, sweet tea. A bank, where women also work, will have no electronic security devices, but one or more men in vaguely military khakis and carrying well-oiled shotguns; these are certainly more impressive than any number of cameras in the ceiling. Campa-Cola stands for Coca-

Cola, by the way: nothing is imported if an equivalent can be manufactured in India, and India does manufacture nearly everything, from plastic water pots in the traditional shape of clay pots to jet fighters and the ubiquitous sturdy Ambassador and Maruti cars that make their way through teeming bicycles and bullock carts by a constant exertion of their horns.

Out in the country, mechanization is severely limited, so the huge numbers of landless farm labourers are not robbed of work; the smallholdings of one to two hectares, or less, are beautifully worked, seemingly with nothing other than a short-handled hoe, and every inch is put to use. One piece of borrowed mechanization, as it were, is the custom of spreading unthreshed grain on the bitumen of a village road to be threshed by the tyres of passing cars and trucks. In the villages, houses range from solid brick and plaster bungalows (the word comes to us from India after all) to the tiny one-roomed huts of farm labourers. It is amazing, though, just what can emerge from the smallest Indian dwelling. A house no bigger than your laundry may send forth a girl in a beautifully pressed cotton sari, off to work on her bicycle.

Indian landscapes can fascinate an Australian, because of their overlay of the strange on the familiar. Around Bangalore and Mysore, in the south, the country looked hauntingly like parts of central Queensland; the same red soil, the same rocky hills, the same vivid tropic greens. The sandstone Red Fort in Delhi, the Mogul seat of power which the British as the next conquerors tried and failed to outdo in their grandiose government buildings, seems to be made of the same material as the Kimberleys. It is a reminder that our continents were once joined, before India split off and slipped north to crash into primeval Asia and throw up the Himalayas in that great collision. That was many millions of years ago, though, and is unlikely to explain the hosts of dark faces in South India which look for all the world like Aboriginal faces. Indians sometimes assume a link, but there is no evidence for it in language or elsewhere. One real link, though it is only a century old, is the presence of gum trees all over the place. They are called Nilgiri trees, from the hill country where they were first planted by the British. Indians have mixed feelings about them: they produce timber and firewood very quickly, but farmers complain that they rob the soil, giving back little or nothing in the way of compost – unlike, say, the beloved mango, which gives delicious fruit as well, or the ubiquitous gulmohar, called the poinciana in Queensland.

Religion is all pervading in India, as it must have been in pagan

Greece and Rome. I visited a number of Hindu temples and found them cave-like and creepy, with their polymorphous gods and lack of windows. Like other ancient architectural styles, India seems not to have hit on the window, developing the veranda and the inner courtyard instead. I did notice an interesting contrast, though, with mosques. These were apt to be more attractive, with an airy lightness provided by open-plan building and lots of cool archways, but the faces around them tended to be distant, even quietly forbidding, in contrast to those around Hindu temples, where a welcoming tolerance seemed to invite one to share in the blessings of a holy place.

In south India, churches were common even in quite small villages, and the handsome Gothic Cathedral of St Philomena in Mysore had the best choir I've heard in years. Gregorian chant goes very well with a spicing of the eternity-hum of Indian music. It was my first experience of Mass in a totally unknown language – in this case Kannada, the local language of Mysore and surrounding Karnataka State – but the well-known gestures of the sacred ritual carried me along without difficulty in the standing-room-only congregation. Although there are more Christians in India than Jains, or Parsees, or even Sikhs, ours is a minority religion there, and the tone of society is strongly Hindu. This comes out, I gather, even in the marriage customs of local Catholics, because no one ever forgets what caste one was, or one's ancestor was, at the time of conversion to Christ.

Hindu shrines are found, and venerated, on any street corner, and the commercial streetscape of an Indian city can seem overwhelmingly religious, with the names of gods and goddesses invoked in most business names: Lord Krishna Suitings, Sri Saraswati Bookshop, Sivaram Provisions. Even the buzzing diesel auto-rickshaws which transport lazy Westerners around will often have an effigy of the elephant god Ganesha on their rudimentary dashboard, garlanded with sweet-smelling flowers, though I have seen garlanded St Christophers too.

In the cities we visited, I did not see many Western seekers after enlightenment: I think I noticed only a single blond Rajneeshee. All that peaked in the early 1970s and may have its lasting effects only in the sphere of diet. All the stories about the sacred status of Mother Cow proved true, however. She wanders everywhere at will, and it is auspicious to be kind to her and unthinkable to hurt her. Her brother the bullock often has a much thinner time of it, with work to do and a sharp-pointed goad to encourage him along. Slaughter of cattle is illegal in Karnataka and many other states, but people in

Mysore seemed to know where the bootleg beef market was, down a back street between the Cathedral and the main mosque.

I do not idealize India: there are strains and volatile passions in the society, as in any other. There is caste, too, formalized and rigid in a way the West no longers dares to have it: Christianity and its offshoots have at least made it covert and slightly malleable in our world. And there are horror stories, worrying to the Indians themselves, of untouchables beaten to death for asserting their rights, or infertile wives – or maybe just the wives of infertile rural men – who have mysterious accidents with the family kerosene cooker and burn to death, making way for a new bride and a fresh dowry.

Now, though, I am talking about things I didn't see on my two-week visit. What I remember most warmly is a busy but still slow-paced rhythm of life that seems to leave a lot of room for casual human warmth and friendly contact. Out on the country roads, men in workstained turban, long shirt and dhoti are quite likely to offer the strolling Westerner a lift in their trundling bullock cart, and a boy may offer to double you on his pushbike. And there is the fascinating way in which the constant honking of motor vehicle horns among the dreamily suicidal pedestrians and cyclists manages not to sound aggressive, but somehow co-operative.

That is something to set alongside my lasting gratitude to scholars who travelled up to four days on trains and rickety buses to hear us read our work and discuss Australian literature with them, and my warm thanks to officials, Indian and Australian alike, who showered kindness and hospitality on us.

Catholic Leader, Brisbane, 13 September 1987

The Trade in Images

Making images of Australia is arguably something we do too much of. Making images of themselves is something very many countries do too much of, even Old World countries you would think should by now be secure in their identity. America does far too much of it, though we have to remember she is a Noble Experiment in human self-government. Here in Australia, the making of national images is a major journalistic and literary industry. It has been a growth industry for at least two generations, if not longer. The Australian Emptiness, the Australian Ugliness, the Lucky Country, The Land of the Long Weekend, The Great Australian Stupor, The End of the Dreamtime: along with all the coffee table books and treatises on every facet of Australiana, we have had a seemingly insatiable appetite for those often tartly hectoring sociocultural studies of our country. We have indulged gluttonously in mirror staring and navel gazing, avid for more and more angles on our own fascinating image. Other countries have learned the hard way the terrible dangers inherent in out-and-out nationalism; it is a Moloch which can swallow incredible amounts of tormented human flesh. We have, thank God, largely been spared an education in this at first hand, but perhaps that very fact has stunted the growth here of a genuine humility. We have got carping instead, which differs from humility in not including oneself. It can sometimes seem that the note of denunciation in most of our serious studies of Australia is a dash of bitters, put in to disguise the sweet taste of endless self-regard and persuade us we are consuming adult beverages. Harsh strains of criticism, of our sloth, of our indifference, our unsexiness, our slowness to take up the latest and most refined items of High Culture, these serve as a guarantee that our indulgence in national narcissism is respectably intellectual. If capitalism tends to turn all things into consumer goods, and radicalism tends to turn all things into inquisition, the commerce in Australian images contrives to reconcile the two rather marvellously. The standard paperback study of Australian mores really has it both ways, at once commanding respectable sales and allowing the author a generous measure of self-righteousness and hectoring zeal.

Someone, somewhere, is eventually going to suggest that much of this image-mongering is rather transparently late-colonial (cf. late adolescent) and parvenu. That person is going to make themselves very unpopular, especially with the writers of the sort of books I'm talking about. Maybe not with the readers of them, but definitely with the writers. And especially, perhaps, with those writers who have only a polemical point of view to offer, and not some properly grounded new perspective, some genuinely fresh discovery. They will also make themselves an odium to publishers, for the formula is such a sure-fire seller that it has tended to crowd out most other sorts of non-fiction writing here. Who wants to take a risk on an Australian book about universals when there is easy money to be made from a mix of photogenic Australian Views and denunciations of the Myth of Mateship? If you doubt what I'm saying, ask yourself how many Australian philosophers you can think of, working and publishing here. Or how many Australian historians with original and cogent theories about some supra-national question or other. I can think of a few of the latter, just a few – but they didn't publish in Australia. They published overseas, in that big outer world where we are still led to believe all truly original thinking is done. That's the traditional division of labour: new ideas are imported, and it is our part to re-jig them for local use, applying them to the benefit and the apathetic backs of our fellow citizens.

A good many of the images we make are graven ones. Firmly inscribed, in hard prose, they are meant to be admired, to become the touchstones of debate, to be influential. They are tokens of power, sometimes effective in bringing about changes, including changes their proponents may come to regret. Blessed, at least initially, are those whose cause they further, and woe betide those who stand inconveniently in their way. If you suffered under White Australia, you may yet be maladroit enough to get run over by Multiculturalism. Or by the Creole idea, which I predict will be its successor. Some of these images last longer than others, but all eventually pass away. Few, in Australia anyway, now remember the workingman's paradise. And the empty continent that we had to populate or perish has suffered a complete reversal. As we leave late colonial reality, more of these formulations get invented. Merely as crutches for lazy minds, these successive conditioning visions are the blight of quality journalism and dinner parties alike, though they do power a busy commerce in conferences; as climbing ladders seized and set up by aspiring politicians, though, they can cause havoc not only to the subtler weave of difficult truth, but to actual human lives. An image, we should remember, is a description shaped by an inner intent. Damage to human lives and communities is likely to happen when one image is being more or less forcibly replaced by another.

I learned this law (we may call it the Law of Loaded Descriptions) the hard way when I came to the city from the bush. I came along just at the moment when the bush was beginning to plummet out of favour and become very unfashionable. Australia had become Urban, and it behoved her to get Sophisticated as quickly as possible, casting off all earlier Dad-and-Dave simplicities and even much of the romance of the Outback. The complex, time-layered realities of the bush hadn't been fully explored or described, but suddenly they were impatiently 'understood' and dismissed. We had become obsolete, just as individuals now do before they die. In a decade or two, the whole of the bush, including the Outback, would become the Environment, which all but its earliest inhabitants had despoiled, and in which nothing more should ever be built. I had also made the mistake of coming from the world of struggling small farmers, a caste our élites have loathed from the start. Epithets such as hick from the sticks, peasant, rural idiocy, and pejorative uses of that pretentious belch-word 'bucolic', these helped me to find my own identity and even lent my writing some of its impetus, so I guess I have something to thank our image-makers for. Many of my relatives would have less reason for gratitude, as a bitterly engineered diminution of sympathy with their struggles against a difficult continent slowly robbed them of government services and self-esteem alike, and eroded any willingness to alleviate the very social deprivations they were derided for. Paradoxically, the perennial attractiveness of the bush for many Australians has not gone away, despite the propaganda. We are now getting a new settlement pattern in the country, partly made up of the holiday houses and hobby farms (the Soviet term is *dachas*) of privileged urban people, but more typically a pattern of disguised unemployment, by which the bush absorbs, as it has always done, some of the strain of industrial restructuring. People from the city sell their one large asset, their suburban house, and move on to a few acres in the country, where they build often quite handsome houses for themselves. It takes a while to realize that in those houses many are living quite precariously on savings or superannuation, on expedients or pick-up work or the dole. They are less productive in volume terms than farmers were, but they do bring variety: of genetics, of social experience and ideas, as well as new crops and occupations. They also bring an attractive innocence about the wellsprings of ancient community friction, in long-settled places. And since the bush is a great and powerful spirit, many of them, if they last long enough, eventually become country people themselves, and join the rest of us in the sorrow of watching our children sucked out of our communities into the cities, where the Action is supposed to be and where most wait around in vain for some worthwhile slice of it. This last, of course, is part of a vaster worldwide pattern, in which the ethic of the Interesting wins out over the ethic of the Good, but we have been slow to discern any but a fairly standardized range of worldwide trends operating in our society.

If much of the foregoing sounds like the soured confessions of a reformed image-monger, I have to plead guilty. I have done my bit of prose image-making, in the past, though I've only been polemical in essays, never in a full-length book. By the time I reached the stage of writing a prose book, I had grown very mistrustful of the conceptual poverty and stereotyping that bedevil the Australian Identity industry, and tried as far as possible to steer clear of any sort of predictable polemic. Even when the game had seemed fun, I was always uneasily aware of something our religion gets itself hated for reminding people of: that every proposal is likely to have its dark as well as its bright results, just as every criticized reality is likely to have its hidden virtues and rationales as well as its vices. It may represent the decay of some initially noble impulse, or the deposit of some formerly pressing need. In Australia's case, the escape of many of the poor from the conditions of the Industrial Revolution, or of the terrorized from the power imagery of tyrannical governments, have been supremely powerful motives – just as, in the case of the bush, we have seen the power of a simple longing to escape even the most honoured and politically romanticized servitude and be one's own boss, at almost any cost in poverty and deprivation. If the suspiciously free-flowing afflatus of polemical argument didn't remind me of these things, my other and true vocation of poetry did. Poetry has a way of reminding us, through its very inexhaustibility, that there are always more sides to a thing. You can't be in its presence long without feeling the pull of that.

Another thing which kept tugging me away from national image-mongering was its pervading acrimony, its frequently dismissive and contemptuous tones, its readiness to bury things before they were dead. If, as our religion teaches, the spirit is inseparable from the body, there seemed ample reason to be worried by the tone of social criticism here. The tone in which a thing is proposed may easily become the atmosphere of its realization, and the spirit in which it is enforced. I would add, not entirely as an aside, that our Church is partly to blame for this. By abandoning the field of higher intellectual life in Australia, or being browbeaten out of it, and not even having a high-quality magazine in which Catholic and Christian perspectives could be published, it left some of us either silenced altogether or forced to slip our thinking into journals highly antipathetic to it. By electing not to have an intellectual presence in the society, the Church removed its people from the sphere of intellectual debate, because no one else was going to give them more than the barest sufferance. As a result, no criticism of the tone and style of Australian polemic has been possible, and no alternative spirit in which to describe our society has had a natural home. The position is the same in book publishing. A Catholic press for books now barely exists, except as a few tiny operations with no access much to distribution or review and certainly no mainstream influence. I know from hard experience the short shrift which serious Catholic manuscripts usually get from secular publishers. None of what I've been saying is meant to denigrate the few small Catholic magazines and book publishers that do exist in Australia. The pity with these is that they are in-house journals, not equipped to challenge the wider society. Also, they are apt to be riven by the internecine battles of left wing versus right wing, that desolating alien terminology which an intellectually vigorous Catholic culture should have been to the fore in opposing.

The theology of the commandment against graven images is fascinating but utterly remote from most people in the Western tradition; it was thrashed out mainly in the Orthodox tradition over a thousand years ago. But if one is around the arts for a time, one discovers that the commandment contains crucial wisdom. You cannot make an image of any large reality. You can't make an image of Australia and do justice to all its aspects. You will inevitably do great injustice to the parts you think less important, and dismiss or leave out, and you can't even see the reality of the country from all the angles you would need to see it from. The dimensions of the subject are too great to observe, and an accurate report on them would take more time to give than anyone has to give it or listen to it. We can only draw images from the reality, and gradually we find that the number of these potentially there to draw is infinite. The whole can't be described; it can only be *evoked*, which is essentially why our church allows images. What we share in practice (and such sharing is what makes a nation) is a rough but poignant *sense* of the reality we live in, a sort of signature tune only partly in words, made of common experiences and family references. No single part of this tune is likely to be shared by all, but there will be a fairly large degree of commonality overall. One modulation of the Australian tune which used to be shared by a broad majority of us used to be a habit of seeing our society in caricature terms that were a subtle and partly amused reaction to how Britain and Europe saw it, when they bothered to look. We had a liking for slum effects, in part because society had largely escaped from its earlier slums and was good at modulating its nostalgia for them. The modern ocker sensibility is nothing like as subtle or sardonic as that older spirit; it's a parody and a crude take-off of it. The Church understood the society which shared this slum joke, and was well adapted to it. But then the society began to be gentrified, and the Church was left floundering. Gentrification is a morally complex process, with many vehement pretensions, and the Church didn't catch on that the old tune had altered. Getting an intellectual presence now might seem a belated piece of gentrification by the Church itself, but it's something you need in gentrifying times, in order to understand them and comment on them, on the way to being able to minister to those they hurt and neglect and exploit. You can only talk to gentrifying people in terms their gentrification obliges them to respect.

As a native of the old half-mythical Australian slum (rural division), still partly in thrall to the delight and disgust of its tune and unable to make the necessary repudiations of loved things on demand, my position in the image business was always precarious, and now I think I've been dropped from it. Journalists no longer ring me up for my opinions on the Australian republic, possibly because of the puzzlingly spiritual answers I give them, starting from the premise that it has in effect come, at least to the extent we're comfortable with for the moment. I sometimes grow apprehensive, as I know many other people quietly do, as to what sort of an ideological whited sepulchre a fully realized Australian republic might be. What would it draw on for its dimension of vision and public panoply? Whose dreams would it exalt, whose images? Not Catholic ones, we may be pretty certain. An American poet asked me a few years ago a question that seemed to me both simple and crucially difficult. The question was: Why don't Australians kill each other like Americans? This isn't merely stereotype; the figure of over 20,000 deaths by gunshot per year in America is admitted to be accurate. Our population is about one fifteenth theirs, and our annual rate of deaths by gunshot rarely exceeds fifty, though it may have begun to climb. I had to ponder the question for quite a while, since it wasn't simply a matter of centralized state police forces versus elected local police forces and a tangle of overlapping jurisdictions. It was a difference in the spirit of the two societies. I finally suggested that it might be because in the past we weren't a republic for bringing things to a head. We weren't actors in a political drama of world significance, in which we felt that what we did counted. We thus lacked the principled American determination to see all conflicts resolved, all questions decided. I don't know whether that is the answer – and I doubt it's the whole answer – but just after I gave it, we had the first of a series of horrific mass slaughters by gunfire. Please God this is not a straw in the wind of the spirit here. Getting back to the image business, I suspect that the only lasting contribution I made to the socio-political side of it was to get the term Anglo-Saxon altered to Anglo-Celtic, which seemed to me obviously more accurate. There we poor downtrodden Celts were, about to become respectably Ethnic, and Murray has to go and re-yoke us to the Anglos, the dread lords of the Establishment. A strange house, the Establishment: everyone enters it facing backwards. In the longer term, it may prove even stranger than that: it may be non-existent even as it stands there, and someone may show that it was built of nothing but rhetoric.

If I am out of the prose national-image stakes, and perhaps I only think I am, I still draw on Australian imagery for my poems. In a way, I hope this may be more responsible of me. Images are at their least disruptive in art, where they are at their most mysterious and many sided and inexhaustible, food for contemplation rather than precipitate action. In art, imagery and conflict alike are raised beyond embodiment in action to a more perpetual embodiment where their life needs nothing further from the world to feed itself. Art is thus, in Christian terms, effectual but vicarious. It has arrived, without having to find its way there through tyrannies, at the true ambiguity of things, and can let all things, even opposites, be true at once.

Address to the International Liturgical Assembly, Hobart, January 1988

A Generation of Changes

I lived away from my native region for some twenty-nine years, keeping in touch with it only by visits and intense recollection. When I went away to university in Sydney, in 1957, my region was still in the pervasive slump that followed the disappearance of coastal and river shipping. That was the meaning, though we were oddly unaware of it, of all the somnolent or dying villages up the road from their derelict wharves. The boats had gone, and motor traffic was still growing to replace them, along what were mostly still gravel roads. By the time I moved home again, on the last day of 1985, the region was well into the era of subdivision, of brick houses standing incongruously on hillsides that had once been pea patches or grazing land. The car reigned supreme, roads were liable to have official names, and the railways that had deliberately finished off coastal shipping after the Second World War were themselves contracting their operations and starting to look bygone.

Some months after coming home, I began to think about, and then to list, all the large and small changes that had taken place during the long generation I had spent in the cities. I would take out a clutch of scribbled sheets and add items as I thought of them, or sometimes as other people mentioned them. After quite a while, I decided to add one more column, for things that had vanished before my time but still lived in the memories of old people. Those memories gave life back to derelict structures rotting up grassed-over bush roads, or to the queer trombones of carbide-lamp piping I'd once made into guns for childish war games. The main work, and fun, was summoning up once-common objects and ways that had slipped almost unnoticed into the crevasses between jostling epochs and vanished, and trying to bring into consciousness the new things and ways which lost their newness and became so quickly commonplace that it's hard to remember when they were not there. The way in which the world looks sensible and final at any moment masks the vertiginous process of its continuous creation and destruction. Our feeling of being somehow above that, or a beneficiary of it, lasts at best until middle life.

I didn't know whether I'd ever publish my lists – but of course pretty well everything a writer writes is in some sense meant for publication, or at least wears its clean underwear in case. All the same, I have left my lists as I wrote them down, feeling that the less I marshalled my items, the more free they were to speak for themselves. Thus I have refrained from internal commentary, beyond the briefest clarifications. There was always something of a problem deciding which innovations were too ubiquitous to put into a regional list – the nationwide advent of television was such a case – and which had a place in my lists because there was at least some trace of regional or maybe just rural relevance about their coming. I don't think I managed to be entirely strict or consistent about this, but I'm not worried; being inclusive might prove truer to the shape and flavour of what was going on than being restrictive. At times, too, the movement of some innovation into and fairly quickly out of local usage may have some meaning in itself; a case in point is the terrible unselective vermin poison 1080, which many farmers now refuse to have on their farms. I didn't speculate, in this or other cases, what that meaning might be. Interpretations are apt to have an even faster turnover time than material gadgets do.

The centre of my field of observations is of course my home district of Bunyah, which lies fifty-odd kilometres south of Taree and about twenty kilometres as the crow flies from the Pacific Ocean. In essence, the district comprises the whole upper catchment of the small Wang Wauk river. The Wang Wauk, the name of which meant 'crows' in the local Kattang language, actually behaves more like a real river, or a real crow, and wanders a bit, before reaching the ocean along with three other rivers by way of the beautiful blue and cream tidal estuary that lies between Tuncurry and Forster. The larger region in which I feel and am accepted as native extends from just north of the Manning River down to the top end of the Myall Lakes, and west beyond Gloucester to the foothills of the Dividing Range. This is the wider purview of the changes I've been mapping. It is the very southernmost end of the New South Wales north coast, a countryside of splendid beaches and coastal lagoons, of forests and shaly hills and mostly poor soils, beautiful but often surprisingly remote even though it is only a short distance from the Pacific Highway and the coastal resort towns. Given the surge of interest in recent years in local and oral histories, my simple lists may suggest a framework for recollection in other regions. And maybe, taken singly or together, such listings might add up to a resource.

Things which have increased or become prevalent

kangaroos
scrub turkeys
echidnas
elastic-sided boots
moleskin pants
brick houses in towns
bookshops and public libraries
dams and waterbirds
concrete and high-level bridges
domestic geese
slashing rather than burning of pasture
tradespeople living in the country
wine drinking
dandelions
fireweed daisy (*Senecio madagascarensis*; variable groundsel)
asphalt roads
steel fenceposts (star pickets)
cattle grids
roast chicken without stuffing
the word 'chicken' in place of 'poultry' or 'fowl'
wearing of underclothes by men
eels in creeks, dams etc.
Friesian cows
ornamental and shade trees, especially exotics
sheep on coast country
bandicoots
king parrots
concrete water tanks and more domestic water storage
absentee landowners
shoes on schoolchildren
contract farming arrangements (to grow a crop on someone's land
    or the like)
bathrooms in rural houses
swamp pheasants (coucals)
fresh fruit
fresh meat
kitchen sinks (in the real sense, with drain plugs)
cattle raising on former dairy farms
secondary schools
bullnose veranda roofs (reappeared)

the loom of artificial light along horizons at night

the word 'lunch' in place of dinner and 'dinner' in place of 'supper' or 'tea'

goannas

town employment for country residents (new and old)

Things which have decreased or become less common

rabbits

flies

fish in creeks

Jersey cows

ringbarked trees

stumps with board slots

googeries (small shelter sheds on farms for making fire in; from the local Kattang word 'gugri', meaning house or shelter)

post-and-rail fences

outside lavatories

soil erosion

canvas waterbags

timber mills

yarning and storytelling

small local post offices

one-teacher schools (virtually all gone)

railway sidings

blackberry bushes

tennis and private tennis courts

pole barns (stockade barns)

use of 1080 poison

dingoes

sleepouts

cattle bells and horse bells

Greek cafés and milk bars

corned beef

home-killed beef

accordions

wire-rope 'flying foxes' over creeks

milk cans

linoleum

pigsties and pig farms

manual telephone exchanges

dairies and dairy farms

collarless flannel shirts

termites

local sports days

the corkwood tree (*Duboisia myoporoides*, almost cut out in the 1950s
when it provided an extract for pharmaceutical use)

share farming

early graves on farms

quince, China pear, loquat and persimmon trees (all associated with
abandoned farms)

fear of wasting water

tin or enamel wash dishes, with towels, for washing hands before
coming inside

hilltop cultivation of peas for market

the term 'feed', meaning either a meal or a rough measure of some
foodstuff, eg, 'There's another two feeds of tomatoes left, and
then they're done.'

tinned fruit

fountain pens

co-operative societies

death adders

broadaxes (for sleeper cutting)

pie melons (jam melons)

child labour on farms

Things which appeared during my absence

brick houses on holdings in the country

capsicums

4-wheel drive vehicles

chainsaws

video cassettes

soy bean crops

electricity outside towns

1080 poison

zucchini

frozen foods (and home freezers)

'health' foods and associated phenomena

houseboats

brown snakes

Kiwi fruit

marihuana

fixed showers in rural houses

septic tanks
drinkable coffee
television on farms
ear tags on cattle
galahs
concrete watering points for stock
local FM radio stations
Aboriginal citizenship
Aboriginal families living in towns
Aboriginal children in high schools
beards (reappeared)
cooking oil
deodorants
hobby farms and rural retreats
bush fire brigades (volunteers)
the blue native waterlily (*Nymphaea brownii*)
toy and tax-concession breeds of cattle (Charolais, Droughtmaster,
    British White, etc.)
antique shops and art or craft galleries
indoor flush toilets

Things which vanished during the same period

bullock teams
enamel advertising signs
milk boats on rivers
zinc butter coolers
meatsafes
shingle roofs
bark roofs
Stockholm tar
poultice mixtures
picnic races
most fixed timber verandas over town footpaths
cream separators
most hand-powered implements (eg, corn shellers, mincing
    machines)
Indian and other hawkers
the last dirt-floored house I knew of
horse-drawn implements and most draught horses
dripping
blacksmiths shops

coppers for boiling clothes
kero lamps, especially ornate hanging ones
the term 'Yankee hash' for shepherd's pie
mosquito coils (these have recently reappeared)
the *Bulletin* in its old true form
boots worn without socks
iron hot water fountains
utility trucks cut down from cars
rural tennis clubs
corn plasters
corn-bag quilts ('Waggas')
nearly all buggies, sulkies and similar vehicles
aspidistras in strapped metal planter pots
motor drivers' dustcoats
hand-operated petrol bowsers
greasing of working boots, usually with dripping or mutton fat
public recitation of poems
provisions sold in bulk, eg, hessian bags of sugar, crates of tea, etc.
friendly societies, eg, the Oddfellows
the term 'budget' for a magazine
use of eucalyptus oil on a spoonful of sugar as a treatment for disease
use of pumpkin seed kernels as a cure for intestinal worms
the last wells for domestic water supply
cyanide gas for rabbit burrows
Bogan sinks (made from an opened-out kerosene tin framed with
    boards)
tin kerosene pumps
segregation of Aboriginals at the pictures

Things which had vanished before my time but are still remembered

shoulder yokes (for humans carrying paired buckets of water, etc.)
goldmines and prospectors
revolvers and muzzle-loading shotguns
pademelons
pommage (porridge made from cracked corn)
sale of corn to cities for horse feed (principal industry there till World
    War I)
river and coastal shipping
chewing tobacco
home-grown tobacco
home-grown arrowroot

eating of native birds and animals (parrot soup, Wonga pigeon pie, kangaroo rissoles, stewed possum, etc.)

house parties three and four days long, with dancing by night and courting and horseplay by day

Friar's Balsam

Pain Killer (a patent medicine with opium)

practical joking

carbide lamps

drinking of schnapps

cooking with chained pots and camp ovens over open fires

open-fire chimneys with slots to receive a whole log fed in progressively as burnt

pet carpet snakes to keep down rats in houses and barns

homemade soup

itinerant dentists

fireflies

homemade bread, as distinct from damper

geebung jam

use of three drops of kerosene on a teaspoonful of sugar as a preventative for diphtheria

typhoid fever

timber getters' tramways with steam locomotives or horse-drawn trucks

burning lampers (hard lumps) off horses' gums with a red-hot iron

First published in *Blocks and Tackles*

A Tribute to Old Delight

Penguin Book of Welsh Verse, edited by Tony Conran (Poetry Wales Press, 1986)

When Anthony Conran's *Penguin Book of Welsh Verse* came out in 1967, I was living in Penarth and exploring Wales and nearby southern England in my green Cortina. On an earlier brief visit to Britain, I had made some close friendships in Cardiff, and had been captivated by Wales. It was natural that when I got a chance to embark on that poor man's Grand Tour which tens of thousands of young Australians had started making in those still-affluent times, I would gravitate first to Wales. There were things about the country which I wanted to understand, and a mood of national cultural revival was in the air, seemingly reversing the usual sad story of Celtic decline. A personal preparation for my amazed delight in Conran's pioneering Penguin book, and its importance in the development of my own writing, was that I'd already begun feeling my way into the poetic traditions of a Celtic sister-culture, that of my own remote Gaelic forebears, and had at least got a bit beyond the coarser misinterpretations of that slippery term 'bardic'. This wasn't entirely ancestor-worship on my part, because Gaelic lay at least three centuries behind me, in my paternal descent. The Old Murrays had been Borderers for a couple of centuries, between being Highlanders and becoming Australians. I had been badly stymied, though, by uncertainty about proper Gaelic pronunciation; well-trained teachers were hard to find in Australia, and the orthography, even in modern Irish, can be nearly as misleading to the novice as that of English. The clear phonetic orthography of Welsh allowed me to sound the language and pronounce it with an accuracy which native judges approved, once I had sorted out the important difference, well explained in all its metrical implications in Conran's new edition, between penultimate stress and that tonic accent which marks final syllables and gives words their well-defined boundaries. Although Conran's Penguin book didn't have facing page texts in the original Welsh, the sheer quality and verbal music of his translations would become my highroad into the all-important formal side of Celtic poetry, and the basis of any understanding of this which I would attain.

I had read a lot of translations, and a lot of original texts in languages I knew well enough, but I had never seen translations as brilliant and immediately convincing as Conran's. Accurate or not, they were poetry of a high order in themselves and reflected a tradition that was clearly of major importance. In all the years since that Penguin book came out, I have never again struck translations of poetry with so powerful an effect; Conran's versions of Welsh classical poems remain a unique memory for me. I have since seen translations by other hands of some of the same poems, and none has moved me in any comparable way. I have been moved by some translations of Irish and Scottish Gaelic poetry, especially those of Kuno Meyer and Flann O'Brien, for Irish, and Roderick Thomson's versions of Scots Gaelic poems. Sadly, though, not even these have moved me to the same extent; I still don't get enough of the music from them which I know must be there, and I haven't mastered Gaelic well enough to extract all the music for myself. For that, I'd probably have to develop a native ear, or something close to it. For Welsh (though this is something I obviously can't check directly upon) I have the impression Tony Conran developed one for me, and shared it fully with all his readers. Friends of mine in Wales told me when the book came out that it was a revelation to some of them too.

The effect of that Penguin book was bodily. The poetry clung in the ear, but it also went through the mind of the body's realm of dance and gesture. It did the same things to me as the poetry of Fr Hopkins SJ, whose work had turned me on to poetry itself when I was a schoolboy, and it did them from the same authoritative source. I had seen the isthmian canal of Hopkins' verse, and its excitingly difficult locks: now I was getting a sense of the aural ocean that had moved behind it. I was also imbibing a lasting corrective, ultimately beyond the grasp or at at least beyond the traditions of my own language, but important as an ideal-absolute case, to the slackness of the *vers libre* and *vers libéré* which had pretty well taken over modern poetry in English. I began to see *that* as an intellectual's poetry, dependent on the aesthetics of *interest*. Poetry, in its fullness, requires more than that iconic quality which a text begins to have when conscious and unconscious thinking are brought into concert with each other; it also requires the sympathy of the body, the ghostly activation of ear and breath and muscles. When thought and dream harmonize with the element of gesture, of the dance, poetry becomes what I call Wholespeak, an utterance of the whole person, capable of addressing the wholeness of the person who receives it. Compared with this, most other utterance is Narrowspeak, of a lesser fullness which merely administers the world. And which may be needed, and indeed exist, to regulate the excesses which poetry can bring in its train. This may be the real meaning of administration, to buffer poetry or at least to counterbalance the iconic when it comes seeking embodiment.

Another aspect of Welsh classical poetry which worked powerfully on me through Conran's translations was a sense of ramified chiasmus, though I certainly didn't know that term back then. Chiasmus, for those who share my slackness about learning the names of technical poetic devices, is derived from the Greek letter chi (X) and really means cross-linkage, X-ing things together. John Hollander's excellent 1981 primer *Rhyme's Reason: A Guide to English Verse* gives several examples. One, not a verbal-musical one but one which works intellectually, is his line 'Speech which in part reflects on parts of speech'. What echoed continually and fascinatingly for me out of Conran's translations of Welsh classical verse was all-over patterning of cross reference and cross resonance, a kind of ever-growing crystal lattice of sound and sense at once. I was amazed by the continual fine shifts of key, of vowel colour, by how a sequence of consonants would appear with dark vowels between them, then immediately recur with an infilling of light vowels, shadow and sunlight chasing each other across a rippling current. It was a powerful, ever-recurring mantra against randomness and chaos, this rapid miming of complex inter-relatedness, and it gave me the fascination with chiasmus that has been a feature of my own writing ever since. I don't think my continuing passion for masculine-feminine rhyme (fence/patience, fluttered/bird) arose precisely from Conran's Penguin book, since I had already encountered it in Gaelic poetry I had read; the Penguin book did, however, immensely sharpen my appreciation of it as a tripping, leaping, sometimes even limping alternative to the stiffer march of English rhyme, with its ever-successive finalities, its continual stoppage. I saw that rhyme, in the hands of its inventors and first masters, was a more flexible, resourceful thing than I had imagined, and capable of more nuance.

Equally, I was struck by the almost *cloisonée* quality of images and epithets in the older verse, the way they were packed tightly into the tense lacing of the verse, or displayed like quarterings in a complex heraldry:

> Son of Gruffudd, valor in battle,
> Your violence long, dragon of Ewias,
> For your fullness of rank, I praise you,
> Everyone praises you, kingdom's head!

I notice this heraldic imagery has been reflected in the new jacket design of Conran's anthology, where the original Penguin book carried an equally native and suggestive imagery of fitted stone walling.

Beyond these impressions, as much visceral as intellectual, Conran's Penguin book gave me the delight of discovering a whole ancient and in the full sense classical tradition. For that, I needed the help of a detailed introduction, and the one he gave did not seem overlong to me. In a book of contemporary verse from one's own culture, too much prose guidance can be obtrusive and school-masterly, muffling the impact of the poetry itself, but with a survey of an unfamiliar literature or period, guidance isn't out of place. Also, Conran very tactfully kept the prose parts of his book separate from the poetry. The lecture ceased when we entered the gallery to view the works of art. In this, he constructed his book more wisely than most of the editors of that deservedly popular Penguin series. For example, one wasn't, while reading the poems, obliged to think about the problem, for modern anti-aristocratic tastes, of a poetry based for hundreds of years on eulogy and elegy addressed to warrior overlords.

It is possible that Anthony (now Tony) Conran worries at this matter a bit too much in the new 1986 version of that splendid 1967 anthology. All poetry in all periods is substantially in hock to the class and sensibility which gives it patronage and a focus; the point doesn't need to be laboured. In our age, much good and nearly all mediocre poetry which gets published is obedient to the class sensibility of secularizing university intellectuals, and deviates from their expected attitudes only gingerly or for deliberately naughty effect. What matters more is how far beyond what we may call the commissioning class a poetry may spread and how freely poets elaborate their own art, either on their own or within some sort of poetic guild-tradition powerful enough to contain and refine the iconic needs of both their sponsors and of any wider public there may be beyond the sponsors. The old bards of Wales must have built their tradition well, for poetry to remain so strong a feature of Welsh life for centuries after the defection of the native lords who once upheld it. As Conran wrote in the introduction to the Penguin book:

The Welsh poet is still a leader in his community, a national figure who appears at public functions and is constantly called upon to give his opinions on questions of the day. He is therefore able to talk, in his poetry, of political matters (and even international affairs) with the certainty that a lot of influential people are going to listen. No English poet has been able to do this since Tennyson.

I can't seem to find that passage repeated in the 1986 rescension of his book. It did interest me very strongly in 1967, though, as a model for something which sporadically did happen in my own society and might be developed further. British readers sometimes profess a rather patronizing scepticism when I tell them how influential poetry can at times be in Australia, and what a broad readership the best of it can attain, proportional to our population. Verse is also a medium which many Australians have always reached for to express things about their society; a strong current of 'light' newspaper verse overlapped with the evolving ballad tradition right through the nineteenth century and well into this one and was a powerful shaper of attitudes. This verse was protected from the deadening conventions of contemporary High Art verse by the very fact of being regarded as light verse, and had a vastly wider readership than the stiff formalities of most of our early academic poets. Indeed the coming of Modernism had the effect of killing off the real modernity of that tradition, at least in great part, and channelling it into academic obedience, though it sometimes reappears, as for example in the work of an excellent poet like Bruce Dawe. A rather ghastly parody of poets' influence is played out, here as elsewhere, when poets are invited to lend their name and pen to designated left-wing causes in return for good reviews and freedom from harassment at festivals, but that is the academy militant, a hangover from the Vietnam War period, and may pass away with that generation. Getting right away from the situation, and the generation I am caught up in, it seemed clear to me, in Wales two decades ago, that the noble courts and the *eisteddfodau* of Wales had created and preserved a highly trained public for poetry, a model for what might be created again.

The new rescension of Conran's anthology contains a good deal more explanatory prose, and I'm frank to admit that I need all the additional data too. The wholly new appendix on Welsh metrics is particularly welcome, and is as easy to follow, probably, as a treatise on so intricate a matter could ever be. Having said this, though, the proportion of explanatory prose to poetry does now seem high; the cliffs do beetle a bit, and threaten to fall in on the stream as it glitters on its way. I may be imagining things, too, but the prose itself now seems a shade heavier and fussier, despite the brilliance of the many fine historical and stylistic distinctions it draws. I wonder if this is not in part a result of the great disappointment of St David's Day, 1979, when the voters of Wales, for their own reasons, knocked down a whole heap of clangorous furniture in the path of their own independence just as it seemed about to reach a measure of consummation. It's very presumptuous of an outsider even to mention these things, but I remember with some nostalgia that sunny hopeful mood that seemed to be abroad in Wales twenty years ago when I lived there. The right to plead in Welsh in the courts had not long been conceded, personal documents could be in Welsh or English, the Red Dragon was visible on public offices everywhere. Anglophone students in Cardiff were starting to attend Welsh-language classes – now when I go back to see my friends, much seems sadder, more dour, more embattled. Perhaps an outsider can be forgiven if he mistook a sectional revival for a national one, and mistook hope and energy for portents of a real shift in the deep mood of a society not his own. The emergence of the language into a modern sort of visibility may have *been* the consummation, rather than the national independence it seemed to presage.

If the updated version of Conran's anthology has a touch more of the museum about it, and a little less of the atmosphere of an exciting exhibition in a newly opened gallery, perhaps I should remember that its editor and I are both a couple of decades older now, and point out that the exhibition has been augmented by some excellent new work, particularly by women poets. In particular, I am bowled over by the work of Ann Griffiths (1776–1805). Even on a small sampling from a small output, she seems to have been a mystical poet worthy of at least some comparison with St John of the Cross. Again, if I was fascinated twenty years ago by the Welsh classical styles, and drew most from them, I was well aware even then that there were some modern poets of world importance in Welsh too. I am happy to see more of both Saunders Lewis and David Gwenallt Jones in the updated edition, just as I have been happy, in both editions, to note an absence of that freezing condescension towards religion and religious poetry so common in present-day scholarly books. It is a pity, though, that the book has changed publishers, and lost the worldwide Penguin distribution. Even if I had not been living in Wales twenty years ago, at exactly the right time and place for Conran's translations to come into my hands,

I would have bought the original Penguin book and been knocked sideways by it; I suspect that its effect on me would still have been profound, even if I hadn't been able to track down so many of its allusions in my battered green Cortina. On the other hand, we never see Poetry Wales Press books in Australia unless we somehow learn of their existence and order them specially; I wouldn't have seen the updated edition if I had not been asked to write this memoir-review of it. I hope this isn't a symptomatic shrinkage of the Welsh presence in the wider world, for the essence of so ancient and brilliant a poetic tradition deserves to be kept before readers everywhere.

A Folk Inferno

Two features of the celebratory mode in poetry which occur to me are refusal of alienation and a species of humility. Unlike poetries of formula and definition, the celebratory doesn't presume to understand the world, at least never reductively, and so leaves it open and expansive, with unforeclosed potentials. Or so I've mostly observed. Celebration is very much a spirit and a tone, and comes out of the poem we live in and are trying to write, at least as much as out of the particular poem we're writing. I don't, however, want to speak to our theme of celebration in generalities; rather, I want to present a case in which it is involved. The poem I want to present is, I think, celebratory, but in a left-handed, paradoxical way that may test the definitions a bit. It was written by a convict shipped from Ireland in 1832 to penal servitude in New South Wales and later in Van Diemen's land, and it is entitled 'A Convict's Tour to Hell'.

Francis MacNamara, or Wilton, or Goddard – convicts often gave false names to the penal authorities when they could, so as to confuse the records and maybe slip through the documentary nets they were caught in – seems to have been born aroud 1811 and to have been reasonably well read in the English-language poetry of his time. He certainly knew Burns, and Swift, and the Bible, and was an adept composer of biting ballads. His sentence was for stealing a piece of cloth, and he did not contest the charge, perhaps because it was trumped up to get rid of a known, witty opponent of landlordism and payment of tax to the Church of Ireland. Whether he was Catholic or Protestant is not known, ironically, and internal evidence in his poems is apt to suggest both possibilities in turn. What is certain is that in the eyes of his gaolers he was a total recidivist, being sentenced to a number of further terms in Australia and seeing the inside of several of the harsh secondary punishment stations set up to torment the recalcitrant. A core group of his poems, though, refers to his time as labourer assigned to the Australian Agricultural Company's ventures in the Hunter Valley north of Sydney. There is an eloquent refusal, doubtless unavailing, to work in the company's underground coal mines, and a versified petition to the authorities at Newcastle to remove a flogger named Duffy from the post of cook because the men on the chain gang can't forget the human flesh the man is more adept at carving. Capable of playing the merry stage-Irish clown to placate authority – he is said once to have charmed a prison commandant who had sentenced him to twenty-eight days on bread and water for drunkenness by instantly composing the quatrain:

> Ah, Captain Murray, if you please,
> Make it hours instead of days;
> You know it behoves an Irishman
> To christen the shamrock when he can –

MacNamara none the less wore his self-conferred title of Frank the Poet like a coat of arms, often proclaiming his personal slogan: 'I'm Frank the Poet, from Cashel in the County Tipperary, and while I live I'll crow.' His career in and out of irons seems finally to have ended in Van Diemen's Land in the early 1850s, and late in life he seems to have written out his whole opus in longhand for a family named Calf who gave him a home. This homemade booklet, bound in leather, was presented to the Mitchell Library in Sydney in the early 1950s and is known as the Trimingham Manuscript, from the name of the family which presented it.

For over a century, Frank the Poet led a shadowy life as a convict balladist. Under that odd imperial system of literary apartheid by which 'folk' poetry and pukka, officer-class poetry still frequently appear in different anthologies, MacNamara's verse has mostly been included only in collections of balladry and folksong, sometimes under his full name, more often under his title only, often enough under Anon. It was not until 1978 that the folklore scholars John Meredith and Rex Whalan in a remarkable piece of literary detective work drew together the scattered facts of MacNamara's life and presented a coherent short biography of the man who wrote, in the 'Tour', the first important poem composed in English in Australia. All my facts in this talk are drawn from their book *Frank the Poet*, published by Red Rooster Press in Melbourne in 1978. Amongst other claims they make for him is that his ballads meant for singing form practically the whole foundation of at least one very important strand of Australian folksong which persists down to our own day. It may be possible to claim him as the father of Australian folksong, out and out, and to see his work as the reason why older Australian ballads sound Irish rather than English or Scottish. Most importantly, their book gives him a place in and a possible renewed influence on our literary history.

The 'Tour to Hell' is a powerful early celebration, necessarily a totally underground one, of attitudes which were going to be persistent and influential in Australia. How much the 'Tour' itself contributed to an emergent popular tradition, though, we may never know. Certainly songs by MacNamara such as 'Bold Jack Donohue', 'The Capture of the Cyprus Brig' and 'Moreton Bay', the last-named set to the tune 'Boolavogue', were widely sung despite official bans and floggings, and did have a powerful effect. They were still being sung in an authentic way into the middle of this century, when versions of them were collected by folklorists. It may be that the 'Tour to Hell', as MacNamara's longest and most ambitious poem, is best seen as the summation of his thinking, his essential crow, celebrating his amazingly undefeated sense of justice. Its early performance history is by now almost certainly impossible to trace. Although he claims to have *written* it in 1839, Frank the Poet may also have stored it in his memory and the memories of fellow convicts for twenty or more years. It would have been difficult enough, though not impossible, to write it down on purloined bits of paper in the brief intervals of his work as a slave labourer for the A.A. Company, and harder still to keep the manuscript safe from warders' inspections as he was shunted around. We know that others could recite it, because it was from their recitations rather than from the Calf-Trimingham manuscript that it was first collected, late last century.

As you will hear, the Tour is a dream-vision belonging, if we are of a classifying turn of mind, to the genre of the world-turned-upside-down, the Saturnalian and Medieval trope of Misrule, in which absurdities are revealed and the world refreshed by inversion. The convict poet views his gaolers undergoing punishment in hell, and not liking it. As is often done, the vision is explained, though not explained away, as a harmless daydream. There are compressed ironies in this; for one thing, it suspends the vision as a potent thought-balloon above the everyday; for another it mocks the potential fury of the ridiculed penal authorities with a patently insincere repudiation of itself; for a third it undercuts seriousness and assists that lightness of tone necessary if so biting a wish-fulfilment is not to bog down in its own anger. And after all that, how sad it is too, in its suggestion that imagination as the refuge of the oppressed is maybe no more *than* imagination. A wry note, and only momentary, but it registers too.

What strikes me about this poem, and causes me to see it as essentially celebratory, is its liveliness and its utterly undefeated tone.

Also, there is its amplitude and its vivid imaginative scene-painting, all done in the teeth of a system intent on reducing men to a broken submissiveness. '*Die Gedanken sind frei*', as the old German song goes, for once accurately. A man so brutally treated as MacNamara was might easily have absorbed more of his oppressors' sanctimonious cruelty and let it darken his spirit. The poem's enormous catharsis of indignation can only work, for the poet and others, if it doesn't in any deep way resemble the suffering he has undergone, or share the spirit in which it has been inflicted. A slower-moving poem might have mimed the authorities' use of time to break a rebellious spirit, and made the vision fatally heavy. Instead, each tormentor is visited with appropriate pangs, but 'visited' is the right word: each is only touched on at suitable length, and very little revelling in their anguish is allowed to clog the rapid vivacity of the poem's movement. The action flickers along like a cartoon strip, helped by the dancing metre, the short lines and the insouciant rhyming which draws half of its effect from being often forced and sometimes outright bad. The end result of this rhyming is as much a satire on classical correctness and a piece of complicity with human haplessness as it is a defect, and for me the former two strengths of it swallow up the defectiveness. It can be seen as a proletarian version of Byron's airy manner, and it mimes the informality of a free settler's hut rather than the fitted regularities of a commandant's house or a Georgian prison barracks.

The poem covers a vast imaginative space and a very large cast of characters, and perhaps the subtlest revenge it takes on the tyrants is that it reduces their full humanity not by detailed Dantean cruelty, which might imply respect and make them tragic, but by turning each into a brief comic figment of himself, a grotesque worth only a moment's viewing and maybe a cheerful mocking word. That is what each has reduced himself to. Here, his use of alienation is masterly, because it is consistently aimed in the right direction, against the tormentors rather than against the world; in other words, he alienates them rather than himself. Frank punishes and approves punishment, but he doesn't mime it in sensuous descriptions and so take part in it. His is a healthy-minded *fiction* of retribution, not the sticky personal indulgence it might have been if given shading and evocative realistic description. The eternity the bad people have landed themselves in is undercut by its being presented as a fantasy, by the brevity with which we see each one there, and by the fact that nearly all were alive when the poet was writing his poem. Some of them indeed are famous figures in our history, and have bits of the geography named after them.

It is crucially ironic that the religion whose tragic fragmentation drove MacNamara into the jaws of official justice should also provide the framework for his vision of real justice. That irony, though, is nearly as old as the Emperor Constantine. I find a sort of extra irony in the way Frank the Poet pours genial scorn on the idea of Purgatory, and then embraces it, having both Satan and Jesus as good as say that life as a convict is sufficient expiation for anything. Excusably enough in his circumstances, the poet doesn't manage forgiveness of his enemies, but another potential of Christianity, one too often latent rather than active wherever that faith has got deeply entangled with secular power, emerges in the amiable ordinariness of the authorities on the Other Side. They reflect the whole theology of casting down the mighty and raising up those of low degree, and exhibit in their very demeanour what has recently been called a preferential option for the poor. Charon, the Devil and even St Peter turn out to be reasonable fellows an old lag can get alone with. Jesus, in turn, is the very soul of decency, fair-minded and not at all forbiddingly awesome. Divinity with a human face can be pagan and Classical, but this is divinity with a working man's face, as in the original Christian concept. The poor in spirit aren't humbled afresh by such figures, as they might be by the haughty doctrines of official prison chaplains. All is understanding brotherliness and festivity, with cruel pomposity overturned and consigned to the pit, and that is an unterrifying wattage of Divine love a plain man might not find too strong for his blood. A not-too-royal Kingdom of Heaven, instinct with decency and welcome. I think the poem finally celebrates that sort of hope for this world or the other, and that its tone and its triumph are fed by a lack of alienation which that hope makes possible despite the worst that man can do. Lack of alienation expressed in a half-joking folk eschatology both draws on and makes possible the sharing of vision by which the poem must have been preserved in its first decades.

That sharing, of course, also draws on shared language and a shared attitude to registers of speech. The poem's language draws on many registers, from legalese ('contiguous to the River Styx') and contemporary literary diction ('in flames of brimstone they were toiling') to sporting vernacular and racy slang ('about six feet of mortal sin'), but its ruling voice is a middle one, made to be shared widely. This very use of language also enacts the humane vision of the poem, refusing to let intelligence or justice be confined to upper registers and their tainted solemnities. Such a mixture and fusion of registers is also characteristic of the popular newspaper verse, which had got started in Australia by the 1820s and lasted till it was eclipsed by literary modernism in the 1930s. This sort of verse, which by contrast with our folksongs tends to sound English rather than Irish, may well have influenced the young convict from Tipperary, reading such second- or third-hand colonial newspapers as came his way in the various up-country prison stockades he did his time in. That older modernity of tone and vernacular balance still emerges in our country today, in battles against a judging, policing mandarin tendency present in our High Art poetry from its earliest correctional beginnings.

Here, now, is the text of MacNamara's poem:

A Convict's Tour to Hell

Composed at Stroud A.A. Co. Establishment Station New South Wales

> *Nor can the foremost of the sons of men*
> *Escape my ribald and licentious pen.*
>
> Swift

Composed and written
October 23rd day, Anno 1839

You prisoners of New South Wales,
Who frequent watchhouses and gaols
A story to you I will tell
'Tis of a convict's tour to hell.

Whose valour had for years been tried
On the highway before he died
At length he fell to death a prey
To him it proved a happy day
Downwards he bent his course I'm told
Like one destined for Satan's fold
And no refreshment would he take
'Till he approached the Stygian lake
A tent he then began to fix
Contiguous to the River Styx
Thinking that no one could molest him
He leaped when Charon thus addressed him
Stranger I say from whence art thou,
And thy own name, pray tell me now,
Kind sir I come from Sydney gaol
My name I don't mean to conceal

And since you seem anxious to know it
On earth I was called Frank the Poet.
Are you that person? Charon cried,
I'll carry you to the other side.
Five or sixpence I mostly charge
For the like passage in my barge
So stranger do not troubled be
For you shall have a passage free
Frank seeing no other succour nigh
With the invitation did comply
And having a fair wind and tide
They soon arrived at the other side
And leaving Charon at the ferry
Frank went in haste to Purgatory
And rapping loudly at the gate
Of Limbo, or the Middle State
Pope Pius the 7th soon appeared
With gown, beads, crucifix and beard
And gazing at the Poet the while
Accosts him in the following style
Stranger art thou a friend or foe
Your business here I fain would know
Quoth the Poet for Heaven I'm not fitted
And here I hope to be admitted
Pius rejoined, vain are your hopes
This place was made for Priests and Popes
'Tis a world of our own invention
But friend I've not the least intention
To admit such a foolish elf
Who scarce knows how to bless himself
Quoth Frank were you mad or insane
When first you made this world of pain?
For I can see nought but fire
A share of which I can't desire
Here I see weeping wailing gnashing
And torments of the newest fashion
Therefore I call you silly elf
Who made a rod to whip yourself
And may you like all honest neighbours
Enjoy the fruit of all your labours
Frank then bid the Pope farewell
And hurried to that place called Hell

And having found the gloomy gate
Frank rapped aloud to know his fate
He louder knocked and louder still
When the Devil came, pray what's your will?
Alas cried the Poet I've come to dwell
With you and share your fate in Hell
Says Satan that can't be, I'm sure
For I detest and hate the poor
And none shall in my kingdom stand
Except the grandees of the land.
But Frank I think you are going astray
For convicts never come this way
But soar to Heaven in droves and legions
A place so called in the upper regions
So Frank I think with an empty purse
You shall go further and fare worse
Well cried the Poet since 'tis so
One thing of you I'd like to know
As I'm at present in no hurry
Have you one here called Captain Murray?
Yes Murray is within this place
Would you said Satan see his face?
May God forbid that I should view him
For on board the *Phoenix Hulk* I knew him
Who is that Sir in yonder blaze
Who on fire and brimstone seems to graze?
'Tis Captain Logan of Moreton Bay
And Williams who was killed the other day
He was overseer at Grosse Farm
And done poor convicts no little harm
Cook who discovered New South Wales
And he that first invented gaols
Are both tied to a fiery stake
Which stands in yonder boiling lake
Hark do you hear this dreadful yelling
It issues from Doctor Wardell's dwelling
And all those fiery seats and chairs
Are fitted up for Dukes and Mayors
And nobles of Judicial orders
Barristers, Lawyers and Recorders
Here I beheld legions of traitors
Hangmen gaolers and flagellators

Commandants, Constables and Spies
Informers and Overseers likewise
In flames of brimstone they were toiling
And lakes of sulphur round them boiling
Hell did resound with their fierce yelling
Alas how dismal was their dwelling
Then Major Morriset I espied
And Captain Cluney by his side
With a fiery belt they were lashed together
As tight as soles to upper leather
Their situation was most horrid
For they were tyrants down at the Norrid
Prostrate I beheld a petitioner
It was the Company's Commissioner
Satan said he my days are ended
For many years I've superintended
The An. Company's affairs
And I punctually paid all arrears
Sir should you doubt the hopping Colonel
At Carrington you'll find my journal
Legibly penned in black and white
To prove that my accounts were right
And since I've done your will on earth
I hope you'll put me in a berth
Then I saw old Serjeant Flood
In Vulcan's hottest forge he stood
He gazed at me his eyes with ire
Appeared like burning coals of fire
In fiery garments he was arrayed
And like an Arabian horse he brayed
He on a bloody cutlass leaned
And to a lamp-post he was chained
He loudly called out for assistance
Or begged me to end his existence
Cheer up said I be not afraid
Remember No. Three Stockade
In the course of time you may do well
If you behave yourself in Hell
Your heart on earth was fraught with malice
Which oft drove convicts to the gallows
But you'll now atone for all the blood
Of prisoners shed by Serjeant Flood.

Then I beheld that well known Trapman
The Police Runner called Izzy Chapman
Here he was standing on his head
In a river of melted boiling lead.
Alas he cried behold me stranger
I've captured many a bold bushranger
And for the same I'm suffering here
But lo, now yonder snakes draw near
On turning round I saw slow worms
And snakes of various kinds and forms
All entering at his mouth and nose
To devour his entrails as I suppose
Then turning round to go away
Bold Lucifer bade me to stay
Saying Frank by no means go man
Till you see your old friend Dr Bowman
Yonder he tumbles groans and gnashes
He gave you many a thousand lashes
And for the same he does bewail
For Osker with an iron flail
Thrashes him well you may depend
And will till the world comes to an end
Just as I spoke a coach and four
Came in full post haste to the door
And about six feet of mortal sin
Without leave or licence trudged in
At his arrival three cheers were given
Which rent I'm sure the highest Heaven
And all the inhabitants of Hell
With one consent rang the great bell
Which never was heard to sound or ring
Since Judas sold our Heavenly King
Drums were beating flags were hoisting
There never before was such rejoicing
Dancing singing joy or mirth
In Heaven above or on the earth
Straightway to Lucifer I went
To know what these rejoicings meant
Of sense cried Lucifer I'm deprived
Since Governor Darling has arrived
With fire and brimstone I've ordained him
And Vulcan has already chained him

And I'm going to fix an abode
For Captain Rossi, he's on the road
Frank don't go till you see the novice
The magistrate from the Police Office
Oh said the Poet I'm satisfied
To hear that he is to be tied
And burned in this world of fire
I think 'tis high time to retire
And having travelled many days
O'er fiery hills and boiling seas
At length I found that happy place
Where all the woes of mortals cease
And rapping loudly at the wicket
Cried Peter, where's your certificate
Or if you have not one to show
Pray who in Heaven do you know?
Well I know Brave Donohue
Young Troy and Jenkins too
And many others whom floggers mangled
And lastly were by Jack Ketch strangled
Peter, says Jesus, let Frank in
For he is thoroughly purged from sin
And although in convict's habit dressed
Here he shall be a welcome guest
Isaiah go with him to Job
And put on him a scarlet robe
St Paul go to the flock straightway
And kill the fatted calf today
And go tell Abraham and Abel
In haste now to prepare the table
For we shall have a grand repast
Since Frank the Poet has come at last
Then came Moses and Elias
John the Baptist and Mathias
With many saints from foreign lands
And with the Poet they all join hands
Thro' Heaven's Concave their rejoicings rang
And hymns of praise to God they sang
And as they praised his glorious name
I woke and found 'twas but a dream.

Addendum

After I had delivered this paper, the Gaelic poet Seán Ó Tuama, who was chairman of proceedings at the conference that afternoon, pointed out that Frank the Poet might be regarded as the successor in English, of a line of MacNamara bards belonging to Tipperary in early times, adding that some of his turns of phrase and thought closely resembled those in Irish-language poems from the region. I was very interested to hear of this, and immediately remembered something that I should not have forgotten, that is, that I had in fact read Joan Keefe's translation of 'Eachtra Ghiolla an Amaráin' (The Adventures of a Luckless Fellow') by the eighteenth-century poet Donncha Rua Mac Conmara, as published in her book *Irish Poems: From Cromwell to the Famine*, published by Bucknell University Press in 1977. Mr Ó Tuama confirmed that Donncha Rua (Red-headed Donald) was one of the poets he had in mind, though this member of the great MacNamara family in fact came from County Clare. When I came home, I re-read the 'Eachtra' to compare it with the 'Tour to Hell'. I could not compare actual turns of phrase carried over from Irish into English, but there was considerable similarity of tone and a similar rapidity of narration; Donncha Rua's poem also contains an inset visit to an otherworld that mingles elements of the classical Elysium, of Hell and of the Fairyland of Celtic myth, but this seems far less unified in structure than Francis MacNamara's elysion. The only stanza I found which immediately reminded me of Frank the Poet was the one in which Eevul, the poet's guide in the underworld, says:

> Take a good look at Luther who changed religion
> And at thick-skinned Calvin sweating off the lard,
> At Henry the Eighth and beside him his queen
> All swinging by chain from gibbets harsh.

Cruder stuff, on the whole, but it may have seeded an idea. And it does raise the question of how far MacNamara the convict poet may have been influenced by the copious *aisling* (vision) literature of Gaelic Ireland.

Talk delivered at the International Writers' Conference, Dublin, Ireland, 14-17 June 1988. The theme of the conference was 'Literature as Celebration'.

The Suspect Captivity of the Fisher King

'Scholars help us with our immortality – they have to, if they're to have any themselves.'

1   The first 140 years in the development of Australian literature in English, from Barron Field's 'Kangaroo' to the early 1960s, proceeded without significant academic involvement or help.

2   The establishment of other lines of patronage before the universities took up Australian literature in any large or convinced way may yet save our literature from a wholesale repudiation of the 'common' reader.

3   An academic-led literature is a gentrified suburb, but the unconstrained reader is the objective correlative.

4   If academic studies in Australian literature arose mainly as an expression of a decolonizing phase in our history, they may fade or diversify as that phase is left behind. If, on the other hand, they arose mostly out of a need for fresh texts to study and comment on, they are likely to continue and even to burgeon. And attempts to manage the canon of approved authors will tend to run afoul of the need for grain to feed the mills.

5   The spirit of the age, as sedulously cultivated in universities and among their graduates, makes it curiously hard to admit that Australian literary studies can be undertaken out of love.

6   Whatever they may pretend out of foolish obedience to that spirit, writers all expect that any study of their work shall be done out of love. Nothing less excuses the intrusion, or balances the element of judgement.

7   Studies in Australian literature, or even the fact that some people were studying it, undoubtedly helped to legitimize our literature for many Australians. Such legitimation, however, removed an older test of cultural and personal independence, by which people simply read and loved Australian works.

8   When universities looked down their noses at Australian liter-
     ature, writers ran more of that literature, and their magazines
     were more alert to literary values than are our present publish-
     or-perish outlets or the mental Pyongyang of our contemporary
     socio-political magazines.

9   Present-day 'literary' magazines carry texts pretending to be
     poetry surrounded by other, longer texts pretending to be based
     on something more solid than poetry.

10   The little magazine as we have known it is a relic of the era of
     literary modernism and now artificially prolongs that era.

11   Universities, like any patron, can determine the subject matter,
     the attitudes and the tone of all but the strongest and most
     individual writing – and thus to study any but the strongest
     and most independent of current writing is merely to admire
     oneself in the mirror.

12   If I'm correctly informed, regular courses in Australian litera-
     ture abroad began a few years before Australian literature
     courses were inaugurated at home. Commonwealth literature
     courses have so far been of vastly greater direct benefit to
     Australian authors, in providing a ladder by which a few, at
     least, have been able to get their work out of the deep well of
     late-imperial scorn and to secure distribution and notice
     amongst that vastly greater readership which the English lan-
     guage potentially affords any author who writes in it. Authorial
     gratitude for this deserves expressing, and I express mine right
     here.

13   Literary studies are vital in establishing and maintaining accu-
     rate texts. Authorial intention has been shown as a fallacy in
     criticism, but not as yet in the textual-editorial sphere. Where
     discoverable, it should be respected, except where it is wrong.

14   It is the special glory of academics not to set or follow fashion,
     but to counteract it on behalf of texts which it injures or
     obscures. They exist to keep the unread read, and to defend its
     real qualities. For a literary academic to treat any author as
     bygone is a betrayal of trust.

15   We all desire taste to be relative in respect of our failures and
     absolute in respect of our successes.

16 Modernist art is asserted to be different in kind from all earlier art, and the qualitative divide between them is claimed to invalidate any comparison. This is only true to the extent that, unlike other art, all but the best of modernist art is merely a function of its own critique, and subservient to the takeover polemic which carries it.

17 Failed authors are liable to blame their failures on anything at all, even on tenured employment in a university. Such authors are, however, more likely to punish successful full-time writers than fellow academics.

18 Apparently inexplicable literary hatreds arise more often from the prick of an editorial pencil than from that of a critical pen, and ancient rejections return to haunt former editors.

19 Academics and authors despise each other most when each has it in mind to exploit the other; when this impulse is dormant, each merely considers the other his dependant, if not his natural servant.

20 Publishers, in turn, despise both academics and authors because they depend on both but effortlessly exploit both.

21 Publishers can exploit academics and writers alike because the former have an assured income and the latter do not.

22 I have never known academics to excel my fellow authors in any vice whatsoever. It is apposite here to mention Jardine's Law, devised by my friend the philosopher Brian Jardine some decades ago: The meanness, skulduggery, backstabbing and general human viciousness of any pursuit increases in direct proportion to the stated high-mindedness of its objects. The claims of literature are loftier than those of scholarship.

23 For savagery, dishonesty, bullying, ill-will and poorly disguised jealousy, I have never seen a piece of academic criticism quite equal that regularly practised by authors on each other. Literature just seems to be informed by this greater *joie de vivre*.

24 In private, writers and scholars alike refer confidently to a standard of literary excellence, but in our country few of them now dare to invoke this standard in public. There, hype and special pleading prevail.

25   Too much agreement between authors and academics on matters of value is more dangerous than too little. The result can be, and in Australia strikingly is, a cabal which rules the intellectual life of the nation, promoting a received sensibility and those authors obedient to it, cracking the whip for an agenda of causes and social attitudes.

26   The real Australian divide is not between authors and academics, but between this cabal and the wider population, which it scorns, patronizes and seeks to reform, or to relegate altogether.

27   The cabal is both the church and the Inquisition of the Enlightenment here, and serves to instruct students and others within its influence in the less physical aspects of terrorism, policing, mind control and the enforcement of unwritten laws. It is now ageing, but is still so well entrenched that it can prevent publication of books and other works contrary to its beliefs, and its confidence is such that it has been known to 'go public' indignantly when it has failed, as it rarely does, to fix a literary prize in accordance with its agenda.

28   The outstanding Australian trait of our time being moral cowardice, any individual set upon by the cabal is instantly abandoned by everyone, to be defended only obliquely and much later, when the heat is off.

29   By an odd sleight of language, academic art in Australia is called modern or modernist. In much the same way, 'avant garde' here signifies persons advancing resolutely into the ethos of early twentieth-century European bohemia.

30   Literary modernism is totalitarian politics in a literary disguise, while totalitarian politics is modernist literature with no disguise at all.

31   The atmosphere is the forecast, and the tone of a work of art is the tone of the regime that would canonize it.

32   It has been suggested that as soon as universities turned from the classics and took up contemporary vernacular literature, they crippled it, or its reception by the broader public, in order to gain and keep control of it. Australian experience may contradict this: the crippling here occurred well before universities showed any interest in Australian literature, which scholars were trained to regard as an oxymoron.

33 The real succession of events is probably better put in mythic terms: the Fisher King in the legend of Parzifal, whom we may take as personifying poetry, saw that aristocracy was finished alike as a way of life and a source of patronage; its natural replacement seemed to be the highbrow. Knowing that while aristocrats can't abide a maimed thing, highbrows can't truly love anything that is whole, the Fisher King carefully shot himself in the foot, rather than tramp the roads with proletarian balladeers. As an old courtier, he believed he needed a castle for his subtleties.

34 Now, in his castle of refuge amid the barren lands, the Fisher King wonders whether his great wound refuses to heal because of a corruption within himself, or whether it is kept open by his nurses for their purposes. All academies are police academies, and he has allowed poetry to be taken over and used by the police.

35 The Enlightenment is a Luciferian poem, that is, one in revolt against poetry itself. Its claim to power in the world is based on the claim that it arises from something more solid than poetry – reason, intellect, science are candidates it frequently proposes, and it confirms their mana with repeated bouts of human sacrifice. One such secured our country for us.

36 In a world ruled by such a paradigm, poetry has not only to be explained, but explained away, and a rationalist equivalent for it developed.

37 Poetry is an atavistic, fertile remnant in the Fisher King's present sterile self-exile, and thus its every officially noted occurrence must instantly be surrounded by a dense barbed wire of commentary and exegesis. A classifying taxonomy should be added to this, to relativize the poem and defuse it even further.

38 No matter how woefully bad the prose of a critical introduction may be, some students will prefer it to the text it introduces.

39 Commentary expands to fill the space occupied by the text itself.

40 Any true poem is greater than the whole Enlightenment, more important and more sustaining of human life.

41 In modernist literature, a very frequent attempted substitute for poetry is called experiment. This is in fact a key ritual of modernism, and its ritual nature is revealed by the confinement

of such experimentation within a tightly circumscribed tone and sensibility which have undergone only very minor changes during the whole twentieth century. Real experiment would be Baptist, or funny, or popular, or charitable in spirit and tone – something unthinkable like that. But of course modernism is obsessive, and ritualistic, and hostile in tone, because at its heart lies the pathological state depression, of which it is either a vector or a result, and probably both.

42   All cultural relativism is an act of condescension towards all actual cultures.

43   To discuss a work of literature by living authors in terms unclear to those authors is to treat them as anthropologists used to treat 'primitive' tribesfolk, and to pretend that any Enlightenment terminology is superior to or has rights over the terms of the work itself is to vandalize the work.

44   Any true work of art is inexhaustible in its suggestions, its implications and its recoveries of freshness; the potentials for commentary on it and interpretation of it are therefore infinite. This is a form of infinite regress, but probably only becomes questionable if taxpayers are being asked to fund it.

45   Criticism has a seeming authority to which weak and inexperienced readers succumb. Like all of education, it converts such individuals into mediocrities and robs authors of them.

46   Reading a text may be as creative an act as writing it, but it's still an author who initiates that creativity, and sets all or most of its terms.

47   If literary analysis and criticism can be applied as productively to a bus ticket as to a work of literature, there is no longer any need for literary texts to be involved in criticism at all. Nor is there any need for specifically literary studies to be funded.

48   A dead end in criticism does not signify the discrediting of literature.

49   Intensely elaborated theory is clearly yet another attempt to trump poetry and to replace it with a principle amenable to Enlightenment values. Earlier contenders include wit, terror, snobbery, drug abuse and affluence, with fashion as a constant. All of these can be controlled and directed against target groups, since all are about power.

50   In an atmosphere where the Interesting (or the Intense) is intended to drive out the Good, literary excellence becomes the true underground.

51   Those who say the author is dead usually have it in mind to rifle his wardrobe.

52   One of the simplest ways of reducing poetry and its effect in human lives is to make it a part of the exam process, by which humans are graded and in which most undergo a measure of humiliation. The atmosphere of that never-to-be-admitted humiliation then attaches to poetry and may immunise a person against it for life. The gamble here is, though, that people so immunised may be prone to seek a true equivalent of poetry from an even more proscribed source, namely religion.

53   The unadmitted humiliation and modification of dreams suffered by perhaps a majority in university also attach themselves to things the academic élites hotly espouse, and so may erode those too. And yet the very humiliation suffered by many victims of the academy make them defend it fiercely.

54   Poetry is the one principle in education which can countervail the dimension of exams, grading and relegation. More essentially, it is not just the poetry of poetry that sustains people in the jostling, politics and rivalry of academic life, but also the poetry of scholarship itself. A scholar who loses this is liable to punish poets especially hard.

55   The only response to a poem, finally, is a poem, though authors naturally prefer that the poem in response to theirs be slightly inferior (greatly inferior is no fun at all). Criticism in its usual modern forms practically guarantees a response which doesn't outshine the original, but it sometimes nettles authors by discovering which of their poems are themselves responses.

56   The authority of literature resides in poetry, that of criticism in the threat of social relegation.

57   The Enlightenment will crumble and disappear because its disappearance can be imagined. One day it will be seen as a strange, cold-hearted interval between self-pity and hard drugs.

58   The large number of 'common' readers who never approved poetry's abandonment of rhyme foresaw, if not always in detail, all of the sorrows and betrayals of poetry listed above, and

poetry's current tentative return to rhyme is an admission of error and an attempt at restitution, as well as a guiltily covert death sentence on rationalism.

59   The truest praise is conceded praise, spoken through gritted teeth – but to speak it, the utterer must possess integrity, and politics now exist to silence that.

60   To conclude where we began, Australian literature is now mostly written about and even approved of at home in contemptuous and threatening terms. The very tones of its acclamation are suffused with hostility.

Offered to the Conference entitled 'Writers and Academics – An Australian Divide?' held at the University of New South Wales, 13–14 August 1988

From Bulby Brush to Figure City

I enjoyed my schooldays, partly, perhaps, because I had comparatively few of them. By accident rather than design, I managed to spend only seven years in schoolrooms. And yet I emerged with my leaving certificate and matriculation to university. Where I grew up, in a part of the country that had remained quite remote, there was initially no local primary school at all. There had been two or three one-teacher schools within walking distance of our farm, but the slump in the birth rate which the Depression brought with it had closed them all down.

It was the late 1940s before Bulby Brush Public School re-opened with an enrolment of fifteen pupils, and by that time I was nine years old. I had learned to read around the age of four, and got into habits of dreamy, bookwormish self-education that would never leave me; I had also done a couple of years of correspondence school by way of the buff envelopes sent out by Blackfriars in Sydney, but those lessons could be done in a day, leaving the other six days of the week for playing down the creek or helping fitfully around the farm. For an only child in the bush, nine is a late age to start socialization, or to start acquiring habits of numeracy and externally imposed discipline. I'm still deficient in all those, and look like never acquiring them now. I'll never be a good employee.

Full of unreal expectations about school, I started off at Bulby Brush on what could have been a disastrously wrong foot. I turned up on the first day with a long essay on the Vikings, written on white butcher's paper I'd lined for myself with a pencil. I was interested in the topic, and thought this was the sort of stuff schools did. The nineteen-year-old teachers' college graduate, whose first posting this was, read the essay in some bewilderment and praised it uncertainly to the other children. In a less innocent place, this would very likely have branded me forever as a 'Brain', a swot and a crawler, but all such terms were unknown to the barefoot farm children who would be my schoolmates for the next three years, and they received it with the same wondering indifference that they

337

gave to most things that happened in that constrained space between eight or so in the morning, when they finished milking and set off for school, and the resumption of real life and farm labour after half-past three. As in Miles Franklin's day, many of them would often go to sleep during class because of the long hours of work they had to do before and after school hours. My own parents were quite indulgent of me in this respect, though I did have my jobs to do, feeding and locking up the fowls, husking and shelling corn, turning the cream separator and many more, and I did my whack of milking on non-school days.

Looking back, I can sympathize with the hellish isolation our teacher must sometimes have felt, among adults who regarded him as a kid and a city weakling, and forgive him for the only four cuts of the strap I ever received in school, although I long resented the fact that two of them came my way on my eleventh birthday.

The Manning-Myall region of NSW now has seven high schools, but in my childhood there was only one, at Taree. I had no sooner started there when my mother died, so I spent the rest of my first year at home, and the following year I entered a school which was much more of a continuation of the ethos of Bulby Brush. This was Nabiac Central School, only twenty-nine kilometres from home, which counted some 150 children of all ages from kindergarten to ninth grade, the stage at which those of us who stayed that long sat for the intermediate certificate. As it was expected by the department that we would all either be farmers or bush workers, or at most enter the bank, our subjects were slanted towards home economics, business principles, woodwork and agricultural biology; glamour subjects such as languages never came our way. On the other hand many of us, probably a majority of the boys in fact, came to school barefoot, prolonging that blessed freedom from foot-distorting constraint which even bush children now lose at the very start of their schooldays.

I travelled to school by milk lorry, working my passage by slinging fifty-kilogram milk cans under the cheerful raillery of the driver's offsider. On quite a few days, I would drop off the lorry short of town and find myself a cosy hide down a creek to read or daydream, and an understanding headmaster silently abetted me in this, knowing I could keep up readily by attending two or three days a week and that I never got myself into trouble anyway. I could be relied on to attend on Wednesdays, as that was the day we had educational films; in those pre-television days, I would watch literally anything on a screen, and I've since seen many intense human dramas there which fell short of the sheer wonder of watching a seed germinate, unscroll and waver upwards to florid maturity in a minute or two, or icebergs calving off looming glaciers in inky Arctic seas. The themes of later movies about humans were all too often only complexified equivalents of these processes anyway and it took a natural solitary a long time to grasp the pathos of that.

I don't remember that we were notably vicious to each other, at Bulby or Nabiac. Anything like outrageous behaviour was constrained by our mostly being related to each other, or at least well within the reach of each other's parents and of community opinion. Real human vileness is safer either in the home or practised on strangers – and anyway it was still easy, in those days before myxomatosis, to take our savagery out on rabbits. Many of us shot them by the hundreds, or trapped them for pocket money in an ecological war which the humans were steadily losing. Earlier, walking the four miles around Deer's high hill to Bulby school, I and George Maurer and my cousin Ray Murray had sometimes caught bunnies by hand, running out wide and then closing in on them from three sides, confusing their poor brains.

Human cruelty only began to come my way as a dreamy fat hillbilly kid at my next and final school, Taree High. That was the first place I learned the nicknames that are used to punish obesity, and the peculiar cultural rituals of townspeople *vis-à-vis* countryfolk. In my own culture, I had never been persecuted for being fat, or for anything else. Now, almost every sentence addressed to me referred to my figure, and many were uttered only for the derisive nicknames they contained. This went on for two straight years, and I learned to regard as a friend any boy who derided me only in public, to protect himself, and was sensible in private. One miraculous friend, called Colin McCabe, never derided me at all, and even mostly called me by my first name. No girl was ever a friend in any sense; it was made clear, with ornamentations of contempt and frost even by those who didn't go in for loud jeering, that this was unthinkable in my case. It was a firm training in self-sufficiency, and immunized me against any herd-animal leanings I might have developed. The sexes were much farther apart in spirit then, in a way that only misogynists and hardline feminists try to revive nowadays. To be fair, my schoolmates may have found me insufferable in ways they could not express directly. I was an impoverished, deeply naïve rural child who lacked all polish, disdained the First Fifteen, talked of sex in medical terminology and tried, by hypothesis, to grasp the Rules by which reality worked. This is always most irritating to those who already know the rules. Looking back, I suppose prolonged mob harrassment arises from a counter-evolutionary instinct we share with other animals, a drive to castrate the aberrant individual so that the species isn't changed and its average members made obsolete.

While at Taree High, I boarded first among butter-factory workers who were apt to hold a boy down and 'grease his bearings' with black shoe polish, and then shared a room with a railways' telegraphist who sometimes brought girls home off the late-night trains and romanced them gaspingly in his bed while I tried to stay asleep. That, my final year at school, was the year of 'Blackboard Jungle' and 'Rock Around the Clock', but I never became a teenager, out of scorn for what would have been denied me anyway. Much more importantly, it was the year in which two English teachers and the sports master introduced me to modern poetry. That fitted in with everything I'd always been, and sealed my fate.

The *Age*, 20 August 1988

Poems and Poesies

In an article published posthumously in the Canadian magazine *Writing* in 1985, Basil Bunting takes strong exception to the opinion of Pound and Eliot that poetry is a useful art, purifying the dialect of the tribe and keeping words sharp-edged and precise. He argues that they were in thrall to the utilitarianism of Jeremy Bentham and Benjamin Franklin, unable to escape from that tradition into the real world. He writes:

> Utilitarianism is the extreme case of humanism, for what they mean by 'useful' is 'what ministers to the material needs of man' – that's Franklin – 'of mankind in general' – that's Bentham. If religion is what we are taught from our youth up, what is meant to influence all our behaviour and most of our thoughts, utilitarianism is the religion of the West in this century as it was through most of last century: a religion that has put an abstraction called Man in the place that used to be occupied by a foggy idea called God. The fellow who makes two blades of grass grow where one grew before is the greatest benefactor (therefore it was right for the Italians to conquer Libya, and it is right for Jewish farmers and manufacturers to drive out nomad Arabs, and it was right for the settlers on this continent to starve or shoot the Indians). It is wrong to loaf and gawp about instead of working steadily at something useful, and of course it is wrong and foolish to write poetry unless it can be seen to purify the dialect of the tribe or keep the plebs in order or perform some other useful function.

Bunting goes on to argue that in fact poetry contributes nothing much to the process of thought, being mostly silly or thoroughly conventional in its philosophical content, or else borrowing any worthwhile system of ideas it may contain from some prose writer – Dante from St Thomas, Lucretius from Epicurus and Democritus. Many poems we consider masterpieces contain little or no thought at all. But none of this detracts from the pleasure we get from poetry,

341

even if it is poetry woven around ideas we thoroughly disagree with. An atheist or a Calvinist can read Dante with as much pleasure as a Catholic. Bunting locates the effect of poetry in its *sound*, its musical effect upon the emotions, and posits the dance as the remote ancestor of all the arts. At bottom, he holds that art, ultimately based on sound and movement, is something we instinctively produce, a part of the definition of being human. It is inherent, like birdsong. 'Birds sing,' he writes, 'even when they are not courting, or warning each other. They sing because birds *do* sing – it is a pleasure to use their throats (as any child knows, singing to itself). Men dance because it is in their nature...' He adds that another age, with a different diction, might have said that we dance and sing, write poetry and play music, to the glory of God. And every time we allow some other purpose to intrude into the work, we are robbing God of His glory. 'A drunken soldier singing "Bolicky Bill" is serving God, while a minister preaching temperance and thrift is serving only man.' As a Quaker, Bunting subscribes to this view, and adds that he is horrified by Benjamin Franklin. I very largely subscribe to it myself, but I don't think, any more than Basil Bunting would have, that it is all one can say on the matter. I think, without wishing to save the grimmer reaches of utilitarianism, that there are senses in which poetry can be seen as useful. Or rather, speaking descriptively rather than teleologically, in which it is essential.

As I see it, poetry exists to provide the poetic experience. Depending on whether you accept or reject the idea of purpose in things, that is either what it is for, or what it does. Everyone knows, and certainly anyone likely to be reading this essay should know, what the poetic experience feels like. It is a datum, a given thing, as distinctive as the experience of sex or eating. Being as fuzzy at its edges as those two, or indeed as any other primary experience, it is easier to point to than to define or delimit, but at any intensity it is quite unmistakable. Anyone reading a Shakespeare play who has come on a passage that made their breathing tighten and alter in a way resembling fear, and felt their mind gripped by a crowding excitement in which vivid activity and arresting awe seemed to struggle with each other, has experienced poetry. It is temporary possession, the Apollo of the ancients; 'it is what makes my toenails twinkle' as Dylan Thomas said, and similar descriptions abound. It is the verbal version of the aesthetic experience, the thing which brings us up short in the face of a great painting, or enraptures us in music. In its verbal form, it is what people read for, as much as for information, though they may be shy about saying so, in an age which distrusts 'mystical' talk and prefers to dissemble its spiritual needs. It is what people mean when they ask how much poetry a text has got in it, and it is not, of course, found exclusively in verse. In another way, it is that in a book or a piece of verse that can't be summarized, or put into other words; we feel a constraint about doing so, a feeling that we would violate something. Where the experience is intense, we find it extremely attractive, fascinating, and yet quickly exhausting; we want it, and more of it, but we have to take frequent rests from it: if we stay focused on it, resisting this urge to take rests, it will itself seem to come and go. It is an experience we can have repeatedly, but find it hard to take in steadily, to sustain. The realms of gold, it would seem, oscillate – or our mind does, when we behold them.

In another way, though, and this is perhaps even more striking in cases where the intensity is not so high, poetry has an odd quality of inexhaustibility. We can experience, it, go away from it, analyse it, try to order it tidily among the other phenomena of our life – but as soon as we come back to it and quiet down in its presence, as even a low-intensity piece of real poetry will make us do, we find it to be as mysterious and pregnant with elusive significance as ever. We can't get to the end of it, somehow, though we may affect to. We are used to things which alter and change their significance for us, but here is something that seems to live with real but utterly unchanging life, and anomaly in time, a hiatus through which new meanings unceasingly flow without any alteration to its surface. Each interpretation or understanding we put around it, each container, will wear through and go out of date, but the standing event poetry will remain. We don't exhaust the aesthetic experience; it exhausts us, or at least our manoeuvres and calculations. And when it is very intense, it can almost knock us out. I remember my reaction to the breathtaking upstairs gallery of the Van Gogh Museum in Amsterdam; after a first look around, I sat down on one of the benches in the middle of the gallery and went to sleep for a while. Only then could I examine the paintings in their individual detail. I hadn't been tired when I went to the museum. I was simply overwhelmed.

The oscillation characteristic of aesthetic experience gives us an important clue to its nature. Humans have two main modes of consciousness, one for waking life, one we call dreaming. The one is said by psychologists to relate to the recently evolved forebrain, the other to the older so-called limbic levels of the brain, sometimes called the reptilian brain. Sleep studies suggest strongly that we need to experience both, and that with very rare exceptions we become distressed and finally psychotic if we are prevented from dreaming. A remarkable poem by the Western Australian Philip Salom which I was happy to include in the *New Oxford Book of Australian Verse* describes waking consciousness and the dream as our two lives, each of which balances the other. Writing of the dream, he says:

> It is wiser than us
> but has no manners
> it's as modern
> as modern poetry
> and always has been
> it's as ancient
> as cave paintings
> and always will be.
>
> – 'The World of Dreams'

He also points out that thought is linear, while dream is holistic. Dreaming of course is not confined to the world of sleep. We speak of day-dreaming, and we are conscious of an undercurrent of dream mentation running below our waking consciousness all the time. I once tried to describe this in a poem, one of four sonnets titled 'The Dialectic of Dreams':

> And that otherworld incongruence
> spindling faintly through the day,
> heightening thought, blanking it,
> silvering, beckoning away

This is reverie, which in my experience informs and influences all of our mental life. In those same dialectical sonnets, I first stumbled on something which, while an ordinary enough discovery, may have something important to say about the aesthetic process:

> The daylight oil, the heavier grade of reason,
> reverie's clear water, that of the dreamworld ocean
> both agitate us and are shaken, forming the emulsion
> without which we make nothing much. Not art,
> not love, not war, nor its reasoned nightmare methods,
> not the Taj, not our homes, not the Masses or the gods

As people knew in ancient times, and as we have known since Freud and the other early psychoanalysts, neither of our two lives is wholly subordinate to the other – or if it is, we're likely to be in trouble. For ordinary mental health, let alone any sort of fullness of life, we need a measure of harmony between them. The aesthetic experience, I suggest, presents us with this harmony in a heightened, sometimes supremely heightened way. It is a fusion of the two, and delivers us into wholeness of thinking and of life. Or at least it models that wholeness vividly for us.

If this is so, it immediately points to a difficulty in writing criticism. The daylight mode of linear expository prose in which most criticism is necessarily written is simply not as *complete* as what it is on about. It is typically what we might call *forebrain* writing, in which the contribution of the older levels of mind is absent or played down.

The pleasure of the poetic experience, as distinct from other species of the aesthetic event, probably lies first of all in its high fusion of the waking attribute of language with the almost pre-verbal mode of the dream. It is impossible to prove that the deep dreaming of sleep contains any language at all; we may gather the supposed words of dreamlife from deeper levels of awakening consciousness on our way out of the dream state, picking them up like strands of near-surface kelp as we rise from the deeps. There does, admittedly, seem to be a modality of language involved in reverie and the continuing sub-consciousness of waking life. There is certainly language in the other dream states of vision and delirium, though perhaps it isn't truly theirs. More typically, though, there is an atmosphere we recognize as belonging to dreamlife, one which we find fascinating or scary according to our nature and, probably, our psychic stability. Where a work of art lacks at least some trace of this atmosphere, it strikes us as dead, as lifeless, as merely explanatory or prosy. On the other hand, too much of the dream atmosphere without corresponding rational strengths is apt to strike us as suspect, and explains the resistance of a great many people to all but very good examples of surrealism. It is as if the others were merely privileged indulgence of an effect, one we can learn to fake, and something which falls short of the full fusion which art demands. I remember many of us young Psych I students in the 1950s doing what a couple of generations of students had already done before us, avidly reading Freud's theories and cases and getting from them a creepy sort of excitement which stood to real aesthetic experience as moonshine stands to cognac. We were indulging in what may be called *hindbrain* experience, though only at second hand. Kids seek the same sort of thrills from horror stories and the dizzy-fizzy surrealism of rock clips. Artistic satisfaction seems to require not the representation of the dream atmosphere in words or some other daylight medium, but its marriage with some degree of logic, measure and design, things which we think of as forebrain matters, though they may not be so exclusively. We seem to be able to sense when the dream component is merely an effect, and to be able to judge, even in the teeth of criticism, when a work is truly dreamed as well as truly thought. In much of art, of course, the consonance of dream with surface structure and thinking may involve not much more than a faint perfume, a slight aura that alerts our subconscious and may not be immediately apparent to our conscious mind. It does not take a heavily obvious lathering on of dream effects. It is only essential that what I term the *vatic divide* between dream-life and waking consciousness be bridged and that the two be felt as present together.

The dimension of dream in art ought, one might think, to be especially interesting to Australians, given its crucial importance in Aboriginal culture and the growing awareness of all of us of terms such as the Dreamtime, dreamings, sacred sites and the like. As I understand it, the categories of the Dreamtime and the sacred are coterminous for Aborigines. A sacred site is one in which the Dreamtime inheres. 'It is Dreamtime there,' in the words of the late tribal elder Sam Woolagoodjah, when instructing his children and grandchildren about his own Wandjina site in the film *Lalai*. The Dreamtime is also a tense, or rather it is all tenses apart from the immediate present and near past; it encompasses all things far away in the future, the past or in conjecture; it is the mythological tense over against the factual, and the place where they meet is the place of ceremony, of art and of law. In Western culture, I suggest, the same is true, though the matter is rarely so clearly expressed. A work of art is a fixed or movable sacred site, what the late Mr Woolagoodjah would describe as a *Wunger*, that is, something which gives health. Hence the great anxiety of some of our criticism to encompass and control art, even to the point of putting it on an implied lower plane, as a primitive irruption needing rational interpretation and other leaden shieldings. Rather as if otherwise land claims might be based on it.

In Western culture, though, we do not usually try to live by existing works of art. These may in part discern and express the law of things, but we don't take that law as binding in any simple or obvious way. We move on past it, or fall back from it. I wrote in the next few lines of the dialectical dream sonnets:

> – but the fusion persists in the product, not in us.
> A wheel shatters, drains our pooled rainbow. It was a
>   moment:

> the world is debris and museum of that moment,
> its prospectus and farm. The wheel is turned by this engine.

In poetry, if not in every art, the fusion of dream and reason is not by any means the only fusion involved. Just as important, in all the language arts but most obviously in verse poetry, is the harnessing of breath and bodily movement. Poetry, in the form of verse or in the rhythms of properly tuned literary prose, alters our breathing and submits it to the laws of the dance. Where this does not happen, where there is an absence of what Alan Gould calls 'some rhythmic principle' or other, poetry tends not to be fully achieved. The full poetic experience is short circuited and replaced at best by what may be its humanistic substitute, interest. And that is the animating principle of what I call a *poesy*, rather than a poem, but we will come back to these terms a little later on. Another element essential to the fusion out of which the poetic experience flows is emotion or feeling, which may be strongly evident or only subtly present, but must be convincing, true to instinct and intuition, capable of stirring involuntary sympathy in the beholder. The easiest way to 'do' that sort of effect is with sincerity, or else so unstudiedly that it disposes itself through the language more or less by itself. Any degree of faking, or lying to oneself or other species of shonk will tend to have dreadful results in the ensemble of the work, at its finest tolerances. It offends against the integrity of the work and frustrates its consummation; the reader senses that something is dragging and jamming inside. Something's wrong. I have always had this feeling, for example, about the last line of Kenneth Slessor's otherwise beautiful last poem, 'Beach Burial', which speaks of the dead sailors of the North African campaign as 'enlisted on the other front'. It smacks of writing something one doesn't quite believe in order to finish a poem. The emotion suddenly becomes compromised, uncertain and weak, and the line doesn't convince. The poetic experience thus vanishes before the poem ends, and we are dropped out of the poem uncomfortably, rather than being escorted to the door still full of the atmosphere and events we have shared inside.

The usefulness of poetry, then, or the way in which it is of the essence, lies in what it models and maybe consummates in the wider range of our life. I suggest that it models the way we really think. Certainly it does that better than forensic logic, which only models how we talk when we want to win arguments and avoid mistakes. It also models something much wider than the simple conveying of information. What it does model is the whole simultaneous gamut of reasoning, envisioning, feeling and vibrating we go through when we are really taken up with some matter, and out of which we may act on it. We are not just thinking about whatever it may be, but savouring it and experiencing it and wrestling with it in the ghostly sympathy of our muscles. We are alive at full stretch towards it. Poetry models the fullness of life, and also gives its objects presence. Like prayer, it pulls all the motions of our life and being into a concentrated true attentiveness to which God might speak. 'Here am I, Lord,' as Samuel says in his book of the Bible. It is the plane or mirror of intuitions. Poetry may lead on to action, but it is equally likely not to, because in a way it *is* the action. It enacts its matter, often more fully and satisfyingly than it could ever be enacted in the world, though active people may resist that fact strongly. In relation to this question of action, though, the Chicago sleep studies have revealed something suggestive about one of art's great components, the dream. It seems that when we dream in sleep, our muscles are immobilized, though we also have an erection or its female equivalent. We are thus potent but immobile when we're dreaming. The same doesn't go, of course, for the waking process of art, when we are writing or painting or composing or experiencing what others have created. But it is a suggestive image to have in the backs of our minds as we think about art.

It follows from what I've been saying, I think, that a great deal of what we may call high-order thinking occurs in ways so analogous with art that we are justified in referring to religions, say, or large-scale theoretical systems as poems, or quasi-poems. They will usually evince the same sorts of intuition, broad grasp, excitement and rational dreaming as poems do, though only rarely will they achieve comparable passages of concentration and presence. Unless they incorporate actual poems of their own, of course, as many of them do. The scriptures of the great religions usually contain many of these, both as set pieces and in passages of text, and perhaps they would never have become great religions if they did not. Overarching these, though, is the larger 'poem' of the religion or theoretical system itself. Marx's great poem of compassionate action on behalf of the exploited. Freud's poem of sexuality, death and the roots of action, with its rescension of ancient myths. The great evolving Jewish poem of God. The large post-war poem of the Third World, which has authors ranging from Mohandas Gandhi and Dr Evatt to Gamal Abdel Nasser and Jomo Kenyatta. The balance of dream, reason, emotion, instinct, dance and presence in a religion, of course, is apt to be closest to that in a poem, and I recently attempted to deal with the relations between them in a short poem of my own which I will quote in full. Its title is simply 'Poetry and Religion':

> Religions are poems. They concert
> our daylight and dreaming mind, our
> emotions, instinct, breath and native gesture
>
> into the only whole thinking: poetry.
> Nothing's said till it's dreamed out in words
> and nothing's true that figures in words only.
>
> A poem, compared with an arrayed religion,
> may be like a soldier's one short marriage night
> to die and live by. But that is a small religion.
>
> Full religion is the large poem in loving repetition;
> like any poem, it must be inexhaustible and complete
> with turns where we ask Now why did the poet do that?
>
> You can't pray a lie, said Huckleberry Finn;
> you can't poe one either. It is the same mirror:
> mobile, glancing, we call it poetry,
>
> fixed centrally, we call it religion,
> and God is the poetry caught in any religion,
> caught, not imprisoned. Caught as in a mirror
>
> that he attracted, being in the world as poetry
> is in the poem, a law against its closure.
> There'll always be religion around while there is poetry
>
> or a lack of it. Both are given, and intermittent,
> as the action of those birds – crested pigeon, rosella parrot –
> who fly with wings shut, then beating, and again shut.

Different religions and systems will, naturally, vary in the degree of their likeness to poetry, by varying in the completeness with which they mirror that complex balance I've been describing. Myths, real ones from the ancient world or the genuinely mythic ones of surviving peoples who haven't as yet been totally modernized, will tip the balance in the direction of dream and perhaps the dance, while strongly intellectualizing secular systems will lean towards abstraction and tend to short change the dimension of presence.

Where they fall away from the riveting wholespeak of poetry they will descend into the narrowspeak of forensic argument, prose exegesis and exhortation. This is fairly graceless terminology I admit, but it may have some utility. We may perhaps crystallize the distinction in this way: Narrowspeak is readily translated between languages belonging to a common large culture, while wholespeak is difficult or impossible to translate. It requires re-creation in the other language. Narrowspeak, pretty obviously, refers to language in which the whole person is no longer (or not yet) truly engaged, and which therefore can't fully move us, though it may hurry us about. It comprises most of the language by which the world is administered from day to day, but not that by which it is ultimately ruled, if I am right about the centrality of poetry, the sphere of the famous unacknowledged legislators. Narrowspeak is not quite the same thing as ordinary speech, in that it tends to contain fewer fragments and beginnings of poetry.

It is clear that some systems will start out without much poetry in them and only acquire it, and with it their persuasive force for non-specialists, fairly gradually. Renaissance astronomy, for instance, which is still developing in our own day, has gained a good deal of imaginative force and resonance as it has gone along, but it still isn't a full poem. It is still hard to feel, with full emotional consent, that the sun doesn't rise in the east and set in the west. Carl Sagan and others are trying to create an emotionally moving mythos of the vast stellar universe, but the job is taking time, largely because its presentations usually have a highly forebrain quality, despite frequent efforts at generating awe. It is probably truer to say that Science itself, with a capital S, is a poem-mythos of real power for some people, with an atmosphere of its own to which they deeply respond.

Again, and equally clearly, the near-identity of theories and systems with poetry isn't confined to the vast constructs of the mind and heart. It is equally true of, say, the tradition and vision of service of a local ambulance unit, or the mystique of a sport, or the work and the legend of a saint. Love between persons is often experienced by them as the unique poem of Us. I remember one friend of mine telling another: 'You'll never be a skindiver till you've got the vision of the sea.' He could equally have called it the poem of the sea and of skindiving. In the past, many chieftains have grasped the importance of this principle and had bards to make poetry of their exploits and themselves, poems in which some hard man, half farmer and half military goon, has been transmuted into something noble, strange, ever-living and inspirational. We need only look at figures such as Ajax or Achilles or Skanderbeg. Sometimes there isn't just one bard, either; the poem or myth arises around the person partly by their own efforts, partly not, and comes to contain actual poems of its own. Napoleon is a good example, with the poems of Victor Hugo and others trailing in his lurid wake. The figure of Bonnie Prince Charlie was partly created by the poet Alasdair MacMhaighstir Alasdair, partly by a milieu of social pain and bardic prophecy and partly by his own actions, and has pretty well outlasted even the later tragic poems it gave rise to, such as 'Soraidh leis an-tSuithneas Ban' ('Farewell to the White Cockade'), though I suppose 'Loch Lomond' and the 'Skye Boat Song' are still vigorous. National histories often contain many such powerful poems and of course the nation will usually function as a poem of its own, the more dangerous the more solemn.

In this view I have been presenting, the whole world resembles what Australia was to its first people: a great field of poem-stories. The world we have inherited, though, is not the orderly network of localized poems that was ancient Australia, but a vast texture of overlaid and overlapping poetries, often competing with each other inside individual human heads. It is possible that we never see the world as it is, through this clamant texture. Or that if we do see odd details, we immediately begin ordering them into poetic structure, our own or an existing ready-made one. Loyalty, that extremely labile and vigorous human emotion, quickly wraps itself around almost any instance of vision or purported inspiration and defends it sturdily. This accounts for much of the density and resilience of the world. Proponents of change are, somewhat naively, surprised ever and anon by the resistance of other people's visions to their own, as poem contends with poem. And everyone, just about, makes the mistake of assailing the other person's poem in the narrowspeak of criticism, as if that were likely to avail against the wholespeak the other may not be able to utter, but which he or she hears deep within. Only a poem can combat a poem. Written poetry, the model and analogue of all this activity, is proportionally only a small adjunct to it, and its creators are surprised, though they perhaps should not be, to find themselves pushed aside by the multifarious energy of the process their art crystallizes. We need not be tempted to megalomania. All things do not aspire to the condition of poetry. Indeed, they typically aspire away from it, moving energetically towards action and power.

Many of the powerful poem-cores of activity in the world are, to outward appearance, only partly verbalized and fitted with a few symbols which may look incongruous in the extreme to people outside their particular aura. Many of the poem-visions that occupy human heads and hearts are treasures of a figure I've always had a soft spot for, and whom I call by a name borrowed from the language of the 1960s and 1970s: the groover. This is the person whose poem remains•forever unwritten, or written only in his or her life, not in words. A groove is a body of objects or images which take up the loving energy and fascination of a human soul. It may be Second World War aircraft, or Egyptian antiquities of the Old Kingdom, or 1950s costume, or systems of formal logic. Grooves may not always be unequivocal or harmless. Grooving on the naked female form may be productive of art photography or of less wholesome results, and the populous groove of Nazi relics, or that of torture devices down the centuries, may be worth keeping an eye on. To the groover in his or her groove, though, the beloved subject matter is the poem of their life, ceaselessly summoning up profound intimations and the quivering pleasure of ever-unfolding significance. There is no morality in the groove. A great many scholars, including many of the best, live there lifelong; so too do vast numbers of other people, for many of whom life would be unlivable without the groove to which they return as soon as they come home from the grey narrowspeak of employment. The groove is one of the great heat-sinks of human energy, and the world might catch alight without it. Totalitarians often begin their rule by trying to pry everyone out of it – this is the stage of compulsory sharing of their own poem – and then realize their mistake and encourage them to go back. Other rulers know to leave them undisturbed in the first place. Some practising poets, perhaps many, are themselves groovers, on poetry in general or at least on their own, and an unknown proportion of our readers are too. I would not be surprised if the proportion were quite high. The groove is one of the great shelters of the individual soul, precisely because individual cases are so often dismissed as eccentric and trivial. It is even largely proof against fashion, which may have something to say about which grooves to enter, but becomes largely inaudible once you are in one.

Both the poem held in common and its solipsist equivalent the groove differ crucially from a principle, essentially aristocratic in its origins and dating back only to the eighteenth century in its Western form, which we usually term *interest*. This is not at all directly the interest earned from financial investments, but an activity of the mind. In a way, it is a cool form of love, one which may show even exaggerated signs of emotional involvement, but which proves to have these firmly under control when closely examined. It is normally accompanied by 'cool' aristocratic (even Lumpen-aristocratic) demeanours and pays close attention to style and gesture, with extreme reluctance ever to be caught at a disadvantage. It is in fact narrowspeak risen socially, full of judgment and scorn, terrified of death. Where poetry and grooving are devoted to their object, interest is devoted to itself, and can switch away from any given object the moment it threatens to become passé. Where poetry and grooving are obedient to the behests of their object, and serve it in season and out, interest feels trapped and flees abruptly when too much is asked of it. It subordinates, and will not be subordinated. It seeks ravishment, but will resist fiercely even as it affects to surrender, and so knows nothing of attentive, truly receptive silence. The bearer of interest is typically a consumer, not celebrating objects and honouring their life, but absorbing them and discarding them, often only partly digested. Where poetry seeks fusion, interest avoids it and substitutes excitement for the poetic experience. The linkage with dream is often absent, and where it is present we feel the underlying dream is not in harmony with the surface utterance. When interest turns away from something, it believes that thing has utterly vanished and no longer counts. As I have remarked elsewhere, it can be as great a disaster for a people or a culture to be taken up as interesting as it is for them to be dismissed as unimportant. In the days of the empires, Westerners frequently conquered native peoples as it were in silence and behind their own backs, dismissing them as savages and nobodies. They would then often turn right round and encourage the conquered to go on being colourfully and interestingly primitive, enacting alien and sometimes orgiastic fantasies the conquerors were not prepared to act out for themselves. Be interesting, it says by implication; be a poetry for us. Work in the factory, but do beat your little tomtoms after work; don't modernize and become proles like *our* working folk. A cloudy form of love, of impatient concern, is visible even in this, of course. And it is fair to point out that interest may sometimes be a fastidiousness displayed onn the way to poetry, one which says Is this it? Is this? No, this is not yet the Beloved, the end of my quest. Poetry and interest may sometimes encounter each other working along the same groove, the one crying This is it! I have seen the vision of numismatics. Coins are the blessed thing! While interest asks excitedly Is that really true? Is it coins? Let me look!

I don't wish to pour scorn on interest, by any means. Nearly all of us are now more or less prone to it. It can be discriminating and

courageous in refusing to settle for the perhaps hectic, perhaps silly
safe haven of a poetic vision. It protects itself from premature commitment, and may help to protect us all from power-seeking myths.
And it is nothing if not entertaining. It can, however, be a destructive
hunger in itself, inciting people to be unsettled, to demand stimulation and confuse that with meaning. It empties the country and
chokes the city – until the backwash of urban people comes searching
the countryside for whatever of interest it may hold. It is as capable
as poetry of dismissing things or people as trivial or irrelevant, but
far less constant in its defence of them when it does take them up.
Poetry makes them present and ever-living, hard ever to dismiss
again, while interest merely makes them – I almost said briefly pregnant, and doomed to be relegated again. It is interesting, not quite
parenthetically, to observe that it is quite easy to find an antonym
for interest. It is boredom, a word scarcely used in the vernacular
languages of the West before the eighteenth century, and not exces-
sively common in its Latin forms *taedium* (a word which also signifies
loathing and disgust) or *acedia*, a medieval usage derived from the
Greek word for sloth. For art and poetry, though, it is very hard to
find an opposite. It is not ugliness, for art often has a vital relationship
with the ugly, transmuting it and revealing its unexpected glories.
It is not chaos, since that is often the very province of art's freedom
and renewal. It is not botched work, because one person's botch is
often another's art, full of authentic oscillation. And so on. It is
perhaps a conundrum worth pondering, this question of art's opposite. I don't think it is quite interest, though the thought does cross
the mind.

If interest, then, resembles poetry cut off at the neck, out of touch
with heart and body alike, that does not mean that it fails to generate
a voluminous literature of its own. This ranges all the way from
smart journalism to a high, often preponderant share of the verse
printed in literary magazines and slim volumes worldwide. An insistent voice intrinsic in Western culture since the days of early modernism says to every intending writer: 'Remember: be Interesting.
Find a ploy, any ploy, but be striking, within the permitted range
of strikingness. And never forget the received sensibility they allow
us as respectably Literary. Play games with that if you want, for
that is one road to being interesting, but don't ever fundamentally
disobey it. It will not be flouted.' At one pitch of the aesthetic of
interest lies experiment for fame's sake, at another lies the defeated
gambit of wishing at least to be of documentary or historical interest.
Even real poems will very often include a few obeisances to interest,

as distinct from the natural ways in which genuine poetry is genuinely interesting without trying to be. Indeed, a poet may write a true poem in which interest-signals abound – but then they are transmuted by their medium and become part of the pleasure the poetry gives.

The crucial difference probably doesn't lie in intention. It is a matter of presence. In the wholeness of poetry, interest can take a valuable place, and experimentation is just as valid a way into the wholeness of poetry as any other. It is possible that we need a term, by now, to distinguish between texts that are poetry and those which aree animated by the aesthetic of interest. I would favour calling the latter *poesies*. It may be possible, I suggest, to put the distinction between poems and poesies in terms of surprise, roughly as follows. There are themes and subjects which seem intrinsically to belong to the wholespeak of poetry, and which can't really be talked about usefully in narrowspeak terms. God and the great matters of religion are an example. The real depths and extents of our world, both outer and inner, are another and problematically related one. These are the inexhaustible realm, which language at its highest can only evoke, not encompass, and which can't be encompassed by the meta-languages of paint or image or music either, nor by the enormous composite 'word' which a ceremony comprises and utters. Coming back to speakable language, however, it is clear that the vocabulary of literature is available to poems and poesies alike – if not, without great strain, fully available to narrowspeak – so that both may deal with these subjects. However, only genuine poetry will tend to say truly memorable or truly surprising or truly illuminating things about them. Poesy may well say striking things, and will frequently strain to say things meant to surprise, even batter the mind into acceptance. But the effect will wear off. It will not, like Randolph Stow's horse, hear the landscape it has come through as a grievous music, or see gestures as stars in sacred dishevelment, as in Francis Webb's 'Wild Honey'. And when any of its statements about sacred things is examined closely, it will turn out to be in open or secret conformity with the reigning literary-intellectual sensibility. It will not be telling us anything not somehow approved. And this will remain equally true whatever the ensemble or approved views might be. Interest is a human mode which has no soul of its own. And thus perhaps no soul at all. It doesn't think there is one, nowadays, and so only appeals to the mind. That is, to the forebrain.

Age Monthly Review, December 1986. Reprinted and expanded in *PN Review*, 1987.

Poemes and the Mystery of Embodiment

Humans are not rational, but poetic. For this reason, the world we have inherited is a vast texture of overlaid and overlapping poetries, often competing inside individual human heads. It is possible that through this claimant texture we never see the world as it is. Or that if we do see odd details, we immediately begin ordering them into a poetic structure, our own or a ready-made one. Loyalty quickly wraps itself around almost any instance of vision or purported inspiration and defends it sturdily. This accounts for much of the density and resilience of the world. Proponents of change are somewhat naively surprised by the resistance of other people's visions to their own, as poem contends with poem. And just about everyone makes the mistake of assailing the other person's poem in the narrow-speak of criticism, as if that were likely to avail against the whole-speak the other may not be able to utter, but which he or she hears deep within. Only a poem can combat a poem.

I have spoken of the larger and lesser vision-constructs that move humankind as poems, not because I confuse them with the texts we experience as poetry, but because the resemblance is so close as to go beyond a metaphor to a degree of identity for which the term 'model' is appropriate. This, however, is as close as the relationship does get, for the most part, so ultimately we need to guard against its becoming complete. There is still a gap of difference, seen crucially in the matter of exhortation. A poem-construct will often demand that the world conform to it, a true poem never needs to. It presents the conformity that already exists, or which at least exists within the world it creates. It thus never needs to police anything. Those truly devoted to the mythos of a vision-construct are themselves somewhat *like* poetry, in being unfazed by obsolescence. They serve a timeless event in their souls – one that may well be replaced by another timeless event later on – while actual poems live on in their real timelessness, which they had from the start and will keep as long as their text survives.

The matter may be put simply by comparing, say, the concept of the *Pax Romana* with Catullus's elegy for his drowned brother. The idea of the *Pax Romana* is a recurring political motif, and has come around several times in history – as the Holy Roman Empire, the Pax Americana, the Pax Sovietica – while Catullus's poem has simply continued to exist, utterly unchanging in its original words and shape, its still dance needing no further actualization. A term may be needed to establish the difference: I would suggest *poeme*, not taken from the French but constructed on an analogy with terms such as phoneme or tagmeme. Thus the *Pax Romana* is a poeme, or perhaps more accurately a theme or stanza of the larger poeme of *Romanitas*, while Catullus's elegy is a poem in the proper sense, fully realized once and for all. No further embodiment of its ensemble of thoughts, emotions and somatic effects is necessary. This is a consistent difference, and we will come back to it a little later, after we have deepened its implications by examining the role of the body in aesthetic experience.

I have already described the somatic effects of reading or hearing a real poem, receiving the impact of any other sort of real art. They may be subtle or quite marked, and may in fact last longer and have a more profound effect if they are subtle: the fierce discharge of a work which transports us may leave less behind, and in fact do less to us, than a work which, as it were, implants itself in our long-term memory and acts upon us ever afterwards from there.

The ensemble of effects in a poem calls into play our autonomic nervous system, the one we don't consciously control, by bringing about a state of alert in us. This is the state balanced between the urge to fight or flee and the urge to surrender, and in it we mime movements and gestures presented to us by whatever has caused the alert. It is a mirror state, or an echoic state, in which we half-consciously imitate the dance that is danced before us, and we probably flicker in and out of this state very rapidly, alternating it with other states such as intellectual receptivity.

A work of art separated from its creator is a suspended alert, only needing the body of a reader or spectator to play itself over and over again. Poetry subtly takes command of our breathing and dances with it; a sob built into a line will reverberate in the diaphragm and cause it to signal the brain for tears, and laughter can similarly be produced without any joke needing to appear in the text. The more purely mental operations can be lulled or provoked by what is done to our breathing; it is the great chord on which we must play if our other effects are to come alive. If it is badly played upon, the rest of the poem will jar to pieces, or never come alive in the first place.

My wife once made what I think was an essential critical point when she said of one very famous novelist that his breath-pauses, expressed through a very idiosyncratic and unsubtle syntax, gave her a sensation like bronchitis; she found his writing unreadable as a result, simultaneously thought and dreamed though it may have been.

The mimetic mysteries that take place inside an alert are not confined to the breath. Very exact reproduction of any sense impression in any medium calls up that sensation afresh in a kind of ghost reality that echoes through body and mind, perhaps bypassing the conscious mind altogether. It is possible to take a person on an artistic journey that exhilarates and even exhausts them without once letting the conscious mind know what is going on. That can be a deeply welcome holiday for them; we can, by mime or using the deep structure of language, go for a romp in the Old Kingdom, among the eloquent wordless animals, faster than you can start to wonder whether you should intellectually approve what you are feeling. Opportunities for counterpoint and dissonance abound once we begin to play on both sides of this divide.

One final example of the phenomena of an alert approaches the repertoire of sport, and particularly that of spectator sports; we may call it the vicarious mode. Watching a supremely clever performance of any feat we intuit or know to be difficult, we are drawn at once into an intense sympathy that is barely intellectual at all, but is almost literally ecstatic. We not only put ourselves in the performer's place, in imagination, but at the same time we stand back from the performance and drink it in thirstily. The oscillation between these two contradictory states brings us to a tension that can approach nausea. We are juggling the plates and the daggers, but at the same time the juggler is juggling them for us: if he dropped a plate or cut himself with one of the knives, it would be our failure, though we would punish him with our scorn. Our life would have crashed to pieces because he fumbled it, and his life would suffer wreck because we couldn't keep all those things aloft and dancing. All of this is experienced instantaneously and profoundly, before conscious thought can snap back into play and integrate its indelible import, protecting us from what we have seen and done. While it is in abeyance, even the teetering in a performance is deeply exciting and probably essential, drawing us into closer identification with it because it echoes what we know of ourselves.

The Enlightenment spirit has tended to play down this aspect of art, trying to dismiss it as *déclassé*, but the effect of this tactic has been merely to divide art and impoverish its 'High' realms, losing from literature (as from 'serious' music or the dance) a whole register of essential enactments and a vast number of potential readers, who still signal this deprivation, in part, when they complain that poetry seems to have abandoned rhyme and metre. The same people are apt to look elsewhere for the lost stimulations and transactions, among purveyors of ecstasy and frenzy whose performances are not balanced by responsible feeding of the mind or the kind of concern for truth and value inherent in worthwhile literature. To the extent that the Enlightenment and its various subordinate poemes are in revolt against the very poetry they arise from, and criticism is their weapon for conquering poetry, such febrile substitutes as drugs and frenzy are bound to flourish.

As the receivers of a work of art, we may be more privileged than its creator, in that we experience as a totality what he or she may have put together out of scattered moments of fusion interspersed with periods of frustration, or losing the thread, or jarring descent into banality. During some of these, other unconscious work may have been going on. During a period when daylight logic may have got snarled and refused to work, the other, non-verbal side of the forebrain – the right hemisphere in right-handed people – may have been functioning full out in its sphere of design, trying to get its contribution right. All that we might consciously experience might be a sense of busyness in the head, a sensation that interfered with the repose we perhaps sought and thought we were having. As surely as a work of art has to involve the hindbrain, the seat of dream mentation, it also has to satisfy the non-verbal hemisphere of the forebrain. If it doesn't, the shape of the work will be wrong and the necessary fusion will not be present.

Narrowspeak may be less aware of this aspect of unconscious thinking than it is of the better-advertised hindbrain unconscious, the realm on which Freud and others have laid their interesting but by definition futile grids of daylight classification in an attempt to conquer and colonize one more Dark Continent. Even where narrowspeak is aware of the other dimensions we have been speaking about, it persists, as good art does not, in behaving as if its formulations were somehow more final and more true than any other, because it has the words and a particular concept of time. If we accept the authority of verbalized reasoning at its own high valuation, the results can be desolating in ways that the whole, integral utterance does not echo. None of the provinces of our thinking is explicable in the terms of any of the others: dream can't give an account of conscious thought, any more than the latter can explain or delimit dream-life; nor does either speak for the body, or the non-verbal mind that knows it best. As I put the matter recently in a poem:

> It's only the left mind
> says before you die
> you and all you love
> will be obsolete –
> our right mind, that shaped
> this poem, paper, type-face,
> has powerful if wordless
> arguments against it.
>
> – 'From the Other Hemisphere'

Unfortunately I lack sufficient knowledge of medicine, or of the special lore of gesture and rhythm in arts not my own, to trace all the somatic concomitants of aesthetic experience. Maybe it is enough that I am sometimes able to set up structures in which they come into play, and must therefore know something of them in a 'craft' way, which is to say, in their own terms.

There are suggestive dimensions and ecstasies in the sphere of rhythm that I'd like to be able to elucidate: there is prayer there, and prophecy, and profound refreshment. Witness the effect of these quatrains by the fourteenth-century Turkish poet Yunus Emre, with the marvellous repeated kick-start verb at the beginning of each fourth line, like the foot of a whirling dervish maintaining the ecstatic spin that mimes the cosmos and evokes eternity:

> While some shall eat and others drink,
> The angels spread God's grace about,
> The raiment will be by Idris
> Sewn, the name of God repeating.

> Its trees are everywhere of light,
> And every one with silver leaves,
> And as they grow their tender buds
> Shout, the name of God repeating.

> Clearer than any moon each face,
> Their every word a perfumed thing,
> The blessed maids of Paradise
> Stroll, the name of God repeating.

> Whosoever loves God truly
> Never ceases from his weeping,

Within, without, illumined, he
Speaks, the name of God repeating.

What you seek, from God alone seek,
Give guidance to the one true way,
The nightingale that loves the rose
Sings, the name of God repeating.
           – translated by John R. Walsh

Studies in the pathology of perception tell us that for some human brains there is a trance-like pleasure bordering on epileptic seizure to be had from certain regular rhythms. The regular flickering of daylight between spaced palings of a fence may sedate motorists and cause them to lose concentration; people may become addicted to certain patterns of drumming in rock music, or uncritically watch any and every film simply because of the unconscious bliss produced by the flickering frames. The heart of this sort of thing is hypnosis, which is a powerful imprinting agent. Hitler more than once attributed the success of his rhetoric to the hypnotic effects he was able to orchestrate, exulting that what people heard while in an ecstatic, hypnotized state became part of them forever. Clearly, we are dealing here with the magical techniques of a poem, not those of a poem (Nazism brought forth singularly few poems, and I know of none that was first-rate), and with a major case where the general Enlightenment strategy of denying and denigrating magic of all sorts succeeded only in weakening the salutary magics that might have countered the rise of a thoroughly vicious poem-vision.

Nazism is perhaps instructive also in having laid stress on the body as a part and as source of its inspiration. It spoke not only of the purported imperatives of race and soil but, like quite a few poems arising around the earlier part of the twentieth century (including the better-lasting poem of Lawrentianism), also of the wisdom of the body and the blood. It admired robust health, and claimed to represent the imperatives of sturdy youthful vigour, seen as daring and rightly ruthless, not to be made decadent by too much intellectual sophistication. Poems with broadly similar preferences have been holding their skirts away from this set of values ever since.

Indeed, in aesthetics and elsewhere, a repugnance to Nazi values may have inhibited balanced examination of the wordless and somatic dimensions of the world-views that people actually hold. The non-verbal art forms such as music and painting and ballet retain and enrich their own special traditions of the bodily dimension, but within the sphere of the word the influence of the somatic has been discussed for the most part in terms of sex and sexualities; both are perhaps felt to be safe, being aspects of the matter that the Nazis did not stress and may even have persecuted. We might say that the body, having been implicated in ghastly crimes, was displaced into its own genitals, or allowed as mainly a walking advertisement for them. And representing sexual flaunt as an underdog in Western culture legitimized afresh all the old Nazi repugnances towards deformity, old age, weakness and general lack of dash. Another place into which Nazi beliefs about human nature have been displaced is the animal kingdom, with poems about territoriality and dominance among animals. A certain amount of the same atmosphere is occasionally detectable in the idealizing interspecies mysticism of some ecological writing, though, to be fair, a degree of secularized Franciscanism is often present too, in that yearning for some Edenic blood-comradeship of all life-forms.

All the mental operations we are capable of are conditioned by the body. Put into deeper jargon, that obvious truth might go: all mental operations are based on somatic substrates. That might not seem worth stating, except that nowadays, as in the ancient Hindu and Buddhist poemes, material things and even other dimensions of our mind are seen as properties or appearances, and however we may honour particular selections of them at different times, we envisage felicity and even health in terms not of harmony with exterior and interior entities, but in terms of presiding over them through the power of articulate reason. We, and it is very much an abstract 'we', want to be beyond their demands, or at least in control of such of their demands as we choose to accede to. They are not admitted to the sphere of freedom; rather, anything like freedom on their part is feared as chaos or disintegration, and we hope to be free in relation to them. This is the fruition of a long spiritual history in the West, and is what I mean when I write elsewhere that the Enlightenment is a Luciferian poem. Lucifer is the light-bringer, and even sleeps with the lights on.

Writing about what he calls 'documentary' poetry, the English poet David Wright has noted:

> What will probably strike anyone... is the vigour and immediacy of medieval poetry wherever it deals with the mundane. Freshness of experience is registered and paralleled in freshness of language. After Marvell some of the bloom and brio goes off; neither the plain workmanship of Swift's verse nor the exquisite technique of Pope can quite compensate. After all, the technological world

that was nourished in the womb of the Industrial Revolution and born fully armed around 1918 had its conception in Marvell's day.

Concepts such as psychic adjustment and the right to 'own' one's own body alike have their origins in this changed picture of the world, as surely as resistance to community demands and to the ceremonies that articulate these demands. We resist ceremony because it takes us over, lulls us and exacts things from us, including a tacit admission that we are mortal. What has happened is that aristocracy, developing out of a feudal brutality that it did not for a long time relinquish but merely put out of its own sight, steadily wore down the idea that things should be *in* common, the Christian ideal exemplified in the vision of Piers Plowman and a thousand other works of art and of sainthood, and declared most things to *be* common. There is profound cultural history in that word 'common'. Attempts to restore the older concept increasingly operated on the terms of the new so as not to arouse its condescension and all ended up fatally confused, undermined by the fear that they were being somehow gauche and uncool. All remain at the mercy of a sensibility that at its heart still resembles that of Sherlock Holmes at the end of *The Sign of the Four,* when he says: 'But love is an emotional thing, and whatever is emotional is opposed to that true, cold reason which I place above all things. I should never marry myself, lest I bias my judgment.' Others may marry, or have the credit for Holmes' detective feats – the whole scene echoes with an unspoken Let the servants live for us, and the text has no comma between 'marry' and 'myself'. 'For me,' concludes Holmes, 'there still remains the cocaine bottle.' And he stretches his long, white hand up for it.

We have since moved much farther into the special world of cocaine, in Western and especially in American society, and may be seeing it win out over the 'warmer' old-time drugs and hallucinogens alike, delivering us into an era where life is narrowed and intensified in its essentially disembodied coolness, without the older tragicomical stumblings and commonalities. Fully to say what I am trying to express about this cultural direction requires me to shift to the wholespeak of poetry, and I did so recently in a poem titled 'The Billions':

> At the whizz of a door screen
> moorhens picking through our garden
> make it by a squeak into the dam
> and breasting the algal water

resume their gait and pace on
submerged spectral feet, and they nod
like that half-filled Coke bottle
we saw in the infant river

as it came to its affliction
in the skinny rapids. There
it made a host of dinky bows,
jinked, spun and signalled

till it was in the calm again.
Riding wet in a wide reach of glare
it made us think of icebergs
towed to a desert harbour

for drink and irrigation,
stranded incongruous wet mountains
that destroy the settled scale there,
but, imported in a billion pieces

that's how the coke world is.
And though, as immemorially,
all our dream-ships come,
and go, to Cervix Paradise,

now when day puts us ashore
we walk on gritty ice
in wideawake cities
with tower flats and smog horizon

and there we work, illusionless,
scared lest *live* rhyme with *naive*
till the evening lights come on.
That's the Enlightenment: Surface Paradise.

It cures symptoms, and is fun,
but almost any warmth makes floes
those caught on them must defend
as the inner fields expand,

floes with edges like a billion.
Strange, that wanting to believe
humans could full awaken
should take away the land.

Embodiment begins as a metaphor for the realization of a poeme in material form. I do not say realization in exterior material form, because not all poemes achieve that: it is possible to imagine a poem-vision being formed in the mind of a dying person and never being expressed to outward view by a single gesture. Such a poeme is still embodied, though, in the person whose fading pulse it quickens and whose muscles it may tighten in a last unnoticed excitement. Most poem-visions do attain some degree of exterior expression, though, even if it is only the occasional gesture or word of the person who conceives them, or in the arrangement of furniture in a room. It may be a truism, but it is crucially important to note that the first embodiment of a poeme is in the body of its creator. Many people discover the external embodiment of their poem-vision already made when they come to it, and it itself causes the event of poetry in them. This is especially true of the people I call 'groovers': human souls whose loving energy and fascination are taken up by a particular body of objects or images. Groovers discover the racing car, or landscape gardening, or ornithology, and these become never-failing wellsprings of wonder and contemplation. They may tinker with the cars, or lay out gardens of their own, or make flight cages for birds and perhaps go in for breeding new strains of songsters. Or they may simply enjoy these objects as they are, perhaps recreating the original inspiration of the maker, and perhaps going beyond it, perhaps coming at the object from an entirely new direction of their own and making their own unwritten poem of it. Any exterior comment they make on it may be stumbling, or drawn from some 'cool' poeme that maddeningly prevents them from speaking their love of it in appropriate words: this is often the fate of scholars in writing about their beloved subjects. So often, their love has to be inferred from the anxiety and strictness with which they monitor others' reception of the beloved material.

Beyond the groove, of course, there is an ever-shifting galaxy of poemes which people realize by creating external embodiments for them. They may do so once, or in successive embodiments which they make by themselves or with the aid of helpers, who may or may not be inspired by the same vision. The materials they use may be themselves, as in the young Snowy Mountains stockman sedulously forming himself into the very image of the tough, laconic bush horseman of the high country, perfect down to the last kangaroo-hide boot and sardonic joke, with never a gesture out of character. People may gradually discover and perfect their poeme by at first idly and then in growing fascination deepening the outline of animal shapes they have drawn with a piece of dry clay on the weathered surface of a sandstone platform; the account they give their people of this, and of the animals, may become the basis of stories in which they themselves still figure by name thousands of years later as the creator of that place and of those species. A person may, like Mother Mary McKillop, embody her vision of the ancient poeme of Catholic Christianity in a new and distinctively Australian style of monasticism and of schools. Henry Ford's poem-visions found their embodiment in cars, in automotive components such as his pioneer automatic transmission, in systems for manufacturing cars, and finally in a whole social revolution arising not by chance but out of his own developing poeme of American and human society, which he was able to embody by making cars in a particular way.

Some of the above are examples of fairly integral, consistent poems embodied in similar ways over a lifetime, but of course there are probably just as many people who pursue and manage to embody many different poem-visions wholly or partly, as Leonardo da Vinci did with varying degrees of exterior success. And very often a person may contemplate and refine their vision for most of a lifetime, as Niccolò Machiavelli did, before giving it is final embodiment in a book that resembles a poem in the usual sense (and perhaps is one) in that it is finally beyond the falterings, mishaps and dangers attendant upon embodying its content in action.

Of all the terms we might use to describe how a fusion of thinking and dreaming acquires some sort of exterior form, I think embodiment is both more precise and more pregnant with productive suggestivity than others such as realization, expression, externalization or even the very technical-sounding word reification. Because, whatever other materials we may use, our own actual body goes into the process. When, to pluralize Shakespeare's phrase, we 'give to airy nothings a local habitation and a name', the first local habitation they have is our own flesh and blood, and we do not exteriorize them without lending them some of our own intimate bodily nature, our gesture and breathing, our hurryings and hesitations, our very temperament and sexiness and weight. Again, just as our body is something of a constant, modifying the flights of our thoughts and dreams, and just as its very wordlessness is a property shared with the rest of speechless life and so serves as the representative of that life in the parliament of ourselves, fusions of thought and dream also arise from it without being called into existence by external stimuli. Just as external purposes borrow our body, its work and sweat and needs, to serve their embodiment, so it borrows from the infinite repertoire of externals to embody its inspirations. Love poetry provides a myriad examples. If a poeme is not embodied in art, it may well requisition other people's bodies to give it some embodiment. Don Juan's poeme did; so did Napoleon's.

In the inextricable cross-lacing of its possible meanings, the word embodiment seems to reflect the complex mutuality and ambiguity of what actually goes on. In a way, everything we make, especially if it is with passion, is a new body for ourselves. In all developing personal poemes, and vastly more so in achieved actual poemes, we can detect an evolution of the body running counter to the devolution that nature imposes. We create our body of work, our *corpus operarum*, a very ancient metaphor, and we try to load every rift with awe, since that is the only fuel which can power its journey into future time. Australian Aborigines say that a sacred site, the ritual objects connected with it and the charged verses that pertain to it, all are the actual body of the Dreamtime ancestor to whom the site belongs. And it is a living body, not a dead one.

Everyone has a sacred site somewhere in their life, even if modern language makes them shy about speaking of it readily. This is the place, perhaps having no physical location outside themselves, where awe inheres for them; the commonest Western term for this place is the soul. Wholespeak is the soul's language, and it can only be spoken about effectively in that integral language. I don't believe that the soul consists merely of that language, but I don't know this in any terms communicable in narrowspeak. What I can say from observation of others, as well as myself, is that the soul seems to know what truth is, and where morals come from. It speaks with the authority of that knowledge when we hear from it. When addressed in language which does not carry that knowledge, or affects not to for reasons of obedience to some poeme or other, it mostly does not reply. Or not for a long time. When it does reply, gradually or in one overwhelming timeless moment of truth, the results are apt to be shattering. This, the soul, is the principle that moves us to create or join in poemes, and also tells us when they are exhausted, and it exercises command over what we remember.

There is a principle in nature that the soul knows well, and is itself threatened by, though everything else is even more threatened by it. This principle has its most crystalline secular formation in our time in the brief words of Colonel Edwin Murphy USAAF (ret.), who stated that if a thing can go wrong, it will. Everything I know of on earth with one exception seems to be subject to that law, and we will examine that exception at the end of this essay. In the meantime we may say that all the poemes which make up human culture have their particular ways of dealing with Murphy's Law. The groover barely notices it, in the rapture of contemplating his beloved objects, or else, like the creator of embodiments that are subject to it, he continually reaches for new embodiments to replace those that fail. The larger poemes often formulate attitudes to it, and not surprisingly, for some of them arose largely from a contemplation of it. For example, there are the mainly South Asian traditions that regard it as evidence that all things are illusory, and that peace is to be found by giving up on human life and human needs altogether. Christians and Jews regard it as our fault, to be atoned, but possibly a good fault in that it is the condition of our freedom and continually renews the creation. Some modern secular poemes deny its reality, or hold that it is the fault of their enemies the bourgeoisie or the imperialists or whomever, while others ascribe it to inner contradictions in the evolving doctrine. Almost any new, freshly created poeme cast in modern terms offers a refuge from Murphy's Law, and this is often a powerful motive for its coming into existence. As the poeme matures, in the light of experience, a consciousness of the shadow that lies on all things and shifts maddeningly around them tends to return.

As an example we may look at the poeme of science, whose less thoughtful devotees would deny it is a poeme, though in fact its vision conditions even the greatest of its strengths, that of meticulous observation, and prescribes what shall not be seen. When we first approach science, especially if we admire it and draw from it without practising its austere disciplines, it seems to be the god whom multitudes had longed for, the one who actually answers prayers. After a while, though, we see that it answers any and every sort of prayer, for petitioners of whatever intent. And its answers are merely supplies, with the fateful ambiguity of externals we alluded to a moment ago. It not only supplies both heart transplants and Hiroshimas, but also DDT and the case against DDT. We come to see that science has replaced magic, not spirituality, and that it pours out gold which changes into straw within a few decades. Science turns out to be a vortex of Murphy's Law, not only because it continually turns out productions that prove to be flawed, but because career needs within science accelerate the failure of earlier productions by clearing them away to make room for new hypotheses, new breakthroughs. To the older, natural process of inevitable crack-up it adds the synthetic failure called obsolescence, by which things that are still sound don't go wrong but are put in the wrong and discarded – and almost anything can go wrong with dazzling speed if that is the criterion of failure! Science lives by continually ripping out its organs and growing new ones in fresh shapes, and poemes from outside its ambit who have hitched their wagon to its star are in for the same painfully bewildering treatment, as orthodoxies shift under continual re-examination. The whole process is enormously interesting, however. If you ask science for a song, it will reel off drily exciting poesies of gripping interest that can almost silence the soul. What they don't do for the soul is nourish it or satisfy its needs, and in the end all the dazzling masteries turn back into mysteries.

Whether in its native free form or harnessed into the corollary modern form of obsolescence, which says that if a thing can go wrong it *must* go wrong, Murphy's Law tests every production and conception of mankind. One class of things that seems to stand up well to its testing is objects and artefacts surviving from the past. Not things that have just entered the past, since those look obsolete and comical for a while, stripped of their dignity by changing fashion. After a few decades, though, they begin to take on a contained, timeless look. James Laver's Time Spirit theory of diachronous perception holds that once-fashionable clothes look 'hideous' after ten years, but 'amusing' after thirty, 'quaint' after fifty, 'romantic' after a century and 'beautiful' after a century and a half. I think his timespans are over-long. In the American motor trade, a car is classed as an antique after twenty-five years, which seems short. We may argue about the rates at which artefacts pass through the stage of obsolescence and enter the curious inviolability of history, when they cease to look exhausted and take on the momentous dreampatina of a relic. But even here a form of Murphy's Law operates: things that were not good in the first place, not honestly made, not truly conceived and truly dreamed and fittingly embodied, are slowest to take on this patina. Some may never acquire it; junk merely becomes old junk, perhaps eventually instructive for archaeology, but rarely numinous, rarely of interest to the soul. A bundle of ancient legal documents is of merely passing interest to any but a scholar immersed in the period they come from, but a medieval pewter jug may have a lumpish strangeness of form that speaks of remote but vigorous life and the mystery of lost commonplaces; it draws to itself hints of the weirdly different thinking that lay behind its shaping and manufacture, and the irrecoverable tastes of drinks that filled it long ago. It thus gives off a perfume of poetry. Sometimes, especially in images of dead people, even an absence can be very evocative. Recently I found myself moved by the absence of so ordinary a thing as sweaters or any sort of knitwear in photographs of American Civil War soldiers. In the books I was looking at, the men of 1861-65 did not yet smoke cigarettes, and though they were wearing much the same clothes I remembered from my own childhood – lanky tubular pants and homemade shirts and rough serge jackets, always called coats back then – their rifles were thinner and longer, and they belonged to a time before knitting wool had really come on the market. This immediately set up a tension between half-remembered past time and wholly unfamiliar past time. This tension is quietly inexhaustible, because all human productions contain elements that we continue to have in common, along with features that grow remote and strange; we might call it a numen of differentiation between the two. Often enough, an extinguished poeme will be absorbed entirely into some relic it would never have considered central to its life, as in the case of the Shaker sect, forgotten now in its intricate doctrine but surviving in the lovely plainness of the furniture it produced.

As relics approach the quality of art, their numen at once clarifies and becomes more mysterious. Bad art of one period never becomes good art because of the effluxion of time, but even good art may be obscured for a time by the turbulence of obsolescence. This does not always happen, though. Some works never become obsolete at all, but merely and quite suddenly assume a finality, memorializing a mode of thought and dream and gesture that, perhaps because of the very perfection with which these are fused, can never be re-entered in the same way. And sometimes high-order art assumes and replaces the action of a poeme, in a way that at once preserves it and closes the door on its ever being embodied in action again. The Spanish Republic of the 1930s will never return again as it was; in its place we have a sheaf of great poems, a few great novels and Picasso's *Guernica*. People who were closer to the reality have many more relics whose poignancy may outlive them, but here another distinction should be made, between the poignancy of documentary and relic on the one hand, and the stage of solace which lies beyond that. If documentary moves us, and especially if it harrows us, it is in part by a paradoxical impulse to action, a sort of grieving impossible urge to *rescue* the past. We may call this jammed art. Real art breaks this impasse, with a final transition we will examine in a moment.

Getting back to Murphy's Law at last, if we had ever left it, it is in part the incommensurability and inexhaustibility of a work of art that preserves it. Or anyway preserves the inside of it. The outside of a work, by which I mean its existence and prestige and interpretations, can be put to all sorts of uses in the world, and all these uses are apt to come to grief sooner or later. The existence of classic works of Western culture was long used by the European empires to justify browbeating and oppressing peoples considered provincial or primitive. Readings of these classics were elaborated to help in the job, and the nimbus of narrowspeak that surrounds great art at all times took on this useful new tendency. But then the empires crumbled away and, as had already happened perhaps many times in their history, the same works began to be interpreted in new ways. Inside the works themselves, nothing had changed, this time or any of the other times. Not a chair had moved, not a speech had been rephrased, not a leaf had dropped its burden of dew. This interiority is deeply mysterious, when we can bear to think of it, in its ability to cross time and admit no intruder. Destruction can come to it, but destruction's purchase on a fully embodied work is tenuous even when near-total. We know the quality of Sappho only from a handful of incomplete poems and fragments of her verse, but how inexhaustible these are, and how complete their numen is! Inside a perfectly embodied work, whether the manner of its embodiment is smooth or rough, Murphy is helpless, because nothing can go wrong there; that danger is forever past. The work now can only be annihilated, as we can be sure every work will be eventually. While it lasts, though, it is in the world but it is of another order of existence. It is, finally, preserved by its death to this world. An artist can be defined as one who makes things the value of which is located beyond death, and which are seen through the impalpable glass of death. A numen of this sort is an anomaly which forces even those who hate it and would relativize it and master it to entertain it within their gates – and we can never presume to know, perhaps not even when they are strangling us, which fingers are clinging in terror and hope and which clawing with destructive intent. A work of real art is thus a final distillation of the oldest human poeme we know of, the one revealed by implements and meat-bones reverently laid in Neanderthal graves, and it is a body that has survived the crossing, even begun its life there. It silently challenges the rest of reality to join it there, in that state we might imagine Heaven to resemble, a place where life is lived at the level of poetry and the writ of Murphy no longer runs. At the very least, we see that it has taken a momentous slight step away from the ordinary, and on to solid ground.

Meanjin, April 1988

In a Working Forest

Only strangers, the very poor and the dead walk in the bush. Of the living, no one who belongs to the bush walks any further in it than they can help. It is an old, subtle taboo, compound of pride and unease.

Here, I am using the word 'bush' in the sense which most bush people attach to it. In its widest sense, 'the bush' is the most common word for all places that are not urban or peri-urban. It is our nickname for the country. Affectionate or contemptuous, it means everything from provincial cities to the far outback. As an adjective, it signifies everything from rural to improvised to primitive to inept to idiotic-through-inbreeding. These are all metropolitan usages, urban as gelato or orienteering. Country usage overlaps with them, but the emotional tonings of the world will in every case be different. They will be reminiscent, proud, sardonic, self-respecting, or else know-ledgably bitter. As I have heard old people say, 'I come from a bigger place than Sydney: I come from the bush.'

Where I live, on the lower north coast of New South Wales, the bush means forest, as distinct from farmland. We speak of going 'out in the bush' when we mean entering one of the many state forests or private forest tracts around our region. The bush, entered beyond a rusty fence at the edge of paddocks or down a gravel road edged in stumps and high blady grass, is set over against civilization and the household. To do 'bush work' can mean to be engaged in any rural occupation, but to work in the bush means to be involved in some aspect of timber or forestry. To be *up* or *down* or *out* in the bush is to be nearby but in a different element, and one 'comes in' from the bush when work is over. Also, one camps in the bush, as my father and many more used to camp in old tramcars down the lower Myall River while cutting for the Masonite Corporation, but one doesn't live in it. To live out there permanently is to court death by bushfire. Some are said to live out in the bush when we really only mean they live in relatively uncleared country, or on the fringes of a state forest. They too come in, for supplies or to collect their mail.

These usages would be understood all over Australia, though in drier parts the word might be 'scrub'. Two words that have altered their meanings since I was young are 'bushwhacker' and to be 'bushed'. In Australia, a bushwhacker was originally nothing more than an uncultured country dweller, a hillbilly; now, under the influence of television, it is acquiring its American meaning, of one who shoots from ambush. 'That ole cuss bushwhacked me!' In the same way, to be bushed once meant to be lost; now it is coming to mean merely tired out. I hope 'brush' doesn't go the same way. At home, it means the opposite of its American significance of low scrubby growth: it is rain forest, and people speak of standing brush, green brush and black brush, depending on the degree to which an unbroken upper canopy cuts the sunlight and produces a moist, still, itching twilight below, home to leeches, and stinging trees, catbirds and cunjevoi lilies.

The reluctance of countryfolk to do much walking in the bush, except from one felled tree to the one they mean to fell next, or in search of some specific product such as staghorn ferns or fruiting puddenie (*Billardiera*) vines, is one that goes back a long way and is hardly ever fully conscious. It carries a suggestion of being abandoned, or lost, not sufficiently in control of things. Even seeing a neighbour or a fellow country person walk along a road without offering them a lift is frowned on, for it humiliates them. A person in bushwalking clothes and carrying a rucksack has declared their intentions, but a person without baggage, or with the wrong baggage, may well be in some sort of need. And all of this becomes the more true if there is forest on either side of the road. Then the ancient law applies, that one's species must not be abandoned to the wilds. It is also a matter of caste, and that is ancient too. Walking is only really stylish amongst fairly privileged urban people; bushwalkers are just a shade below joggers and squash players, and may be coterminous with them. Among working people, to walk means one has no better means of transport, or is not at liberty to use transport. The Aborigines walked everywhere for thousands of years, but gradually after settlement they saw that this put them on a similar footing to convict gangs and soldiers, who shuffled or marched along while their overseer or their officer lounged along on horseback. As their ancient skills were devalued by encroachment on their lands, they too adopted the horse or the camel, where they could acquire them or be issued with them, and many became legendary riders. Nowadays they travel by car or train or bus like the rest of us, and get about their tracts of restored tribal land in Land Cruisers and on dirt bikes. Even their outback hunting trips are apt to be mounted on four-wheel-drive vehicles. To walk the roads or tramp the bush meant the same thing, and carried overtones of penury and failure, echoes of depression times, or of humping Bluey long ago, on the weary tucker tracks of the nineteenth century. Even back then, rural workers very often used a bike or a horse, if they could afford one. And bushrangers, who often began their depredations on foot, would take care to acquire fast horses just as soon as they could, perhaps during or immediately after their first hold-up.

A memory persisted for a long time in my region of one proud Aboriginal who resisted assimilation and continued to walk the bush in the ancient way. Long after the local Biripai or Shark section of the Kattang people had lost their best land and become dependent on wages or handouts from the whites, a few solitary hunters kept to the high country along the eastern fall of the Dividing Range, maintaining themselves by traditional means. One such lone warrior was captured at Johnston's Peak outside Wingham in the early 1880s. A powerfully built man, wholly naked, speaking no English at all, he was suspected of cattle spearing and may have been lucky to have escaped some cattleman's rifle. Lodged overnight in Wingham lockup, he was brought before magistrate Joseph Cochrane the next day. The 'camp blacks' on the fringe of Wingham were said to be terrified of him, but perhaps their apparent fear was tinged with respect and shame. We do not know how much of tribal life and ritual might still have been going on – initiations certainly occurred until the 1930s – nor the role of such a man in Dreaming matters. Nothing was proven against the 'wild blackfellow' in court and he was released to go back to the mountains. He went unhurriedly, with dignity. Wingham people could still see his campfire two nights later winking away on the mountain, and then he vanished, perhaps to meet with a cattleman's bullet after all. He was the end of a world, and no one like him was ever to be seen again.

When that man was a child, and back before his life, trees were fewer and larger, and distributed in a way that would only be re-established with enormous labour. Regular burning by his people kept the valley bottoms and lower hills open, for ease of hunting, and thicker forest clung to hilltops and the moister shady sides of hills, where rainforest swelled out of steep gullies in its perpetual seesaw struggle with open gum forest. My aunt Grace, mother of my cousin Stewart Murray, who is himself an active ninety years old, was told by an old Aboriginal man with the European name Boney, who lived on my great-great grandfather's farm at Kimbriki on the upper Manning, that when he first knew our district of Bunyah it was all open grassland with few trees and much game. The creek there, which becomes the Wang Wauk River, is still called Horses Creek. Originally it was Wild Horses Creek, for the brumbies that roamed there. An old brumby catcher named Woodward told an early settler named John Griffis tales of rounding up the wild horses in the early days. When Mr Griffis remarked that it must have been dangerous chasing horses at a gallop through thick bush, the old man explained that there were then no logs on the ground and no scrub, such as there would be in plenty a few decades on. Kurrajong and rough-barked apple trees (*Angophoras*) grew there, typical trees of open country. By the time settlers arrived there in 1870, regular burning had long been neglected and the forest would have sprouted and begun to look primeval and formidable. As late as my father's teens, though, after the First World War, it was still possible to see through the bush for a mile or more in any direction, and possible to drive a bullock team in a straight line through the timber with no need for a road. Now it's barely possible to move through the regrowth on foot in some places, and a bullock truck would be impossible to manoeuvre through much of what locals call the 'State'.

One man who walked in our forest before settlement is said to walk there still. Folklore has lost his Christian name; he is known now only as Bingham. He seems to have been a cedar cutter, one of that wild underworld of escaped convicts, runaway sailors and dungaree immigrants who within less than a century stripped the fragrant ginger-red softwood of *Toona australis* out of a face along the whole east coast of Australia. In autumn the cutters would walk or ride the hills looking for the browning leaves of their prey, one of the very few deciduous trees in our forests, and in spring they would spy out the russet leaves re-clothing the giant trees; each season gave them work to last till the next, if they were lucky. After one such season, Bingham's partner Cassidy, likewise known only by his surname now, came in alone to the tiny river port of Coolongolook; when asked where Bingham was, he replied that his mate had chucked cedar-getting and gone off to work somewhere down on the Hunter River. Locals noticed that Cassidy's nature had subtly changed: he had become jumpy, and hated to have anyone walk behind him. As if in answer to their suspicions, and perhaps arising from them, travellers on the then main north road up the Myall River valley and over the Manning Hill to the Manning Valley via Bunyah began to meet with Bingham himself on the high cuttings of the range's north side. Seen always at night, the lost cedar cutter would be walking along the road towards Bunyah, or standing in one of the dark corners of the descent, and when greeted or merely approached, he would disappear. My Murray grandfather and a man named Jack Dorney caught up with him one night and, not remembering the tale of the ghost, bade him good night, which can be a greeting as well as a farewell in our region. 'Good night!' they chorused again when he failed to answer or look around. 'Answer, you bugger,' snapped my grandfather, 'or I'll crack the whip over you!' And at that the figure ceased to be there. Allan and Jack became very quiet for a while, then voluble, as they rode on down the switchback turns of the road. Others who saw him were sometimes drunk, sometimes as sober as Allan and Jack had been. The last person I knew who saw Bingham was my cousin Jack Murray, sometime in the late 1930s; by his own admission he was 'three parts full' when he encountered the apparition in a dark corner of the road. Jack became very sober immediately. In all accounts of Bingham except one, he is seen wearing an old workman's coat and frieze trousers with all the pockets hanging out. The exception was an encounter many years ago, probably around the beginning of the twentieth century, when a bullocky named Matt Hogan camped on a tributary of Horses Creek, now known as Bingham's Creek. During the night, he was terrified by desperate shouts and screams, and a fearsome splashing in the water. 'In spite of all my gameness,' he averred, 'the hair stood up on my head. I'd never camp the night in that place again!'

The newly luxuriant woodland my great-grandparents John and Isabella Murray encountered when they took up their land at Bunyah in 1870 is now pretty well confined to State Forest number 295, Wang Wauk, and to the high ridges of the Kyle range which run down into it from the north-west. This is the forest I have known all my life, the one I walked in first and the one I'm likely to walk in most often in the future. Together with Bulahdelah State Forest, number 296, it forms a gigantic prone figure of a deep-sea diver or a hooded man straddling Boolambayte Lake and the Pacific Highway with two long legs. This map-figure lies on the landscape with its big head in Bunyah and an arm crooked down behind Coolongolook Mountain cradling a detached forestry block that was once the site of the abortive Telararee gold rush. Embracing 8651 hectares, State Forest 295 comprises all the government forest preserve which drains by way of the Wang Wauk and Coolongolook rivers into Wallis Lake and thence the ocean. Bulahdelah State Forest, the two legs, hips and one shoulder of the map giant, takes in 10,166 hectares and drains by way of Boolambayte Creek and the Myall River into the Myall Lakes. High on the more northerly thigh of the giant, shared by both state forests, is the superb O'Sullivans Gap Flora Reserve with its cabbage-tree palms growing between the beige to milk-blue boles of tall flooded-gum trees, and its rainforest patches; when returning by road from the south, I always regard this twisting arcade of luxuriant bush as the gateway to the north coast. Further south in the same leg, just inside State Forest 296, is the Grandis, the tallest tree in New South Wales, a flooded-gum some seventy-six metres (or two hundred and fifty feet) in height and as big round the base as the average second bedroom. Pinned on to the south leg, behind roughly the knee, is Bulahdelah Mountain Forest Park, a protected habitat of the rare subterranean orchid *Cryptanthemis slateri*, an endangered species. The small rocky mountain there was once the world's chief source of the chemical alum, formerly used as an astringent in medicine and a mordant in dyes; now its main use is as an absorbent in catbox litter. My mother's father Fred Arnall started work up there, in drives that opened on near-vertical skips and blue sky, when he was a sixteen-year-old Cornish orphan, and he stayed in the district long enough to marry Emily Worth, daughter of a Coolongolook family whose name has been represented in local timber-getting since the beginnings of settlement.

The first time I entered Wang Wauk State Forest lies well before conscious memory, but it was almost certainly on Black Saturday in February 1939, when I was five months old. I was taken to a swimming hole in the already burnt-out forest to stay with the women and the other small children of the district, while the men and big boys fought to save as much as they could from the terrifying, irresistible bushfires that were now sweeping through the farms. Since then I've gone there for picnics, for solitary rambles, to cut poles and fence posts, to help my father search unsuccessfully for a lost gold claim in a gully overgrown since the claim was filed in the 1930s, to botanize, to be quiet among the trees and birds. Sometimes when driving about the roads in there, Smedley's Cutting Road or Horses Creek Road, Worths Road or the steep pinch up Possum Pie, or the exhilarating Koolonock Road that hangs cornice-like on one side and then the other side of the high steep spinal ridge dividing Wang Wauk from Bulahdelah forest, I indulge a kind of soundless visual symphony, watching the tree species change in response to the different soils. High up there will be forest oaks, whose non-deciduous needle leaves turn bronze in autumn and used to be taken

by the black people as their signal to move away from the coast to
winter in the sheltering hills. With these will be greyish-mauve spot-
ted gums, then white mahogany and grey ironbark and seasonally
orange-streaked grey gum, telling of stony ground; a brush box or
two will indicate moister shaded soil, and then perhaps the warm
chestnut trunks of soaring tallowoods will take over, with black
ironbarks and maybe a shift to blackbutt on drier soils, then these
will give way to dizzying bluegum, flooded-gun and turpentine far
down on the creek levels. Often the symphony will be faster and
more complex than this, and a flowering vine, say wild hops or
native clematis or creamy-belled wonga, will bring me to an admir-
ing stop, or I will slow down to drink in the swarming scent of
bloodwood trees in bloom. Always, too, I pay heed to the grassy
tunnels of abandoned roads, and the many ancient stumps, fluted
with decay, which still show the neat slots cut into them with three
or four skilful swings of the axe sixty or eighty or a hundred years
ago to take the improvised 'boards' on which men ascended to fell
or even to top soaring trees, working five or ten or a hundred feet
up with no thought of safety harness. And I find myself thinking
of an age I saw the very tail end of, the era of bullock teams and
trundling iron-shod jinkers, always called trucks by the men who
used them. The very last team working in our bush ceased operations
only a little over twenty years ago; it belonged to Eric Bennett, of
Coolongolook, a quiet, gentle man who was for a while my uncle
my marriage.

Men who cut and drew timber in the 1930s and through the boom
time of the Second World War, when vast tonnages of timber went
to build wharves all over the Pacific for the forces that were driving
back Japan, all agree that the logs they felled, or 'fell' as they say,
were the second generation, sticks that their fathers and predecessors
would have disdained, though they were still mighty logs, often
three or four feet in diameter at the butt. The truly great trees, giants
surviving from away back in Aboriginal times, and often having a
girth greater than that of a thousand-gallon iron water tank, were
cut down and drawn to the mills by men whose names still, but
only for a little while longer, ring in local tales. Ned Toms was
admitted by all to be the finest judge of timber of his generation,
as well as one of the hardest workers: his bullocks were worn out
in a couple of years, and had to be replaced continually. Albert
Worth was his pupil and successor, a man said to be able to smell
white ants in the crown of a tree when standing at its base. Other
mighty men were the Holdens, Herb and Albert, Bill and Stan,

whose trucks had 'cottonreel' wheels, not spoked but solid timber cut in the round from a log; Frank, Percy and Bailey Bunt, whose surname endures in Bunts Creek; Archie, Jim and George Carter; Stan Mills, John Griffis; Jack, George and Billy Mitchell, and Harry and Dargan Mitchell too; Tom and Jim Batchelor, sardonic jesters who also cut and drew in the state forest to the east of Coolongolook that now bears their family name; Don and Frank Worth; Jake and Billy Newton; Bucca Wauka Bob Paterson; Jack Tull; Albert McDean; Billy Newman, who has a road named after him in the forest; Mick Ronan; the Burnses, Arthur, Billy and George; the Aboriginal family of French, Harry and Morgan in the older generation and then their sons Clarrie and Bill, the latter of whom was always known as Plugger. And then there were Gomer Woodward and Stewart Murray senior, and Jack Woodward whose head was crushed by a loop of bridle chain as a log slipped off the skid up which it was being snigged on to his bullock trucks. This tragedy occurred in the teens of the century, and an identical accident almost killed my father Cecil Murray in the 1930s; if the log and the skid had fallen to the ground, rather than lodging on the nave of the truck's wheel, I would never have existed. Bailey Bunt, by contrast, caught himself around the head with a lash of his bullock whip, and for many weeks wore a vivid scar as if his face and his very scalp under his hair had been cut in half and soldered back together. In a way, they had been. Many of the men I have named began work in the bush well before the turn of the century, and often they shifted over to full-time farming after a decade or two in the timber. Very many of the early settlers in fact used the sale of timber off their selections to set up in dairy farming, and that was after they had used some of the timber to build their original dwellings. A typical case was Henry Tagg, whose son George was a bullock driver for many years; Mr Tagg senior was a punt captain in the Myall River timber trade, until he bought a block at Willina that had taken his eye. He was nicknamed Peter Positive, for his assured demeanour, and the quality was probably a godsend in the hard scrabble of a selector's life.

When Jim, Sandy and Allan Murray gave up bullock driving, and Allan's sons entered the timber business in the late 1920s, most private cutters and teamsters were concentrated in the northern half of Wang Wauk forest. The southern end and much of Bulahdelah forest was the preserve of Allen Taylor's logging tramway, which ran from Horses Creek over the steep little Mayer's Range where the Wang Wauk Forest Way now runs, and thence down to the now-dying village of Wootton, and on to Mayer's Point, on the main Myall Lake. From there, steam punts carrying huge layers of logs would chug down the deep Myall River to Winda Woppa, on Port Stephens, whence the timber would be transferred into deepwater ships to go to Sydney, Newcastle, New Zealand or California. The tramway was first powered by horses, which crossed the many bridges on close-fitted decking; later they were replaced by narrow-gauge steam locos. The tramway ran from 1900 to 1944, employing hosts of men from Wootton, Bulahdelah and all the districts round about, and it only died when the river boats and the coastal steamers they served were killed off by the war. Now, only a few relics of the tramway remain. On Horses Creek, a bridge still carrying its rusted steel rails has survived bushfires by virtue of the shady moist creek bush around it. To city eyes, it probably looks like a smallish mouldering sister of the bridge on the River Kwai. There is now a small cleared picnic area at one end, with barbecues and labelled trees, and large yellow-flecked black goannas there compete with the currawongs and noisy miners for tourists' scraps, often coming out to demand them even before the sausages are cooked. The leeches, for their part, don't have to wait; for them, the tourists themselves are the picnic.

The teams drawing out of the north end of Wang Wauk State Foest used to haul their logs in to Bunyah and down to Coolongolook, at first to the mills there, later mainly to the wharf, or else they would follow a now-disused road down the Wang Wauk to just past where it becomes a tidal saltater river. In either case, much of their timber went to Wrights' mill and shipyard at Tuncurry. Hundreds of sailing ships were built from native hardwoods on our rivers, and timber construction lasted well into the era of steam. In early times, millions of super feet of ironbark went to make paving blocks in the cities; turpentine went to construct wharves, and the cabbage-tree palm had its role in providing stakes for oyster leases, as it still does. Another unlikely-seeming timber consumed by the bullockies themsleves was grass tree (*Xanthorrhoea*), from which they cut the brake shoes for their trucks; no other timber had so little slippage. In that age and before, rainforest trees weren't protected as they are nowadays, and from private and Crown lands alike went coachwood, rosewood, the rare brown pine (*Podocarpus elatus*) and many more, lumped in with the hardwoods. At the same period, of course, rainforest was still being routinely cut and burnt to clear it. Nowadays, the only native softwood in commerce from our part of the coast is the coastal callitris (*Callitris macleayana*) or coast cypress pine, not present, as far as I know, in either of the two state forests dealt with here.

When the teams were using it, the Bunyah road, never a showpiece thoroughfare, degenerated into a morass of deep trenches and liquescent or sundried clay scarps; no other vehicle, whether car or sulky or bike, could negotiate it, and most traffic went round by other roads. Ironically, the beginning of the end for the teams, and the victory of mechanization, began with something as simple as gravel. When Stroud Shire first gravelled the roads in the mid-1930s, bullocks that used them began to go lame. The going was too hard and sharp for their feet, while at the same time the thick loose surface absorbed the inertia of the trucks' wheels and meant that the bullocks had to pull harder and more constantly to move their great tonnages of load. Soon, the teamsters began to bring their loads only to the edge of the forest, establishing dumps with huge permanent loading skids over which to slide the log onto the first motor lorry jinkers. Archie Fenning and Jack Saxby were among the first lorry drivers to cart logs, though tabletop lorries had long been going into the bush to haul sleepers, girders and suchlike smaller timber. The log dumps, a few still used but mainly derelict now, are still a striking feature of the bush, squat cliffs and bunkers of grey timber and dirt. In their heyday, the dumps were apt to look like brontosaurian paving, or a vast corduroy laid on the ripped, deliciously raw-smelling bush soil. I can still just remember them like that, back when what are now called sawlogs, American style, were still known universally by their Australian term, mill logs. 'Mill logs today?' snort the old men. 'They're bloody telephone poles! We wouldn't have looked at anything that small.'

Those who walk the forest in the memory and reverie of my region include many who made, very late in Western terms, the momentous step across from the age of muscle power to the age of the machine. Men still alive remember riding into bush in the mists of dawn and hobbling their horses to browse all day on the rich kangaroo grass between the trees, while they swung their axes and drove their wedges with scarcely a break till sundown. Often their bullocks would be nearby, located by their bells' iron music as they grazed together. It was the work of only half an hour or so to round them up, put on their yokes and bows and link up the snig chains to draw a hundred-foot barked spar to the trucks for loading. The bullocks moved slowly between the trees, avoiding obstacles, and the log following behind made little more than a groove in the soil, because it was narrower than the team and so couldn't smash much that they had avoided. When bulldozers arrived at the end of the Second World War, they crashed straight through, up slopes and down gorges, destroying twenty future trees and three or four present ones to extract a single log. But they were much faster, and so earned more money for their operators. Most timber-getters have always been contractors, rather than employees on wages, and they tend to come from families with a fierce love of personal independence. The ancient steam traction engines had been as slow as the bullocks, and a fire risk to boot, so they worked mostly outside the forest and were never serious competition. When the bulldozers came, and the last bullock teams disappeared, as usual a host of subtleties vanished. There was, for example, no more need for men who could judge the strength and potential of a bullock, or select which should be leaders, no more call for training animals to respond to voice and tone, and no more use for the tricks of psychology which overcame the animals' fears and occasional jibbings. To cite just one such, it used to be well known that if a load became stuck, bringing the team to a halt, their first pull when re-starting would be the most powerful. Their next would lack heart, though it would still be energetic; the third would be despairing and weak, and there probably wouldn't be a fourth. The way to get a further powerful effort, after a short spell, was to lengthen the slack of the chains considerably, then gee the team into motion; they would move tentatively, register the joyous lightening of their load, and be in full, confident motion when the chains tightened. This was particularly effective when, as so often happened, the second of two linked loads became stuck in a creek or a mudhole. Putting the first into motion established a heartening inertia, and the management of inertial forces was as much at the heart of bullock drivers' skills as it was central to those of dozer drivers. Sometimes inertia would do most of the work, by accident or design. Two men hauling a bloodwood log up Pappinbarra mountain north of Taree, well into the caterpillar age, saw their load slip out of its bark smoothly as a leg out of a stocking and begin a sizzling end-on descent, splitting some trees, riding up through the high foliage of others in momentary arcs, till it plunged down through the tangled vines at the mountain's foot and buried its entire length almost parallel with the surface of the soil And there it stayed. In the bullock era, logs were regularly drawn by block and tackle to the top of a steep hill and 'speared' down, or else drawn down festooned with knotted chains that 'grabbed' in the earth and prevented their racing down past, or over, the bullocks. One log that got away from my father and his brother Eric on

Martin's Mount, just north-west of the state forest, skied down with such impetus that it leaped over the cleared flat at the bottom, cleared Darling's Creek and plunged fifteen feet deep into the soft soil on the other side. It took both teams together to joggle it free.

Few farmers ever used bullocks for ploughing; compared with the fine control of line given by a bit in a draught horse's mouth, driving bullocks by whip and command was a poor way to get, say, a perfectly straight furrow, though George Harris managed it with two giant Devons which he steered with reins attached to halters. Those two would have weighed 1000 lb each, like those in the short twelve-bullock team of silent Billy Mitchell, famous for his ability to log a paddock with scarcely a sound 'like as if he was thieving the timber', though he never was. Few men flogged their bullocks, or even swore at them much, though there were hot-headed exceptions. One maniac was famous, in his rages, for lashing the very logs of his load and the wheels of his trucks, and would gouge his animals' eyes in his frenzy. Another had regularly to unyoke the most savagely flogged bullocks out of his team before entering Coolongolook, for fear of being arrested for cruelty. He was also liable to conscript odd beasts out of paddocks as he passed by: a heifer of Stewart Murray's served a short season in the purgatory of his service, as did my grandfather's Jersey bull. All this to make up the sixteen or eighteen beasts in the average team. Contrary to their stolid reputation, cattle are in fact rather emotional, flighty creatures, prone to curiosity and panic. Fussy, too: I've seen them walk a mile, through creeks and past clay-water dams, to drink from a sophisticated new concrete watering system. In work, bullocks were apt to shy at strange phenomena, and what every teamster feared was a team 'ringing up', that is, running in a circle so tight that necks came under tension in their yokes and began to break. Most of a team could be killed in this way within a minute or two, and drivers had to brave high winds and slashing hailstorms in the open, preventing their panicked beasts from starting the fatal circling. Particular teams had particular habits, too: that of the Salter brothers was famous for waiting its chance when being hooked on to a fresh load, and bolting, sometimes to be caught only miles away. Unlike Western teamsters, few local men used offsiders; either they worked alone, or a whole family group with similar skills worked loosely together. One man who did serve as an offsider, though, was Bob Salter, whom one of the savage drivers once lashed squarely down the back with his whip in an access of rage. 'I tell you, it was nearly enough to make a man fight,' Salter related.

Minor injuries were, and remain, commonplace in the bush, to be borne with stoicism and humour. Relatively few of the old generations of cutters and bullockies seem to have been killed or maimed in the course of their work, and the Horses Creek tramway in its forty-four years of operations had just one fatal accident. A deflected axe, wedges popping out of a log, a tree kicking back past the stump as it fell, all these were menaces to watch for, but really the men's skills became so profound and instantaneous that before a bad accident could happen they had usually stepped away from it to watch the play of forces, perhaps with a curse or a laugh. 'Go it, you bastard!' 'By jabers but that was close!' Death and maiming were always more likely in the sawmills than the bush. To name just two cases out of many, my grandmother's brother George Payne lost his arm in an instant in a mill at Moto. And a man named Hector Newton was feeding a log past the guide rollers of a mill at Nabiac when, as can happen if a log develops even an imperceptible skew as it rides into the saw, the outer scantling ran out, flew up and was flung by the screaming blade end on like a shovelnose spear. Newton was impaled through the heart and died instantly, and he was not the only victim of this exact pattern of accident. The coming of the chainsaw, so much swifter than the old man-powered axe and crosscut saw, brought an increase in horrendous injuries to the bush, as well as a new source of close-shave stories. The man who trod on a black snake on a steep pinch and slid down its entire length while desperately holding a revving chainsaw away from his body survived unbitten by either, to be laughed at as a liar by all except timbermen, though their belief also didn't prevent them from laughing. A nearer thing happened the day the same man put his saw into a thick branch that had a 'bind' on it, that is, one which was under tension; it's often impossible to detect the presence of tension in a tangle of branches or a lodged tree. When the branch was severed, the strain it had been under released, tossing man and saw a dozen feet. Its trigger jammed, so that the blade was still chewing furiously at the air, the saw fell on its handle end between the man's sprawled legs, and stood upright for a long millisecond. If it fell backwards, he would be split in two, or at the very least torn open in hideous death. If he raised a hand, he would lose it and the arm too. And then the blade fell away from him, and gnawed at the soil between his feet. Another man, working alone as no one should ever do in the forest, was noticed by a Masonite Corporation supervisor named Clarrie Dawson to be sitting oddly hunched on the ground near his camp, so that Dawson felt impelled to put his utility truck into reverse and go back. It turned out the man had somehow dropped his whizzing chainsaw in his lap, and was proceeding to bleed to death. Rushed to hospital, he was saved, and even his genitals were eventually restored to full working order. At the Masonite factory's offices in Raymond Terrace, though, none of the men who had rushed to help Dawson with the injured man really wanted to dictate the contents of the accident report to the pretty young typist. Dawson had to do that himself. 'Er... extensive lacerations,' he paused, 'to the penis...' 'Poor man,' said the typist, never missing a beat in her rapid typing. Nowadays, the various forestry district offices have chainsaw examiner-instructors on staff, who check and brush up the skills of all workers wishing for a license to cut timber in the various state forests.

Men working in the bush are also nowadays required to wear yellow plastic safety helmets. No such protection existed in September 1938, when my father's brother Archie, an experienced sleeper cutter and just three months married, was killed by the falling top of a dead tree. My father had refused to fell a certain tallowwood, just before retiring from the bush to start working a dairy farm of his father's, on the grounds that it was too difficult to haul out and anyway dozy, that is, afflicted with subsurface rotting, at one or more spots high up. His father, who supervised operations from horseback, was stubbornly convinced the log was good, and could be secured. As he rode off after breakfast, my grandmother, afflicted all her life with flashes of the bad gift of prescience, rushed out, calling and calling to him to warn him of a terrible foreboding she had. He failed to hear, and at three that afternoon, as the disputed tree fell, it brushed against a tall dead one beside it and set up a whipping vibration in it. Hearing a cry of 'Look out!', Archie made his only mistake, and ran without looking up. The long snapped-off top section of the dead bole hit him squarely in the head and burst his brains out. Handsome, waltzing Archie was so well liked and bitterly missed that over a thousand crowded Krambach cemetery for his funeral.

When the colonial forestry authority came into existence in the 1870s, it was thought that the native forests would be rapidly cut out. If the country was being cleared anyway, the Crown might as well make some money from the process before releasing its thus cleared lands to selectors. Licenses began to be granted and royalties to be paid for felling timber on Crown land, and it was only later that state forests as such were proclaimed. Those of Bulahdelah and Wang Wauk had to wait till it was decided whether the planned north coast railway line would pass that way and so compete directly with the coastal shipping, or go by the much easier inland route from Maitland via Mammy Johnson's River and Craven to Gloucester and the upper Manning. The railway eventually went that way, and by that time the forestry authorities had begun thinking in terms of sustained yield from the forests; the notion of a timber mine had been replaced by the idea of a crop to be managed and harvested. After eighty-odd years of this paradigm, the forest is generally dense, except on the stonier heights where grass replaces undergrowth or ferns under the patchy shade of tall ironbarks, yellow box and grey gums. This return to something like ancient parkland conditions is secured by controlled burning, by bushfires and by grazing animals; kangaroos and wallabies are much commoner there than below in the thick growth. Cattle help, too; turned out to graze illegally in the state forests, they are tolerated de facto by the forestry authorities except when they destroy too many young seedlings and saplings. The bush has furnished cover for all sorts of skulduggery with cattle, over the years, though usually nothing major. Odd pools of blood on the ground, the edges of a hide still smouldering in a fire, unlikely movement by cattle trucks, all these are mentioned occasionally. Once, a long time ago, an undercover policeman camped in the Wang Wauk forest; a strong, cheery, well-built man, he was a pitifully inept sleeper cutter, and he received long brown envelopes through Bunyah post office, so his cover was diaphanous indeed. Trees in a given section or block of the forest will tend to be similar in size and age, though this is more noticeable in some parts than others. The regime is that trees should be harvested sequentially as they reach full size, without letting too many become over-age; deterioration under the assaults of bacteria and parasites is apt to set in quite early, in gum trees. Little or no planting has taken place in the two forests that form the great blue giant, so there are no sad ranks of little old trees languishing on the wrong soil. Eucalypts are by and large extremely fussy about their requirements for drainage and soil chemistry, and really the best way to 'plant' them is to fence grazing animals out and see what comes up. Heads of trees are left on the ground after felling, to shed their masses of seed and replenish the forest with their species; it's messy for a while, but effective and ecologically responsible, and anyway the casual car-driving tourist doesn't see the mess, since nothing is supposed to be cut down within twenty metres of a main forest road. A few very big trees remain, rejects from earlier eras, but the healthy diversity of scale they give to the forest is contradicted at many places by jammed masses of saplings weltering in vines.

Although officialdom denies it, there is often an air of not exactly neglect but of decrepitude in the state forests. Botanists, foresters and soil chemists alike have told me that our forests and all the rest of the northern coastal forests are in fact well on the way back to a rainforest regime perhaps older and vaster than in Aboriginal times. And you can see it, in the decade-by-decade spread of rainforest up gorges and gullies. All but a few Forestry roads are in need of repair; surfaces are pot holed or crumbling, and some roads are almost closing in under South American blueweed, tobacco bush, lantana and wattles, the precursors of recapture by the forest proper. It seems the district forestry office simply can't extract the funds from their department to do roadworks, despite the comparatively recent stress on tourist and recreational value in the forests. In the future, facilities that have been provided free of charge to tourists may have to be charged for, though how the moneys will be collected without hiring more staff than such payments could support remains a conundrum. Bulahdelah district office used to employ over thirty staff, now the number is down to eleven. Mill logs are still the principal product of the forest, but even on its fringes people now often build in brick, because timber has become too dear, especially given the extra cost of repeated coats of paint; fashion has long left behind the beautiful silvery effect of unpainted timber still to be seen on very old sheds and houses. Royalties which used to be linked to the CPI are now well above it, adding to the cost of timber, but the Forestry Commission has little choice, if local forests are to pay for their own administration. Only two men, Ray Worth and Alan Miller, both of Coolongolook, are still cutting sleepers in Wang Wauk, and girders and wharf timebers are well down on earlier days. A sign of the times, perhaps, is the steel frame of the newest timber mill in Bulahdelah. The only flourishing new product is wooden pallets, used wherever forklifts are employed. Pit props are still being ordered, though most new coal mining is open-cut. Logs for chipping by firms such as Masonite are now going out of the forests again, though in much smaller numbers than before the great economic slump of the mid-seventies which put nearly all contractors out of a job, and the forests continue to be drawn on for such miscellanea as oyster stakes, fence posts, (though steel star pickets compete with those), native plants collected under license, bee farming and the like. Far fewer farmers can now rely, as they once did, on the forest as a source of supplementary income in winter or in bad times, and quite a few older uses for timber have vanished. The old culverts and road bridges built of hardwood up until the early

1960s are now being replaced by new concrete ones, and in this generation no one has cut firewood for the steam engines of a butter factory, let alone for those of river shipping. And that used to be a very handy fall-back, though it probably drew more on private stands of timber, including dead stuff, than on the state. The only two enterprises from which the Forestry can expect to make a significant profit nowadays are, sadly, from logging its exotic softwood plantations and from mass export of woodchips for papermaking to Japan and elsewhere. Thankfully, the nearest the green blight of pine plantations has come to my home region is just north of Raymond Terrace, and those were torched by an arsonist several years ago. No plans exist to alter the ecologically sensible regime of timbergetting in our region; for one thing, the forests in our area are too varied and rich in species to justify clear felling, which is claimed to be the only way to regenerate a forest crammed with mature trees of just one or two species, like those of the eastern foothills of the Snowy Mountains.

The forests near home function as a concentrated habitat for wildlife that was once more thinly spread through the Aboriginal open parkland. Scores of bird species, from the minute but confiding grey-green weebill to the bell miner and the whipbird to the black, showy-necked scrub turkey, can only really exist there. Logging doesn't have a large impact on them, but out in the farms the isolated cattle camps and forested creek fringes wouldn't afford them the means of life in competition with the species that have adapted well to the agricultural and now in fact largely pastoral landscape of the coastal hills. The same is true of many animals, too, from sugar glider possums to goannas, though the once heavy population of dingoes there seems to have dwindled almost to nothing. A century ago the sons of my great-grandparents at Bunyah, who ran a beef business in conjunction with their farming and grazing, used to have to throw heads and offal to the dingoes on Bulby Mountain as they drove over the pass there, to save their horses from being savaged by the packs. Several men were bailed up by dingoes on remote tracks, and had to defend themselves with their axes, and John Startin of Bunyah, now middle aged but a national champion axeman all the same, was almost taken by dingoes out in the paddock next to the state forest boundary when he was a toddler; only prompt intervention by his father Tony saved him. No one of the older generation around home doubts the ability or the readiness of a dingo to take a small baby such as Azaria Chamberlain. Another and grimmer beast which has been largely confined to the state forest is bushfire.

The Big Red Steer has hardly visited the farms in any serious way since Black Saturday in 1939. That conflagration burnt up tens of thousands of ringbarked trees, the long roots of which smouldered away underground for months afterwards; no fire since then has had comparable fuel, and relatively few dead trees are now standing. The bulldozer and the chainsaw have made obsolete the ugly practice, understandable on the part of poverty-stricken settlers needing grass quickly, of ringbarking trees and leaving them to fall on the next generation. Burning off, slashing and grazing itself reduce the risk of grass fires, and few leave many native trees close to their buildings. In the forest, control burning is done, but a bad summer will still explode, as in 1968, stripping away undergrowth, killing myriad seedlings and damaging hosts of trees, and the open country has more to thank the foresters and volunteer bushfire brigades for in the way of protection than its people sometimes realize. They might say, of course, that if the forests harbour a monster, their keepers are morally obliged to restrain it themselves.

'The past is never dead. It's not even past,' wrote William Faulkner. It is in search of this sense of things that many come to the forests and wander the grassy tunnel-trails. The perpetual dimension, though, needs knowledge to furnish it with imagery – and the imagery, once realized, is ever-living, and creates energies and responsibilities. After a while, shapes and patterns aren't enough: you need the names, and the words those people used to name things. At Bulahdelah Show last year, my wife and I lighted upon a fascinating exhibit of what some would call 'primitive' paintings. Each depicted some aspect or scene from the local past, and nearly all were to do with the world of timber-getting. Old slab-built houses, ponderous steam punts loaded with logs moving out onto moveless tan-green river water, smoking steam traction engines drawing loads of poles, men holding whips taller than themselves and walking beside teams of Ayrshire and brindle-roan bullocks: we were drawn into each in turn, arrested not by the painstaking realism but by the sourceless dream light in which each scene was bathed. That unconcern with the pedantic rendition of shadow is one of the surest marks of an untutored painter, and is at best a liberating gesture in itself. It signals our own depths, if the things thus freed from relativity are painted well, that here is something important. After some enquiry, we found that the painter was a Mrs Jean Onley, president of the local historical society. In her paintings, she had no artistic ambitions at all, but a purely documentary purpose: she was mainly enlarging, transcribing to colour and in effect preserving old photographs of the region, though a few paintings were of surviving buildings as it were 'taken' directly. We couldn't help feeling that her very unconcern with artistry had helped her to make very real art. As we talked with her, it emerged that she could name every place, every person and building and machine in her paintings, and regarded it as natural and necessary to do so. No bullock driver was a stock figure; he was a man who once existed, with a name and a character. So was every shop in the town of a century ago. This is completely true to the way a community preserves its history, being concerned not with patterns or ideologies, but with the living quiddity of each person, each being, each object. Where that concern is realized, there is no background or foreground, nor is anything either aggrandized or relegated. I can't remember any of Mrs Onley's paintings being located inside the forest proper; after parts of the bush were fenced off to become forest, women and cameras for a long time stayed out in what was becoming the country, or the towns. This is changing now, well beyond decorous picnic visits. The spoken rather than the written form of local history, on which Mrs Onley has largely based her paintings – for the camera arguably reflects the culture of its users, and the photographs she draws on were taken by people whose culture was oral and musical – and on which I have largely based this article, is well fitted to a quality of the bush itself. It is a quality not so much alien and indifferent, as too many literary authors by now have parroted, but rather sober, subtle and uncorrupt, with a curious remote decency about it. As you move and work there, or as you die there, you do so in an intense spare abundance which sheds its perfumes and its high riddled light on you equally. This is what often misleads outsiders into thinking it necessarily ancient: away from the marks of human incursion, it is always the first day. One in which you are as much at home as a hovering native bee, or the wind, or death, or shaded trickling water.

First published in *Gone Bush*, edited by Roger McDonald (Transworld Publishers, 1990)

Also available in Minerva

LES MURRAY

Collected Poems

'One of the finest poets writing in English, one of a superleague that includes Seamus Heaney, Derek Walcott and Joseph Brodsky'
  Blake Morrison, *Independent on Sunday*

'The Australian Les Murray is one of the most widely admired poets writing in English . . . (His) apotheosis is the *Collected Poems* . . . Read him and see a new zone taking shape, a territory created by a generous and expansive sensibility – the Kingdom of Sprawl'
  Peter Forbes, *Independent*

'Les Murray is a major Australian poet of our time, full stop'
  Douglas Dunn

'The true spokesman of the whole nation, the custodian of its soul, but also the witty Theophrastus of its peculiarities and customs'
  Peter Porter

'There is so much of a world in Murray's poems, so much linguistic life and intellectual energy, so many tones, moods, clever ideas, amusing anecdotes, and a presiding presence . . . His talent clamours to be fed'
  London Review of Books

JILL KER CONWAY

The Road from Coorain

'A small masterpiece of scene, memory and very stylish English. I've been several times to Australia; this book was the most rewarding journey of all'
John Kenneth Galbraith

'This beautifully written narrative of Conway's journey from a girlhood on an isolated sheep-farm in the grasslands of Australia to her departure for America (and eventually the Presidency of Smith College) is both new and universal. If few of us have known an eight-year-old drought in New South Wales, many of us have felt the despair of an ambitious young woman facing a constrained female destiny. This book, an extraordinarily gripping and inspiring work, will take its place as one of the few heroic stories of girlhood'
Carolyn Heilbrun

'*The Road from Coorain* is the work of a writer who relentlessly tugs at the cultural fences around her until they collapse, leaving her solitary under an immense Australian sky, enlarged to herself at last'
New York Times Book Review

'Immensely readable, elegant and well crafted'
Sydney Morning Herald

JULIAN EVANS

Transit of Venus

'This gem of a book . . . Julian Evans describes memorably an assortment of villains and comedians for which only the South Pacific can provide a home. His prose is magical, his wit gentle, his stories eminently repeatable, his touch sure and graceful'
Simon Winchester, *Guardian*

'The Americans use [the Pacific] as a firing range. Kwajalein has been turned into a slice of golf course suburbia for the officers of the range and their families. The Micronesians, whose island it is, have been moved off to a slum atoll nearby . . . Not far away is Kili Island, where the people of Bikini atoll were dumped so that their own islands could be cratered and partly vaporised by the first H-bomb in 1954 . . . The triumph of Evans's slow, questioning journey toward Kwajalein through the islands of the South Pacific is to make it clear that those gross and careless crimes are no aberration'
Adam Nicolson, *Sunday Times*

'Evans's writing [is] jaundiced but sharp, quick to tick off the mess that's been made of things but still attentive to those too-few moments when the old dream of islands asserts itself . . . *Transit of Venus* presents a vivid inventory of corruption and loss'
Times Literary Supplement

'Brilliant . . . a wickedly sardonic account . . . the best travel book I've read in years'
Bruce Palling, *Country Life*

WILLIAM LEAST HEAT-MOON

Blue Highways

'When "Least Heat-Moon" (the translation of the tribal name in his mixed blood) lost his job in a college in Missouri, he got a half-ton Ford van, packed a few necessaries including *Leaves of Grass* and Neihardt's *Black Elk Speaks*, and set out to follow the track of various ancestors and write a book about America. The book is called *Blue Highways*, and it is a masterpiece . . . Least Heat-Moon has a genius for finding people who have not even found themselves, exploring their lives, capturing their language, and recreating little (or big) lost worlds, or moments. In short, he makes America seem new, in a very special way, and its people new. *Blue Highways* is a magnificent and unique tour'

Robert Penn Warren

'Least Heat-Moon is a witty, generous, sophisticated, and democratic observer. His modesty, his subtle, kindly humour, and his uncanny gift for catching good people at good moments make *Blue Highways* a joy to read'

Annie Dillard

'Least Heat-Moon watches the details of the backwater American landscapes and the people who inhabit them with a startling, poetic scrupulousness . . . Turn to any page of *Blue Highways* and it's filled with vivid details of sights, tastes, smells, wildlife, weather, topography and talk, especially down-home talk'

New Society

ZINOVY ZINIK

The Mushroom Picker

'An extravagant farce set between the over-heated, cramped tenements of Moscow, which nourish a vigorous, uninhibited life, and the lawns of southern England, which nourish little at all. The story centres on the courtship – if seduction by pepper vodka and gherkin counts as courtship – and marriage of Kostya, a Russian for whom there is no greater good, in physical and spiritual terms, than the experience of eating, and Clea, a withering English liberal . . . Zinik's seemingly inexhaustible ability to make the metaphorical and symbolic profit from Kostya's obsession means that his novel is as inventive as it is witty'

James Campbell, *Observer*

'Zinik has both a great comic gift and an intricate critical mind . . . [He] is at his best when he allows himself to float way over the top'

Literary Review

'Zinik is well aware that national modes of humour contrast as much as anything else, and he exploits this as effectively as every other ingredient in his sexual and gastronomic farce. Seriousness and humanity are not mentioned in the recipe, but they help to season the brew; and deep down is the notion that communality survives socialism in the Soviet Union, but has not yet reaches our shores'

Times Literary Supplement

ANDRÉ BRINK

An Instant in the Wind

In early 1749 a white woman and a black man are stranded in the wilderness of the South African interior. She is an educated woman, totally helpless in the wilds. He is a runaway slave. They know only each other. At first their relationship is guarded, poisoned by the black and white in them both. But slowly and breathlessly there emerges between them a fellowship that engulfs their most private selves, as they face the long trek back to civilisation.

'It is difficult to see how any South African novelist will be able to surpass the honesty of this novel or the real courage – both as an artist and as a political man – that enabled Brink to write it'
World Literature Today

'Memorable'
Times Literary Supplement

'Brilliant'
Capetown Argus

ANDRÉ BRINK

A Dry White Season

Ben du Toit is an ordinary, decent, harmless man, unremarkable in every way – until his sense of justice is outraged by the death of a man he has known. His friend died at the hands of the police. In the beginning it appears a straightforward matter, an unfortunate error that can be explained and put right. But as Ben investigates further, he finds that his curiosity becomes labelled rebellion – and for a rebel there is no way back.

'The revolt of the reasonable . . . far more deadly than any amount of shouting from the housetops'
Guardian

'Impossible to recommend too highly'
Time Out

'Excellent . . . [a] harrowing and surprising story. The ultimate power of the book comes from an authoritative meditation on the traps that open up for someone who answers to himself before society'
Scotsman

'André Brink's writing is built on conviction . . . A *Dry White Season* describes the triumph of tyranny'
The Times

UMBERTO ECO

The Name of the Rose

'Imagine a medieval castle run by the Benedictines, with cellarists, herbalists, gardeners, young novices. One after the other half a dozen monks are found murdered in the most bizarre of ways. A learned Franciscan who is sent to solve the mystery finds himself involved in the frightening events . . . a sleuth's pursuit of the truth behind the mystery also involves the pursuit of meaning – in words, symbols, ideas, every conceivable sign the visible universe contains . . . Umberto Eco has written a novel – his first – and it has become a literary event'

New York Times Book Review

'The late medieval world, teetering on the edge of discoveries and ideas that will hurl it into one more recognisably like ours, its thought, its life-style, its intense political and ecclesiastical intrigues . . . its steamy and seductive currents of heresy of thought . . . all these are evoked with a force and a wit that are breathtaking'

Financial Times

'This novel belongs with Voltaire's philosophical tales . . . in the entertaining guise of an erudite fiction story, it is also a vibrant plea for freedom, moderation and wisdom'

L'Express

'A novel of stunning intelligence, linguistic richness, thematic complexity'

Il Giorno

A Selected List of Titles Available from Minerva

While every effort is made to keep prices low, it is sometimes necessary to increase prices at short notice. Mandarin Paperbacks reserves the right to show new retail prices on covers which may differ from those previously advertised in the text or elsewhere.

The prices shown below were correct at the time of going to press.

☐	7493 9137 5	**On the Eve of Uncertain Tomorrows**	Neil Bissoondath	£5.99
☐	7493 9050 6	**Women In A River Landscape**	Heinrich Boll	£4.99
☐	7493 9921 X	**An Instant in the Wind**	Andre Brink	£5.99
☐	7493 9147 2	**Explosion in a Cathedral**	Alejo Carpentier	£5.99
☐	7493 9109 X	**Bodies of Water**	Michelle Cliff	£4.99
☐	7493 9060 3	**Century of the Wind**	Eduardo Galeano	£4.99
☐	7493 9080 8	**Balzacs Horse**	Gert Hofmann	£4.99
☐	7493 9093 X	**The Notebook**	Agota Kristof	£4.99
☐	7493 9174 X	**The Mirror Maker**	Primo Levi	£4.99
☐	7493 9143 X	**Parents Worry**	Gerard Reve	£4.99
☐	7493 9172 3	**Lives of the Saints**	Nino Ricci	£4.99
☐	7493 9003 4	**The Fall of the Imam**	Nawal El Saadawi	£4.99
☐	7493 9924 4	**Ake**	Wole Soyinka	£5.99
☐	7493 9139 1	**The Four Wise Men**	Michel Tournier	£5.99
☐	7493 9092 1	**Woman's Decameron**	Julia Voznesenskaya	£5.99

All these books are available at your bookshop or newsagent, or can be ordered direct from the publisher. Just tick the titles you want and fill in the form below.

Mandarin Paperbacks, Cash Sales Department, PO Box 11, Falmouth, Cornwall TR10 9EN.

Please send cheque or postal order, no currency, for purchase price quoted and allow the following for postage and packing:

UK including BFPO	£1.00 for the first book, 50p for the second and 30p for each additional book ordered to a maximum charge of £3.00.
Overseas including Eire	£2 for the first book, £1.00 for the second and 50p for each additional book thereafter.

NAME (Block letters) ....

ADDRESS ....

....

☐ I enclose my remittance for ....

☐ I wish to pay by Access/Visa Card Number ☐☐☐☐☐☐☐☐☐☐☐☐☐☐☐☐

Expiry Date ☐☐☐☐